M. J. Moran

NORMAL AND
DEFICIENT CHILD LANGUAGE

Normal and Deficient Child Language

Edited by
Donald M. Morehead, Ph.D.
and
Ann E. Morehead, Ph.D.
San Francisco, California

University Park Press
Baltimore · London · Tokyo

UNIVERSITY PARK PRESS
International Publishers in Science and Medicine
Chamber of Commerce Building
Baltimore, Maryland 21202

Typeset by The Composing Room of Michigan, Inc.
Manufactured in the United States of America by Universal Lithographers,
Inc., and The Maple Press Co.

Library of Congress Cataloging in Publication Data
Main entry under title:

Normal and deficient child language.

Bibliography: p.
Includes index.
CONTENTS: Phonology: Ingram, D. Current issues in child
phonology. Lorentz, J. P. An analysis of some deviant phonological rules of
English. Compton, A. J. Generative studies of children's phonological
disorders: clinical ramifications. [etc.]
1. Children—Language—Addresses, essays, lectures. 2. Speech
disorders in children—Addresses, essays, lectures. I. Morehead, Donald
M. II. Morehead, Ann E.
P118.N6   401'.9   76-9114

ISBN 0-8391-0857-5

Contents

Contributors

Julian de Ajuriaguerra
Department of Clinical Psychiatry
University of Geneva
Geneva, Switzerland

Elizabeth Bates
Department of Psychology
University of Colorado
Boulder, Colorado

Melissa Bowerman
Bureau of Child Research and
Department of Linguistics
University of Kansas
Lawrence, Kansas

Arthur J. Compton
San Francisco Hearing and
Speech Center
2340 Clay Street
San Francisco, California

Richard F. Cromer
Developmental Psychology Unit
Medical Research Council
Drayton House, Gordon Street
London, England

Hans G. Furth
Department of Psychology
Catholic University of America
Washington, D.C.

David Ingram
Department of Linguistics
University of British Columbia
Vancouver, British Columbia

Bärbel Inhelder
Institute of Educational Science
University of Geneva
Geneva, Switzerland

Judith R. Johnston
Department of Psychology
University of California
Berkeley, California

James R. Lackner
Department of Psychology
Brandeis University
Waltham, Massachusetts

Patricia L. Looney
Children's Hospital Medical
Center
Boston, Massachusetts

James P. Lorentz
Department of Linguistics
University of California
Berkeley, California

Paula Menyuk
Department of Psychology
Boston University
Boston, Massachusetts

Donald M. Morehead
180 Mallorca Way
San Francisco, California

Teris Kim Schery
Office of Los Angeles County
Schools
Los Angeles, California

James Youniss
Department of Psychology
Catholic University of America
Washington, D.C.

Preface

Linguistic theory has dominated much of the research in language since the appearance of Chomsky's *Syntactic Structures*. From the beginning, Chomsky maintained that linguistics was part of human cognition and that an adequate theory of language must account for the implicit knowledge of every native speaker as well as the requisite knowledge that a child brings to the task of learning language. This emphasis on competence directed attention to those aspects of human knowledge that relate to the predisposition for acquiring language and to its structural organization and is largely responsible for the particular directions taken in the study of language since the late 1950's. Initially, abstract syntactic structures were viewed as the basic knowledge underlying linguistic competence. Although this position was greatly revised and extended during the mid-1960's, the more general theoretical constructs were not basically altered until the end of that decade, when the emphasis in language study shifted to meaning and its relation to other psychological processes, particularly cognition.

Chomsky was concerned with a number of conditions that a universal theory of language must meet in order to account for language acquisition. Three aspects of these general conditions had a significant impact on directions in child language research: describing linguistic competence in the child, understanding the operational procedures the child uses in acquiring a language, and determining the nature of the linguistic input. Most research in child language did not begin with attempts to specify the nature of linguistic input or the knowledge required for learning a language because Chomsky had maintained that linguistic input was restricted and of poor quality and that the procedures which the child uses were largely dependent upon innate linguistic capacities that develop relatively independent of intelligence. Consequently, the early research explored the acquisition of syntax or the child's grammatical competence.

At the same time that meaning was displacing syntax as the central focus in the study of language, research in child language was undergoing a similar change in direction. Both Schlesinger and Bloom concluded that children have certain intentions when they use language and that these intentions are best described by semantic rather than grammatical relations. They also agreed with the proposition of Sinclair that these early semantic relations are dependent upon previous developments in cognition, and, furthermore, that the uniformity of early linguistic structures across different children is the result of more general universal cognitive functions. The fullest discussion of these important transitions is found in Brown's *A First Language*. As a result of these changes, there is now a general interest in semantic characterizations in child language and in the relationship between language acquisition and cognitive development. Specifically, researchers are attempting to determine which linguistic acquisitions develop in close relation to cognition and which acquisitions develop independent of it.

Only recently have investigators been concerned with the precise nature of linguistic input; the evidence to date suggests that the linguistic data received by the child are not as impoverished as they were once believed to be. In fact, both adults and children modify the general complexity of their utterances as a function of the linguistic competence or style of their listener. Although little cross-cultural research has yet been done, the work that does exist suggests that adult speakers in all languages adjust their speech when talking to children.

A number of basic operating procedures used by children to construct the grammar of a language have been postulated by Slobin from cross-cultural studies of children learning different languages. In addition, alternate strategies for acquiring early multi-word constructions as well as specific strategies used by older and retarded children in processing complex constructions have been identified by several investigators. Brown has found that alternate strategies used in early constructions are the same as those that children use to expand these early constructions and that these methods for expansion hold for children learning different first languages. The claim that basic operating procedures are inherent to the child has also resulted in an interest in the biological prerequisites to language. Recent research in the biological aspects of language has included both renewed exploration of the comparative linguistic abilities of higher primates, particularly the chimpanzee, and an expansive attempt by Lenneberg to provide supporting evidence for the thesis that language is specific to humans.

Another important but often overlooked aspect of Lenneberg's approach was his inclusion of speech and language disorders in children to clarify major theoretical issues and to illuminate the process of normal language acquisition. Lenneberg did not concur with the view that any failure in a major aspect of development such as talking or reasoning results in a modification or distortion that makes the study of deficient systems more difficult. Instead, he argued that it is unlikely that most deficits obscure the general structure of developments in systems as basic to humans as language and cognition and that the study of these deficits is, in fact, informative. He studied children with various abnormalities to establish that the onset of language is regulated by maturational processes and even included the study of normal children born to deaf parents to support this position. He used congenital and acquired deafness, congenital and traumatic aphasia, and language arrest in retarded children to specify the critical period for language development. His study of language acquisition in mongoloid and deaf children showed that neither severe intellectual limitations nor extreme auditory deprivation fundamentally changes the course of language development. Finally, his often-cited study of a child who was incapable of producing intelligible speech but who nonetheless understood language at a level comparable to his intellectual development raised serious questions regarding the position that appropriate verbal responses are necessary for learning language.

The present edition brings together a group of studies and discussions on both normal and deficient language as a reaffirmation of Lenneberg's approach to the study of language acquisition. In contrast to the extensive work on normal language acquisition, comparatively little research has been carried out with that minority of children who experience difficulty in learning language. The research that has been done with language-deficient children has been largely comparative and concerned primarily with the cross-sectional study of morphology and syntax. The evidence from this work suggests that language-deficient children show a grammatical competence similar to that of normal children of the same level of linguistic development—a finding that supports Lenneberg's earlier work with retarded children. To date there has been no research reported on linguistic input to deficient children although it seems reasonable that modifications in speech style to those children are even more dramatic than those made for normal children. Research on the strategies used by language-deficient children has just begun and nothing has yet been reported to indicate whether or not they construct grammars using operating procedures similar to those of normal children. Deaf and dysphasic children—children whose intellectual development is often normal until early adolescence—have been natural subjects for the study of the relationship between language and cognition and key aspects of that work are reported in this edition.

The invited papers and reprinted articles in this collection all share a double view of language acquisition and development. The papers on normal language development discuss current theoretical positions and recent research in phonology, grammar, semantics, cognition, and pragmatics and relate each of these areas to the study of deficient children. The papers on deficient child language demonstrate the efficacy of studying atypical populations: these studies explore important theoretical questions, provide insights into the normal process, and suggest new procedures based on research findings for the assessment and habilitation of language-deficient children. The editorial comment which prefaces each article in the collection attempts to place that study in a general theoretical framework and to cross-reference it to other current research. A bibliography for both this preface and the comments is included at the end of the edition.

In preparing this edition we have had much help from friends and colleagues. Our greatest debt is to Elizabeth Bates, Melissa Bowerman, Arthur Compton, Richard Cromer, David Ingram, Judith Johnston, James Lorentz, and Teris Schery—researchers who shared our view that the study of normal and deficient child language should be complementary and who prepared original papers for this edition. We are also grateful to Julian de Ajuriaguerra, Hans Furth, Bärbel Inhelder, Patricia Looney, James Lackner, Paula Menyuk, and James Youniss, who allowed us to reprint their previously published work in this vein. We also thank Kate Cooper and Sophia Vlamis for their assistance in translating the papers which were originally published in French. Finally, special thanks to our daughter Kerstin, who showed amazing patience, ingenuity, and resilience while her best friends were compiling and editing this work.

to Kerstin

PHONOLOGY

Current Issues in Child Phonology

DAVID INGRAM

In the study of phonology, there have been few attempts to apply recent developments in phonological theory and analysis to the evolving system of the child. The Stanford Phonology Project (Ferguson and Farwell, 1975) and the work of Ingram (1974), Smith (1973), Menn (1971), Moskowitz (1970), and Stampe (1969) represent major exceptions. Moreover, aside from Jakobson's (1968) detailed treatment of child phonology, most discussions of phonological theory include only passing reference to child phonology (Chomsky and Halle, 1968; Ladefoged, 1971; Schane, 1973; Anderson, 1974). In fact, Ingram's discussion opens with the observation that the study of child phonology is now in a position not unlike that held by syntax in the mid-1960's. In this paper, he places phonology within a general developmental perspective, a perspective already taken in the study of syntax and semantics (Bowerman, this volume; Cromer, this volume). The influence of Piaget's theory on the study of child language has been extensive, and Ingram proposes that major shifts in phonological development may well parallel aspects of Piaget's stages of cognitive development. As a result, this paper provides a broad coverage of child phonology, spanning development from infant speech perception to late phonological acquisitions, and discusses current positions that challenge previous theoretical assumptions, including those of Jakobson (1968).

—DMM

PURPOSE

A renaissance of sorts has taken place in the last 15 years in the study of language acquisition in children. Although this trend has generated research in nearly all aspects of child language, the renewed interest in child phonology is even more recent in its origin. A glance at the linguistic studies of phonological development will show that most have appeared in the last 5 years, e.g., Stampe (1969), Moskowitz (1970), Menn (1971), Kornfeld (1971), Waterson (1971), Smith (1973), Ingram (1974), and Ferguson and Farwell (1975). In many ways, this attention to phonology can be attributed to the English translation in 1968 of Jakobson's classic work on child phonology entitled *Child Language, Aphasia, and Phonological Universals.*

Because this area is recent, active, and growing, we are currently in a period of transition. Although the relevant questions are being asked, it is not always clear what the more substantive issues will be. In many respects, it is possible to say that child phonology today is at the point where child syntax was in the mid-1960's. At that time, initial studies by Miller and Ervin (1964), Brown and Fraser (1964), and Braine (1963) had produced some degree of understanding of grammatical development. Then, between 1966 and 1968, it became clear that these initial studies had hardly begun to capture the richness of the child's system. Since that time, several studies have begun to account for some of this richness, e.g., Bloom (1970) and Brown (1973). This recent work has taken this field into the very exciting area of cognitive development and its relation to language.

Like child syntax circa 1968, child phonology has arrived at some initial observations on the nature of the child's system. It has become clear that children rely on a fairly common set of phonological processes to simplify adult speech for their own productions. In some respects, the isolation of these processes can be compared to the discovery of pivot-grammars in the study of child syntax. When pivot-grammars were first proposed, people felt they had discovered a significant phenomenon until they realized that these represented merely the tip of the grammar iceberg. Evidence is already beginning to appear suggesting that phonological processes may have a similar position historically. For example, it is becoming evident that children vary greatly in the use of those processes so far described to simplify speech. Perhaps more important, children seem to use these processes for "higher" goals, such as a general treatment of syllables or the creation of specific contrasts in their own speech. All of this suggests that research in the next few years will reveal that phonological processes are just one part of a very complex development in the child.

Given this state of the art, one cannot provide a conclusive overview of our current knowledge in this area. It is possible, however, to show how the study of child phonology has reached this point and to suggest where it is going. To show this progression, this chapter is divided into three major sections: 1) historical background; 2) stages of phonological development; and 3) some current controversies. The first section presents a brief historical overview, pointing out some of the major works on the acquisition of English phonology and the kinds of data that are available. The second section, which forms the central part of the chapter, explains how a child acquires phonology through various stages of acquisition. Although some attempts have been made to propose stages of syntactic development, there has been virtually no work of this kind on phonological development. With stage or level representation in phonology it can be seen that some issues in child phonology actually result from describing behavior at different stages of acquisition. It is shown that phonology, like syntax, is also subject to general stages of cognitive development. The final section concentrates on some specific theoretical and methodological controversies current in the literature. The theoretical issues revolve around two central questions: 1) whether or not the child has a system of his own construction, at times quite different from the adult's; and 2) the relational development of perception and production. The methodological issues concern ways in which data are elicited and recorded. In an attempt at neutrality, this presentation discusses the views of several researchers representing various alternative approaches.

HISTORICAL BACKGROUND

Although a flurry of research in child phonology has recently taken place, the study of this topic has been pursued intermittently for the last 100 years. However, most of this older work has been neglected by recent researchers who usually limit their references to Velten (1943), Leopold (1947), and possibly Templin (1957). There are two apparent reasons for this restriction. One is that most research in child phonology has been done on languages other than English. For example, an excellent early paper on phonological development is that of Franke (1912). Second, most of the early work on English uses very poor phonetic transcription (e.g., Foulke and Stinchfield, 1929).

The research to date can be divided into three historical periods: Period of Diary Studies (1876–1929); Period of Large Sample Studies (1930–1957); Period of Linguistic Studies (1958–present). Each of these can be characterized by a method of data collection that dominated the period. The word "dominate" is important here because it does not mean that these methods haven't been used in other periods.

Diary studies, for example, have been conducted throughout the study of child language.

A *diary study* is one in which a parent-observer makes notations on a child's utterances over a period of time. There may be no specific timetable for observations and even in recent years a tape recorder is not often used. This method has continued to be the primary one for the collection of phonological data. In the Period of Diary Studies, there were several excellent phonological diaries in other languages, especially French (e.g., Roussey, 1899–1900; Deville, 1890, 1891; Bloch, 1913; Vinson, 1915; and Ronjat, 1913). In English, however, only a handful appeared. Some of the better ones are Humphreys (1880), Hills (1914), and Holmes (1927). There have been in all of this time only two major diaries, that of Leopold (1947) of his daughter Hildegard from around 0.8 (8 months) to 1:11 (1 year, 11 months) and that of Smith (1973) of his son A from 2:2 to 4:0. Although these two studies are rich sources of data, the children observed both had unusual linguistic backgrounds.

The best data on how children acquire language over several years came from studies collecting samples from a cross-section of a large number of children. The Period of Large Sample Studies between 1930 and 1957 was highlighted by several studies that attempted to provide norms for language acquisition. These studies were not concerned with how individual children structured language, so that the results quantified data for selected age levels. In the area of phonological development in English, the major studies in this period were those of Wellman et al. (1931), Poole (1934), and Templin (1957). The norms for the acquisition of English sounds suggested by these studies are reviewed in Winitz (1969). A recent study of 100 children that qualifies in many ways as a large-sample study is that by Olmsted (1971).

These two methods of data collection are in certain respects at extreme poles. One method looks at only one child, while the other looks at hundreds of children. In recent years, attempts have been made to combine the strengths of each method. The result has been the use of *longitudinal studies*. The studies by Bloom (1970) and Brown (1973) are examples of this approach. Instead of using just one child, several are selected; each of the above studies used three. The children are then systematically visited at predetermined intervals, and their speech is tape recorded. This approach has led to some rich data on the syntactic development of children.

Unfortunately, longitudinal study has yet to be seriously applied to the collection of phonological data. Although this method sets syntactic studies apart from those done before 1958, it does not separate phonological ones. The characteristic that sets off recent phonological studies from previous ones is the use of formal linguistic analyses. Papers like the one by Menn (1971) are dominated by linguistic rules and notations. The recent diary by Smith (1973) differs markedly from Leopold's (1947) by its use on linguistic formalism. Recently, there has been a trend away from formalism, as it becomes more and more apparent that there are limitations to the value of purely formal descriptions.

Another trend in recent years has been the construction of theories of phonological development. The most widely cited theory continues to be that of Jakobson (1968). Looking at data from very young children, Jakobson has argued that language develops through the establishment of a predictable series of contrasts. Recently, a serious contender with the theory is the one proposed by Stampe (1969, 1972). Stampe's theory, which he calls Natural Phonology, emphasizes the existence of an innate set of hierarchically structured processes that simplify adult words. The focus is on the adult word and the child's attempts to produce it. Acquisition is seen as the gradual suppression or elimination of these simplifying tendencies. Other recent works geared towards theoretical explanations include those of Waterson (1971), Smith (1973), and Ingram (in press). An overview of several alternative approaches, including the two just mentioned, is found in Ferguson and Garnica (1975).

STAGES OF PHONOLOGICAL DEVELOPMENT

To understand the relevant issues in child phonology and the direction of current and future work, it is necessary to place the acquisition of phonology in a general developmental perspective. This is possible through the establishment of stages of acquisition. The first attempts to do this for syntax have been made by Brown (1973). In regard to phonology, virtually no stages have yet been proposed. The following section provides a first step in characterizing stages of phonological development. These stages are then related to syntactic and cognitive development.

Role of Cognitive Development

Recent work has made it clear that child language has to be considered within the broader framework of a child's cognitive ability. As a result, stages of language acquisition are best seen as part of stages of cognitive ability. Let me provide one example of how the influence of cognition affects language development in both syntax and phonology. In syntax, one of the important steps in acquisition is the development of complex sentences, such as those with relative clauses as in example (1).

(1) *The boy who came here* was very tall

This sentence actually reflects two different sentences, (2) and (3), which have been combined into one.

(2) The boy was very tall
(3) The boy came here

To learn to produce sentences like (1), the child needs to be able to understand the relation between these two, and use a process to combine them. Sentence (1) can also be compared with sentence (4), which is derived from a structure like (1) through a rule of Extraposition from Relative Clause.

(4) *The boy* was very tall *who left early*

The child needs to compare adult sentences like these and determine from them the transformation involved. Children do not acquire rules like this until after age 6 (Ingram, 1975a).

In the area of phonology, English has a complex system of morphophonemic rules, many of which are outlined in Chomsky and Halle (1968). One widely discussed rule is the Vowel Shift, which relates forms like those in example (5).

(5) a. div*i*ne - div*i*nity   - [ay] ~ [ɪ]
    b. expl*ai*n - expl*a*natory - [ey] ~ [æ]
    c. ser*e*ne - ser*e*nity   - [iy] ~ [ɛ]

Morphophonemics refers to sound changes that result from the joining of one morpheme with another. For example, when the morpheme *divine* is added to the morpheme *-ity,* the second vowel in *divine* changes from [ay] to [ɪ]. To learn a rule like Vowel Shift, the child needs to compare pairs of words like these and determine that they share a particular morpheme. In the process the child needs to isolate the sound change that takes place and establish a rule to explain it. A recent study on Vowel Shift by Moskowitz (1973) has demonstrated that this rule is not learned by children until after age 6.

One could say that it is coincidence that these two complex patterns are acquired in the same period. There is, however, a more principled explanation for this fact. To compare sentences and words like these to determine their relationships requires the ability to perform *reversible operations*. The child needs to go from one to the other and back again to link two separate items to each other. Piaget (Flavell, 1963), in a number of classic experiments with the conservation of liquids, mass, and volume, has shown that this ability to perform concrete operations does not occur until after age 6. The explanation of these linguistic developments resides in the cognitive abilities of the child.

This is a rich and exciting area of future research in the study of child phonology. Hopefully, the next few years will provide some solid information on the relation of cognition to the various stages of linguistic development, syntactic as well as phonological. The following overview is a first attempt to do this.

Stages

Piaget (Flavell, 1963), in his numerous works on cognitive development, has developed a theory outlining three major periods of cognitive development, covering the time from birth to age 16:0. In addition, the second of these, the period of concrete operations (1:6–12:0), can be divided into three subperiods. There are specific phonological stages that correspond to each of these periods. A brief summary of these is provided in Table 1.

Preverbal Vocalization and Perception (Birth to 1:0)   Piaget's (Flavell, 1963) first period of sensorimotor development covers the first 1.5–2 years of age. In this time, the child learns that it is but one of many objects in the world. It explores objects and comes to know their various properties and functions. During this period, it is possible to identify two stages of phonological development. The first one of these covers the first year of life and is marked by the development of preverbal vocalization and perception.

Important developments take place in preparation for the later appearance of words. As for perception, recent research has shown that infants as young as 1 month of age are making fine perceptual distinctions (Morse, 1974). This is an important skill required for the identification of adult words and those sound features which are distinctive. This is a popular and quickly growing area of research.

The child also is producing sounds at an increasing rate in the sensorimotor period. This production of speech is commonly referred to as babbling. The segmental characteristics of these sounds have been extensively studied by Irwin in a series of studies throughout the 1940's (cf. the review of these in McCarthy (1954) and Lewis (1951)).

Table 1. A comparison of Piaget's stages of cognitive development with six major stages of phonological development

Piaget's stages	Phonological stages
Sensorimotor period (birth–1:6)	1. Preverbal vocalization and perception (birth–1:0)
The child develops his sense and motor ability; he actively explores his environment until the achievement of the notion of object performance.	2. Phonology of first 50 words (1:0–1:6) Child gradually acquires his first words.
Period of concrete operations (1:6–12:0)	
Preconcept subperiod (1:6–4:0)	3. Phonology of simple morphemes (1:6–4:0)
The onset of symbolic representation. The child can use a system of social signs to refer to the past and future, although he primarily lives in the here and now.	Vocabulary increases rapidly as child develops a system of speech sounds. The child uses a variety of phonological processes to simplify speech. Most words consist of simple morphemes.
Intuitional subperiod (4:0–7:0) The child's play begins to mirror reality rather than change it to the child's own structures. Child begins to solve tasks such as the conservation of liquids by use of perception.	4. Completion of phonetic inventory (4:0–7:0) Most speech sounds are acquired by the end of this period. Simple words are by and large pronounced correctly. First appearance of more complex words which are poorly pronounced.
Subperiod of concrete operations (7:0–12:0) The ability to solve tasks of conservation is developed as the child can now perform reversible operations. He no longer needs to rely on perception.	5. Morphophonemic development (7:0–12:0) The more complex derivational morphology of language is acquired. Rules such as Vowel Shift become productive
Period of Formal Operations (12:0–16:0) Appearance of the ability to reflect abstractly. Child can now solve problems through reflection.	6. Acquisition of spelling Child develops the ability to spell the complex words of the language. Development of linguistic intuitions.

The role of babbling has been controversial, largely because of Jakobson's claim (1968) that these sounds are unrelated to actual language development. Broader studies of babbling and language, however, have shown a relationship. Piaget (1962) has studied in detail the development of babbling in its relation to the ability to imitate. Imitation of adult words is necessary to acquire an adult language. The child at first can only imitate sounds made by adults that are similar to his own. Eventually this ability increases until the child can imitate new models. This occurs toward the end of the first year along with the appearance of the child's first words. Recent research on the comparison of babbling with later phonological development by Oller et al. (1974) has shown that even similar simplifying processes may be in use.

Phonology of First 50 Words   Children's first words appear around the end of the first year. This marks the onset of a definable stage of language acquisition that lasts for approximately 6 months, from about 1:0 to 1:6. During this time, the child gradually acquires words until approximately 1:6 when his vocabulary reaches a size of about 50 words (Nelson, 1973). The child also uses one-word utterances during this stage. The end of the period is marked by two abrupt linguistic changes—the rapid increase in vocabulary and the first use of two-word utterances.

This 6-month period covers the last part of the sensorimotor period. For Piaget (1962), true linguistic development does not begin until about the age of 1:6 with the onset of a wide range of symbolic behavior. The words that are used before this time are not the arbitrary social signs used in the adult language. Instead, they are the child's first attempt at symbolic behavior. Through the development of imitation, the child begins to retain mental images of words and uses these to signify meanings. However, the child's ability to coordinate these images with objects is very unstable. At this point, the meanings of these early words are very personal for the child. Because of the instability of these coordinations between image and object, overextensions such as those described by Clark (1973) take place.

Since the child's cognitive ability from 1:0 to 1:6 represents a different level from that which follows, this suggests that the nature of the child's phonology at this time would also differ from that which follows. However, most linguistic analyses of children's phonology have assumed a gradual and continual development, beginning with the onset of the first word. For example, Jakobson's (1968) classic theory assumes that children use contrast in their speech from the very beginning.

Some recent studies are beginning to show that phonological development during this period of the first 50 words deserves separate study from the one that follows. Since this stage appears before the onset of language as a system of social signs, one should expect to find evidence that the child does not have a system of contrasts at this time. Also, one would expect the use of segments and words to differ in some ways from those in the next stage.

One way that words differ in the stage from 1:0 to 1:6 is the use of *advanced forms* (or "progressive idioms," a term coined by Moskowitz and cited in Ferguson and Farwell, 1975). These are pronunciations of words that are better or more advanced than their later productions. Moskowitz has noted that Hildegard Leopold pronounced the word *pretty* rather well for several months (e.g., 0:10 [prəti], 0:11 [prɪti], 1:1 [prɪti], [prəti], 1:4 [pwɪti], [pəti], [pyɪti]). The next few months it stabilized to [bɪdi] and remained so for quite a while. The varied pronunciation of this word is consistent with the use of symbols during the last months of sensorimotor development. Once a linguistic system began to develop, the pronunciation was stabilized to [bɪdi].

Another way that words differ in this stage is that occasionally the consistent phonological processes that characterize later speech do not apply (Ingram, 1974). For example, young children have a tendency to voice consonants before vowels, e.g., *pie*[bay]. Hildegard did this for *pretty,* but only at age 1:9 after several months of using [p].

It is also questionable whether children are productively using sounds to contrast meaning in this stage. Braine (1971) conducted a simple experiment to test this. His son at the time had acquired five words: *see* [di:], *that* or *there* [da] [dʌ], *juice* [du:], *no* [do], *hi* [ʔai]. Braine wanted to see if the use of [d] versus [ʔ] was contrastive for the child, i.e., could be used to distinguish new words. He tried to teach his son two new words, [i:] and [dai]. The child, however, learned these as [di:] and [da] or [dʌ]. Braine concluded that these sounds did not have contrastive value.

An excellent source of information on this stage is a recent study by Ferguson and Farwell (1975). The authors studied the phonologies of the first 50 words of three English-learning children. When looking for contrasts in the speech of these children, they observed a great deal of variation. For example, one of the children was in the midst of acquiring [m] and [n]. In some words the children used only one or the other, whereas in other words the children showed free variation between them. The children were acquiring this contrast very gradually and only in certain words. This led Ferguson and Farwell (1975) to conclude that on the basis of their data it would often be impossible to make claims about the existence of phonological contrasts in these early stages.

Given these observations, more research is required to compare the nature of phonological development at this stage with the one that follows. It may be that the real onset of a phonological system does not occur until around age 1:6 or the onset of representational behavior.

Phonology of Simple Morphemes   Strong evidence of representational behavior appears around ages 1:6–2:0 with several changes in the child's language. At this point the child begins to enter into dialogue, commences to use two-word utterances, refers to past and future events, rapidly acquires vocabulary, and engages in symbolic play. The onset of rapid linguistic development marks a stage in which the child moves from simple two-word utterances at 1:6 to fairly well formed utterances by age 4:0. At age 4, the yound child has enough language to be capable of communication with strangers.

Over this period, there are some characteristic developments in the child's phonological system. One of these is that the child's *perception* of adult forms improves. A few studies have attempted to trace this ability in children (Templin, 1957; Shvachkin, 1973; Garnica, 1973; and Edwards, 1974). In regard to the question of how rapidly this ability progresses, some people feel that it is very much ahead of production (Smith, 1973).

A second characteristic of the period from 1:6 to 4:0 is that the child acquires a substantial part of the *phonetic inventory* of English sounds. At the beginning of phonological development around 1:6, the child will predominantly use CV or occasional CVC syllables for words. A typical vowel and consonant system at this age might be selected from the ones shown in example (6). The consonants would be mostly syllable initial.

(6) i   u   b   d
             a   p   t
                            f   s   h
                            w   y
                            m   n

Soon after this, the child masters the production of vowels. The production of consonants improves in all syllable positions, and consonant clusters emerge. Templin (1957) and Olmsted (1971) have shown that most consonants are acquired by age 4:0 with the exception of several fricative sounds. These consonants and their position, according to Templin, are given in (7).

(7) p-, -p-, p   t-, -t,   k-, -k-, -k
     b-, -b-, -b   d-, -d-, -d   g-, -g-, -g
                                        ǰ-
     f-, -f-, -f   s-, -s-,   š-, -š
          -v-   -z-
     m-, -m-, -m   n-, -n-, -n   -ŋ-, -ŋ

     w-, -w-   y-, -y-
                      l-, -l- r-, -r-

Templin also found the following initial clusters acquired by this age:

(8) sm- sn-   pl-   kl-
     sp- st- sk-   pr- tr-   kr-
          tw- kw-   br- dr-

The number of correct productions allows a relatively high level of intelligibility.

    A third aspect of phonological acquisition in this stage is the use of a number of *phonological processes* or procedures to simplify speech. In attempting to produce adult words, the child reduces them to simpler patterns. For example, a child might say [da] for *dog* by deleting [g] and changing the vowel to [a], the first vowel usually acquired by children. Study of these procedures has shown that there are systematic and recurring processes across children. Table 2 presents a list of the more common ones that have been observed from young children and examples of each process.

    The detailed study of the nature of processes such as these is an exciting area of current and future research. There are several directions that the study of these processes may take. We need to know more about each of the processes mentioned in Table 2. Knowledge on each will answer questions concerning when they first appear, how long they last, how they gradually are eliminated, and how widely they are used across children. Other processes besides these more common ones also need to be isolated and studied. Furthermore, it is

Table 2. Some common phonological process found in the speech of young children

---

Syllabic structure processes
1. *Deletion of final consonant*—e.g., *out* [æw], *bike* [bay]
2. *Reduction of clusters*—the reduction of a consonant cluster to a single consonant, e.g., *floor* [fər], *step* [dɛp]
3. *Deletion of unstressed syllables*—e.g., *banana* [næna]
4. *Reduplication*—e.g., *rabbit* [wæwæ], *noodle* [nunu]

Assimilatory processes
5. *Prevocalic voicing of consonants*—consonants tend to be voiced when preceding a vowel, e.g., *pen* [bɛn], *tea* [di]
6. *Devoicing of final consonants*—e.g., *bed* [bɛt], *big* [bɪk]
7. *Nasalization of vowels*—vowels tend to take on the nasality of a following nasal consonant, e.g., *friend* [frɛ̃]
8. *Velar assimilation*—apical consonants tend to assimilate to a following velar consonant, e.g., *duck* [gək], *tongue* [gəŋ]
9. *Labial assimilation*—e.g., *top* [bap]
10. *Progressive vowel assimilation*—an unstressed vowel will assimilate to a preceding stressed vowel, e.g., *apple* [ʔaba]

Substitution Processes
11. *Stopping*—fricatives and occasionally other sounds are replaced with a stop consonant, e.g., *seat* [tit], *soup* [dup]
12. *Fronting of velars*—velar consonants tend to be replaced with alveolar ones, e.g., *book* [but], *coat* [towt]
13. *Fronting of palatals*—similar to above, e.g., *shoe* [su], *juice* [dzus]
14. *Denasalization*—the replacement of a nasal consonant with an oral one, e.g., *no* [dow], *home* [hub]
15. *Gliding*—the substitution of a glide [w] or [y] for a liquid sound, i.e., [l] [r]; e.g., *rock* [wak], *lap* [yæp]
16. *Vocalization*—the replacement of a syllabic consonant with a vowel, e.g., *apple* [æpo], *flower* [fawo]
17. *Vowel neutralization*—the reduction of vowels to a central [a] or [ə], e.g., *bath* [bat], *book* [ba]

---

important to establish the relations that exist between specific processes and whether the existence of one implies that of another.

Although the processes in Table 2 are shown with examples in which the process is clear-cut, often more than one process will apply in a child's word. For example, the child who says [gɪk] for *tick* is using two processes to produce the initial segment, prevocalic voicing and velar assimilation. Little research has been done to determine how many processes may apply simultaneously in a word. Stampe (1972), for example, has argued that Joan Velten's (1943) word for *lamb,* [bap], can be explained by proposing multiple processes. Using

the terminology of Table 2, example (9) shows the simplification of
this word.

(9)   / l æ m /

b	Denasalization - 14
p	Devoicing of final consonants - 6
y	Gliding - 15
z	Frication (not discussed)
d	Stopping - 11
b	Labial assimilation - 9
a	Vowel neutralization - 17

[b a p]

While it is possible to do this, it is also evident that children usually do
not apply so many processes at once. The extent and limits of this
metamorphosis need to be determined.

Completion of Phonetic Inventory   The development between
ages 4:0 and 7:0 is transitional in some respects. On the one hand, the
child completes much of the development that began in the preceding
period. One striking feature is the completion of the phonetic inventory. The sounds that were not acquired at 4:0, which were primarily
fricatives and affricates, are pronounced correctly by the end of the
stage. Also, the child uses phonological processes less frequently. By
the end of this stage, the child produces most of his words correctly.
This has led to the assumption that phonological development is
completed by age 7.

During the first three stages, another aspect of acquisition begins. The child begins to acquire and use some of the morphologically
complex words of English. This development anticipates the rapid
morphophonemic development of the next stage. While the child
produces most words in their adult forms, the longer ones are much
less precise in pronunciation. Here are some examples of three
children between ages 5:6 and 5:8 producing the words *thermometer,*
vegetables, and *zither* (based on Ingram, in 1976, Chapter 2).

(10) *child*	B.B. (5:6)	B.M. (5:6)	G.S. (5:8)
thermometer	[θəmánəbɽ]	[θɽmámapɽ]	[θámpətu]
vegetables	[vɛ́staboz]	[vɛ́jəblz]	[vɛ́nčtəb̩z]
zither	[zízu]	[zɛ̆sɽ]	[ðɪ́sa]

Even though the initial segments are mostly correct, the words still
differ from the adult model. Most longer words will have inaccurate

productions during this stage. These words will need to be correctly pronounced before an accurate morphemic analysis can be done.

The first morphophonemic rules are acquired, but the evidence to date suggests that this knowledge does not progress very far. Berko (1958), in the classic study on the acquisition of morphophonemic rules, found this to be the case when she tested 5- and 6-year-old children on a variety of morphological endings. One of these was the difference between [-s], [-z], and [-əz] on English plurals, possessives, and present tense. While the children used [-s] and [-z] productively, [-əz] was not extended to the nonsense words in her task. The conclusion that this performance failure was the result of incomplete morphophonemic development rather than phonetic considerations was supported by differences in performance on the three places where these endings appear. Children used [-əz] better on present tense and possessive forms than on plurals. The productive development of these and other morphophonemic alternatives awaits the next stage of phonological development.

Morphophonemic Development   The transition to more complex lexical items that begins between ages 4:0 and 7:0 blossoms in the period from 7:0 to 12. This development is apparently assisted by learning to spell and read (Moskowitz, 1973). Complex rules such as Vowel Shift become productive parts of the child's system.

Research into the development of phonological rules during this stage is just beginning and promises to be a fruitful source of information. A recent study by Atkinson-King (1973) demonstrates very nicely the type of development that takes place. English has a system of contrastive stress which differentiates compounds from noun phrases.

(11) *Noun compound*   *Noun phrase*

gréenhouse	green hóuse
rédhead	red héad
híghchair	high cháir
bláckboard	black bóard

To learn these patterns, the child needs to relate pairs like these to one another in order to relate them by rule. In this case, the rule is that phrases take primary stress at the end of words whereas compounds take it on the first word. The child needs to be able to perform a reversible operation. Testing these as well as other stress patterns through a variety of tasks, Atkinson-King (1973) found that children at age 5 did not know these rules but that the older children did. "In general, a child of five does not yet show ability with these stress contrasts but one of twelve does, and the closer to twelve a child is, the more likely he is to have acquired it" (p.v.). Research like this shows that phonological development is not complete even when the child has acquired the phonetic inventory.

Spelling With the advent of formal operations, the child's reasoning is now free of the effects of what is perceived. The child can now reflect on problems that are not immediately in front of him and arrive at a reasoned solution. In the area of phonology, the prime development that results from this ability to think abstractly is the completion of learning to spell. This ability begins before age 12.

SOME CURRENT CONTROVERSIES

Currently, there are two topics in the study of child phonology that are receiving a good deal of attention: the role of perception in acquiring phonology and the claim that the child develops a phonological system of his own. A certain amount of data has been proposed in support of opposing positions in each of these topics. Hopefully, future research will add to our understanding of them.

A less controversial, but nonetheless interesting, area is that of method in the collection and transcription of a child's productions. Until recently, much has been taken for granted in collecting a child's speech. However, evidence has been recently accumulated which suggests that one has to be very careful in the procedure used to guarantee that transcriptions accurately reflect the child's actual speech.

Theory

Jakobson (1968) emphasized the claim that the child constructs a system of contrasts within his own system. This led to a general assumption in the 1940's and 1950's that the child develops a phonological system of his own, independent from the adult system. This independence is implied in Chao (1951), for example, who refers to the Chinese spoken by his grandchild Canta as "the Cantian dialect." Velten (1943) is another who makes this assumption, specifically pointing out ways that his daughter used contrasts that did not exist in the adult language.

Stampe (1969) has recently challenged this assumption: "Most modern students of child phonology have assumed that the child has a phonemic system of his own, distinct from that of his standard language. So far as I am aware, no evidence whatsoever has been advanced to support this assumption. There is, on the other hand, abundant evidence that the child's representatives closely conform to adult speech" (p. 446). He argues that aspects of the child's speech can always be traced back to information contained in the adult words. This position has been strongly supported by Smith (1973).

In examining this issue, it is necessary to clarify what is actually being claimed. In proposing that a child has a system separate from the adult one, at least two positions could be intended. The first position would be a very strong version:

(12) *Child System: Strong Version*
     The child has a system of contrasts in his speech that is not
     related in any significant way to the contrasts that occur in
     adult speech.

This version claims that the child develops language independently from the language being learned. Although this interpretation may occasionally be understood as claiming that the child has a self-constructed system, this author knows of no research that has ever taken this position. Jakobson (1968), for example, was quite aware that the child uses his sounds as substitutes for adult ones. For instance, in discussing the acquisition of affricates, he states, "Before the child acquires affricates, he substitutes either corresponding stops or fricatives for them, e.g., *t* or *s* for *ts,* and *p* or *f* for *pf*" (p. 56).

A more realistic version of the claim that the child has his own system would be one of these weaker versions:

(13) *Child System: Weak Versions*
     a. The child will use sound to contrast meaning, and occa-
         sionally sounds will be used for contrasts that differ
         from those used in the adult models.
     b. The child's use of sounds contrastively will occasion-
         ally be unrelated to segments in the adult words.

Of these two versions of this position, the one in (13)b is stronger than that of (13)a.

These two positions can be understood by looking at Joan Velten's use of vowel length in her speech. At one point in her development, she had several words like those in example (14).

(14) a. *beat* but   c. *foot* fut
          beat bu·t   *food* fu·t
      b. *bite* bat
          bed   ba·t

In these words, the vowel length is the sole means used to distinguish each of these pairs. Velten (1943) took this as indicative of position (13)a, in that the child used a contrast that is not contrastive in adult English. A way that a child could use a contrast of the adult system would be in hypothetical forms like *map* [mæ] and *nap* [næ].

Stampe (1969) has criticized this interpretation on the grounds that the vowel length is predictable from the adult words. English lengthens vowels before voiced consonants. Stampe argues that the actual contrast for the child is in the final consonants. The production of pairs such as (14)a would be as in (15).

(15) /bit / *beat*   /bi·d / *bead* Child's under-
                                          lying forms
      but   bu·d Vowel substitution
      ———   bu·t Devoicing of final con-
                                sonants
      but   bu·t

The child's underlying form is the same as the adult form and therefore it is not necessary to claim that the child has a system of his own construction.

A number of factors need to be considered before this issue is resolved. One is that (14)a does not deny that the child's contrast may be traceable to the adult word. The point is that since the child does devoice final consonants, he relies on another aspect of the adult word to maintain a contrast. In this sense, the explanation in (15) does not necessarily provide counter-evidence to (14)a.

Another factor is that evidence showing the existence of (14)b would be a strong indication that children do use sounds contrastively, and these may differ from expectations based on the adult models. Ingram (1975b) has presented some preliminary data suggesting that children occasionally have minimal pairs that are not obviously predictable from the adult words; (16) provides two examples of these.

(16) Philip *plane* me   Jennika *Mark* mək
              plate pe   *milk* nək

Philip nasalized the initial segment in *plane,* resulting in a contrast between [m] and [p]. Curiously, other words with nasals at the end do not cause nasalization of initial segments. They either occur or are deleted. The unique nasalization appeared to have one purpose, that of creating a contrast in the child's own system. Without nasalization, *plane* would have been [pe], the same as *plate.* The situation is similar in Jennika's example. All other words except *milk* have the appropriate use of [m]. The unique use of [n] allows the child's own system to maintain a contrast. Research into the way children change adult words into their own speech is required before it can be decided whether or not children do construct a system of their own.

This issue is closely related to a second one having to do with the child's ability to perceive adult speech. The claim that the child does not have a separate system implies that the child has a more or less accurate representation of the adult word. Both Stampe (1969) and Smith (1973) have argued that perception of words is far advanced over production and complete at an early age. Those who have argued that the child does structure language in his own separate system have claimed that perception is not complete (Kornfeld, 1971; Waterson, 1971). The latter argue that children select certain features of the adult word and use these to create their underlying forms of words. Since only certain perceptual features are selected, the child's system will differ from that of the adult. An example of this would be Jennika's use of [wəŋik] for *music* at age 1:6. The child only selected certain features of the adult word, e.g., "labial," "sonorant" for the first segment and "nasality" from the first to the second.

Arguments against incomplete perception are based on the observation that children are often aware of their mispronunciations. Smith's (1973) son A, for example, was quite aware that his production of [sip] for *ship* was not correct. "No, I can only say [sip]" (p. 137). Second, it is argued that once a child does learn to produce a new sound, it occurs in all of the instances where the old substitution also appears.

Although examples like these show that perception can precede production, they do not suggest that this is always the case. Some recent research has attempted to test the young child's ability to perceive sounds in words. Based on earlier work in Russian by Shvachkin (1973), Garnica (1973) and Edwards (1974) have shown that perception is not complete as late as age 3:0. This position directly contrasts with claims made by Stampe (1969) and Smith (1973).

There are two further points worth noting about the issue of perception and production. One has to do with the finding mentioned under "Preverbal Vocalization and Perception" that infants as young as 1 month show fine perceptual distinctions. In studies like that of Garnica (1973), the children were tested on "linguistics perception." The sound tested appeared in nonsense syllables (e.g., [mʌk] vs. [bʌk]) that were taught as names of objects. These were linguistic signs in that they were sounds paired with meanings. This method differs greatly from the testing with infants where the discrimination is between meaningless pairs. The introduction of meaning changes the task from a sensorimotor one to a symbolic one. This change from one level to another results in what Piaget (Flavell, 1963) calls a décalage, i.e., the child has to relearn the ability at the new level of development.

The second point concerns one's definition of system. If the child between 1:0 and 1:6 is still not operating on a representational level, it is not clear what is meant when referring to the child's linguistic system during that period. A discussion of a child's perceptual abilities refers to different levels of these abilities during the acquisition of first words. As noted earlier, more research on this early stage is required to better understand how it differs from later development.

Method

While theory tends to attract much attention in child phonology, there have also been important methodological issues raised and discussed in recent years. These deal with both the elicitation and transcription of data. Understanding in these areas will eventually lead to a much sounder data base than we currently have.

There are two basic alternatives available to elicit a child's speech. The most common among published accounts is the collection of spontaneous speech. This method has been used in the diary studies mentioned earlier. The other method is to construct an elicitation task of some kind. The most common alternatives are to have the child identify a picture or imitate the experimenter. The issue here is *whether children imitate a word differently than they produce it spontaneously*. The facts on this issue are far from clear. Templin (1947) and Edwards and Garnica (in preparation) have argued that normal children do not change their production in imitation. Data from children with language problems (summarized in Ingram, 1975b, Chapter 4) indicate that they do.

A second question has to do with whether or not children learn sounds dependent on the word in which those sounds occur. Stated another way, *do children's productions of a sound vary according to the word in which it appears?* Templin (1947) has argued that the acquisition of a sound is independent of the words in which it is used. Consequently, she feels the ability to produce a sound can be established from observing it in a single word. If this were true, it would lessen the number of words needed to obtain a representative sample of a child's speech. Recent data reported in Ingram (1976), however, suggest that Templin (1947) was not correct. Example (17) presents the percentage of correct production of some initial fricatives by children between 3:0 and 5:11.

(17)   a.   *shelf*   81%   (33/41)
           shampoo   81%   (33/41)
       b.   *vase*   84%   (32/38)
           volcano   55%   (21/38)
       c.   *thief*   33%   (13/40)
           thermometer 63%   (25/40)

The first pair shows what Templin (1947) found, that production can be the same across words. The performance on the next two pairs, however, demonstrates that other factors can cause variation. For initial /v-/, the monosyllabic word resulted in a much higher correct production than did the longer word. The examples in (17)c show that length is not the only factor involved. The final /-f/ in *thief* caused many of the children to assimilate /θ-/ to /-f/. These data suggest that this issue is far from settled and that it requires further investigation.

A particularly troublesome aspect of method is transcription of the child's speech. For one thing, children often produce sounds that are not like those commonly found in the adult language. Bush et al. (1973) have been developing a special system of diacritic symbols specifically designated for child phonology. These will need to be tested and refined. Also, evidence suggests that a single transcriber may not be very accurate at objectively recording the finer aspects of a child's speech. This was noted a long time ago by Henderson (1938). Recently Johnson and Bush (1971) have observed that multiple transcribers will vary from one another in their recording of the same forms. A further insight has been added by Oller and Eilers (in press), who found that transcribers altered their transcriptions when they knew what the child was trying to say. Interestingly, the changes were toward a more accurate transcription. Early results suggest that more than one transcriber should be used, and that more than one instance of a form should be elicited so that crucial decisions do not need to be made from one instance.

CONCLUSION

The next few years should be a period of great advances in child phonology. We have now reached a point where the stages of acquisition are being isolated and the general characteristics of each are being formulated. This has permitted a better understanding of the results from diverse studies which show the acquisition of different skills at many different ages. The infant of 4 months, for instance, can hear fine discriminations of sound, and yet the 6-year-old cannot tell the functional difference between *hotdog* and *hot dog*. Piaget's (Flavell, 1963) theory shows, however, that each requires very different skills.

There are several specific areas that should be receiving special attention. The slow and unique development during the acquisition of the first 50 words suggests that this is a qualitatively different stage from that which follows. The very active period of development between ages 1:6 and 4:0 provides several interesting areas of research. The question of linguistic perception and its relation to production still requires close examination. With the establishment of a basic set of phonological processes, it is now possible to learn more about the developmental patterns of each. Less common processes need to be observed and understood. These processes especially need to be compared to their effect in creating contrasts within the child's own system. We need to resolve the conflict about whether the child has a system of contrasts of his own.

While most work has concentrated on acquisition before age 4, it is now clear that phonological acquisition is far from complete at this age. An especially important issue is the way in which morphophoneme acquisition progresses. This includes information and comparison on development during the period from 4 to 7 as well as the one from 6 to 12.

It is of course impossible in a single chapter to cover each of the various areas that research has addressed in the last few years. At a time of such active work, it is also difficult to predict with total confidence the directions of future research. What is clear, however, is that more reliable data are required on the actual speech of young children at each of the stages described earlier. With a rich body of phonological data, many of the theoretical controversies should fall into perspective. The insightful and elegant theory of Piaget (Flavell, 1963) provides a good example of what can result when facts and theory go together.

REFERENCES

Atkinson-King, K. 1973. Children's acquisition of phonological stress contrasts. UCLA Working Papers in Phonetics. No. 25.

Berko, J. 1958. The child's learning of English morphology. Word 14:150–177.

Bloch, O. 1913. Notes sur le langage d'un enfant. Mem. Soc. Ling. Paris 18:37–59.

Bloom, L. 1970. Language Development: Form and Function in Emerging Grammars. M.I.T. Press, Cambridge, Mass.

Braine, M. D. 1963. The ontogeny of English phrase structure: The first phase. Language 39:1–13.

Braine, M. D. 1971. The acquisition of language in infant and child. In C. E. Reed (ed.), The Learning of Language, pp. 153–186. Appleton-Century-Crofts, New York.

Brown, R. 1973. A First Language. Harvard University Press, Cambridge, Mass.

Brown, R., and C. Fraser. 1964. The acquisition of syntax. In R. Brown and U. Bellugi (eds.), The Acquisition of Language, Monogr. Soc. Res. Child Dev. 29:43–79.

Bush, C., M. Edwards, J. Luckau, C. Stoel, M. Macken, and J. Petersen. 1973. On specifying a system for transcribing consonants in child language: A working paper with examples from American English and Mexican Spanish. Unpublished paper, Child Language Project. Stanford University.

Chao, Y. R. 1951. The Cantian idiolect: An analysis of the Chinese spoken by a twenty-eight-months-old child. Univ. Calif. Publ. Semitic Philol. 11:27–44.

Chomsky, N., and M. Halle. 1968. The Sound Pattern of English. Harper and Row, New York.

Clark, E. V. 1973. What's in a word: On the child's acquisition of semantics in his first language. In T. Moore (ed.), Cognitive Development and the Acquisition of Language, pp. 65–110. Academic Press, New York.

Deville, G. 1890. Notes sur le développement du langage. Rev. Ling. Philol. Comp. 23:330–343.

Edwards, M. L. 1974. Perception and production in child phonology: The testing of four hypotheses. J. Child Lang. 1:205–219.

Ferguson, C., and C. Farwell. 1975. Words and sounds in early language acquisition: English initial consonants in the first 50 words. Language 51:419–439.

Ferguson, C., and O. Garnica. 1975. Theories of phonological development. *In* E. Lenneberg and E. Lenneberg (eds.), Foundations of Language Development. UNESCO.

Flavell, J. 1963. The Developmental Psychology of Jean Piaget. Van Nostrand, New York.

Foulke, K., and S. Stinchfield. 1929. The speech development of four infants under two years of age. Pedag. Seminary 36:140–171.

Franke, C. 1912. Uber die erste Lautstufe der Kinder. Anthropologischer 7:633–676.

Garnica, O. 1973. The development of phonemic speech perception. *In* T. Moore (ed.), Cognitive Development and the Acquisition of Language, pp. 215–222. Academic Press, New York.

Henderson, F. 1938. Objectivity and constancy of judgment in articulation testing. J. Educ. Res. 31:348–356.

Hills, E. 1914. The speech of a child two years of age. Dialect Notes 4:84–100.

Holmes, U. 1927. The phonology of an English-speaking child. Am. Speech 2:219–225.

Humphreys, M. W. 1880. A contribution to infantile linguistics. Trans. Am. Philol. Assoc. 11:5–17.

Ingram, D. 1974. Phonological rules in young children. J. Child Lang. 1:49–64.

Ingram, D. 1975a. If and when transformations are acquired by children. Monograph Series on Language and Linguistics. Georgetown University. No. 27.

Ingram, D. 1975b. Surface contrast in children's speech. J. Child Lang. 2:287–292.

Ingram, D. 1976. Phonological Disability in Children. Arnold, London.

Jakobson, R. 1968. Child Language, Aphasia, and Phonological Universals. Mouton, The Hague.

Johnson, C., and C. Bush. 1971. A note on transcribing the speech of young children. Papers and Reports on Child Language Development 3:95–100.

Kornfeld, J. 1971. Theoretical issues in child phonology. *In* Papers from the Seventh Regional Meeting of the Chicago Linguistic Society, pp. 454–468. Chicago.

Leopold, W. 1947. Speech Development of a Bilingual Child: A Linguist's Record. Vol. 2. Sound Learning in the First Two Years. Northwestern University Press, Evanston, Ill.

Lewis, M. 1951. Infant Speech: A Study of the Beginnings of Language. Kegan Paul, London.

McCarthy, D. 1954. Language development in children. *In* L. Carmichael (ed.), Manual of Child Psychology, pp. 492–630. Wiley, New York.

Menn, L. 1971. Phonotactic rules in beginning speech. Lingua 26:225–51.

Miller, W., and S. Ervin. 1964. The development of grammar in child language. *In* U. Bellugi and R. Brown (eds.), The Acquisition of Language. Monographs of the Society for Research in Child Development 29:9–34.

Morse, P. 1974. Infant speech perception: A preliminary model and review of literature. *In* R. Schiefelbusch and L. Lloyd (eds.), Language Perspectives: Acquisition, Retardation, and Intervention, pp. 19–53. University Park Press, Baltimore.

Moskowitz, A. 1970. The two-year-old stage in the acquisition of English phonology. Language 46:426–41.

Moskowitz, A. 1973. On the status of vowel shift in English. *In* T. Moore (ed.), Cognitive Development and the Acquisition of Language, pp. 223–260. Academic Press, New York.

Nelson, K. 1973. Structure and strategy in learning to talk. Monographs of the Society for Research in Child Development, 38:Nos. 1–2.

Oller, D., and R. Eilers. Phonetic expectation and transcription validity. Phonetica. In press.

Oller, D., L. Wieman, W. Doyle, and C. Ross. 1974. Child speech, babbling, and phonological universals. Papers and Reports on Child Language Development 8:33–44.

Olmsted, D. 1971. Out of the Mouth of Babes. Mouton, The Hauge.

Piaget, J. 1962. Play, Dreams, and Imitation in Childhood. Norton, New York.

Poole, I. 1934. Genetic development of articulation of consonant sounds in speech. Elementary English Reviews 11:159–61.

Ronjat, J. 1913. Le developpement du langage observé chez un enfant bilingue. Champion, Paris.

Roussey, C. 1899–1900. Notes sur l'apprentissage de la parole chez un enfant. Parole 1:870–880; 2:23–40.

Shvachkin, N. 1973. The development of phonemic speech perception in early childhood. *In* C. A. Ferguson and D. I. Slobin (eds.), Studies of Child Language Development, pp. 92–127. Holt, Rinehart and Winston, New York.

Smith, N. 1973. The Acquisition of Phonology: A Case Study. Cambridge University Press, Cambridge, Mass.

Stampe, D. 1969. The acquisition of phonetic representation. *In* Papers from the Fifth Regional Meeting of the Chicago Linguistic Society, pp. 443–454. Chicago.

Stampe, D. 1972. A Dissertation on Natural Phonology. Unpublished Ph.D. dissertation, University of Chicago.

Templin, M. 1947. Spontaneous versus imitated verbalization in testing articulation in preschool children. J. Speech and Hear. Disord. 12:293–300.

Templin, M. 1957. Certain Language Skills in Children: Their Development and Interrelationships. Institute of Child Welfare Monograph No. 26. The University of Minnesota Press, Minneapolis.

Velten, H. 1943. The growth of phonemic and lexical patterns in infant language. Language 19:281–292.

Vinson, J. 1915. Observations sur le développement du language chez l'enfant. Rev. Ling. 49:1–39.

Waterson, N. 1971. Child phonology: A prosodic view. J. Ling. 7:170–221.

Wellman, B., I. Case, I. Mengert, and D. Bradbury. 1931. Speech sounds of young children. University of Iowa Studies in Child Welfare, No. 5.

Winitz, H. 1969. Articulatory Acquisition and Behavior. Appleton-Century-Crofts, New York.

An Analysis of Some Deviant Phonological Rules of English

JAMES P. LORENTZ

The level at which a phonological form is represented—regardless of whether or not it is acceptable—is determined by the degree of abstraction possible in the analysis used (Anderson, 1974). Few studies of children with defective speech or deviant phonologies have gone beyond the level of phonetic representation (i.e., what the child actually says) in limited environments. Recent work in speech pathology (summarized in Ingram, 1976; McReynolds and Engmann, 1975; and Singh, 1976) has included distinctive feature analysis but primarily at a phonetic rather than a phonemic level. The research reported by Lorentz is the first to include not only phonemic representations, which posit underlying forms for phonetic representations, but also phonological rules derived from specifying the various shapes these morphemes can take in different contexts or environments. He derives several sets of phonological rules from a single phonological sample and provides a detailed discussion of the rationale for accepting or rejecting both these rules and the order in which they must appear. Lorentz's detailed and systematic analysis serves as an excellent example of the methods available for studying both normal and deviant phonologies.

—DMM

There have been a considerable number of investigations directly concerned with the normal phonological development of the child. Numerous older accounts exist, mostly in diary form, and during the last several decades increasing interest has been devoted to this

This chapter is a revised version of a paper presented at the Second Annual Summer Linguistics Conference, University of California, Santa Cruz, July 1972.

question, as exemplified in Velten (1943), Leopold (1947), Chao (1951), Albright and Albright (1956), Burling (1959), Stampe (1969), Moskowitz (1970a and 1970b), Kornfeld (1971), Edwards (1971), Ingram (1971), Shvachkin (1973), and Smith (1973). Very little work of a comparable nature, however, has been carried out with cases of unusual or deviant phonological development. Jakobson (1968) mentions the investigation of Stumpf (1901), and there have been several more recent accounts that analyze such cases within a linguistic framework, such as Cross (1950), Applegate (1961), Haas (1963), and Oller (1973).

One might suppose that cases of unusual phonological development are quite rare, but, in fact, deviant phonologies are really very common and have fallen traditionally within the investigative domain of the field of speech pathology. For many years, however, speech pathologists have treated all such cases indiscriminately under the general heading of "articulation disorders," a cover term that can refer to almost any kind of speech defect. Recently, speech pathologists have recognized the necessity of distinguishing cases of "functional articulation disorder" or *dyslalia* from disorders of articulation arising from hearing defects, motor defects (dysarthria), developmental failures at the cortical level, and structural abnormalities of the articulatory mechanism (Morley, 1960). In addition, Grady (1963), Hartley (1963), and Simms (1963) have attempted to narrow the definition of *dyslalia* to cover just those cases of "articulatory disorders" for which no physiological cause can be determined. They point out that for such children the term "defect of articulation" is quite inappropriate, since these children experience no *physical* difficulty in articulating sounds. They conclude that differences between the speech of these children and the speech of adults is strictly phonemic in nature. That is, such children have phonological systems that are different from the standard phonology but are consistent and coherent in their own right. This view has been reiterated more recently in speech pathology journals by Crocker (1969), Compton (1970), Weber (1970), and McReynolds and Huston (1971).

Thus, while numerous cases of deviant phonologies have been reported in the speech pathology literature, very few of these studies until recently have demonstrated any real understanding of the nature of such phonological disorders. Traditionally, each sound was treated separately, in terms of both analysis and treatment, and analysis generally consisted of nothing more involved than a listing or classification of the possible substitutions that could occur for a standard sound. One might expect that an increased understanding of deviant phonologies would result in an increased sophistication in the analysis of such phonologies. Unfortunately, this is not the case. Most analyses ignore almost completely the environmental conditions that govern the determination of sound variations in such phonologies. But any analysis of a phonological system that does not attempt to state explicitly the environmental conditions that govern the occurrence of sound substitutions, mutations, or deletions is only half an analysis. Reference is also frequently made to feature analysis, but, in general, the most that speech pathologists seem to have discovered in feature analysis is a more reasonable and insightful method of classifying the deviant phonemes that a child produces. This, of course, is useful but it provides one with only a partial, still rather superficial analysis of the child's phonology.

The only genuinely thorough analysis of such a deviant phonological system that I have been able to discover is by the linguist Applegate (1961). All other accounts have been lacking in one respect or another. For example, the analysis that Cross (1950) gives of a 4-year-old boy's deviant phonology is insightful, but neither explicit nor complete. Cross points out the loss of /l/ in initial consonant clusters (flew → [suu], fly → [sai], sleeve → [siiz]) but does not clarify the condition for exceptions to this rule which, as exemplified in please → [pwiiz], bled → [bwed], etc. and ugly → [ugwi], is simply that /l/ becomes [w] after [+labial] or [+velar] segments. Nor does he point out that this rule must apply *after* another very general rule /f/ → [s], which explains why we have fly → [sai], but not *[swai].[1]

The purpose of this paper is to demonstrate both the feasibility and the utility of doing a complete phonological analysis of such cases of aberrant phonological systems. There is utility in such an analysis for both the speech pathologist and the linguist. A truly thorough analysis of such cases can offer the speech pathologist a sound basis

---

[1]Slashes (/ /) enclose phonemic or underlying segments. Brackets ([ ]) enclose phonetic or surface realizations of underlying segments. Brackets that enclose features in rules (such as in rule 2, Table 3) simply delimit the boundaries of individual segments and do not imply anything at all about the underlying or surface status of a segment. Phonological rules have the following general form: A → B / X__Y which is equivalent to: XAY → XBY. The arrow (→) indicates that some change in A occurs such that A "becomes" or "is realized as" B. This change occurs "in the environment" (/) of some left environment X and some right environment Y. The dash between X and Y indicates the exact position of A in the string of segments under consideration. A and B may be ø; A ≠ B; X and Y may be null.

from which to carry out treatment, regardless of the method of treatment employed. In fact, complete analyses of such aberrant phonological systems will probably result in new, more sophisticated methods of treatment. This has already been suggested by those speech pathologists who have attempted to reinterpret deviant phonological systems in terms of feature analysis. Additionally, it is quite likely that such phonologies are deviant in a systematic and predictable way. Consequently, a logical, central goal of speech pathology ought to be a general characterization of the nature of deviant phonological systems: how they are structured, how they change, and what general or specific restrictions determine the form and the range of application of phonological rules. The greater the number of explicit, well documented accounts of such deviant phonologies that are available for analysis, the more likely the eventual attainment of this goal becomes.

For the linguist, analyses of such deviations from the standard phonology can be useful in helping to determine precisely what the make-up of the norm is. Such nonstandard phonological systems demonstrate alternative sets of rules which, for reasons that will be clarified shortly, must be presumed to operate from the same base as normal phonological rules. This amounts to a natural converging operation that allows us to contrast the processes and elements which have been posited for normal rules with those that must be posited for such aberrant rules. In effect, these cases provide the linguist with the opportunity to double-check hypotheses concerning the generation of normal phonological output. Deviant phonologies are also of interest in their own right. This is especially true when one considers the question of phonological universals, since deviant phonologies document a range of possibilities inherent in the articulatory mechanism and in associated phonological processes that may be quite rare or completely absent in normal phonologies.

Such unusual phonological systems are, of course, closely related to the developing phonologies of young children, but it is not correct to characterize such deviant systems as "frozen" speech of early childhood, as Jakobson (1968, p. 15) does. While it is obvious that a number of rules of deviant phonologies are mere carry-overs from restricted systems of early development, this is not generally true for the entire system, which is the result of a *separate* and *continuing* development. The original impetus for the development of the aberrant system may have been, for example, a set of typical assimilation rules that did not drop out as would be normally expected, but persisted. During subsequent growth of the phonology, newly acquired phonemic elements and processes would be required to adjust to these persisting assimilation rules, and at several points within the system these new elements would also deviate from the norm, thus serving to deepen to an even greater extent the separation between standard and aberrant systems. It is unlikely that any typically complex deviant phonological system would be equivalent in all respects to any normal stage of phonological development.

Another important difference between developing phonologies and typical deviant phonologies is the relatively small amount of variation to be found in such deviant systems. That is, aberrant phonological systems of 4- and 5-year-old children are relatively fixed and consistent in terms of the operation of the rules of those systems.[2] In developing phonologies, on the other hand, there is a good deal of variation in phonological forms and processes. Thus, deviant phonological systems of the type discussed here are best viewed as the summed result of a series of intermediate stages, each one a further development away from the standard phonology, and each stage adding its own set of deviances to those that had existed before. From this point of view, it is perfectly logical to consider the end result of this aberrant development, the deviant phonological system, as functionally equivalent in principle to the normal phonological system manifested by a child of equivalent maturation.

This paper presents an analysis of one such deviant phonological system. Joe, who was 4½ years old when the investigation began, is quite intelligent and very lively, and there is no evidence of a hearing disorder or of any physical impairment of the articulatory mechanism. Joe's phonology manifested a small set of deviant phonological rules which were restricted in application to a quite limited environment. A simple substitution analysis of the data presented in Table 1 yields the following results in word initial position: /sw/ is replaced by [f] and [fw], /sm/ is replaced by [f] and [f] + [Ṽ] (vowel nasalization), /sp/ is replaced by [f], /sn/ is replaced by [s] and [s] + [Ṽ], /st/ is replaced by [s], and /sk/ is replaced by [ks].[3]

---

[2]Of course, during the dissolution of a deviant phonology there will be an increase in variability as the child's pronunciation changes in the direction of the standard system.

[3]In addition /θ/ is replaced by [f] in all positions and /v/ is replaced by [b] word initially. Since these substitutions occur without environmental restrictions they will not be discussed any further.

Table 1. Examples of word initial fricative/−liquid consonant clusters[a]

/sw/	swoop [f]oop; swollen [f]ollen; (nonsense:) 'swoy' [foy]; swallow [f]allow; swamp [f]amp; swat [f]at ~ [fw]at; swine [fw]ine; swam [fw]am; sway [fw]ay; swim [fw]im; swing [fw]ing; swerve [fw]erve
/sm/	smooth [f]ooth; smoke [f]oke ~ [fõwk]; small [f]all ~ [fɔl]; smile [f]ile; smell [f]ell; Smith [f]ith; smirk [f]irk
/sp/	spoon [f]oon; spot [f]ot; sponge [f]onge; space [f]ace; spinach [f]inach
/sn/	snow [s]ow; snap [sæp]; snake [sēyk]; snail [sēyl]; snip [sĩp]; sneak [sïyk]
/st/	Stooy Stinker [s]ooy [s]inker; story [s]ory; stomach [s]omach; stand [s]and; stitch [s]itch; steam [s]eam; street [s]reet
/sk/	Scott's school [ks]ott's [ks]ool; scar [ks]ar; sky [skay]; skunk [ks]unk; scout [ks]out; skate [ks]ate; squash [ks]uash

[a]For convenience, only the affected clusters are placed in phonetic brackets. The rest of the word is spelled out normally.

METHODOLOGICAL CONSIDERATIONS

Before proceeding with the analysis, it is necessary to consider the method employed in gathering the data.[4] The most efficient general method of observing the extent and distribution of a phonological rule is by eliciting specific words, phrases, and sentences from the subject. With young children this amounts to eliciting imitations. In using imitation, however, it is always necessary to be sure that in *imitating* the child is not distorting his own, natural manner of speaking. For Joe it became obvious rather quickly that, in general, no such danger was involved. However, in addition to imitation, a good deal of natural conversation was elicited, with attempts being made to "center" the conversation around certain words or phrases which were of interest. Such natural conversation elicitation acts as a check on the imitation method and brings out any artifacts that might be inherent in imitation as a procedure. Generally speaking, imitation proved to be a quick and bias-free method for gathering the required

[4]Elicitations were done according to instruction by Kendra Bersamin, a friend who knows Joe very well and has excellent rapport with him. I am grateful to her for her help on this project. All sessions were recorded on a Sony cassette-recorder.

data. Two kinds of problems, however, were encountered. In acquiring some data from Joe, several single-word elicitations were obtained at the beginning of one session as follows:

K:	OK, can you say swallow?	J:	[f]allow
K:	Can you say swamp?	J:	[f]amp
K:	swim	J:	[fw]im
K:	switch	J:	[fw]itch
K:	smack	J:	[fw]ack
K:	smack	J:	[fw]ack
K:	smear	J:	[fw]ear
K:	smell	J:	[fw]ell

In the last four imitations we have /sm/ being replaced by [fw]. One might infer from these data that /sw/ and /sm/ clusters behave in the same way. And yet this is quite incorrect. A thorough search of the data did not turn up one other occurrence of /sm/ becoming [fw]. A glance at the first four items in the elicitation indicates what has gone wrong here. The elicitation session began with /sw/ clusters and proceeded through the first four items, all initial /sw/ clusters. When a switch was made to the /sm/ clusters, Joe simply continued to handle them as /sw/ due to the acoustic and articulatory similarity between the two. Joe was "set" to hear more /sw/ initial words and reinterpreted the /sm/ clusters to conform to that "set."

A somewhat different kind of reinterpretation of elicited words can also occur. Consider the following examples:

K: swirl   J: [ksr̩l]
J: I have a [f]aceman... and he's from outer [f]ace.
K: Does he have a flyswatter? Can you say flyswatter?
J: What's a fly[sɔtr̩]?

In the first example we have [ks] subsituting for /sw/ in the original word. If we take this at face value, we have to make a rule realizing /sw/ as [ks], a thoroughly unlikely possibility. What has happened, in fact, is that Joe has reinterpreted the stimulus word "swirl" as "squirrel" and applied the normal rule for initial /sk/ clusters to that word. In the second example, Joe is thinking and talking about spacemen and outer space and is then asked about flyswatters (it happened to be the next word on the list). Within the context of spacemen and flying saucers "flyswatter" can only make sense as some sort of flying saucer. Thus, Joe reinterprets the stimulus word as a variant of flying saucer, a "fly-sauter," and asks what it is supposed to be. Upon finding out what a flyswatter is, Joe quickly reverts to the spaceman game and replies: "Uh, uh, it has a flying saucer with it, got a flying saucer with it so it can go flying."

The above examples show the difficulties involved in working with imitation as a technique for eliciting raw data for phonological analysis. However, such examples are quite rare and, in general, no particular problems were encountered in using this method. These mistakes themselves are revealing and underline the necessity of treating data with great care, regardless of the source. The other sort of danger inherent in an imitation task is that the child's repetitions will deviate from his own natural pronunciation in the direction of the adult's pronunciation. This problem did not occur in working with Joe since the rules that comprise his phonology are so strong that deviations in response to the adult form simply do not occur. This is not to say that if one made a deliberate *effort* to get the child to pronounce the words in an adult manner, there would not be some effect. But this was rarely attempted and when tried met with little success.

ANALYSIS OF THE DATA

The previous substitution analysis is not very revealing, for it does not tell us whether there are any general principles operating, and it is also not capable of accounting for or even suggesting reasons for certain variations noted in the data. One way of beginning an analysis of such data is to look at each case separately, devising rules to account for each "substitution." What happens to the /sk/ cluster appears to be singular enough, and one might be happy to get it out of the way with a simple metathesis rule: /sk/ → [ks] /#__. /st/ clusters could also be accounted for rather readily by simply deleting the following consonant: /t/ → ø /#s__; and an extension of this rule would appear to also cover /sn/ clusters: /nV/→V̂ /#s__. For /sp/, there seems to be a simple assimilation rule operating with a subsequent deletion of the stops: /s/→[f] /#__p, /p/→ø /#f__, and again, a similar phenomenon appears to occur for the equivalent nasal cluster: /s/₀ [f] /#__m, /m/→ø /#f__. Finally, /sw/ clusters could be accounted for by the same assimilation rule, plus an optional deletion rule: /s/→ [f] /#__w. Optional: /w/→ø/#s__. However, a number of important generalizations are simply ignored by such an item-by-item analysis.

A close analysis of the examples given for the /sw/ cluster indicates that, except for the realization of "swat" as [fwat], there is a clear dichotomy between rounded and unrounded vowels and the occurrence of either [f] or [fw]. This is true to the extent that the vowel sound of "swallow," "swamp," and "swat" is taken to be [ɔ] and thus rounded, as opposed to [a], unrounded, as in "swine" [fw]ine. In American speech, the dividing line between [ɔ] and [a] is rather tenuous and this could explain the occurrence of [fwat]. It should be noted that "swat" also occurs without [w]: [fɔt], thus, the only variation which occurs in the realization of /sw/ as [f] or [fw] is precisely with the vowel [ɔ]. The rule to be posited to account for this alternation between [fw] and [f] is simply that /w/ is deleted after assimilation if the following vowel is [+round].

If we consider /sk/→[ks] /#__ a valid description for that consonant cluster, then we can summarize the rules governing fricative initial consonant clusters as follows. Metathesize /sk/ to [ks]. Assimilate the fricative of any fricative initial consonant cluster to the position of a following nonliquid consonant. Nasalize any vowel following initial /sn/ clusters and delete any /w/ that follows an initial fricative and precedes a rounded vowel. Then delete all noncontinuant segments that follow initial fricatives.

Before formalizing these rules it is necessary to consider some additional data that are relevant to the operation of the rules in the environment of word, morpheme, and syllable boundaries. In Table 2, only relevant word (#), morpheme (+), and syllable (−) boundaries are marked.[5] In the middle column is the presumed (approximate) underlying representation of the corresponding word or phrase in the left column. In the right column is the phonetic representation of Joe's pronunciation of each form.

It is generally the case that all word initial clusters of the type under discussion here will follow the posited phonological rules. This is quite clear from the previous examples given in Table 1, and it is also clear from an examination of the first set of examples in Table 2. In those cases in which the /s/ is the last segment of the preceding word ("space country") the rule does not operate. Thus we have [féyskəntriy] but not *[féyksəntriy]. But in those cases where the cluster is word initial ("I spy," "I scream"), the rule does operate, thus: [ayfáy], [áyksriym]. This is even true when the last segment of the preceding word is /s/ (or /z/), such as ("Scott's school," "his stingers," "breaks spiders") where we have [ksɔ́tsksuwl̩], [hɪz

---

[5]There are, occasionally, certain difficulties in determining what boundary is correctly imputed to a young child. In the word "tele+scope," for example, the division between tele- and -scope is marked with a morpheme boundary. But it may very well be that for Joe there is no morpheme boundary present at all, but only a syllable boundary.

Table 2. Examples of fricative/−liquid consonant clusters at word, morpheme, and syllable boundaries

---

Word boundary
  I spy   /ay#spáy/   [ayfáy]
  Breaks spiders   /breyks#spáydr̥s/   [breyksfáydr̥z]
  His stingers   /hɪz#stíŋr̥s/   [hɪzsíŋr̥z]
  I scream   /áy#skriym/   [áyksriym]
  You scream   /yúw#skriym/   [yúwksriym]
  Scott's school   /skɔ́ts#skuwl̩/   [ksɔ́tsksuwl̩]
  Space country   /spéys#kəntriy/   [féyskəntriy]

Morpheme boundary
  Teaspoon   /tíy+spuwn/   [tʰíyfuwn]
  Bedspread   /béd+spred/   [bédfred]
  Outer space   /æwtr̥+spéys/   [æwdr̥féys]
  Displease   /dɪs+plíyz/   [dɪsplíyz]
  Ice box   /áys+bɔks/   [áyspɔks]
  Understand   /əndr̥+stǽnd/   [əndr̥sǽnd]
  Sidestep   /sáyd+stɛp/   [sáydsɛp]
  Lipstick   /líp+stɪk/   [lípsɪk]
  Upstairs   /əp+stérs/   [əpsérz]
  Telescope   /télə+skòwp/   [tʰéləksòwp]
  Roller skate   /rówlr̥+skeyt/   [rówlr̥kseyt]
  Boyscout   /bɔy+skǽwt/   [bɔyksǽwt]
  Ice cream   /áys+kriym/   [áyskriym]
  Blacksmith   /blǽk+smɪθ/   [blǽkfɪf]
  Mistake   /mɪs+téyk/   [mɪstéyk]

Syllable boundary
  Hospital   /hɔ́s−pɪtl̩/   [hɔ́spɪtl̩]
  Aspirin   /ǽs−pr̥ɪn/   [ǽspr̥ɪn]
  (Nonsense:)   /pǽs−pr̥ɪn/   [pʰǽspr̥ɪn]
  Explode   /ɛk−splówd/   [__flówd]
  Explain   /ɛk−spléyn/   [__fléyn]
  Whisper   /wís−pr̥/   [wíspr̥]
  Suspicious   /sə−spíʃəs/   [səfíʃəs]
  Mystery   /mís−tr̥iy/   [místr̥iy]
  Presto   /prés−tow/   [pʰréstow]
  Christopher   /krís−təfr̥/   [kʰrístəfr̥]
  Western   /wés−tr̥n/   [wéstr̥n]
  Distance   /dís−təns/   [dístəns]
  Monster   /mɔ́ns−tr̥/   [mɔ́nstr̥]
  Construct   /kən−strɔ́kt/   [kənsrɔ́kt]
  Astronaut   /ǽs−trənɔt/   [ǽstrənɔt]
  Extra   /ɛ́ks−trə/   [ɛ́kʰstr̥]
  Basket   /bǽs−kɪt/   [bǽskɪt]
  (Nonsense:)   /mǽs−kɪt/   [mǽskɪt]
  Eskimo   /és−kɪmow/   [éskɪmow]
  Excuse me   /ɛk−skyúwz#miy/   [ɛkksyúwzmiy]

---

síŋrz], and [breyksfáydṛz], respectively. If there is any condition that might promote breaking of the phonological rules word initially, it would occur where an /s/ is the last segment of the previous word. Yet, the rules do not break down even in such a tongue-twister as "Scott's school." The only example that I have of the rules not operating word initially is with "I scream" where it is used in the phrase: "I scream, you scream, we all scream for ice cream." I think that the reason for this is transparent: The "I scream" is confused with "ice cream," where the rules do not operate.

But exactly the same thing that is true for word initial clusters is also true of morpheme initial clusters such as in "teaspoon," "bedspread," "understand," "lipstick," "roller skate," "boy-scout," "blacksmith," and "telescope." That is, in all such environments the rules operate just as in word initial position. Also, just as with "space country," the rules do not operate across a morpheme boundary when the last segment of the preceding morpheme is an /s/, such as: "ice cream" [áyskriym], "displease" [dɪsplíyz], "ice box" [áyspoks]. There are no exceptions to this condition in the data that I have collected.[6]

The last boundary to be discussed is the "syllable" boundary. The syllable is a controversial subject in linguistic theory and any data that can shed some light on this question are of value. The general problem in defining a syllable is that syllable boundaries do not necessarily coincide with boundaries that mark meaning elements (i.e., word or morpheme boundaries). Consequently, a syllable must be defined as a strictly phonological/phonetic entity. The difficulty with such a definition is that there do not appear to be any consistent physiological or acoustic parameters which can be correlated with what is perceived by subjects to be a "syllable." The approach that will be taken here is that, in those words in which there is no morpheme boundary present, there is some phonological boundary operating which, depending upon its position in the word, either blocks or allows the operation of the posited phonological rules. This boundary is referred to as a "syllable" boundary. In noting the manner in which the syllable boundary appears to operate I will try to explicate the condition for its placement in the word and consequently the condition for the operation or nonoperation of Joe's phonological rules.

---

[6]This failure of the phonological rules to operate across morpheme boundaries does not necessarily mean that the morpheme boundary has blocked the operation of these phonological rules. In each such case the boundary is simply no longer in initial position.

Consider the examples in Table 2 which are marked with a syllable boundary (−). If we divide these cases up into those which are stressed on the first syllable and those which are not, we discover that all words which are stressed on the first syllable also do *not* allow the operation of the phonological rules on the internal clusters. This is true regardless of whether the /s/ is preceded by a vowel ("hospital," "aspirin," and "basket"), a nasal ("monster"), or a stop ("extra"). That is, if the group of phonological segments that immediately precedes the /s/ is stressed, then the /s/ is apparently drawn into that "syllable" or group of sounds. If, on the other hand, the stress falls on the group of sounds that immediately follows the /s/, then the rule *does* operate: "excuse," "construct," "suspicious," "explain," and "explode."[7]

It is important to point out that if the condition for the determination of the location of the syllable boundary is correct (i.e., that the syllable boundary will fall after the /s/ if the stress is on the first group of sounds, "whisper," "basket," etc.), then morpheme boundaries and syllable boundaries will not always coincide. For example, the morpheme boundary for "teaspoon" is placed before the /s/ and, consequently, the rule operates: /tíy+spuwn/ → [tíyfuwn]. If, however, no morpheme boundary were present, then, by the above stated condition, the syllable boundary would have to occur *after* the /s/, and the rule would not operate: /tíys−puwn/: [tíyspuwn]. Thus, the presence of a morpheme boundary controls the occurrence or nonoccurrence of a syllable boundary, or the placement of that boundary if one were to assume that a syllable boundary is always present.

Based upon the above examples and analysis, it seems reasonable to state that the operation of these deviant phonological rules is dependent upon the placement of a cluster with respect to *any* boundary: word, morpheme, or syllable. Specifically, these phonological rules will only operate when a relevant cluster occurs in any boundary initial position. These rules do not operate across boundaries.[8]

---

[7]Notice that if the word "mistake" were assumed to contain a syllable boundary rather than a morpheme boundary, then Joe's pronunciation of this word would violate the stress condition for the placement of syllable boundaries.

[8]It is interesting to note just how specifically these phonological rules are tied to the boundary initial environment. After the inversion of /sk/ to [ks] in the words "square," "squash," and "squeak," we have [sw] clusters that are not separated by any boundary, but which do not obey the posited phonological rules because there is no boundary that occurs immediately before the [s]. Thus, the [sw] cluster is allowed because the phonological rules are not relevant in this environment. The above three words are pronounced by Joe as follows: [kswér], [kswóʃ], [kswíyk].

Table 3. Phonological rules

1. /sk/→	[ks]	/ B____	
2. [+fricative]→	[αposition]	/ B____	$\begin{bmatrix} C \\ -\text{liquid} \\ \alpha\text{position} \end{bmatrix}$
3. V→	[+nasal]	/ B [+fricative]	$\begin{bmatrix} C \\ +\text{alveolar} \\ +\text{nasal} \end{bmatrix}$ ____
4. $\begin{bmatrix} +\text{glide} \\ +\text{round} \end{bmatrix}$→	ø	/ B [+fricative] ____	$\begin{bmatrix} V \\ +\text{round} \end{bmatrix}$
5. [−continuant]→	ø	/ B [+fricative] ____	

With these additional facts about boundary conditions it is possible to formalize the posited phonological rules in terms of distinctive features. The following abbreviations are utilized in writing these rules:[9] consonant (C) (i.e., any nonvowel); vowel (V); "any boundary" (B).

Rules 1–5 (Table 3) apply only in any boundary initial position. Rule 1 metathesizes /sk/ to [ks]. Rule 2 assimilates the positional value of a following nonliquid consonant onto the fricative. Rule 3 nasalizes any vowel following an /sn/ cluster. Rule 4 deletes any /w/ which follows a fricative and precedes a rounded vowel. Rule 5 deletes any [−continuant] segment which follows a fricative. Rule 1 must precede rules 2 and 5. Rule 2 must precede rules 4 and 5. Rule 3 must precede rule 5.

---

[9]The feature "position" is a cover term for any of the traditional places of articulation, such as "labial," "alveolar," and "velar." The use of the Greek letter alpha (α) before this feature simply indicates the variable selection of these nonbinary positional values. Notice in particular that /w/ is assigned the value "labial." The features "anterior" and "coronal," which are proposed by Chomsky and Halle (1968), are not used here since there is no reasonable way to describe the positional assimilation in /sw/ clusters when using these features. In Chomsky and Halle's system /w/ is assigned the values −anterior and −coronal which are the specification for the velar position; while the labials, of course, are given different values for these features, namely, +anterior and −coronal. Since the labial [f] does not share the same set of features in this system as the glide /w/, it is quite impossible to assimilate the positional features of /w/ to the fricative and produce the required [f]. And yet, this is what the facts demand. It would, of course, be possible to specify the input segment of rule 2 as [+anterior], in which case the assimilation of [αcoronal] would produce [f] from /sw/ clusters. However, this solution is less general and entirely counter-intuitive. Furthermore, as will be seen upon deeper analysis, it is also contradicted by the failure of initial /sk/ clusters to behave in the same way.

The ordering of the above rules is only necessary because the environments that govern rule operation have been written in their most general form. Thus, rule 1 must precede rules 2 and 5 only because 2 and 5 are written without specifying that they do not apply to initial /sk/ clusters. If rule 1 did not precede rules 2 and 5, then 2 and 5 would have to specifically state the exclusion of initial /sk/ clusters from their domain of operation. Additionally, some of the rules are intrinsically ordered, 2 before 5, for example, to the extent that the output of rule 2 (the various forms of the fricative according to the nature of the assimilation) could not have occurred had the stops /p/ and /t/ already been deleted by rule 5.

THEORETICAL CONSIDERATIONS

There is one objection of critical importance that can be raised against the foregoing analysis and against any of the following analyses that are presented in this paper. That objection is simply that all of the data can be much more easily accounted for by the simple expedient of representing in the lexicon all of the affected lexical items in just the same way as they appear on the surface. That is, one can posit the child's own overt form as his underlying lexical representation and do away with all of the posited rules. If taken seriously, this suggestion would certainly simplify things in terms of production rules, but in reality it would do nothing more than shift the entire set of rules to the interpretive component of the grammar. This would be necessary in order for the child to be able to decode the standard phonology (the normal input) so as to relate the overt adult form to his own deviant underlying form. Thus, the only thing that is accomplished by such a shift is to remove the problem from an area of the grammar where we know something to an area of the grammar where we know nothing at all.

There are several other reasons to reject positing the child's overt form as identical to his underlying form. First, one could expect that if a child's underlying form were identical with his overt form, he would have no difficulty in understanding his own phonetic output when confronted with it. It would require nothing more complicated than a simple matching procedure, the two forms to be matched being identical. And yet, it is a common observation that children with deviant phonologies are often not able to understand their own output when it is said back to them, and even if they happen to understand an utterance they do not accept it, but react to it as though it were an impossible thing to say. Both of these facts would seem remarkable if the child's actual underlying form were identical with his output. But if we make the assumption that the child's underlying form is equivalent to the adult's,[10] then such reactions would be completely understandable.

Second, if the child's underlying form is taken to be identical with his own output, and if he has a whole set of interpretation rules that decode the standard phonology into the deviant underlying form, then it is not at all clear how or why the child goes about altering his pronunciation in order to conform to the adult model. For, if everything the child hears is resolved into the deviant underlying form by means of interpretation rules, and everything he says is already identical with that deviant underlying form, then what model would the child employ in readjusting his phonology? If, however, we posit an underlying form for the child that is taken to be equivalent to the adult underlying form, then the possibility exists that at some point the child will recognize a discrepancy between his underlying form and his overt form and adjust his phonology in order to render the two equivalent. In general, then, there is no good reason to posit the child's underlying form as identical with his phonetic output, and there are several excellent reasons for opposing such a position. Consequently, throughout this paper the position is taken that the child's underlying form is equivalent to the adult's underlying form, and that the phonological rules posited here are structurally equivalent in every way to normal phonological rules.

REVISED ANALYSIS OF THE DATA

The most unusual feature of Joe's deviant phonology is the inversion of /sk/ to [ks]. This rule appears to be completely idiosyncratic, and bears no obvious relationship to the general assimilatory processes which occur in the other clusters. If the /sk/ inversion rule could be related in a consistent and natural way to the assimilation

---

[10]To say that the child's underlying form is *equivalent* to the adult's underlying form does not mean that underlying forms of child and adult are identical in all respects. To the extent that *any* child of 4½ has an underlying representation of lexical items or parts of lexical items which is assumed to be the same as that of an adult, then, it is asserted, so does a child with a deviant phonology—as long as that child gives no evidence of discrimination difficulties. With regard to the case under discussion, there is no evidence that 4½-year-old children have underlying representations of such initial clusters which are different from an adult's underlying representation of these clusters.

and deletion rules that determine the output of the other frica-
tive/−liquid (FC) consonant clusters, then we would have a better,
more general explanation of the operation of this deviant phonology.

Such an alternate explanation does exist which relies on the
notion of phonetic constraints. Stanley (1967) has described the way
in which morpheme structure conditions (MSCs) might function in a
generative phonology. In Shibatani (1973) it is explained how the
notion of MSCs can be reapplied at the phonetic level to account for
certain general constraints on the phonetic output of a phonology.
These constraints are referred to by Shibatani as "surface phonetic
constraints" (SPCs). SPCs are intended to express directly those
generalizations about the occurrence of phonetic elements that are
accounted for only indirectly within the traditional generative
framework by means of morpheme structure conditions and
phonological rules. As Shibatani points out, these generalizations
were accounted for by structural linguists with the use of allophonic
rules and phonotactics. A typical example of an SPC is the requirement in German that a word final obstruent is always unvoiced. This
is expressed by Shibatani with the same formalism that Stanley
applies to morpheme structure conditions, namely, with *if-then* constraints:

IF: [−sonorant] ##
$$\downarrow$$
THEN: [−voiced]

The above constraint can also be expressed as a negative constraint:

$$\sim \begin{bmatrix} -\text{sonorant} \\ +\text{voiced} \end{bmatrix} \#\#$$

In the case of Joe's phonological rules, the use of negative
surface phonetic constraints allows us to draw up a more general set
of rules regarding the realization of fricative initial consonant clusters, and provides a partial motivation for the resultant phonetic form.

From the viewpoint of surface phonetic constraints the most
salient feature of this deviant phonological system is the prohibition
of fricative/−liquid clusters in all boundary initial positions. This is
not true in normal English, either at the phonetic level or at the
underlying lexical level. Consequently, since we are obliged to posit a

normal lexical representation as Joe's underlying form we must state this generalization about Joe's phonology as a surface phonetic constraint which must be realized by the operation of various phonological rules. Thus, the negative SPC that prohibits the occurrence of initial FC clusters can be viewed as triggering the entire set of deviant phonological rules. In general, these phonological rules operate to assimilate the positional feature of the following nonliquid segment to the /s/, and then delete that second segment. But here again, there is an SPC operating which does not allow the realization [x], a voiceless velar fricative. If the /s/ assimilated the positional feature of the following /k/, it would become [x] which, however, is not allowed phonetically in English. This SPC, having blocked the realization of /sk/ as [x], triggers a further phonological rule that places the /s/ on the opposite side of the /k/, giving [ks]. From this point of view, /sk/ clusters are not treated differently from other initial clusters. There simply exists one more constraint that prohibits realizing phonetically the result of carrying out the assimilation rule on initial /sk/ clusters.

Thus, the metathesis rule that applies to /sk/ clusters is not an arbitrary, idiosyncratic rule but the logical result of complying with two surface phonetic constraints. In fact, if viewed in terms of segment displacement, the rule that places the /s/ after the /k/ is not a metathesis rule at all but merely the last of two segment displacement rules that were triggered by the two SPCs relevant to initial /sk/ clusters. That is, SPC 1 does not permit /s/ to occupy its original position, and SPC 2 does not allow /s/ to merge with /k/ to form [x]. Consequently, if /s/ is to be realized at all it must occupy the segment position immediately after /k/, an option that is apparently allowed in Joe's phonology. In the following revised set of rules (Table 4), the two SPCs are stated first and considered to be in effect throughout the rule sequence.

SPC 1 states that boundary initial +fricative/−liquid consonant clusters may not occur. SPC 2 states that the segment [x] cannot occur. Rule 1' assimilates the positional value of the nonliquid consonant onto the fricative. SPC 2 blocks the operation of this rule on /sk/ clusters. Rule 2' takes any case where the positional value of the fricative is not identical with the positional value of the nonliquid consonant and places the fricative to the right of that consonant. After the previous assimilation rule, of course, this is only true for /sk/ clusters and we have, consequently: /sk/ → [ks]. Rules 3, 4, and 5 are the same as in Table 3. Rule 1' must precede rule 2'.

This revised analysis which utilizes SPCs is superior to the first

Table 4. Surface phonetic constraints and revised phonological rules

Surface phonetic constraints:

1. $\sim$ B [+fricative] [−liquid]

2. $\sim \begin{bmatrix} C \\ +\text{velar} \\ -\text{voice} \\ +\text{fricative} \\ +\text{continuant} \end{bmatrix} = [x]$

Phonological rules:

1′. $[+\text{fricative}] \rightarrow [\alpha\text{position}] \quad / \text{ B}\underline{\qquad} \begin{bmatrix} C \\ -\text{liquid} \\ \alpha\text{position} \end{bmatrix}$

2′. $\begin{bmatrix} +\text{fricative} \\ \alpha\text{position} \end{bmatrix}_1 \begin{bmatrix} C \\ -\text{liquid} \\ -\alpha\text{position} \end{bmatrix}_2 \rightarrow 21 \quad / \text{ B}\underline{\qquad}$

one that was proposed because it explains or motivates the phonological rules that are posited to account for the difference that exists between the presumed underlying forms and the phonetic output. It is also to be preferred because it is more general in its application; that is, it treats all of the initial clusters in the same way, not positing an arbitrary metathesis rule for the /sk/ cluster. At that point in the rule derivation where the "normal" treatment of the /sk/ cluster is prevented by a further SPC of English, then a separate rule that applies only to /sk/ clusters is employed.

The above analysis appears to be well motivated except for the fact that now rule 4 (Table 3) contradicts SPC 1 by, apparently, allowing the presence of a +fricative/−liquid cluster ([fw]) in initial position. A close consideration of the environment for the operation of this rule, however, provides us with a hint regarding the actual nature of this apparent contradiction. According to rule 4, the [w] is allowed to remain after the fricative only before unrounded vowels. A [w] is itself "rounded," that is, during the articulation of a [w], the lips are protruded and contracted. There is no physiological reason that prevents the occurrence of a /w/, rounded vowel sequence. This is true even when this combination follows an /f/, which is the resultant fricative from the operation of assimilation on the /sw/ cluster.[11] If, however, the [f] had also acquired rounding during the positional assimilation which occurred, then it would be considerably more difficult to articulate a "w" between the rounded [f] and the rounded vowel. This suggests that what we are dealing with are not 3 segments f-w-V but only 2 segments, a rounded [f] (represented as f^w) and a following vowel.[12] The transitional sound which is heard as a "w" when the [f^w] is pronounced before an unrounded vowel is not itself a segment and is therefore not subject to SPC 1. When the [f^w] occurs before a rounded vowel no such transitional sound occurs because there is no transition in going from rounded to rounded. These considerations require a number of changes in the rules that

---

[11]Mel Greenlee has pointed out to me that in a developing phonology which she is studying there are occurrences of [fw] (derived from both /sl/ and /sw/) before rounded vowels, such as: swoop → [fwuwp], float → [fwowt], flute → [fwuwt].

[12]Notice that the same type of analytical problem exists when trying to determine the set of phonemes of a language. In Hausa, for example, there are syllable initial phonetic sequences of velar stop + glide [kw], [ky], etc. Some authors treat these phonetic sequences as clusters of two phonemes, whereas Greenberg (1941, p. 317) points out that these "clusters" must be "unit phonemes" (labialized and palatalized velars /k^w/, /k^y/, etc.) because the syllabic structure of Hausa prohibits initial consonant clusters.

were posited. First, rule 1' must be rewritten to assimilate the feature "round" onto the fricative:

Rule 1'

$$[\text{+fricative}] \rightarrow \begin{bmatrix} \alpha\text{position} \\ \beta\text{round} \end{bmatrix} / \text{B}\underline{\quad} \begin{bmatrix} \text{C} \\ -\text{liquid} \\ \alpha\text{position} \\ \beta\text{round} \end{bmatrix}$$

Second, rule 4 is dropped and a late phonetic rule is put in the grammar which inserts a nonsegmental "w" between a rounded consonant and an unrounded vowel.

Notice that the presence of this late phonetic rule implies the very interesting consequence that there is a level in the phonetic derivation after which SPC 1 (and by implication surface phonetic constraints in general) do not apply. What this level appears to involve are the acoustic reflexes of certain physiological constraints. In English, for example, the partial nasalization of vowels before nasal consonants is best described as the simple acoustic reflex of the advanced opening of the velum in anticipation of a following nasal consonant. This is a physiological fact which should be described in physiological terms, a situation which appears to apply equally well to the transitional "w." But I think that it is also clear that a physiological explanation is quite inappropriate in describing the bulk of the deviant phonology presented in this paper. Thus, I can think of no physiological explanation that can suitably motivate assimilation in fricative/−liquid clusters or the eventual inversion that occurs with the /sk/ cluster, since there exists no *physical* difficulty for Joe to articulate such clusters (as is demonstrated by the fact that they occur in nonboundary initial positions). We appear then to be dealing with two sets of facts and consequently with two separate levels of description: a phonological level that must account for the way in which the sound system of a language is organized and eventually realized in interpretable segments at the phonetic level, and a physiological level that accounts for the way in which the articulatory mechanism functions in the real-time production of speech. There is no reason to believe that all facts concerning the sound pattern of a language can be accounted for best by an analysis at only one or the other level of description. With regard to Joe's deviant speech, an analysis at both levels allows us to discriminate between those factors of the phonetic output which are the result of the rules of the phonological system and those factors which are the result of purely physiological contingencies.[13]

Notice that the nasalization of vowels after original /sn/ clusters (and occasionally after /sm/ clusters) can also be treated in a very natural way within the framework of the revised analysis. In this analysis the response to SPC 1 is to merge the "manner" feature of /s/ with the "place of articulation" feature of a following nonliquid consonant. If we suppose the existence of a third SPC:

$$
\sim \begin{bmatrix} +\text{fricative} \\ +\text{nasal} \end{bmatrix}
$$

which states that no segment can occur which is both [+fricative] and [+nasal], then it is clear why "nasality" could not be incorporated directly into the fused cluster segment. If nasality were, then, to be expressed phonetically the only option left would be to "graft" this feature onto the next segment which, after /sn/, is always a vowel. From the data it appears that this process has occurred most widely with initial /sn/ clusters and only in part and quite sporadically with /sm/ clusters.

ORIGIN AND DEVELOPMENT

This revised analysis also provides a basis for making a reasonable guess about the possible evolution of this deviant phonology. It is very common for young children at one stage of their development to represent consonant clusters with only one member of the cluster. And /s/−initial clusters appear to be most commonly represented at this stage by the second consonant of the cluster. At one time, then, we may assume that Joe pronounced only the second segment of fricative/−liquid consonant clusters. Then, at some later date, [s] began to appear in consonant clusters that were syllable, morpheme, and word final. For some reason, however, a surface phonetic con-

---

[13]Several related remarks must be made about the phonetic realization of initial /sk/ clusters. In slow or careful pronunciation [ks] is quite distinct. In more rapid speech this phonetic cluster is realized very often as [ᵏs] which is intended to represent a lightly articulated "k" followed by [s], and even sometimes as [ˣs], a slight velar fricative followed by [s]. These varying pronunciations of [ks] are due to purely physiological factors. There is no evidence that these various acoustic effects are due to phonological rules.

straint prohibited [s] from occurring in the same clusters in syllable, morpheme, and word initial position. At this point, a rule was introduced into the grammar that had the effect of merging the positional value of the nonliquid segment with the "manner" value of the /s/. Since there existed in Joe's English another, quite normal SPC that did not allow the phonetic realization of an [x], the /s/ could not merge with /k/ but was forced into the only segment position left to it if it were to be realized at all: that position immediately following the /k/. Finally, since, by SPC 3, "nasality" could not be realized in the fused fricative segment, it was eventually incorporated into the vowel after original /sn/ clusters, and sporadically after /sm/ clusters. This is, in essence, a recapitulation of the analysis just presented but from an ontogenetic point of view. It seems to me, at this point, to be the most reasonable explanation of the evolution of Joe's deviant phonology. Also, from a psycholinguistic point of view the posited rules appear to be the most reasonable guess about the actual mechanisms that are operating in the real-time production of Joe's phonetic output. It appears to be a case of certain prohibited sequences (represented by the negative SPCs) being replaced by a fusion of the two segments where possible or an inversion of the two segments where a fusion is not possible.

It is also possible to make several reasonable predictions about the likely development of this phonology. During the period of time when the data were collected vowels were consistently nasalized after underlying /sn/ clusters. However, there are also several occurrences of actual [sn] clusters in initial position and also one case with concomitant full nasalization of the following vowel: "snake" [snẽyk]. After underlying /sm/ clusters, on the other hand, there is only sporadic nasalization of the following vowel and there are no examples of an initial [sm] cluster. One would predict that, in time, vowels following /sm/ clusters would also be consistently nasalized. One would also predict that the emergence of initial FC clusters would first take place with /sn/. There are also two examples from the data of genuine initial [st] clusters with the words "stand" [stænd] and "stuff" [stəf]. This is evidence that it is at the alveolar position in general that one can expect to observe the initial emergence of FC clusters. There appear to be several reasons for this. First, there already exist initial fricative/+liquid clusters at the alveolar position: [sl] and [ʃr]. Second, the articulatory position for both the fricative and the following segment in /sn/ and /st/ clusters is identical, namely, alveolar. In all other cases (sm, sw, sp, and sk) the articulatory position of the fricative is different from the position of the following nonliquid segment. For these clusters there is no evidence for predicting which cluster would emerge first in the subsequent development of the phonology.

EXPERIMENTS

Several informal experiments were carried out in order to see whether it would be possible to defeat the operation of these phonological rules. It was hypothesized that very rapid imitations of a word or nonsense syllable might allow Joe to bypass his normal encoding procedure and actually produce in response phonetically genuine imitations of the input. The idea behind this procedure was that, if Joe could be induced to perceive only *sounds* for imitation, not sounds within a linguistic context, then it seemed reasonable to suppose that he would imitate the actual sound and forego the application of his phonological rules. On the first attempt, this method completely failed to bypass the phonological rules. Apparently, on first hearing the presented word or syllable, Joe immediately analyzed it for output in terms of his phonological rules and then, regardless of the number of repetitions or the speed of repetition, he would simply pronounce the word in his deviant manner. Consequently, a different, more devious method was employed in the next attempt. Stetson (1951) pointed out that if a VC(C) cluster is repeated over and over again rapidly enough, the consonants will be transposed to the front of the syllable. Thus, if a word like "ask" were presented to Joe for imitation he would encode it for production in terms of his phonological rules (which would produce a correct pronunciation since the deviant rules do not apply in final position) and then, if the hypothesis were correct, the "sk" cluster would shift to the front of the "word," and the phonological rule would, at least in one sense, have been bypassed. This is, in fact, what did happen. Presented with "ask" and told to repeat it rapidly, Joe produced:

ask ask asskas as kas *skas skas* ask

where the two italicized utterances were preceded by a significant pause. Such an experiment clearly demonstrates the essentially phonological nature of the rules that govern Joe's output. If, by such a devious method, no base is provided on which the phonological rules can operate then a normal pronunciation is obtained which perseveres even when the consonant cluster is gradually moved to "initial" position.

Another little experiment was carried out which demonstrates rather clearly the reality of SPC 1. In this experiment, an epenthetic vowel, ə, was inserted between the two segments of the initial FC cluster, first in reversed order, then in the normal order, and then it was simply deleted. The idea behind this experiment was to defeat SPC 1 by approximating an FC cluster and hope that the effect of this approximation would carry over to the pronunciation of a genuine initial FC cluster. The experiment did not work, but merely served to demonstrate the strength of SPC 1. Here are some examples:

K:	[təsíŋkiy]	K:	[pəsɔ́ts]	K:	[mɨsɔl]
J:	[təsíŋkiy]	J:	[pəsɔ́ts]	J:	[mɨsɔl]
K:	[sətíŋkiy]	K:	[səpɔ́ts]	K:	[səmzɔ́l]
J:	[sətíŋkiy]	J:	[səpɔ́ts]	J:	[s(ə)mɔ́l]
K:	[stíŋkiy]	K:	[spɔ́ts]	K:	What's the name of that
J:	[síŋkiy]	J:	[fɔ́ts]		cowboy that you know?
				J:	Cowboy [fɔ́l].

In Joe's response to [səmɔ́l] it is difficult to hear even a trace of the [ə]. That is, the response sounds virtually identical to the normal pronunciation of the adult [smɔ́l]. But this is only possible because what was encoded was [səmɔ́l], a form that is not subject to SPC 1, since a vowel was inserted between the two consonants. In the actual physical pronunciation this vowel is hardly realized and a form is actually pronounced that would appear to violate SPC 1. In the next response, cowboy [fɔ́l], the rule operates normally. In the other examples, Joe has no difficulty in imitating the pseudo-clusters, but there is simply no carry-over when a real initial cluster is to be pronounced.

MOTIVATION OF DEVIANT FORMS

In the preceding analysis, SPCs were conceived of as motivating the various phonological rules. But negative SPCs of the type discussed here can only determine what is *not* allowed phonetically; they cannot predict the actual form of the phonological rules or the resultant phonetic output of those rules. But if we state the possible kinds of adjustments that *can* occur in response to an SPC, then it might be possible to motivate one of those adjustments on independent grounds as being more likely than the others.

In general, there appear to be two ways to reduce a two-segment cluster in order to conform to SPC 1. First, only one of the original segments is retained while the other is deleted. That is, either the /s/ is retained and the second segments of these clusters are deleted (w, m, p, n, t, k), or the individual second segments are retained and the /s/ is deleted. The second possibility is to merge compatible features from *both* original segments of the cluster into just one segment. In general, such a merger would appear to be possible only if the "manner" features of one segment are combined with the "positional" features of the other segment. This again gives us two possibilities with respect to the clusters under discussion. Either the positional feature of the /s/ is merged with the manner features of the second position segments, giving /sw/→[y]; /sm/→[n]; /sn/→[n]; /sp/→[t]; /st/→[t]; and /sk/→ [t], or, as actually occurs, the manner feature of the fricative is merged with the positional features of the second position segments, giving /sw/ → [fʷ]; /sm/ → [f]; /sp/ → [f]; /sn/ → [s]; /st/ → [s]; and /sk/ ↛ *[x].

It is reasonable to ask just why the latter solution was chosen rather than the solution which retained the positional feature of /s/ and the manner features of the other segments. Earlier, an hypothesis was offered regarding the possible evolution of this deviant phonology. It was assumed that at one stage Joe realized all FC clusters with only the second segments w, m, p, n, t, k. At some later stage, when /s/ began to occur in FC clusters in noninitial position and when it began to appear in initial position before +liquid segments, we may begin to speak of an SPC which specifically blocks the occurrence of initial fricative/−liquid clusters. It is most likely that the immediate solution to the occurrence of SPC 1 was simply to retain the already present second segment of the cluster and delete the /s/, which is one of the possibilities suggested above. This, however, would appear to be only a temporary solution, since the auditorily most stable element of these clusters, the /s/, is not phonetically realized in any manner at all. Consequently, in order to realize this most significant and stable element of the clusters, and still retain some information about the nonliquid segments, a merger occurred which combined the relevant auditory feature of the /s/ with the positional features of the second segments. Where this was not possible, such as with /sk/ clusters, then the full /s/ segment was simply transposed to the other side of the /k/. The other solution, which combines the positional values of the /s/ with the manner feature of the second segments, is ill motivated for two reasons: the auditorily most stable element of the cluster is not phonetically realized, and the positional features of the already established nonliquid segments are displaced in favor of the positional values of the nonestablished /s/ segment. Thus, the actual solution appears to be the best solution when compared with the other possible adjustments to SPC 1, since it maximizes in one segment the most important auditory cues of the cluster but still retains some information about the second position segments of these clusters.

REVISION OF PHONOLOGICAL RULES

One problem remains with regard to the actual form of the posited phonological rules. SPC 1 states that any boundary initial [+fricative] [−liquid] consonant cluster is prohibited. And yet, rule 1′ which is said to be "triggered" by this SPC does nothing more than assimilate the positional features of the nonliquid segment onto the fricative. But what SPC 1 requires is the elimination of the sequence [+fricative] [−liquid] in boundary initial environments. This is accomplished by rule 5. Thus, rule 1′ appears to be quite arbitrarily motivated since it does not appear to accomplish anything directly in response to the requirements of SPC 1. The very same criticism can be made of rule 3 which assimilates the feature [+nasal] onto any vowel that follows an initial /sn/ cluster. Again, this cannot be viewed as any sort of direct response to SPC 1. In fact, the real function of rules 1′ and 3 is to *preserve* information about the nonliquid segment of the consonant cluster before that segment has been deleted by rule 5. In this sense, rules 1′ and 3 are motivated by SPC 1, but in an indirect way.

It seems, however, that a more reasonable way to handle rules 1′, 3, and 5 is to make them all part of the same rule process. That is, rather than write rules 1′ and 3 as assimilation rules, they should be incorporated into the segment deletion process as feature *transfer* rules. In this way, transferring the positional feature of the nonliquid segment to the fricative (or in /sn/ clusters, the feature [+nasal] to the vowel) would perform the double function of preserving information about the nonliquid segment and removing certain features of that segment to other segments in direct response to SPC 1. This is most reasonably done by utilizing the kind of rule employed by Chomsky and Halle (1968) to handle contraction. This same formal structure can also be used to describe the metathesis of /sk/ → [ks]. As before, SPCs 1, 2, and 3 are considered to be in effect throughout the entire rule sequence.

The rules in Table 5 are written in the form of transformations. First, the structural description (SD) is given and then the structural

Table 5. Phonological rules in the form of transformations

Surface phonetic constraints:

1. ~ B [+fricative] [−liquid]   2.

$$\sim \begin{bmatrix} C \\ +\text{velar} \\ -\text{voice} \\ +\text{fricative} \\ +\text{continuant} \end{bmatrix} = [x]$$

3.

$$\sim \begin{bmatrix} +\text{fricative} \\ +\text{nasal} \end{bmatrix}$$

Phonological rules:

1″.

SD: B   [+fricative] $\begin{bmatrix} C \\ -\text{liquid} \\ \alpha\text{position} \\ \beta\text{round} \\ <+\text{nasal}> \end{bmatrix}$ $\begin{bmatrix} <V> \end{bmatrix}$

        1   2   3
        1   2   3

SC: B $\begin{bmatrix} \alpha\text{position} \\ \beta\text{round} \end{bmatrix}$ [ø] $\begin{bmatrix} <+\text{nasal}> \end{bmatrix}$

Condition: <when the positional variable is designated as +alveolar.>

2″.   SD: B   [+fricative] $\begin{bmatrix} C \\ -\text{liquid} \end{bmatrix}$

                    1   2
    SC: B   12→21

---

change (SC) is shown. In the structural description of rule 1″ we have any boundary followed by a fricative, a nonliquid consonant with certain relevant features included, and a vowel which is tied to the presence of the feature "nasal" in the nonliquid segment. The structural description of rule 1″ is equivalent to SPC 1. Thus, a certain structural change will have to occur in order to bring the relevant segment sequence into conformity with this SPC. In the process, two other SPCs must be observed, SPC 2 which prohibits the segment [x], and SPC 3 which prohibits the occurrence of a segment that is both [+fricative] and [+nasal].

The structural change of rule 1″ *transfers* the features [αposition] and [βround] to the [+fricative] segment. Since SPC 2 prohibits the results of merging a fricative with a velar, /sk/ clusters are unaffected by this structural change. SPC 3 does not allow the incorporation of a nasal with a fricative and consequently, if the nasal is to be preserved, it must be grafted onto the vowel segment. The angled brackets around the nasal feature, the vowel, and the "condition" stated below the rule delimit the environment in which such a transfer of the nasal feature can occur, which is only in an initial /sn/ cluster before a vowel.

Rule 2″, which must be ordered after rule 1″, takes any +fricative/−liquid cluster in any boundary initial position and metathesizes the [+fricative] and [−liquid] segments. Since /sk/ is the only such cluster that was not affected by rule 1″ (because of SPC 2), rule 2″ has the sole effect of converting /sk/ to [ks].

CONCLUSION

What I have tried to demonstrate with the above analysis is that it is possible to give an explicit, complete description of the rules governing Joe's deviant phonology. Wherever possible, I have motivated these rules in terms of surface phonetic constraints which are conceived of as prohibiting certain phonetic realizations. That is, the presence of the SPCs triggers adjustments in the phonetic output which are carried out by the deviant phonological rules. The actual output of these deviant rules appears to be determined by the auditory significance of the component parts of the cluster. Thus, the manner feature of the /s/ which is the acoustically most stable element of the clusters is preserved, but in combination with the positional features of the nonliquid segments. This particular solution appeared to be the best solution when compared with the other possible adjustments that could be made in response to SPC 1, since it maximizes the significant information from both segments of the cluster. Of the posited surface phonetic constraints, only SPC 1 is deviant for English. SPC 2 is a normal surface phonetic constraint in English, and SPC 3 is probably a universal constraint placed on the phonetic output of all languages.

The use of SPCs would appear to be of significance for the speech pathologist since it can pinpoint that part of the phonological process that may be viewed as initiating the deviant development. Some changes in the phonology have been seen to occur at a level of phonetic analysis which is no longer subject to SPCs. This level, which appears to be physiological in nature, produces modifications in the phonetic signal that are seen as reflexes of the real-time operation of the articulatory mechanism.

A number of theoretical issues have been taken up in an attempt to clarify the nature of underlying forms in deviant phonologies. I have concluded that the child's underlying form is essentially equivalent to the adult's underlying form. Finally, it has been seen that the posited phonological rules only operate when a relevant cluster occurs in any boundary initial position. These clusters are not subject to the deviant phonological rules when they occur across boundaries or in any boundary final position. It would appear that both speech pathologist and linguist stand to profit by detailed investigations of deviant phonologies. Some of the processes in Joe's phonology are perhaps unique, but much appears to be quite general, and one would expect to find the same processes occurring in other such cases.

ACKNOWLEDGMENTS

I am grateful to John Ohala, Marilyn Vihman, James Bauman, Mel Greenlee, Meredith Hoffman, Masayoshi Shibatani, and John Crothers for their comments and suggestions.

REFERENCES

Albright, R., and J. Albright. 1956. The phonology of a two year old child. Word 12:382–390.

Applegate, J. R. 1961. Phonological rules of a subdialect of English. Word 17:186–194.

Burling, R. 1959. Language development of a Garo and English speaking child. Word 15:45–68.

Chao, Y. R. 1951. The Cantian idiolect: An analysis of the Chinese spoken by a twenty-eight-months-old child. Univ. Calif. Publ. Semitic Philol. 11:27–44.

Chomsky, N., and M. Halle. 1968. The Sound Pattern of English. Harper and Row, New York.

Compton, A. J. 1970. Generative studies of children's phonological disorders. J. Speech Hear. Dis. 35:315–339.

Crocker, J. R. 1969. A phonological model of children's articulation competence. J. Speech Hear. Disord. 34:203–213.

Cross, E. 1950. Some features of the phonology of a four year old boy. Word 6:137–140.

Edwards, M. L. 1971. One child's acquisition of English liquids. Stanford University, Papers and Reports on Child Language Development 3:101–109.

Grady, P. A. E. 1963. Towards a new concept of dyslalia. *In* S. E. Mason (ed.), Signs, Signals and Symbols, pp. 159–165. Methuen, London.

Greenberg, J. H. 1941. Some problems in Hausa phonology. Language 17:316–323.

Haas, W. 1963. Phonological analysis of a case of dyslalia. J. Speech Hear. Disord. 28:239–246.

Hartley, L. M. 1963. Analysis of the linguistic data of dyslalia. *In* S. E. Mason (ed.), Signs, Signals and Symbols, pp. 152–158. Methuen, London.

Ingram, D. 1971. Phonological rules of young children. Stanford University, Papers and Reports on Child Language Development 3:31–49.

Jakobson, R. 1968. Child Language, Aphasia, and Phonological Universals. Mouton, The Hague.

Kornfeld, J. R. 1971. Theoretical issues in child phonology. *In* Papers from the Seventh Regional Meeting of the Chicago Linguistic Society, pp. 454–468. Chicago.

Ladefoged, P. 1971. Preliminaries to Linguistic Phonetics. The University of Chicago Press, Chicago.

Leopold, W. 1947. Speech Development of a Bilingual Child. Vol. 2, pp. 207–256. Northwestern University Press, Evanston, Ill.

McReynolds, L. V., and K. Huston. 1971. A distinctive feature analysis of children's misarticulations. J. Speech Hear. Disord. 36:155–166.

Menyuk, P. 1968. The role of distinctive features in children's acquisition of phonology. J. Speech Hear. Res. 11:138–146.

Morley, M. E. 1960. Defects of articulation. *In* L. Stein (ed.), Proceedings of the XIth International Speech and Voice Therapy Conference, pp. 15–17. S. Karger, New York.

Moskowitz, A. 1970a. The acquisition of phonology. Working Paper No. 34. Language Behavior Research Laboratory, Berkeley, California.

Moskowitz, A. 1970b. The two-year-old stage in the acquisition of English phonology. Language 46:426–441.

Oller, D. K. 1973. Regularities in abnormal child phonology. J. Speech Hear. Disord. 38:36–47.

Shibatani, M. 1973. The role of surface phonetic constraints in generative phonology. Language 49:87–106.

Shvachkin, N. 1973. The development of phonemic speech perception in early childhood. *In* C. A. Ferguson and D. I. Slobin (eds.), Studies in Child Language Development, pp. 91–127. Holt, Rinehart and Winston, New York.

Simms, R. E. 1963. The data underlying the concept of dyslalia. *In* S. E. Mason (ed.), Signs, Signals and Symbols, pp. 141–151. Methuen, London.

Smith, N. V. 1973. The Acquisition of Phonology: A Case Study. Cambridge University Press.

Stampe, D. 1969. The acquisition of phonetic representation. *In* Papers from the Fifth Regional Meeting of the Chicago Linguistic Society, pp. 443–454. Chicago.

Stanley, R. 1967. Redundancy rules in phonology. Language 43:393–436.

Stetson, R. H. 1951. Motor Phonetics: A Study of Speech Movements in Action. North Holland, Amsterdam.

Stumpf, C. 1901. Eigenartige sprachliche Entwicklung eines Kindes. Z. Paed. Psychol. Pathol. Jahrgang III. Heft 6:419–447.

Velten, H. V. 1943. The growth of phonemic and lexical patterns in infant language. Language 19:281–292.

Weber, J. L. 1970. Patterning of deviant articulation behavior. J. Speech Hear. Disord. 35:135–141.

Generative Studies of Children's Phonological Disorders: Clinical Ramifications

ARTHUR J. COMPTON

The study of phonology has in many ways become increasingly complicated by the extensive use of formalism in the description of phonological systems. A major contribution of Compton's (1975; this volume) research has been his attempt to make more detailed and systematic analysis available to those assessing and treating deviant phonology. While distinctive feature analysis has dominated recent work in deviant phonology, Compton argues for more systematic characterization of deviant sound systems and suggests that any attempt to modify these systems should affect an entire aspect of the system, such as a rule or several related rules, rather than a single phoneme or several phonemes related only by their shared distinctive features (also see Oller, 1973; Walsh, 1974; Parker, 1976; Lorentz, this volume). In addition, Compton provides evidence that periodic reevaluations are necessary to capture the dynamic nature of deviant systems and suggests that therapeutic procedures cannot be dictated by an initial analysis but must be revised following each reevaluation.

—DMM

The very existence of a language implies an underlying organization or grammar, whether or not it has ever been studied or described in any formal sense.[1] Furthermore, so far as the presence of grammar is

---

[1] "Grammar" refers to the system of rules that determine the connections of sound (speech signal) and meaning (semantics) for the utterances of a language and, thus, properly encompasses the phonological, morphological, syntactic, and semantic structure of language, as opposed to the more restricted "syntactic" sense in which the term is sometimes used.

concerned, whether a language is spoken by one or by millions, child or adult, or is designated as regional, idiolectical, educated, substandard, abnormal, or whatever the label, is irrelevant. Structure is an inherent property of language. The linguist who sets out to study some "exotic" or uncharted language safely does so with this fact in mind. Similarly, the speech therapist who sets out to discover the grammar of a child's deviant speech or language can proceed with equal certainty.

This chapter focuses on the grammar of children's deviant speech and the clinical applications forthcoming from systematic phonological analysis (generative phonology). The fact that there will be a grammar present to discover has been amply demonstrated by a number of recent investigations depicting the systematic nature of the phonological processes underlying children's deviant speech. For example, Compton (1970) presented analyses of the speech of two children with severe phonological handicaps and concluded that the defective sounds of speech characterizing an articulatory disorder are part of a coherent and productive system organized by means of phonological principles. Likewise, Oller (1973) studied the speech of five children with speech disorders who were "otherwise basically normal" and noted that "there is much more regularity in abnormal speech than there would appear at first glance," and that the use of generative phonology makes it possible "to capture numerous generalizations which must be left unstated in more traditional frameworks" (p. 36). Similarly, Lorentz (1974) studied the deviant speech of a 4-year-old child and concluded, "these (phonological) processes, which render David's speech almost completely unintelligible, are, however, regular in application and consequently subject to systematic phonological analysis" (p. 55). Furthermore, Ingram's (1972) study of a developmentally aphasic child and Oller and Kelly's (1974) study of a hard-of-hearing child have also demonstrated the systematic nature of the deviant speech of children who have additional handicaps in conjunction with their articulatory disorder. As all of these studies clearly show, children's deviant speech is systematic and rule governed. We can now turn our attention to investigations which will lead to more refined analyses and further contribute to our insights into the nature of childhood phonological disorders and what to do about them.

The purposes of this chapter are: 1) to elucidate further the practical applications of systematic phonological analyses to the diagnosis and treatment of children with phonological disorders; and

2) to present some preliminary normative data on some of the more common deviant phonological processes typical of children with articulatory disorders. The clinical uses of generative-phonological analyses and the normative data presented are based upon an extensive program of research concerning the normal and abnormal development of speech and the nature and treatment of children's phonological disorders.[2] The theoretical foundations and clinical effectiveness of this approach were originally outlined by Compton (1970). In a later report, Compton (1975) presented an elaborated step-by-step strategy for carrying out a phonological evaluation, along with a detailed case study of a 5-year-old child illustrating the clinical applications of the analysis and the consequent effects during successive stages of therapy.

SOME GENERAL REMARKS
ON THE NATURE OF PHONOLOGICAL ANALYSIS

Broadly speaking, there are roughly 45 to 50 speech sounds in English, but so far as actual talking is concerned, this is a gross understatement. The actual task of a child learning to produce the sounds of language obviously far exceeds a mastery of perhaps 50 specific sounds; otherwise, his job would be relatively simple and straightforward, as would ours in describing it, and there would be little point in pursuing a study of the sound system of language: we would not be studying a system but merely a handful of sounds and determining the ages at which they were acquired. Suppose, for example, the word "kick" were recorded and then played backward. Would we still hear "kick"? The answer is no, for the "k" sound beginning the word is not the same as the one that ends it, and such is the case for any other "sound" we might try. Even at the beginnings of words, the "same" sound is not the same as illustrated by the words "keep," "cup," and "coupe" in which the initial /k/ is drawn progressively farther back in the mouth (point of tongue contact with the velum) under influence of the vowels.[3] Furthermore, the [k] in

---

[2]This research is being conducted at the San Francisco Hearing and Speech Center and is supported by Grant HD 07185-03 from the National Institute of Child Health and Human Development.

    [3]Throughout this chapter, the distinction between symbols enclosed by / / and [ ] is as follows: / / denotes the implicit version of a sound which may be thought of as roughly equivalent to the "stored" or "internalized" representation of a sound in its unspoken form, and [ ] designates the overt, phonetic shape that an internalized "sound" takes on when it is actually spoken.

"coupe" has more lip rounding due to the influence of the rounded vowel [u], and should an /s/ be added immediately before a /k/, as in "scoop," it becomes an unaspirated [k=]. These are but a few of the varying forms of /k/, and if we were to continue examining other contexts and expanding our search to other sounds, we would soon discover that English (or any other language) is composed of, not 50, but literally hundreds of different sound variations. Does this mean that a child must somehow commit to memory all of these many sounds in their specific phonetic contexts during the course of learning to talk? Fortunately not, for the sounds of speech do not vary independently of each other but, instead, are organized into various intersecting classes that follow systematic patterns of phonetic realization. For example, /g/ as well as /k/ (the class of velar stops) is subject to the same vowel influences of articulatory placement and lip rounding, and /s/ has no special claim on /k/, for all of the voiceless stops (/p,t,k/) become unaspirated following /s/. The child, then, does not fall victim to hundreds of separate phonetic entities but, rather, quickly discovers and gains control of the unifying principles underlying them.

The sounds of speech are multiply related to one another and fall into various intersecting classes (natural groupings) on the basis of certain shared attributes. For example, /m/ is simultaneously a member of the class of nasal sounds (/m,n,ŋ/) with respect to the attribute of nasality and the class of bilabial sounds (/p,b,m/) by virtue of its place of articulation. Accordingly, speech sounds are not indivisible entities but are composed of various subcomponents or attributes, commonly called features. Some of these features are the carriers of linguistic contrast in that they provide the basis for distinguishing among the utterances of a language. The difference, for example, between "mat" and "bat" is generally attributed to the presence or absence of nasality in the initial segment, and the difference between "bat" and "pat," to the presence or absence of voicing. Features carrying discriminating information of this sort are often said to be phonemic (as opposed to phonetic), i.e., distinctive features.

Many other features characterizing speech sounds do not play a contrastive role, as to distinguishing meaning among utterances, but serve to render them as "natural" or "native" sounding: they are the details or "particulars" of pronunciation of sounds in specific phonetic contexts—as in the previous example of the voiceless stops which incorporate the feature of unaspiration following /s/. Such features, although not serving a contrastive linguistic function, are, nonetheless, noticeably conspicuous when violated, as witnessed in the speech of non-native speakers and of children with articulatory disorders; hence, the notion of linguistically nondistinctive is not to be equated with perceptually indistinct. Furthermore, some of the noncontrastive features of English may be linguistically distinctive in other languages (the contrast between aspiration and nonaspiration in Hindi, for example) as well as in the speech of children still learning to talk and of those with phonological disorders. As an example, many children who omit the /s/ in the blends still apply the rule for unaspirating the voiceless stops, so that a word such as "spin" pronounced [p=in] is contrastive in their phonological system with the word "pin" pronounced [pin], the distinction being marked by the presence or absence of aspiration in the initial segment.

Returning now to the 45-odd speech sounds of English from a somewhat different perspective, it is perhaps clearer that they are not the actual sounds we speak but the skeletons of speech to which the details of actual pronunciation are added. They are unspoken abstractions that embody the essential features of linguistic contrast. The various phonological principles we learn during childhood serve to relate these underlying features to the particular surface (noncontrastive) features appropriate to the actual pronunciation of sounds in specific phonetic contexts.

A characterization of the contrastive features underlying the consonants of English in their abstract or unspoken form is given in Table 1. The feature system presented here is motivated mainly by very practical considerations concerned with explicitly describing normal and deviant speech of children in the most simple and straightforward way. Aside from a few minor differences, the feature system closely corresponds to the traditional classifications of speech sounds which, for the most part, are fully adequate for characterizing the phonological systems of children and have the additional advantage of being readily understood. I have not adhered to a strictly binary feature classification (where features can only asume a value of + or −, indicating their presence or absence), and the features relating to place of articulation are represented by one of six values, each designating one of the major points of articulatory contact of the consonants of English. The manner features, however, are specified in binary form, since they are more readily accommodated to a binary classification.

Each column of the table designates the particular set of feature

Table 1. Representation of the contrastive features underlying the consonants of English

	p	b	t	d	k	g	m	n	ŋ	f	v
Place[a]	1	1	4	4	6	6	1	4	6	2	2
Voice	−	+	−	+	−	+	+	+	+	−	+
Nasal	−	−	−	−	−	−	+	+	+	−	−
Round											
Consonantal	+	+	+	+	+	+	+	+	+	+	+
Friction	−	−	−	−	−	−	−	−	−	+	+
Stop	+	+	+	+	+	+	+	+	+	−	−

	θ	ð	s	z	ʃ	ʒ	tʃ	dʒ	r	l	w	j
Place[a]	3	3	4	4	5	5	5	5	5	4	6	5
Voice	−	+	−	+	−	+	−	+	+	+	+	+
Nasal	−	−	−	−	−	−	−	−	−	−	−	−
Round									+	−	+	−
Consonantal	+	+	+	+	+	+	+	+	+	+	−	−
Friction	+	+	+	+	+	+	+	+	−	−	−	−
Stop	−	−	−	−	−	−	+	+	−	−	−	−

[a]The place-of-articulation features are defined as follows: place$_1$, bilabial; place$_2$, labial-dental; place$_3$, lingual-dental; place$_4$, lingual-alveolar; place$_5$, palatal; and place$_6$, velar.

values or specifications appropriate for a specific consonant. Notice that each consonant differs by at least one feature from every other consonant, a difference that corresponds to the separate or unique identity of each consonant; i.e., they are linguistically contrastive. At the same time, however, all of the consonants have one or more features in common with various other consonants, which in turn gives rise to a variety of multiple groupings by virtue of their shared features. If, in fact, the resulting groupings appropriately delineate those classes of sounds that conform to actual phonological regularities (patterns), they may be said to constitute natural classes.

PHONOLOGICAL ANALYSIS OF CHILDREN'S DEVIANT SPEECH

The major assumption on which the phonological analysis is founded is that the sounds of speech do not function independently but, instead, have an intricate complex of relationships with one another.

These relationships manifest themselves as systematic patterns which in turn reflect the organization of the phonological system. In other words, the existence of observable patterns presupposes the existence of an underlying organization which is internally consistent; i.e., patterning is a surface reflection of the abstract (underlying) structural relationships that characterize the system. Thus, the only way to describe clearly the patterns the system produces (the output) is to characterize the structural properties or relations of the system. Patterns are a product and exist only as a consequence of the structure of the system that generates them.

The purpose of the analysis is to characterize explicitly the relational principles that underlie or give rise to the observable deviant productions in the speech of children with phonological disorders. The method of analysis and specific form in which the phonological principles (rules) are expressed are demonstrated by examining an actual sample of a child's speech. The child, Grace, was 5 years old at the time of the initial evaluation and had a severe phonological disorder (approximately 80% unintelligible speech as judged by the several clinicians working on the project) but otherwise appeared to be relatively normal.

The analysis is derived from close phonetic transcriptions of Grace's naming responses to a series of 84 picture stimuli and samples of her spontaneous conversational speech. The responses were recorded on a high quality tape recorder (Sony 770) and the phonetic transcriptions were done by two trained individuals who first worked independently and then transcribed together to check for agreement.[4]

Tables 2 and 3 present a description of Grace's pronunciations of the consonants and blends at the time of the first evaluation. The second and third columns of Table 2 give her pronunciations of initial and final consonants for the corresponding ones shown in column 1. For example, the first row of column 2 indicates that initial /p/ is either produced normally (designated by [p]) or as unaspirated (designated by [p=]); the numbers following the symbols indicate the frequency of occurrence of the various pronunciations as they appeared during the evaluation. Similarly, the same row of column 3 indicates that final /p/ always occurs normally (designated by [p]).

The substitution of [w] for initial /h/ appears to be a pronunciation oddity for Grace peculiar only to the word "horse"; it did not show up

---

[4]A detailed discussion of the construction of the test items and the procedures for administering and transcribing the phonological evaluation appears in Compton (1975).

in a later recheck of approximately 15 different /h/−words. Likewise, the substitution of [l] for /j/ in "yellow" was limited to just this word. However, in this particular case, over half of the children in the clinical program have exhibited the same difficulty with this word, apparently due to the assimilation influence of the medial /l/ upon the initial /j/. Table 3 gives Grace's pronunciations of the consonant blends in initial position, the second and fourth columns designating her pronunciations of the corresponding blends shown in the first and third columns. Thus, the first row of column 2 shows that the /pr/ blend is produced with a normal [p] or an unaspirated [p=], and the /r/ portion of the blend is pronounced as [w]. As in Table 1, the numbers after the symbols indicate frequency of occurrence.

Table 2. Phonological description of Grace's pronunciations of initial and final consonants for the first evaluation[a]

Underlying sound	Child's productions (initial position)	Child's productions (final position)
/p/	[p] 2, [p=] 5	[p] 6
/t/	[t] 6, [t=] 9	[t] 8
/k/	[k] 4, [k=] 6	[k] 6
/b/	[b] 11	[b] 5
/d/	[d] 4	[d] 2, ø 7
/g/	[g] 5	[g] 6
/m/	[m] 8	[m] 5
/n/	[n] 7	[n] 9, ø 2
/ŋ/	−	[ŋ] 7
/f/	[f] 5	[f] 5
/s/	[s] 8	[s] 12
/ʃ/	[ʃ] 6	[ʃ] 2, [s] 8
/θ/	[f] 4	[f] 8
/tʃ/	[ʃ] 5	[ʃ] 1, [s] 5
/v/	[v] 1, [b] 5	[v] 3, [b] 2
/z/	[s] 4	[z] 5, ([s] 2 inflections only)
/ʒ/	−	[ʒ] 1, [z] 3
/ð/	[d] 5	[v] 4
/dʒ/	[dʒ] 5, [ʒ] 1	[ʒ] 2, [z] 5
/h/	[h] 7, ([w] 2 *horse* only)	−
/w/	[w] 6	−
/l/	[l] 3, [w] 4	ø 4
/r/	[w] 9	−
/j/	[j] 4, ([l] *yellow* only)	−

[a]Numbers specify frequency of occurrence, and "=" following a symbol denotes nonaspiration.

Table 3. Phonological description of Grace's initial position consonant blends for the first evaluation[a]

Underlying form	Child's productions	Underlying form	Child's productions
/pr/	[pw] 3, [p=w] 3	/pl/	[pw] 1, [p=w] 2, [p=] 1
/br/	[bw] 4, [b] 1, [w] 1	/bl/	[bw] 3, [b] 1, [w] 2
/tr/	[tw] 2, [t=w] 3, [t] 1	/kl/	[kw] 2, [k=w] 2
/dr/	[dw] 5, [w] 2	/gl/	[gw] 4, [w] 2
/kr/	[kw] 3, [k] 1	/fl/	[fw] 4, [f] 1
/gr/	[gw] 4, [g] 2	/sl/	[sw] 3
/fr/	[fw] 4, [w] 1	/sp/	[sp] 1, [spᶜ] 1
/θr/	[fw] 6, [f] 1	/st/	[stᶜ] 2
/spr/	[spw] 2, [spᶜw] 2	/sk/	[sk] 5, [skᶜ] 4
/str/	[stw] 2, [stᶜw] 1	/sm/	[sm] 2
/skr/	[skw] 2, [skᶜ] 2	/sn/	[sn] 2
/spl/	[spw] 2, [spᶜw] 3	/sw/	[sw] 4

[a]Numbers specify frequency of occurrence, "=" following a symbol denotes nonaspiration, and "ᶜ" following a symbol denotes strong aspiration.

A simple counting of the various deviant productions shown in Tables 2 and 3 yields more than 60 different misarticulations. Presented in this form, however, these misarticulations constitute nothing more than a collection of observations, for they are only the surface manifestations of the child's underlying phonological system. The purpose of the analysis, then, is to discover the regularities (patterns) inherent in these surface observations, which will then enable us to direct therapy towards the principles giving rise to the misarticulations.

The first step of the analysis is to begin examining the child's deviant productions for patterns encompassing related sounds which consistently reoccur in specific phonetic environments. For example, observe that /p,t,k/ (the class of voiceless stops) may all be produced as unaspirated variants in initial position (Tables 2 and 3). In English, unaspirated stops occur normally only after /s/ as in "spot," "stop," etc., and their presence in initial position in Grace's speech (Table 3) generally gave the illusion that she was substituting the corresponding voiced cognates /b,d,g/. Notice, however, that the voiceless stops following /s/ in the blends may also be aspirated (Table 3), which sounded conspicuously unnatural, creating a general impression of breathy, jerky speech. Also observe the even more general pattern of consonantal omission which may apply to any initial consonant preceding /r/ and /l/ in the blends (Table 3) or, alternately, for the same blends, /r/ and /l/ may be omitted; in all instances in which this latter option (omission of /r/ and /l/) is not taken, /r/ and /l/ are always replaced or substituted by [w]. These examples illustrate the general strategy by which phonological regularities are discovered in a child's speech.

The next step of the analysis is to translate these patterns into an organized collection of phonological principles, i.e., a generative phonology. Tables 4 and 5 present an analysis of the underlying principles characterizing all of Grace's misarticulations shown in Tables 2 and 3. The analysis of initial consonants and blends is shown

Table 4. Phonological analysis of Grace's initial consonants and blends for the first evaluation[a]

Phonological rules

1.	$\begin{bmatrix} p \\ t \\ k \end{bmatrix}$	→	$\begin{bmatrix} p= \\ t= \\ k= \end{bmatrix}$	/#____ opt. 60%
2.	$\begin{bmatrix} p \\ t \\ k \end{bmatrix}$	→	$\begin{bmatrix} p^c \\ t^c \\ k^c \end{bmatrix}$	/s____ opt. 50%
3.	[v]	→	[b]	/#____ opt. 80%
4a.	[θ]	→	[f]	/#____ oblig. /____r oblig.
4b.	[ð]	→	[d]	/#____ oblig.
5.	[z]	→	[s]	/#____ oblig.
6.	$\begin{bmatrix} t\int \\ d_3 \end{bmatrix}$	→	$\begin{bmatrix} \int \\ 3 \end{bmatrix}$	/#____ $\dfrac{\overline{[\text{voice}-]}\ \text{oblig.}}{[\text{voice}+]\ \text{opt. 20%}}$
7.	[cons.+]	→ ø		1 /____r opt. 20%
8a.	$\begin{bmatrix} r \\ l \end{bmatrix}$	→	[w]	/#____ $\dfrac{\text{if /r/ oblig.}}{\text{if /l/ opt. 50%}}$
8b.	$\begin{bmatrix} r \\ l \end{bmatrix}$	→	[w]	/cons.____opt. 80%
8c.	$\begin{bmatrix} r \\ l \end{bmatrix}$	→	ø	/cons.____ opt. 20%

[a]Unless otherwise specified, all initial consonants occur in the context preceding a vowel. Percentages following rules provide an estimate of how often they apply. Opt., optional rules; oblig., obligatory rules.

Table 5. Phonological analysis of Grace's final consonants for the first evaluation[a]

Phonological rules

9.	$\begin{bmatrix} d \\ n \end{bmatrix}$ → ø	/____#	$\overline{[\text{nasal}-]}$ opt. 80% $\overline{[\text{nasal}+]}$ opt. 20%
10.	$\begin{bmatrix} \theta \\ \eth \end{bmatrix}$ → $\begin{bmatrix} f \\ v \end{bmatrix}$	/____#	oblig.
11.	[v] → [b]	/____#	opt. 40%
12.	$\begin{bmatrix} t\int \\ d_3 \end{bmatrix}$ → $\begin{bmatrix} \int \\ 3 \end{bmatrix}$	/____#	oblig.
13.	$\begin{bmatrix} \int \\ 3 \end{bmatrix}$ → $\begin{bmatrix} s \\ z \end{bmatrix}$	/____#	opt. 80%
14.	[z] → [s]	/____#	opt. 50% (inflections only)
15.	[l] → ø	/____#	oblig.

[a]Percentages following rules provide an estimate of how often they apply. Opt., optional rules; oblig., obligatory rules.

in Table 4, and the analysis of final consonants is given in Table 5. An explication of each of the rules shown in Tables 4 and 5 follows:

Rule 1 The voiceless stops /p,t,k/ are produced as unaspirated, voiceless stops [p=, t=, k=], the arrow designating the direction of change. The slash "/" is to be interpreted as "in the phonetic environment of." The "#" symbol following the slash is a linguistic boundary marker which, in this case, designates the beginning of a word, and the "___" following the boundary marker specifies the position in which the sound occurs, i.e., initial position in this rule. The "opt" (optional) restriction indicates that the rules may be applied optionally, that is, other pronunciations are possible; as the rules are presently formulated, "optional" may be interpreted to mean that the sounds can also occur normally. The percentage values following the rules give an approximate estimate of how often the rules apply and are derived from the frequency tabulations given in Tables 2 and 3. Consequently, the percentage value following rule 1 indicates that the rule applies about 60% of the time, whereas about 40% of the time /p,t,k/ occur normally. These percentage estimates, although only approximate, are often quite helpful for determining the relative status of the various deviant rules and for evaluating a child's progress during therapy. For example, if a rule applied 80% of the time and was subsequently decreased to 20% through therapy, the resulting 60% difference would provide an approximate index of clinical progress. It may be noted in passing, that this is an extremely common rule, occurring in all six of the younger children included in our longitudinal studies of normal development and in over 60% of the children in the clinical program.

Notice that the phonological principle characterized by rule 1 does not apply to the /p,t,k/ sounds individually but, rather, to the class of sounds of which they are members, i.e.,

$$\begin{bmatrix} \text{stop } + \\ \text{voice } - \end{bmatrix} \rightarrow \begin{bmatrix} \text{stop } + \\ \text{voice } - \\ \text{aspiration } - \end{bmatrix}$$

The above feature specification of rule 1 more explicitly captures the principle of unaspiration of the voiceless stops and, strictly speaking, all phonological rules should be specified by means of features. However, I have abbreviated the rules by using the more familiar phonological symbols so that they can be read more easily, but it is nonetheless important to read into these abbreviations the actual feature changes being depicted.

Rule 2   The voiceless stops /p,t,k/ may be realized as aspirated stops whenever they occur in the phonetic context immediately following /s/, i.e., the /s/ blends. This is the only context in English in which unaspirated stops should occur (all the time), but in Grace's speech she alternates between aspirated and unaspirated stops with about equal frequency. The fact that the same alternation (and nearly the same frequency distribution) occurs with these sounds in initial position suggests that Grace does not discriminate between aspiration and unaspiration. However, in a later discrimination check, she was able to differentiate systematically between pairs of nonsense words (same or different) containing only this contrast (minimal pairs). This does not, of course, rule out the possibility that she is still unable to make the discrimination in monitoring her own speech as opposed to hearing it in someone else's speech, i.e., "internal" versus "external" discrimination.

Rule 3   Initial /v/ is optionally produced as [b] about 80% of the time.

Rule 4a   The voiceless lingual-dental fricative /θ/ is substituted by the labial-dental fricative [f] in initial position before vowels and before /r/ in the /θr/ blend. The "oblig" (obligatory) restriction indicates that the rule always applies.

Rule 4b The voiced lingual-dental fricative /ð/ is always substituted by the voiced lingual-alveolar stop [d]. Notice that in rule 4a the substitution of [f] for /θ/ involves a shift forward in place of articulation but manner of articulation is held constant, whereas in this rule the substitution of [d] for /ð/ arises from a shift backward in place of articulation, and manner of articulation is changed as well. For most of the children in the program, the substitutions of both the voiced and voiceless lingual-dental fricatives (as a class) follow a symmetrical pattern, with [t] and [d] being the most common substitutions preceding vowels and [f] generally occurring before /r/ in the /θr/ blend.

Rule 5 Initial /z/ is always produced as [s].

Rule 6 The initial affricates /tʃ, dʒ/ are replaced by the palatal fricatives [ʃ, ʒ]. The further specification [voice −] following the rule is a convention for singling out the voiceless member of the pair of sounds, and thus the rule is to be interpreted as applying to /tʃ/ all of the time. Similarly, the optional restriction associated with [voice +] designates that the rule applies to /dʒ/ about 20% of the time.

Rule 7 Consonants preceding /r/ and /l/ in the blends are omitted about 20% of the time.

Rule 8a The liquids /r,l/ are both replaced by [w] in initial position. In the case of /r/, the substitution occurs all of the time, and with /l/, the substitution occurs about 50% of the time.

Rule 8b The liquids /r,l/ are replaced by [w] after consonants in the blends about 80% of the time.

Rule 8c The liquids /r,l/, when not replaced by [w], are omitted in the blends the remaining 20% of the time.

Rule 9 (Table 5) The voiced and nasal, lingual-alveolar stops /d,n/ may be omitted in final position. The non-nasal member of the pair, /d/, is omitted about 80% of the time, and the nasal member, /n/, is omitted 20% of the time.

Rule 10 The lingual-dental fricatives /θ, ð/ are always replaced by the labial-dental fricatives [f,v] in final position.

Rule 11 The final labial-dental fricative /v/ is substituted by [b] about 40% of the time. Observe, also, that the substitution of [v] for /ð/ specified by rule 10 is likewise subject to this rule.

Rule 12 The affricates /tʃ, dʒ/ are always replaced by the palatal fricatives [ʃ,ʒ] in final position.

Rule 13 The final palatal fricatives /ʃ,ʒ/ are substituted by the alveolar fricatives [s,z] approximately 80% of the time. Again, notice that this rule also applies to the palatal fricative substitutions arising from rule 12.

Rule 14   Final /z/ is optionally replaced by [s] about half of the time. This rule, however, applies only to final /z/ when it occurs as an inflectional ending (as a plural or possessive marker) and, thus, it is in reality a variant morphological rule rather than a deviant phonological rule.

Rule 15   Final /l/ is always omitted.

In addition to the consonantal misarticulations covered by the analyses shown in Tables 4 and 5, Grace also had many pronunciation oddities (including vowels) which appeared to be unique to specific words; i.e., they followed no discernible pattern or system. Her flow of conversational speech was also greatly disrupted (staccato-like), resulting from an abrupt onset and termination of words which seemed to be an overriding characteristic of her behavior and bodily movements in general. This characteristic of Grace's speech gradually disappeared as she became calmer during the course of therapy.

CLINICAL APPLICATIONS OF PHONOLOGICAL ANALYSES

The basic assumption underlying the clinical use of phonological analyses is that the elimination of any specific articulatory error effects a change in the principle giving rise to that error. Hence, all of the other articulatory errors arising from that principle will also be eliminated without having to work directly with them. Therefore, by selecting specific key sounds which will have the greatest impact upon the organizational structure of the child's deviant phonological system, the effects of therapy will be maximized. To illustrate the strategy and results of this approach, we shall again return to Grace and follow the successive stages of her phonological development during the course of her therapy program.

Grace is one of 18 children who have participated in the clinical research program and serves only as a typical case in point. She was enrolled for two 45-min sessions of individual therapy twice a week for approximately 1.5 years. At the end of that time she was dismissed from therapy with essentially normal speech.

With Grace, as with all of the children in the program, therapy was focused primarily upon production of sounds within the context of meaningful words and conversational speech. The actual therapy typically follows such traditional techniques as picture-oriented games and keeping a speech notebook, as well as less structured activities such as working with varied art media adapted to the therapy vocabulary. For the most part, "faulty" discrimination has not been a very significant problem among the children in our program, but, in instances where a child's misarticulations do appear to arise from such perceptual failures, then various discrimination exercises are incorporated into the therapy program.[5]

The phonological analyses presented in Tables 4 and 5 serve as the starting point for planning Grace's therapy program. Every 3–4 months thereafter, her speech was reevaluated to reappraise and update her therapy. The analyses accompanying these reevaluations are given in Tables 6 through 9 and, thus, constitute a record or history of her changing phonological system as it evolved throughout the period of therapy. A discussion of the therapy plan and consequent changes in her phonological system for each reevaluation follows.

Reevaluation Period 1

This period covers the intervening time between the initial evaluation and the first reevaluation, during which Grace had attended 25 therapy sessions. Throughout this period, the clinician worked with Grace on the production of initial /p/, final /d/, and final /tʃ/, and all direct therapy was always limited to just these sounds. Thus, aside from possible extraneous influences outside of therapy, any resulting changes in her phonological system would reflect the effects of the specific key sounds included in her therapy program.

The choice of initial /p/ was directed at changing rule 1 (refer to Table 4), the unaspiration of the voiceless stops. In addition, if rule 2 were actually a counterpart to rule 1 arising from a discrimination failure between aspiration and unaspiration (as previously discussed), then working on this contrast with initial /p/ might also have an effect upon Grace's use of aspirated stops following /s/, i.e., rule 2. Final /d/ was chosen to eliminate the omission of the lingual-alveolar stops /d,n/ as specified by rule 9 in Table 5. Final /tʃ/ was selected to provide a means of working with the substitution of the palatal fricatives [ʃ,ʒ] for the affricates /tʃ,dʒ/ (rule 12, Table 5) which would in turn block the substitution of the alveolar fricatives [s,z] arising from rule 13.

The analysis of Grace's phonological system at the end of the first therapy period is shown in the first column of Tables 6 and 7.

---

[5]We do not, for example, blanketly assume that a child's deviant productions result from poor discrimination nor automatically devote the beginning stages of therapy to auditory discrimination training. For further discussions of this issue, refer to Compton (1970 and 1975).

Table 6. Phonological analysis of Grace's initial consonants and blends for the first and second reevaluations[a]

Phonological rules	(Reevaluation 1)	Phonological rules	(Reevaluation 2)
1a. $\begin{bmatrix} p \\ t \\ k \end{bmatrix} \rightarrow \begin{bmatrix} p= \\ t= \\ k= \end{bmatrix}$	/#___ opt. 15%	1a.	No longer present
1b. $\begin{bmatrix} b \\ d \\ g \end{bmatrix} \rightarrow \begin{bmatrix} p \\ t \\ k \end{bmatrix}$	/#___ opt. 50%	1b.	No longer present
1c. $\begin{bmatrix} b \\ d \\ g \end{bmatrix} \rightarrow \begin{bmatrix} p \\ t \\ k \end{bmatrix}$	/___l ___r oblig.	1c.	No longer present
2. No longer present		2.	——
3. NC [v] → [b]	/#___ opt. 80%	3. NC	[v] → [b] /#___ opt. 80%
4a. [θ] → [f]	/#___ opt. 70% /___r oblig.	4a. NC	[θ] → [f] /#___ opt. 70% /___r oblig.
4b. NC [ð] → [d]	/#___ oblig.	4b.	[ð] → [d] /#___ opt. 70%

5. NC	[z] → [s]	/#__ oblig.	5.	No longer present
6a.	[tʃ] → [ʃ]	/#__ oblig.	6a. NC	[tʃ] → [ʃ] /#__ oblig.
6b.	[dʒ] → [tʃ]	/#__ opt. 50%	6b.	No longer present
7. NC	[cons. +] → ø	/__r̄ opt. 20%	7.	No longer present
8a. NC	$\begin{bmatrix} r \\ l \end{bmatrix}$ → [w]	/#__ if /r/ oblig. if /l/ opt. 50%	8a.	[r] → [w] /#__ opt. 90%
8b. NC	$\begin{bmatrix} r \\ l \end{bmatrix}$ → [w]	/cons.__ opt. 80%	8b.	[r] → [w] /cons.__ opt. 80%
8c. NC	$\begin{bmatrix} r \\ l \end{bmatrix}$ → ø	/cons.__ opt. 20%	8c.	No longer present

aUnless otherwise specified, all initial consonants occur in the context preceding a vowel. Percentages following rules provide an estimate of how often they apply. NC designates a rule has not changed from the previous evaluation. Opt., optional rules; oblig., obligatory rules.

Table 7. Phonological analysis of Grace's final consonants for the first and second reevaluations[a]

Phonological rules (Reevaluation 1)			Phonological rules		(Reevaluation 2)
9.	No longer present		9.		
10. NC	$\begin{bmatrix}\theta\\\delta\end{bmatrix} \rightarrow \begin{bmatrix}f\\v\end{bmatrix}$	/__# oblig.	10.	$\begin{bmatrix}\theta\\\delta\end{bmatrix} \rightarrow \begin{bmatrix}f\\v\end{bmatrix}$ /__#	$\begin{bmatrix}\overline{voice-}\rbrack \text{ opt. } 40\%\\\lbrack voice+\rbrack \text{ oblig.}\end{bmatrix}$
11. NC	$[v] \rightarrow [b]$	/__# opt. 40%	11. NC	$[v] \rightarrow [b]$	/__# opt. 40%
12.	$\begin{bmatrix}t\int\\d3\end{bmatrix} \rightarrow \begin{bmatrix}\int\\3\end{bmatrix}$	/__# opt. 50%	12. NC	$\begin{bmatrix}t\int\\d3\end{bmatrix} \rightarrow \begin{bmatrix}\int\\3\end{bmatrix}$	/__# opt. 50%
13.	$\begin{bmatrix}\int\\3\end{bmatrix} \rightarrow \begin{bmatrix}t\int\\d3\end{bmatrix}$	/__# opt. 30%	13.	$[3] \rightarrow [d3]$	/__# opt. 30%
14. NC	$[z] \rightarrow [s]$	/__# opt. 50%	14.	$[z] \rightarrow [s]$	/__# opt. 10%
15. NC	$[l] \rightarrow \o$	/__# oblig.	15. NC	$[l] \rightarrow \o$	/__# oblig.

[a]Percentages following rules provide an estimate of how often they apply. NC designates a rule has not changed from the previous evaluation. Opt., optional rules; oblig., obligatory rules.

Notice, first of all, that of the 21 rules (counting subrules) shown in these tables, 11 have remained unchanged. ("NC" beneath a rule number designates the rule has not changed from the previous evaluation.) Based upon Grace's therapy program, however, we would not have predicted that any of these rules should be affected, so this result is not surprising. However, there are three new subrules (1b, 1c, and 6b) which were not present in the first evaluation. The probable origin of these rules is taken up in the discussion which follows on the effects of therapy.

Rule 1a (formerly rule 1 of Table 4) shows a decrease of approximately 45% in the occurrence of unaspirated stops [p=,t=,k=] in initial position. This is a definite positive change and is attributed to the therapy with initial /p/. The fact that both /t/ and /k/ show an accompanying decrease as unaspirated variants without being direct targets of therapy provides strong support for the theoretical model upon which the therapy is based: namely, working with a single sound within a class effects a consequent change in all of the other sounds in the class, i.e. a change in the phonological principle underlying the misarticulations.

Even further evidence for the model is provided by the introduction of three new deviant rules (1b, 1c, and 6b) into Grace's grammar which appear to have originated in the following way. The distinction between unaspirated, voiceless stops [p=,t=,k=] and their corresponding voiced counterparts [b,d,g] is a very subtle perceptual discrimination which is generally not made by speakers of English and other languages in which the contrast is not phonemic. This is evidenced by the fact that even most trained clinicians are likely to hear unaspirated stops as voiced stops, unless they have had some specific training and practice in making the discrimination. It is highly probable, then, that during the course of therapy to eliminate Grace's substitution of unaspirated stops [p=,t=,k=] for the aspirated, voiceless ones /p,t,k/ (rule 1), she, too, did not make a distinction between unaspirated and voiced stops. Consequently, as she began making the transition from unaspirated stops to the aspirated, *voiceless* ones as shown in rule 1a (resulting from therapy with initial /p/), she also extended the process to include all of the voiced stops (including /dʒ/ which is also specified as a stop, at least in part): hence, the origin of rules 1b, 1c, and 6b. This process can be more explicitly depicted by collapsing these three rules into the more general rule underlying them.

$$\begin{bmatrix} \text{stop} + \\ \text{voice} + \end{bmatrix} \rightarrow \begin{bmatrix} \text{stop} + \\ \text{voice} - \end{bmatrix}$$

Additional evidence of the validity of this hypothesized account is also provided by the clinical results obtained during the second reevaluation period.

The creation of deviant rules as an artifact of therapy is actually not so rare as we might like to think (see Compton, 1970, p. 325 for another example) and is an important issue under study in this research program.

In reevaluation 1, rule 2 (the abnormal aspiration of the stops after /s/) is no longer present; i.e., the voiceless stops now occur in their proper unaspirated form in the /s/ blends. The elimination of this rule also seems to have resulted from working with initial /p/ on the alternation between aspirated and unaspirated stops. Earlier, it was suggested that this alternation might be due to an internal (self-monitoring) discrimination failure, and that learning the discrimination for initial stops would possibly generalize to the stops in the /s/ blends. However, there is conflicting evidence on just how this generalization process might have taken place. Since Grace also began to devoice her previously normal voiced stops (rules 1b, 1c, and 6b) in initial position, it would have seemed equally plausible that this devoicing (and accompanying aspiration) would have actually reinforced the use of unaspirated, voiceless stops following /s/. Perhaps the distinction is more difficult in initial position and is facilitated by the context of /s/. At any rate, the theoretical issue still remains unclear, although the more practical clinical problem for Grace has ceased to exist.

Rule 4a shows a 30% decrease in the substitution of [f] for /θ/ in initial position preceding vowels with no accompanying change in this substitution before /r/ in the /θr/ blend. The positive gain, in this case, has no obvious relationship to the particular sounds included in therapy, and thus, cannot be directly ascribed to Grace's therapy program.

Rule 9 is not present, indicating that the omission of the final alveolar stops /d,n/ no longer occurs. The elimination of this rule is attributed to the therapy with final /d/.

The substitution of the palatal fricatives [ʃ,ʒ] for the afficates /tʃ,dʒ/ (rule 12) has decreased by approximately 50% and this result is interpreted as a direct consequence of working with only final /tʃ/.

Rule 13 shows a substantial increase (also 50%) in the normal occurrence of the palatal fricatives /ʃ,ʒ/, but there has also been a curious change in the form of the substitutions that still occur for these sounds. Previously, the lingual-alveolar fricatives [s,z] were substituted for /ʃ,ʒ/ (compare rule 13, Table 5), but these substitutions have now been replaced by the affricates [tʃ,dʒ]. Thus, rule 13 now appears to be a reversal of rule 12, and both this revision of form and the accompanying decrease in substitutions have apparently resulted from the therapy with final /tʃ/.

Reevaluation Period 2

This period includes the time between the first and second reevaluations in which Grace attended 39 therapy sessions. Her therapy program was based upon the grammar for the first reevaluation as shown in column 1 of Tables 6 and 7. Grace's therapy program included the initial /pr/ and /br/ blends, initial /z/, final /ʃ/, and final /θ/.

The selection of initial /pr/ and /br/ was, in part, intended as a carry-over of the therapy with initial /p/ from the first period to continue working with Grace's use of unaspirated stops (rule 1a). The voiced-voiceless contrast between the /p/ and /b/ in these blends also provided a means of counteracting the newly acquired devoicing of the voiced stops (rules 1b, 1c, and 6b) which had developed as an artifact of the therapy with initial /p/ during the first period. In addition, by incorporating this contrast (voiced-voiceless) into the context of an /r/ blend, it was also possible to work simultaneously with 1) the omission of consonants before the liquids /r/ and /l/ (rule 7), 2) the substitution of [w] for /r/ and /l/ and occasional omission of these liquids in the blends (rules 8b and 8c), and possibly 3) the substitution of [w] for /r/ and /l/ in initial position (rule 8a).

The addition of initial /z/ was chosen to work with the obligatory substitution of [s] for /z/ (rule 5). The selection of final /ʃ/ was directed toward rule 13. This selection was actually a replacement of the therapy with final /tʃ/ from the first period which appeared to trigger the reversal of rule 12 that was projected upon rule 13. This switch from /tʃ/ to /ʃ/, then, was made primarily to combat this reversal, i.e., to avert the possibility that continued therapy with final /tʃ/ would, at the same time, reinforce the substitution of [tʃ,dʒ] for /ʃ,ʒ/ (rule 13). The new addition of final /θ/ was selected to work with the substitution of the labial-dental fricatives [f,v] for the lingual-dental fricatives /θ,ð/ (rule 10).

The resulting changes in Grace's phonological system are shown in the second column of Tables 6 and 7. Rules 3, 4a, 6a, 11, 12, and 15 remain unchanged though not unexpectedly, since the therapy program did not encompass these rules.

Rule 1 (the use of unaspirated stops) is no longer present, and this result is attributed to the therapy with the /pr/ and /br/ blends. Furthermore, the voiced-voiceless contrast provided by these blends has successfully and completely eliminated rules 1b, 1c, and 6b (the devoicing of initial stops), thus giving support to the previously hypothesized origin of these rules as artifacts of the therapy program. The example also serves to point up the importance of keeping close track of the phonological principles underlying a child's misarticulations, not only as a way of optimizing the positive effects of therapy, but also as a means of minimizing potential negative effects.

Therapy sessions with the /pr/ and /br/ blends have also had a rather dramatic effect upon rules 7, 8a, 8b, and 8c. Rule 7 (the omission of consonants before /r/ and /l/) has been eliminated, and the substitution of [w] for /l/ both initially and following consonants (rules 8a and 8b) as well as the omission of /r/ and /l/ in the blends (rule 8c) have all disappeared. The overall effects of working with the /pr/ and /br/ blends dramatically illustrate the potentially sweeping results that can be obtained by carefully selecting *key sounds* for therapy which, in this instance, have affected eight rules (1a, 1b, 1c, 6b, 7, 8a, 8b, and 8c) and at least 40 different surface misarticulations of consonants and consonant blends.

Rule 4b (the obligatory substitution of [d] for /ð/) has decreased by approximately 30%. This decrease mirrors a similar decrease in substitutions for the voiceless cognate /θ/ for the preceding period, again, in the absence of any direct therapy. However, it is possible that the therapy with initial /z/ during this period had some indirect effect upon /ð/, but such a hypothesis is purely conjecture at this point.

Rule 5 (the obligatory substitution of [s] for /z/) has been eradicated entirely during this period as a result of the therapy with initial /z/.

Rule 10 shows that the therapy with final /θ/ resulted in a decrease of about 60% in the substitution of [f] for /θ/ but produced no concurrent effect upon the substitution of [v] for /ð/. This result is closely paralleled by the effects of therapy with final /ʃ/ upon rule 13, which eliminated the substitution of [tʃ] for /ʃ/ but had no impact upon the substitution of [dʒ] for /ʒ/. This lack of generalization of /θ/ and /ʃ/ to their respective voiced cognates /ð/ and /ʒ/ has been typical for several of the children in the clinical program. In similar instances involving different sounds, the most successful strategy appears to be to switch to the voiced member of the pair which seems to generalize more easily to the voiceless member. In the case of /ð/ and /ʒ/, however, this has not been a practical clinical solution because there are so few English words ending with these sounds.

Rule 14 (the substitution of [s] for /z/ for plural and possessive endings) has decreased by approximately 40% without any specific work on final inflections. It is unlikely, for example, that the therapy with initial /z/ had any influence upon this replacement, since the substitution is not phonologically based; i.e., Grace produces /z/ normally in uninflected final position. Furthermore, even when a child's misarticulations are strictly phonological in nature, we have not found any clinical or developmental evidence of generalization (crossover) between initial and final position environments (Compton, 1975).

Reevaluation Period 3
During this period, Grace attended 25 therapy sessions. Her therapy program was derived from the analysis for the second reevaluation which is given in the second column of Tables 6 and 7. Her therapy included initial /θ/, initial /tʃ/, initial /r/, and final /tʃ/ and /ʃ/. Initial /θ/ was selected to work with the substitution of [f] for /θ/, both initially before vowels and before /r/ in the /θr/ blend (rule 4a). Initial /tʃ/ was directed at rule 6a to work on the obligatory substitution of [ʃ] for /tʃ/. The switch to initial /r/ was a continuation of the therapy with this sound (rules 8a and 8b) which had been previously covered by the /pr/ and /br/ blends. While these blends had a great impact upon Grace's overall phonological system during the second period, they did not markedly alter her deviant use of /r/. For many children, the correction of /r/ both initially and in the blends seems to be facilitated by working with it in the context of a blend, but this did not appear to be true with Grace; hence, the change to initial /r/. The return of final /tʃ/ into Grace's therapy program was a reinstatement of the work with the final affricates /tʃ,dʒ/ (rule 12) begun during the first period. Recall that the therapy with /tʃ/ had been discontinued and replaced by /ʃ/, because of its apparent negative effect upon the palatal fricatives /ʃ,ʒ/ (rule 13). Thus, to prevent a possible recurrence of the substitution of [tʃ] for /ʃ/, final /ʃ/ was also retained (an adjunct to /tʃ/) as a precautionary measure, even though final /ʃ/ was no longer misarticulated.

The effects of the therapy program upon Grace's phonological system are depicted by the analysis given in the first column of Tables 8 and 9. Rules 3, 10, 11, 13, and 15 remain unaltered during this period.

Rule 4a indicates that the substitution of [f] for /θ/ no longer occurs initially before vowels and has decreased by about 80% before /r/. Furthermore, rule 4b shows an 80% reduction in the substitution of [d] for /ð/, also apparently resulting from working with initial /θ/. This latter result was an unexpected gain. The therapy with /θ/ was not anticipated to have any pronounced effect upon /ð/, since each of these sounds followed different substitution patterns.

Rule 6a (the substitution of [ʃ] for /tʃ/) has been completely eliminated, and this result is directly attributed to the therapy with initial /tʃ/.

Rules 8a and 8b continue unchanged as to the actual percentage of substitutions for /r/, 90% both initially and in the blends. However, the specific form of the substitutions has been significantly altered (by 60%) in a positive direction ([ɪ] = an unrounded variant of /r/). Observe, too, that the therapy with only initial /r/ has just as effectively generalized to the /r/ blends.

Rule 12 shows a 30% decrease in the substitutions for the affricates /tʃ,dʒ/ due to the therapy with final /tʃ/. There has also been a positive change in the form of the substitution for /dʒ/ previously replaced by [ʒ]. Generally, /dʒ/ is now properly initiated as [d] and then subsequently released as the voiceless cognate /tʃ/, i.e., [dᵗʃ].

Whether or not the precautionary therapy with final /ʃ/ in conjunction with final /tʃ/ was actually instrumental in preventing the recurrence of the substitution of [tʃ] for /ʃ/ is indeterminate. It is clear, however, that the work with /ʃ/ did not affect its voiced cognate /ʒ/ (rule 13) which, again, parallels the lack of generalization from /ʃ/ to /ʒ/ of the preceding period.

Rule 14 (the residual substitution of [s] for /z/ in inflectional endings) has now disappeared, and this loss has no obvious relationship to Grace's therapy program.

Reevaluation Period 4

This was the final period of Grace's therapy program during which time she attended 26 sessions. Her therapy was based on the analysis presented in the first column of Tables 8 and 9. From this analysis it is apparent that most of the remaining deviant productions represent an assortment of infrequently occurring sounds of English and a few

Table 8. Phonological analysis of Grace's initial consonants and blends for the third and fourth reevaluations[a]

Phonological rules	(Reevaluation 3)	Phonological rules	(Reevaluation 4)
1a.	——	1a.	——
1b.	——	1b.	——
1c.	——	1c.	——
2.	——	2.	——
3. NC	$[v] \rightarrow [b]$ /#___ opt. 80%	3.	No longer present
4a.	$[\theta] \rightarrow [f]$ /___r opt. 20%	4a.	No longer present
4b.	$[ð] \rightarrow [d]$ /#___ opt. 20%	4b.	No longer present
5.	——	5.	——
6a.	No longer present	6a.	——
6b.	——	6b.	——
7.	——	7.	——
8a.	$[r] \rightarrow \begin{bmatrix} w \\ \boxed{r} \end{bmatrix} \begin{matrix} = 30\% \\ = 60\% \end{matrix}$ /#___ opt. 90%	8a.	No longer present
8b.	$[r] \rightarrow \begin{bmatrix} w \\ \boxed{r} \end{bmatrix} \begin{matrix} = 30\% \\ = 60\% \end{matrix}$ /cons.___opt. 90%	8b.	No longer present
8c.	——	8c.	——

[a]Unless otherwise specified, all initial consonants occur in the context preceding a vowel. Percentages following rules provide an estimate of how often they apply. NC designates a rule has not changed from the previous evaluation. □ around a symbol denotes the sound is unrounded. Opt., optional rules.

residual misarticulations left over from previous therapy. Consequently, this phase of Grace's program was devoted mainly to "cleaning up" these isolated and lingering misarticulations. Her therapy included initial /r/ (rules 8a and 8b) final /tʃ/ (rule 12)—both continuations from the previous period—and the new addition of initial /v/ (rule 3). Also, two words each were incorporated for the following: initial /θr/ (rules 4a, 4b, 8a, and 8b), final /ð/ (rule 10), final /v/ (rule 11), and final /l/ (rule 15). This latter strategy of limiting Grace's therapy to just a few words was intended as a clinical experi-

Table 9. Phonological analysis of Grace's final consonants for the third and fourth reevaluations[a]

Phonological rules	(Reevaluation 3)	Phonological rules	(Reevaluation 4)
9. ——		9. ——	
10. NC	$\begin{bmatrix} ð \\ ð \end{bmatrix} \rightarrow \begin{bmatrix} f \\ v \end{bmatrix}$ /___# $\dfrac{[\overline{voice-}]}{[voice+]}$ opt. 40% oblig.	10.	No longer present
11. NC	[v] → [b] /___# opt. 40%	11.	No longer present
12.	$\begin{bmatrix} tʃ \\ dʒ \end{bmatrix} \rightarrow \begin{bmatrix} ʃ \\ dˡ \end{bmatrix}$ tʃ /___# opt. 20%	12.	No longer present
13. NC	[ʒ] → [dʒ] /___# opt. 30%	13. NC	[ʒ] → [dʒ] /# opt. 30%
14.	No longer present	14. ——	
15.	[l] → ø /___# oblig.	15.	[l] → ø /___# opt. 30%

[a]Percentages following rules provide an estimate of how often they apply. NC designates a rule has not changed from the previous evaluation. Opt., optional rules; oblig., obligatory rules.

ment to determine whether these misarticulations could be eliminated during this period without overloading her program.

The effects of therapy on the remaining phonological rules are shown in the analysis given in the second column of Tables 8 and 9. Rules 3, 4a, 4b, 8a, 8b, 10, 11, and 12 have been successfully eliminated. Rule 13 (the substitution of [dʒ] for /ʒ/) continues unchanged, but no therapy was directed toward this rule. Rule 15 (the omission of final /l/) has decreased by 70%. Since final /ʒ/ occurs so infrequently in English and the omission of final /l/ had nearly subsided, the continued presence of these misarticulations did not seem to justify further therapy, and Grace was dismissed.

Grace began therapy with a severe phonological disorder which rendered her speech almost totally unintelligible, and she was dismissed from therapy 17 months later with essentially normal speech. She was selected for inclusion here as representative of the 18 children who have participated in the clinical program; i.e., her progress was no more dramatic or exceptional than that of any of the other children. The results of these clinical studies indicate that, by focusing therapy on the underlying principles of a child's deviant phonological system, even severe articulatory disorders can be eradicated within a period of 1.5 years, or less. This approach is to be contrasted with traditional approaches in most clinics and schools where therapy typically extends for periods of 3–4 years for children with disorders of comparable severity.

The case study of Grace illustrates the general strategy for translating a phonological analysis into a motivated plan of therapy. I would like to emphasize, however, that the analysis itself is not a recipe for therapy. Rather, it is more like a map to aid us in choosing the best route to reach a destination. In the process of selecting the specific, key sounds to include in therapy, we are formulating our working hypotheses of the most effective routes to follow in correcting a child's speech; the effects of therapy upon the child's speech constitute a test of these hypotheses. With each child, we are conducting an experiment, the results of which allow us to refine further our hypotheses and, thereby, improve the effectiveness of therapy. In this sense, then, the dichotomy between therapy and research is totally without foundation.

THEORY OF ACQUISITION OF PHONOLOGICAL DISORDERS

An integral part of the present research includes a longitudinal study of the normal acquisition of speech involving six children, beginning with their first meaningful utterances at about 1 year and extending through the 3rd year, the age at which most children have fairly well mastered the sound system of their language. A preliminary summary of the results of this study appears in Compton (1975), and the comparisons of normal and deviant development indicate that the same, or quite similar, phonological processes are operating when children develop speech normally as well as when they fail to do so. The difference, then, does not reside in the phonological processes underlying the development of normal or deviant speech.

The child with a phonological disorder does not deviate from normal phonological development—at least with respect to his form of speech—but, in fact, perpetuates it. A child acquiring speech normally goes through various stages of omission and sound substitution patterns which are subsequently dropped or replaced by others as he moves from one phase of development to the next. However, the child with defective speech appears to be operating according to some sort of rigidity principle by which he retains and thus accumulates these patterns of omissions and substitutions that would otherwise be discarded in moving from one stage to another. In so doing, children with defective speech may also develop various idiosyncratic phonological patterns—often bizarre, but nonetheless quite innovative—perhaps as an attempt to compensate for a phonological system that is failing to meet their communicative needs by rendering them unintelligible. Consequently, the speech of a 5- or 6-year-old child with an articulatory disorder is not simply a case of arrested early normal development; rather, it is a highly integrated system of omission and sound substitution patterns every bit as complex as the phonological system of a child of the same age with normal speech. In this sense, then, such a child is not operating by a simplified or "primitive" phonological system but, instead, has more nearly developed a different phonological system.

ANALYSIS OF FREQUENCY OF OCCURRENCE
OF CLINICALLY DEVIANT PHONOLOGICAL RULES

A long range objective of our clinical research is to establish some firm normative data on the phonological processes (deviant rules) underlying children's articulatory disorders. A preliminary summary of the more common deviant patterns, based upon 20 children, that have emerged to date is presented in this section.

Since the project has begun, analyses of 23 5- and 6-year-old children with severe phonological disorders have been completed. All of the children appear to be relatively normal with the exception of their articulatory handicap. Thirteen of the children are boys and 10 are girls. Their socioeconomic backgrounds range from high to low, and a cross-section of ethnic (second and third generation) and racial backgrounds is represented, i.e., Armenian, Chicano, Chinese, Japanese, Italian, Black, and Caucasian. The various phonological rules present at the time of the first evaluation for 20 of the children have been tabulated according to their frequency of occurrence and converted into percentage estimates of the degree of commonality of deviant rules.

To date, there are about 35 major types of rules (based upon an occurrence of 20% or greater) which appear to be typical of children with defective speech. These more common deviant patterns are summarized in Tables 10, 11, and 12. Table 10 includes those rules affecting initial consonants; Table 11 includes the initial consonant blends; Table 12 covers the final consonants. Thus, rule 1 of Table 10 shows that the initial, voiceless stops were produced as unaspirated

Table 10. Most commonly occurring deviant phonological rules (20% or greater) for initial consonants in 20 children (ages 5–6 years) with severe articulatory disorders

I Stops:		V Frictions:	

I Stops:

1. $\begin{bmatrix} \text{stop}+ \\ \text{frict}.- \\ \text{voice}- \end{bmatrix} \rightarrow \begin{bmatrix} \text{stop}+ \\ \text{frict}.- \\ \text{aspir}.- \end{bmatrix}$ = 65%

2. $\begin{bmatrix} k \\ g \end{bmatrix} \rightarrow \begin{bmatrix} t \\ d \end{bmatrix}$ = 40%

II Affricates:

3. $\begin{bmatrix} t\int \\ d_3 \end{bmatrix} \rightarrow \begin{bmatrix} t \\ d \end{bmatrix}$ = 55% $\Big\rangle$ = 75%^{a}

(a) [d3] → [d]   = 20%

4. [t∫] → [∫]   = 20%

III Liquids:

5. $\begin{bmatrix} r \\ l \end{bmatrix} \rightarrow$ [w]   = 40% $\Big\rangle$ = 95%^{a}

(a) [r] → [w]   = 55%

6. [l] → ø   = 20%

IV Glides:

7. [j] → [l]   = 20%

V Frictions:

8. $\begin{bmatrix} f \\ v \end{bmatrix} \rightarrow \begin{bmatrix} p \\ b \end{bmatrix}$ = 25% $\Big\rangle$ = 80%^{a}

(a) [v] → [b]   = 80%^{a}

9. $\begin{bmatrix} \theta \\ \delta \end{bmatrix} \rightarrow \begin{bmatrix} t \\ d \end{bmatrix}$ = 55% $\Big\rangle$ = 100%^{a}

(a) [ð] → [d]   = 45%

10. $\begin{bmatrix} s \\ z \end{bmatrix} \rightarrow \begin{bmatrix} t \\ d \end{bmatrix}$ = 15% $\searrow$ = 50%^{a}

(a) [s] → [t]   = 20% $\nearrow$

(b) [z] → [d]   = 15%

11. [z] → [s]   = 40%

12. [z] → [d3]   = 20%

13. [∫] → [t]   = 25%

14. [∫] → [s]   = 20%

15. [∫] → [t∫]   = 20%

^{a}These values represent the total composite per cent occurrence of the general form of the phonological rules (designated by numerals) and the more specific or restricted forms (designated by subrules a, b, c, etc.) subsumed under the general rules. Each general rule and its accompanying subrules are mutually exclusive for each child.

variants by 65% of the children. Similarly, rule 3 indicates that /f,v/ were substituted by [p,b] 25% of the time; rule 3a specifies that the same substitution process was also applied, but only to the voiced cognate /v/, which was again replaced by [b] by an additional 55% of the children. The combined total of 80% represents the overall frequency of occurrence of the more general phonological principle underlying rules 3 and 3a; namely, that labial, friction consonants undergo a change in manner of articulation and become labial, stop consonants, i.e., a change from friction to stop with the labial (place of articulation) feature held constant. Likewise, rule 1 of Table 11 indicates that both of the liquids /r,l/ are omitted in blends by 60% of the children; rule 1a shows that an additional 20% omit only /r/, while still another 15% omit only /l/. Thus, the value of 95% represents the

Table 11. Most commonly occurring deviant phonological rules (20% or greater) for initial consonant blends in 20 children (ages 5–6 years) with severe articulatory disorders

---

I Liquids in Blends:[a]

1. $\begin{bmatrix} r \\ l \end{bmatrix} \rightarrow$ ø   = 60%

(a)   [r] → ø   = 20%   = 95%[b]

(b)   [l] → ø   = 15%

2. $\begin{bmatrix} r \\ l \end{bmatrix} \rightarrow$ [w]   = 15%

(a)   [r] → [w]   = 15%   = 45%[b]

(b)   [l] → [w]   = 15%

Consonants and Glides after /s/:

3. $\begin{bmatrix} \text{stop}+ \\ \text{voice}- \end{bmatrix} \rightarrow \begin{bmatrix} \text{stop}+ \\ \text{voice}- \\ \text{aspir.}- \end{bmatrix}$ = 20%
(pseudodeviant rule, i.e., /s/ is omitted)

4.   [w] → ø   = 25%

III /s/ in Blends:

5.   [s] → ø   /____   [cons.+]   = 80%
                                                                = 95%[b]
(a)   [s] → ø   /____ $\begin{bmatrix} \text{cons.}+ \\ \text{nasal}- \end{bmatrix}$ = 15%

6.   [s] → [f]   /____w   = 20%

7.   [s] → [ʃ]   /____l   = 25%

---

[a]The combined percentage for rules 1 and 2 is greater than 100%, because some of the children had the option of both substitution [w] for /r/ and /l/ and omitting these liquids.

[b]These values represent the total composite per cent occurrence of the general form of the phonological rules (designated by numerals) and the more specific or restricted forms (designated by subrules a, b, c, etc.) subsumed under the general rules. Each general rule and its accompanying subrules are mutually exclusive for each child.

total composite percentage of occurrence of the general rule of liquid omission (specified by rule 1) and the more restricted forms of the same omission process (specified by subrules 1a and 1b) subsumed under the general rule.

For the sake of clarity, I should emphasize that each general rule and its accompanying subtypes (rules) are mutually exclusive for

Table 12. Most commonly occurring deviant phonological rules (20% or greater) for final consonants in 20 children (ages 5–6 years) with severe articulatory disorders

I Stops: (substitutions)

1. $\begin{bmatrix} \text{stop}+ \\ \text{frict.}- \\ \text{voice}+ \end{bmatrix} \rightarrow \begin{bmatrix} \text{stop}+ \\ \text{frict.}- \\ \text{voice}- \end{bmatrix}$ = 65%
(devoicing)

2. $\begin{bmatrix} \text{stop}+ \\ \text{frict.}- \end{bmatrix} \rightarrow \begin{bmatrix} \text{stop}+ \\ \text{frict.}- \\ \text{release}- \end{bmatrix}$ = 40%
(unreleasing)

3. $\begin{bmatrix} \text{stop}+ \\ \text{frict.}- \\ \text{voice}- \end{bmatrix} \rightarrow \begin{bmatrix} \text{stop}+ \\ \text{frict.}- \\ \text{voice}- \\ \text{marked} \\ \text{aspir.}- \end{bmatrix}$ = 20%
(over aspiration)

4. $[\eta] \rightarrow [n] = 35\%$
("ing" endings excluded)

II Frictions: (substitutions)

5. $\begin{bmatrix} \text{frict.}+ \\ \text{labial}- \end{bmatrix} \rightarrow \begin{bmatrix} t \\ d \end{bmatrix}$ = 20%

(a) $\begin{bmatrix} \text{frict.}+ \\ \text{labial}- \\ \text{voice}- \end{bmatrix} \rightarrow [t]$ = 15%
$= 35\%^a$

6. $\begin{bmatrix} f \\ v \end{bmatrix} \rightarrow \begin{bmatrix} p \\ b \end{bmatrix}$ = 20%

(a) $[v] \rightarrow [b]$ = 35%
$= 55\%^a$

7. $\begin{bmatrix} \theta \\ \delta \end{bmatrix} \rightarrow \begin{bmatrix} f \\ v \end{bmatrix}$ = 35%

8. $[z] \rightarrow [s]$ = 35%

9. $\begin{bmatrix} \int \\ \mathrm{3} \end{bmatrix} \rightarrow \begin{bmatrix} s \\ z \end{bmatrix}$ = 35%

10. $\begin{bmatrix} t\int \\ d\mathrm{3} \end{bmatrix} \rightarrow \begin{bmatrix} \int \\ \mathrm{3} \end{bmatrix}$ = 20%

III Stops: (omissions)

11. $\begin{bmatrix} \text{stop}+ \\ \text{frict.}- \end{bmatrix} \rightarrow \emptyset$ = 20%

(a) $\begin{bmatrix} \text{stop}+ \\ \text{frict.}- \\ \text{labial}- \end{bmatrix} \rightarrow \emptyset$ = 20%
$= 40\%^a$

IV Frictions: (omissions)

12. $[\text{frict.}-] \rightarrow \emptyset$ = 10%

(a) $\begin{bmatrix} \text{frict.}- \\ \text{voice}+ \\ \text{labial}- \end{bmatrix} \rightarrow \emptyset$ = 20%
$= 30\%^a$

V Alveolars: (omissions)

13. $\begin{bmatrix} \text{cons.}+ \\ \text{alv.}+ \end{bmatrix} \rightarrow \emptyset = 10\%$

(a) $\begin{bmatrix} d \\ n \end{bmatrix} \rightarrow \emptyset$ = 10%

(b) $[n] \rightarrow \emptyset$ = 10%
(c) $\begin{bmatrix} t \\ d \end{bmatrix} \rightarrow \emptyset$ = 10%
$= 50\%^a$

(d) $\begin{bmatrix} s \\ z \end{bmatrix} \rightarrow \emptyset$ = 10%
(e)

VI /l/ (omission)

14. $[l] \rightarrow \emptyset$ = 75%

---

^{a}These values represent the total composite per cent occurrence of the general form of the phonological rules (designated by numerals) and the more specific or restricted forms (designated by subrules a, b, c, etc.) subsumed under the general rules. Each general rule and its accompanying subrules are mutually exclusive for each child.

each child; i.e., no child is represented more than once for any given phonological process. However, in some instances, more than one process may apply to the same sounds for any given child. This is the case, for example, for rules 1 and 2 of Table 11 and is reflected in their combined total which exceeds 100% because some of the children had the option of both omitting the liquids /r,l/ (rule 1 and accompanying subrules) and substituting [w] for these liquids (rule 2 and accompanying subrules).

A few illustrative examples of some common phonological processes which may be inferred from Tables 10, 11, and 12 follow:

1. With the exception of unaspirating voiceless stops and substituting alveolar stops for velar ones, initial stops are rarely misarticulated (Table 10).

2. Except for /f,v/, initial friction consonants as well as the affricates are generally substituted by [t] or [d] (Table 10).

3. In initial position, the voicing feature is highly stable, resistant to change (Table 10). Notice that, with the exception of rule 11 (devoicing of initial /z/), the voicing feature specification (+ or −) of the sound substitutions is preserved in every substitution rule: voiceless sounds are substituted for voiceless ones, and voiced sounds replace voiced ones.

4. Omission of liquids (/r,l/) predominates over substitution of liquids in the blends (Table 11).

5. Initial /s/ in blends is generally omitted (Table 11), with the probability of omission being slightly greater before non-nasal consonants (refer to rules 5 and 5a).

6. Initial consonants are rarely omitted (Table 10), whereas final consonants have a high probability of being omitted (Table 12).

7. The probability of omission of final stop consonants is slightly greater than the omission of final friction consonants (Table 12).

8. The probability of omission of final, voiced friction consonants is slightly greater than the omission of final, voiceless friction consonants (refer to rules 12 and 12a of Table 12).

9. The probability of omission of final alveolar consonants is much greater than for any other place of articulation (Table 12).

10. In final position, the labial feature (sounds involving the lips) is relatively stable, i.e., resistant to change (Table 12). This is reflected by rules 7 and 7a, in which the labial feature is preserved (the substitutions of [p] and [b] for /f/ and /v/) and, also, by rules 6, 6a, 11a, and 12a, all of which carry the feature specification "labial-," indicating that these rules do not apply to labial sounds.

As the study continues, the accumulation and refinement of such normative data will provide convenient guidelines for therapists in analyzing children's deviant speech by pinpointing the types of patterns likely to be present. These data should also serve as a useful clinical guide for planning therapy by establishing priorities for working with deviant rules. In addition, a further related goal is to develop an index of communicative disruption based upon the presence of types of deviant rules. Clearly, this is a more meaningful way of scoring articulatory severity than present practices of simply counting misarticulated sounds. Such indices should take into account 1) the form of misarticulation (contrastive vs. noncontrastive feature changes and magnitude of change in place and manner of articulation features); 2) the generality of misarticulation patterns (rules affecting one or a few sounds vs. rules affecting large classes of sounds); 3) the specific phonological context or environment in which the rules apply (initial, intervocalic, blends, etc.); and 4) the degree of commonality of deviant rules. A discussion of the clinical implications of common vs. uncommon rules is included in the next section.

UNUSUAL PHONOLOGICAL RULES

In addition to the more common phonological rules shown in Tables 10, 11, and 12, there are also a number of rules that occur less often, most of which are unique to specific children, i.e., their own idiosyncratic creations. In general, there appears to be an inverse relationship between the degree of commonality of phonological rules and the extent to which they disrupt intelligibility; i.e., the less common a rule is, the greater the communicative impairment. Furthermore, idiosyncratic rules seem to attract more attention to a child's speech and, thus, may intensify his handicap all the more by rendering his speech more conspicuous. To the extent that these hypotheses are shown to be valid, early therapy directed at such rules would be more effective in minimizing the child's communicative handicap than would be therapy beginning with more common rules.

It is rather typical for relatives, friends, and teachers to report that they more easily understand a speech handicapped child after they have spent some time with him, no doubt because the continued exposure allows them to accommodate or "tune in" to the child's deviant system and intuitively recode or translate his speech. In fact, it is often difficult to distinguish between a child's real progress and the adults' increased awareness without some objective means of evaluation. At any rate, to the extent that such recoding does occur, it would seem to follow that more common deviant rules, perhaps grounded in our own early-normal childhood, would more easily facilitate recoding a child's deviant speech than would more unusual rules.

Unusual phonological rules may take many different forms and generally have no obvious relationship to, or precedent in, the language environment to which the child is exposed. Neither is there any obvious explanation for the way in which they develop other than that they appear to be the unique creations of children with phonological disorders. To date, there is no evidence of unusual phonological rules in the longitudinal data from our studies of children developing speech normally, thus suggesting that they are peculiar to children with phonological disorders. Consequently, the presence of unusual rules in a child's speech may be an important, early diagnostic sign for detecting potential phonological disorders in young children.

A possible explanation of why unusual rules originate in a child's speech has previously been discussed in Compton (1975) as an attempt to compensate for an ineffectual phonological system. A few examples illustrating the nature and diversity of such rules follow.

Example 1   (Anthony, age 5)   In the /sl/ and /sw/ blends, the /l/ and /w/ portions of the blends are both replaced by [r] (extremely uncommon), and the /s/ is replaced by [ʃ] (not uncommon). Thus, the words "swing" and "sling" would both be pronounced as [ʃrɪŋ]. The underlying rules can be characterized as,

Rule A $\begin{bmatrix} w \\ l \end{bmatrix} \rightarrow$ [r] /s___

Rule B [s] → [ʃ] /___r

Example 2   (Robert, age 5)   In all /r/ and /l/ blends with preceding stop consonants (/pr, pl, tr, etc./), the stops are replaced by [f] (extremely uncommon), and the /r/ and /l/ portions of the blends are replaced by [w] (very common); thus such words as "play, tray, clay," etc. would be pronounced as [fwe]. The underlying rules can be characterized as,

Rule A   [stop +]   →   [f]   /__$\begin{bmatrix} l \\ r \end{bmatrix}$

Rule B $\begin{bmatrix} r \\ l \end{bmatrix}$ →   [w]   /f__

Example 3   (Doug, age 6)   All initial, non-nasal consonants are replaced by the nasal consonants [m] or [ŋ] whenever a word contains a later appearing nasal consonant, i.e., regressive, nasal assimilation. If the initial consonant is a labial (/p,b,f,v/), it is replaced by [m], and if it is a nonlabial consonant, it is replaced by [ŋ]. The following vowel then becomes markedly nasalized, and if the later nasal consonant is in final position, it may be produced normally or omitted altogether. Consequently, the word "king" would be pronounced as [ŋĩŋ] or [ŋĩ]; the word "pen" as [mɛ̃n] or [mɛ̃]; the words "Santa Claus" as [ŋæ̃ehəkɔz] (intervocalic consonants become [h]); the word "violin" as [maĩohɪn] or [maĩohɪ], etc. Observe that the nasal assimilation crosses syllable boundaries (as illustrated by "violin"), but there are no instances crossing over word boundaries. The underlying rules can be characterized as,

Rule A $\begin{bmatrix} \text{cons.+} \\ \text{nasal}- \\ \text{labial}\pm \end{bmatrix}$ → $\left\{ \begin{matrix} \begin{bmatrix} \text{cons.+} \\ \text{nasal+} \\ \text{bi-labial+} \end{bmatrix} /[\overline{\text{labial}}+] \\ \\ \begin{bmatrix} \text{cons.+} \\ \text{nasal+} \\ \text{velar+} \end{bmatrix} /[\overline{\text{labial}}-] \end{matrix} \right\}$ $\begin{matrix} \text{cons.+} \\ /\#\_\ldots\text{nasal+} \end{matrix}$

Rule B $\begin{bmatrix} \text{vowel+} \end{bmatrix}$ → $\begin{bmatrix} \text{vowel+} \\ \text{markedly} \\ \text{nasal+} \end{bmatrix}$ $\begin{matrix} /\text{cons.+} \\ /\ \text{nasal+}\ \_ \end{matrix}$ (does not apply to vowels following nasal consonants in true initial nasal words)

Rule C $\begin{bmatrix} \text{cons.+} \\ \text{nasal+} \end{bmatrix}$ →   ø   /__# (optional)

In each of the foregoing examples, the unusual phonological processes are characterized by rule A and are arranged in order of their increasing generality. Thus, rule A of example 1 is very specific, applying only to the /sl/ and /sw/ blends, and is, therefore, of limited consequence in Anthony's speech. By contrast, rule A of example 2 is much more general, applying to all stop consonants occurring in /r/ and /l/ blends, and affects a much greater segment of Robert's speech. Similarly, rule A of example 3 is even more general, since it applies to any initial consonant (followed by a later nasal consonant) and, in fact, was so far reaching that this rule alone nearly devastated the intelligibility of Doug's speech. Furthermore, apparently because of its bizarre nature and sweeping consequences, Doug's speech attracted so much attention that people within hearing distance of him would often go out of their way to have a look at the child with the strange sounding talk. There can be little question of the importance for Doug of eliminating this rule as quickly as possible.

REFERENCES

Compton, A. J. 1970. Generative studies of children's phonological disorders. J. Speech Hear. Disord. 35:315–339.

Compton, A. J. 1975. Generative studies of children's phonological disorders: A strategy of therapy. *In* S. Singh (ed.), Measurement Procedures in Speech, Hearing, and Language, pp. 55–90. University Park Press, Baltimore.

Ingram, D. 1972. Phonological analysis of a developmentally aphasic child. Mimeographed. Stanford University, Stanford, California.

Lorentz, J. 1974. A deviant phonological system of English. Stanford University Committee on Linguistics Papers and Reports on Child Language Development 8:55–64.

Oller, D. K. 1973. Regularities in abnormal child phonology. J. Speech Hear. Disord. 38:36–47.

Oller, D. K., and C. A. Kelly. 1974. Phonological substitution processes of a hard of hearing child. J. Speech Hear. Disord. 39:65–74.

SYNTAX/SEMANTICS

Semantic Factors in the Acquisition of Rules For Word Use and Sentence Construction

MELISSA BOWERMAN

That general intellectual development—particularly during the sensorimotor period described by Piaget (1952)—provides the basis for single-word acquisition and the onset of multiple word utterances is generally accepted in the child language literature. Even though the correspondence between evolving cognitive and perceptual systems and language has been often noted, there is still no detailed account of what the nature of this correspondence may be. In this paper, Bowerman gives a thoughtful and penetrating analysis of categorical and relational development in early language, detailing the semantic content of both aspects. Rather than postulating an innate capacity for a hierarchy of grammatical classes (McNeill, 1970), Bowerman (1973, 1974) explores the relationship between cognitive and linguistic categories and their relative effect on word meaning and sentence construction. Her discussion of the recent literature on early language and her presentation of data from the study of her own two children follow the same measured methods that Inhelder and Piaget (1964) used in studying early logical development. Furthermore, Bowerman's descriptions of early categorical and relational linguistic development have interesting parallels to the Inhelder-Piaget descriptions of "similarity" and "belonging" in early graphic collections.

—DMM

This research was supported in part by Grant NS-10468-1 from the National Institute of Neurological Diseases and Stroke to the Bureau of Child Research, University of Kansas.

A striking shift has taken place over the last decade in the topics that concern investigators of child language. Studies in the early and mid 1960's concentrated primarily on the acquisition of formal syntactic configurations and operations (e.g., phrase structures, transformations). More recent analyses, in contrast, reflect a growing concern for the way form is related to meaning in linguistic development, and, more generally, for the cognitive bases of language acquisition.

The recent interest in cognitive factors in language development comes in part as a reaction to the nativist position that dominated much discussion of child language in the 1960's. According to the nativist view, man's capacity for language is a specialized component of his biological makeup and does not arise directly from more general cognitive abilities. The child is seen as coming to the language learning task equipped with much inborn knowledge of language structure; he requires only a certain amount of linguistic input to activate this knowledge (Chomsky, 1965, 1968; Katz, 1966; McNeill, 1966, 1970, 1971).

Two major lines of attack on the nativist position have been mounted. According to one, the *formal structure* of language is not totally distinct from man's more general cognitive organization. Rather, it is argued, various linguistic categories, structures, and processes, such as word classes, grammatical relationships, concatenation or "adding together" of elements, the embedding of one sentence into another, and the distinction between deep and surface structure, have striking correlates in nonlinguistic modes of conceptualizing experience and acting upon the environment. Thus, the child's learning of language is facilitated by his having established certain basic cognitive abilities during the early months of life (Sinclair deZwart, 1971, 1973a and b; Greenfield, Nelson, and Saltzman, 1972; Goodson and Greenfield, 1975; see Bowerman, 1974a for discussion).

A second cognitively-based counter to the nativist position has concentrated on the possible role played in language acquisition by the kinds of *meanings* children are capable and desirous of expressing at various stages of development. Much of the recent theorizing and research on the role of meaning in language development was foreshadowed by a statement made in 1966 by Slobin, in an argument against the need to ascribe extensive foreknowledge of grammatical categories to the child. Slobin pointed out that many language categories are based on semantic features and that such features are learnable through experience. He went on to suggest that an important component of the child's capacity to acquire language may be the "ability to learn certain types of semantic or conceptual categories, the knowledge that learnable semantic criteria can be the basis for grammatical categories, and... the formal knowledge that such categories can be expressed by such morphological devices as affixing, sound alternation, and so on" (1966, p. 89).

Studies undertaken in the late 1960's began to reflect the growing conviction that the acquisition of syntax cannot be adequately explained without reference to the kinds of meanings children attempt to express in their early utterances (e.g., Bloom, 1970; Schlesinger, 1971b; Kernan, 1969; Bowerman, 1973a). Comparisons of data collected in different language communities revealed striking similarities in the semantic content of children's utterances across languages (Slobin, 1970; Brown, 1973; Bowerman, 1973a, 1975b). Ervin-Tripp (1971), reviewing the early crop of the semantically-based studies, summed up a prevalent viewpoint in her statement that "the findings [from child language data] of universal, or even of common semantic features specifying subcategories or characterizing sentential relations is more than a mere curiosity, an addition to what we know... these semantic features may provide a crucial link in our understanding of how sentences develop" (p. 208). She then pointed out that knowledge of the kinds of semantic categories, features, and relationships that are available to children at various stages of language acquisition can help to account for the *order* in which different aspects of language develop and also aid in determining "which properties of input are irrelevant because incomprehensible to children on the basis of their cognitive development" (p. 209).

After several years of considering the semantic properties of young children's utterances in conjunction with their forms, many investigators have come to a kind of consensus on the early course of language acquisition which may be summarized briefly as follows: during the period before he speaks, the child is busy building up a repertoire of basic cognitive concepts—ways of organizing and understanding his experiences. His task in acquiring language is to discover the linguistic devices by means of which such concepts can be expressed. In other words, acquiring language consists in large part of learning how to map or translate from one representational system (the child's prelinguistic conceptual notions) into another (language) (Schlesinger, 1971b; Slobin, 1973; Bloom, 1973; Nelson, 1974; Clark, 1974a; Wells, 1974). Important mechanisms for expressing meaning to which the child must attend include not only the *morphological* processes mentioned by Slobin in the quote given above but also *words* as devices for representing various kinds of conceptual material and contrastive *word orders* and *intonation patterns* that signal distinctions in meaning, e.g., "the cat bites the dog" vs. "the dog bites the cat," and "Mommy is going out?" (rising intonation) vs. "Mommy is going out" (falling intonation).

The view that a central process in language acquisition is the child's search for links between cognitive concepts and linguistic forms and operations has been strengthened and encouraged by recent developments in linguistics. Many linguists now argue, on grounds quite independent of child language, that the most basic elements of language are not abstract syntactic configurations like grammatical relations but rather a universal set of prime semantic concepts that combine according to general and language-specific constraints to yield both words and sentences (e.g., Fillmore, 1968, 1971; Postal, 1971; Lakoff, 1971; McCawley, 1971). Attention to the role of meaning in language has led to the realization that many syntactic classes, configurations, and operations which were once assumed to be semantically arbitrary—i.e., not constrained by any particular meaning—are in fact governed by various subtle semantic distinctions (e.g., Postal, 1971, p. 252ff; Zwicky, 1968).[1] To the extent that linguistic phenomena are semantically motivated, the proposal that the child's primary concern is to discover consistencies linking variations in meaning to variations in formal structure is an appealing one.

The goal of the present chapter is to discuss and integrate research on the kinds of meanings that appear to play an important role in the initial stages of language acquisition. Specifically, the chapter deals with the way in which children ascribe meanings to words at the

---

[1]For example, Zwicky (1968) argues that English verbs which take an infinitive in their complement (e. g., "*want* to get," "*persuade* John to come") are semantically distinguishable from those that take a present participle (e.g., "*find* John going downtown," "*imagine* yourself flying") in that verbs of the former type refer to events that temporally precede the events specified in their complements while those of the latter type refer to events that are contemporaneous with the events of the complements. A number of investigators have noted that there is a semantic distinction between verbs that can occur either in intransitive contexts or in transitive contexts with a *causative* sense ("the door opened," "John opened the door") and those that cannot (e.g., "sing," "eat") (e.g., Zwicky, 1968; Binnick, 1971). Other illustrations of semantic constraints on possible linguistic structures are found in Zwicky, 1968; Postal, 1971; p. 267; McCawley, 1971. In an earlier era, Whorf (1956) made related arguments about "cryptotypes," or covert semantic categories that constrain the ways in which various linguistic forms can combine.

one-word stage and with the nature of the relational concepts—concepts involving *relationships* between objects and other objects or events—that underlie children's early rules for word combination.

To put the discussions to follow into perspective, it must be noted that although the ability to perceive or construct various kinds of meanings and to link these with appropriate expressive devices is clearly a basic component of the child's language capacity, an adequate account of language acquisition must deal with more than semantic factors. First, many aspects of language structure are purely formal, in the sense that they are apparently not linked to meaning at all. For example, consider the restriction in English that renders sentences like "put the hat on," "put it on," and "put on the hat" grammatical while those like "put on it" are not (McCawley, 1974).[2] Since such constraints are not governed by semantic distinctions, their ultimate mastery by the child cannot be explained by reference to his semantic development. Possibly acquiring such knowledge depends on all-purpose inductive strategies that enable the child to recognize and abstract out regularities in linguistic and nonlinquistic input alike (Dore, 1975; Reber, 1973); alternatively, as the nativist position states and as Cromer (1974a and b) has continued to caution, there may be specifically linguistic (as opposed to cognitive) abilities involved.

A second way in which an account of semantic development is insufficient in itself is that it does not explain how the child takes the step from formulating language-relevant concepts to linking these up with the appropriate expressive devices of his language. Different devices (e.g., word order, affixation) are not equally easy for a child to master; sometimes the expression of a given semantic content must wait not on the child's development of the concept itself but on his ability to figure out how to express it once he has acquired it (Slobin, 1973). In short, an adequate account of language acquisition must take into consideration not only the nature of early semantic development but also the way in which children deal with the formal characteristics of language. These matters are outside the scope of this chapter, however.

---

[2]Most investigators would include basic grammatical relations such as "subject of the sentence" and "predicate of the sentence" as examples of purely formal, non-semantically based aspects of language (see Fillmore, 1968; Brown, 1973; Bowerman, 1973a and b). Schlesinger (1974), however, has argued that although technically these may appear to be independent of conceptual content, psychologically they are assimilated to various semantic notions, e.g., "subject" to "agent."

The contents of the chapter are organized in the following way. The first major section takes up the role of *categorization* in language acquisition. The role of categorization as a prerequisite for creativity in language use is considered here, followed by discussions of the relationship between semantic and cognitive categories and of the origin of the categories children use in the early period of language acquisition (i.e., are they introduced through language or do they arise in the child on grounds quite independent of language?). The second major section investigates the kinds of categories that govern children's early understanding and use of words. The third major section explores the nature of the relational categories that underlie children's early word combinations. In the final section some remarks about possible clinical significance are offered.

LINGUISTIC AND NONLINGUISTIC CATEGORIES: SOME BASIC ISSUES

Categorization and Productivity

The most fundamental ability with which a theory of language acquisition must come to terms is a speaker's capacity to use language in a creative or productive way. In this chapter we will be concerned with two aspects of creativity in language use: the speaker's parallel abilities to use *words* to refer to objects or events that he has never heard them applied to before and to put together words to form novel *sentences*.[3] The development of both these abilities requires that the child be able to perceive similarities between new experiences and the familiar situations in which he has heard or produced particular words and sentences.

The child's attempts to apply known forms or patterns to novel situations along lines of perceived similarity are reflected most obviously in the way he uses known words in connection with new

---

[3]The focus will thus be on *production*, although much of the material to be discussed is relevant for *comprehension* as well. While both production and comprehension can be assumed to tap ultimately into the same conceptual system, the developmental relationship between the two performance modalities is complex (cf. Bloom, 1974; Huttenlocher, 1974, for discussion). In particular, the young child often uses different kinds of information in interpreting utterances than in producing them. For example, his interpretations of language forms that he does not yet completely understand are apparently swayed both by general nonlinguistic strategies (Clark, 1973a) and by the specific characteristics of the settings in which the forms are heard (Donaldson, McGarrigle, 1974).

referents, e.g., the extension of "doggie" from dogs to all four-legged animals and "open" from opening doors and boxes to taking pieces out of jigsaw puzzles. A similar phenomenon is found in the child's extension of patterns for combining words to new situations. For example, a child who has heard a number of sentences of the type "that's Mommy's coat" (Daddy's hat, the baby's shoe, the man's car, etc.) will eventually begin to produce his own version of these, e.g., "Mommy coat," "Daddy hat," etc. As long as these sentences refer to familiar and often-talked-about pairings between a person and an object that the person owns, controls, or typically uses, one cannot be sure that the child really sees any similarity among the various specific relationships involved (e.g., the relationship between Mommy and her coat, Daddy and his hat, etc.). But when the child starts to produce similar sentences that have never been modeled to him, e.g., "Mommy keys," "baby book," and "Grandpa spoon," while in the context of an object owned, controlled, or used by the person mentioned, one may plausibly assume that he has figured out a systematic way (a consistent word order, in this case) to encode an abstract relational notion which might be called "possession." It is abstract in the sense that it is not tied to any particular situational realization (e.g., the relationship between Mommy and her coat). Rather, the child sees the relationship between Mommy and her coat as similar to that which holds between Daddy and his hat, the baby and its book, Grandpa and the spoon he uses, and so on.

Things that are not identical but which are treated as if they were equivalent, at least under certain circumstances, constitute a *category,* or, alternatively, a concept or a class.[4] (By the unsatisfactory word "things" is meant here virtually anything an organism is capable of perceiving or experiencing, such as objects, properties of objects, actions, processes, mental states, relationships between objects and other objects or actions, etc.). The ability to categorize is regarded as one of the most basic cognitive capacities. According to Bruner, Goodnow, and Austin, for example, "virtually all cognitive activity involves and is dependent on the process of categorizing" (1956, p. 246). The grouping of discriminably different stimuli into categories on the basis of shared features is an adaptive way of deal-

---

[4]There are certain problems involved in defining concepts in terms of "equivalence responses" ("similar or identical reactions to different environmental input," Flavell, 1970, p. 983), as Flavell (1970) has outlined. However, even though the definition is not ideal, it will do for purposes of discussing the concepts underlying words and sentence structures.

ing with what would otherwise be an overwhelming array of unique experiences. As Tyler puts it, ". . . . life in a world where nothing was the same would be intolerable. It is through . . . classification that the whole rich world of infinite variability shrinks to manipulable size" (1969, p. 7).

In asking how children learn to use language in novel situations, we are in essence asking what kinds of concepts they have formulated with which to associate words and syntactic devices such as word orders, inflections, and intonation patterns. What kinds of similarities across experiences are children sensitive to in the early stages of language acquisition, for purposes of extending known words to new referents or using familiar structural patterns to build novel sentences? Put more generally, how do children come to construct, from their general experiences (both linguistic and nonlinguistic), those categories that underlie their emerging ability to use language? How do they organize their perceptions of and interactions with the world into the kinds of conceptual chunks or units to which morphemes (words and inflections) may be attached and upon which rules for combining and ordering those morphemes can operate?

These questions have been the focus, either explicitly or implicitly, of a large number of semantically oriented investigations of the early phases of language development. For example, studies of the acquisition of word meaning have investigated children's grounds for referring to a given set of items by the same word and how initial classifications change over time (e.g., Clark, 1973b; Nelson, 1974). Studies of children's early word combinations have explored the nature of the relational categories that underlie children's early rules for combining words (e.g., Schlesinger, 1971b; Bloom, 1970; Brown, 1973; Bowerman, 1973a and b; Braine, in press). The findings of such studies will be reviewed in the sections on word meaning and word combination.

Although most studies have treated children's knowledge of word meaning and of rules for word combination as two separate areas of investigation, acquiring both kinds of knowledge requires that the child be able to associate aspects of language with concepts that specify similarities or invariances across diverse experiences. While the kinds of concepts that underlie children's word meanings are not necessarily the same as those that govern their word combinations, there is no obvious dividing line between them; sometimes, in fact, it is clear the related notions are involved in the two kinds of knowledge. For example, the creative use of the words "my" and "mine" requires that the child be capable of perceiving a type of invariance in his relationship to a number of different objects that is quite similar to the invariance which he must recognize in order to achieve a systematic formula for producing sentences like "Mommy keys" and "Grandpa spoon." Similarly, the child's ability to say "in" in connection with a variety of different stiuations (e.g., someone's getting into a tub, putting a doll into a drawer, or pouring juice into a cup) requires an awareness of an abstract similarity in the way pairs of objects can be spatially related, just as does his ability to produce sentences like "baby tub," "doll drawer," and "juice cup" in a systematic way. In short, the semantic developments affecting the acquisition of word meanings and of rules for sentence construction are related, and similar questions about the nature and origins of the relevant concepts can be asked about both. For this reason they are treated within a common framework in this chapter.

Cognitive vs. Semantic Categories

The search for the semantic categories that constitute children's early word meanings and that underlie their rules for word combination is clearly related to the study of children's developing cognitive structures. However, many investigators have felt a need to distinguish knowledge that can properly be called "semantic" from the child's general understanding of the world. Yet there is little agreement as to exactly how the distinction should be drawn.[5]

Most of the debate over whether particular behaviors of the child reflect "semantic" knowledge or are simply due to the child's cognitive apprehension of a situation has focused on whether simple utterances consisting of one or two words can contract a relational semantic meaning with an aspect of the situational context that is not explicitly mentioned. For example, can the child's word "Mommy," uttered while the child points to Mommy's coat, be considered to express a relational semantic meaning of "possession," in addition to whatever lexical meaning the word "Mommy" may have? Similarly, can "Mommy," uttered while the child observes his mother opening a door, be considered "agentive" in relation to a contextually given but not linguistically specified action? A number of researchers have answered this question affirmatively, documenting with various

---

[5]What counts as "semantic" knowledge is as much at issue in the case of adult speakers as it is for children. Contrast, for example, the views of Katz and Fodor (1963) with those of Bolinger (1965) and Olson (1970b).

kinds of evidence (e.g., Ingram, 1971; Antinucci and Parisi, 1973; Greenfield and Smith, in press).

Such proposals sometimes identify the term ''semantic'' with the notion of what the child intends to *communicate,* in order to distinguish between the ''semantic'' knowledge reflected in an utterance and the child's general cognitive understanding of the situation about which he speaks. For example, Parisi (1974), in discussing his and Antinucci's (1973) model (which postulates complex semantic structures underlying even one-word utterances), states that ''by semantic structure we mean a cognitive structure which is constructed with the intent to communicate it. Therefore semantic structures are a subclass of cognitive structures'' (p. 102).

While recognizing the importance of the child's developing cognitive structures for his ultimate linguistic knowledge, many investigators are nevertheless reluctant to assign a relational *semantic* structure to a single word on the basis of the way in which it is embedded in a nonlinguistic context (e.g., Bloom, 1973; Schlesinger, 1974; Dore, 1975. Brown, 1973, p. 151ff. feels that the kind of evidence that has been advanced so far is not adequate but leaves the matters open). Bloom (1973, p. 2), for example, distinguishes sharply between *semantic* knowledge, which she defines as involving the meanings of particular words and of meaning relations between words, and *conceptual* knowledge, or the underlying cognitive structures that the child uses to represent to himself the relations among persons, objects, and events in the word. Like Bloom, Dore (1975) argues against assigning linguistic significance to such nonlinguistic aspects of context as crying, gestures, etc. He recommends maintaining a clear distinction between ''knowledge of language and knowledge of the world'' to ''prevent basing claims about the former on data about the latter'' (p. 34). Similar arguments have been made by Bowerman (1974b) about the need to make a clear distinction between the general conceptual knowledge that is reflected in a child's behavior at the time of speech and knowledge of the internal structure (i.e., semantic components) of words.

The matter of distinguishing semantic knowledge from cognitive knowledge is clearly a complex one and cannot be analyzed in detail here. However, the position I would advocate, in line with the sorts of arguments made by Bloom (1970, 1973), Dore (1975), Schlesinger (1974), and Bowerman (1974b), is that the term ''semantic'' be reserved for cognitive knowledge that has demonstrably become linked to aspects of *language* for the child—i.e., that has begun to ''make a difference, linguistically,'' to borrow Schlesinger's useful phrase (1974, p. 144). In other words, a concept that the child grasps at the nonlinguistic level achieves semantic significance only if 1) it has an effect on the way in which he selects a word to refer to a situation, or chooses an inflection and determines the class of words to which the inflection can be applied, or selects a word order or intonation pattern, or decides whether or not a particular operation can be performed (such as using a noncausative verb in a causative sense, see Bowerman, 1974b), and so on, or, conversely, if 2) it governs the way in which he *understands* a word, inflection, word order, intonation pattern, etc.

Certain cognitive distinctions which human beings are capable of making are probably semantically significant in all languages in that they are reflected somewhere in the linguistic system, whether it be in the comprehension of or choice among competing morphemes (words, affixes), word orders, intonations, or whatever. Other cognitive distinctions may have semantic consequences in some languages but not in others. For example, in Japanese, the nature of the physical relationship between an article of clothing or accessory and the body part on which it is worn is semantically significant in that it governs the choice of verb used to refer to removal of the object from the body. The removal of objects that *envelop* the body part, such as shoes, gloves, pants, coats, and mittens, is referred to by *nugu,* while *toru* is used for the removal of objects like earrings, bibs, glasses, broaches, and rings that are simply ''perched'' on the surface of the body. (The choice among the two verbs is not learnable strictly as a matter of association between verb and object, since, for example, an object such as a shoe which ordinarily takes *nugu* would take *toru* instead if it were removed from, say, the top of the head instead of from its usual site).[6] In English, in contrast to Japanese, the distinction between enveloping and nonenveloping relations between objects and body parts is not semantically significant. It has no effect either on the selection of the verb referring to removal (''take off'' is routinely used for all these operations) or on choices among other linguistic forms, patterns, or operations. Thus, a child acquiring Japanese must learn to attach semantic significance to a distinction which will remain linguistically irrelevant for an English-speaking child. Nevertheless, we can assume that the English-speaking child is

---

[6]I am grateful to Megumi Kameyama for acting as my informant on this and other topics in the structure of the Japanese lexicon.

just as capable of making the cognitive discrimination as his Japanese counterpart.

To summarize the arguments advanced above, cognitive discriminations are not automatically also semantic ones. They assume significance only when they become linked to one or another aspect of language. (Whether or not the link made by the child is appropriate from the adult's point of view is irrelevant.) When cognitive and semantic knowledge are carefully distinguished, the study of children's semantic development becomes a two-step process. First, we must understand the nature of children's general cognitive development in order to know what kinds of cognitive discriminations and groupings they routinely make or are capable of making at a given point in development. In other words, what is the cognitive repertoire upon which meaning in language can draw? Piagetian theory has provided investigators of child language with invaluable insights into these matters, as is evidenced in the work of Brown, 1973; Bloom, 1970, 1973; Edwards, 1974; Morehead and Morehead, 1974; Sinclair-deZwart, 1971, 1973a and b; and Wells, 1974, among others. Second, we must determine how, out of all the cognitive discriminations a child is potentially capable of making at a given time, some begin to get connected to language and hence to take on semantic significance while others do not. An important question that must be considered in connection with this is the extent to which the child's formulation of the specific categories that govern his use of language is influenced by the particular language he hears. To this issue we now turn.

Origin of Semantic Concepts

Social scientists have long been plagued by the question of how linguistic and cognitive development are related in a child's growth. Are concepts first introduced into a child's thoughts through language, or does language merely express concepts that are formed independently of it? More specifically, does the child come to see experiences (objects, events, etc.) as similar if the language he is learning treats them as equivalent, as instances of the same concept, and as different if different words or different syntactic structures are applied to them? Or does he initially judge similarity or lack of it for himself, on the basis of his own nonlinguistic experiences?

Earlier in this century there was a tendency to regard a child's conceptual development as strongly influenced by or even completely determined by the language to which he is exposed. According to this view, categories—groupings of things that are similar in some way—neither pre-exist in nature, only awaiting discovery, nor unfold naturally as part of man's biologically given way of organizing his experience. Rather, they are arbitrarily imposed on reality and can take almost any form. The evidence advanced for this position, known in its strongest form as the Sapir-Whorf or Whorfian hypothesis, was that there is little correspondence among the semantic categories employed in the lexicons and grammars of different natural languages. Given domains such as colors, relatives, actions, etc. are classified in a variety of contrasting and incongruent ways, such that distinctions that are important in the structure of one language may play no role at all in the structure of another. According to the Whorfian hypothesis, the child's acquisition of his native language not only is the means by which he is initiated into the particular concepts his culture considers meaningful, but also is the medium through which he imposes a basic structure on reality.

The Whorfian hypothesis was heavily debated prior to the mid 1960's (see Carroll, 1964, for a review), but recent years have seen a growing movement away from extreme or even moderate Whorfian views on the relationship between language and cognition. Many investigators now regard cognition as relatively independent of language. Lenneberg (1967), for example, has argued that "the modes of conceptualization that happen to be tagged by a given natural language need not, and apparently do not, exert restrictions upon an individual's freedom of conceptualizing" (p. 334). What limits there are on modes of conceptualizing are seen as resulting from biologically-given restrictions on cognitive organization rather than from knowledge of language. MacNamara (1972), for example, argues that there are cognitive constraints on what will be grouped together, reminding us that "children do not form bizarre concepts to include foot and floor and exclude all else" (pp. 3–4). He suggests that selective attention to certain aspects of the environment may play a role in constraining patterns of concept formation. Related arguments are made by Olson (1970a), who proposes that the structure of the human nervous system gives priority to certain kinds of perceptual cues over others, presumably because of their evolutionary usefulness. Some concrete evidence of restrictions in concept development is offered by Rosch (1973a and b), who found that certain physical stimuli (shapes, colors) are classified similarly by people from different cultures regardless of major differences in their languages.

The currently prevalent view that cognitive development is relatively independent of language is clearly reflected in recent studies of child language, many of which treat Whorfian notions with little sympathy. As noted in the introduction to this chapter, the child is now commonly viewed as coming to the language-learning task well equipped with a stock of basic concepts that he has built up through his interactions with the world. His problem is to discover how these concepts can be mapped into language rather than to learn from language what the necessary concepts are (e.g., Slobin, 1973; Bloom, 1973; Nelson, 1974; Clark, 1974a). According to this position, the child does not learn—and probably does not even attend to—language forms or patterns which encode meanings that he has not already formulated on the nonlinguistic level. MacNamara (1972), for example, states that "it is inconceivable that the hearing of a logical term [by which he means words such as "and," "or," "more," "all," and "some"] should generate for the first time the appropriate logical operator in a child's mind. Indeed the only possibility of his learning such a word would seem to be if he experienced the need for it in his own thinking and looked for it in the linguistic usage about him" (p. 5). (See Cromer, 1974b, for further arguments and lines of supporting evidence for the cognition-first position on language development.)

A modification or softening of the strict cognition-first viewpoint is discernable in some of the most recent literature on language acquisition. A few researchers are now urging that the role played by social factors—including language—in the child's conceptual development not be discounted. Wells (1975), for example, cautions that "attempts to give substance to claims about predispositions for language acquisition in terms of prior cognitive development are seriously limited in their neglect of the social dimensions of cognition." Some of Wells' arguments and related studies will be presented in the section on the acquisition of word meaning.

A view of conceptual development which accepts the hypothesis that language input can have an influence on the child's cognitive structuring of the world from the start of his attempts to make sense of language, (e.g., before the end of his first year), while nevertheless acknowledging the role played by the child's inherent disposition to develop cognitively along certain lines, can be termed "interactionist." According to this position (towards which I shall confess my bias at the outset) there are many relationships possible between language and concept formation depending both on the kinds of concepts involved and on the type of input provided. Some early concepts undoubtedly develop autonomously (i.e., independently of

language), particularly those which are universal (e.g., object permanence; cf. Brown, 1965, pp. 314–315). Other early concepts might be
considered autonomous only insofar as they require a nonlinguistic
potential for recognizing certain sorts of similarities across experiences. However, they would start to develop primarily because the
child's caretakers call his attention to the possibility of grouping along
certain lines by repeatedly using the same word in superficially variable situations (a word acting as a "lure to cognition," Brown, 1956,
p. 278). These possible relationships between language input and
particular concepts will be illustrated and discussed further in the
section on word meaning.

To summarize, this section on "Linguistic and Nonlinguistic
Categories" has examined some basic issues concerning the source of
productivity or creativity in language, the relationship between cognitive and semantic knowledge, and the ultimate source of a child's
earliest semantic categories (independent cognitive activity or linguistic input?). These issues are relevant to studying the acquisition
both of word meanings (how categories underlying word use develop)
and of rules for word combination (how children formulate categories
having to do with the relationships expressed by the juxtaposition of
words in sentences). Let us look now in more detail at issues in the
acquisition of word meaning; sentence construction is taken up in the
following section.

LEARNING THE MEANINGS OF WORDS

With the exception of proper names, the words of a language are not
labels for specific objects but rather are tags for concepts or
categories encompassing a set, often infinitely large, of similar-yet-
different items (Lenneberg, 1967, p. 322). The possession of a concept
has often been equated with knowing a rule—a rule for grouping that
specifies both what the relevant attributes of stimuli are and how they
are to be combined for use in identifying new instances of the concept
(Brown, 1965, p. 309; Bourne, 1967). Learning the meaning of a word,
according to this view, can be regarded as learning a rule which
specifies the conditions that must obtain before the word can be used
appropriately or correctly.[7] For example, in order for the word
"drip" to be used appropriately to refer to the behavior of an entity, it

---

[7]See Fodor, Bever, and Garrett (1974), chapter 4, for a discussion of why the
acquisition of word meaning is better accounted for in terms of *rule* learning than by
competing theories such as the speaker's history of conditioning.

must be the case that the entity is either a liquid or semi-liquid such as mud, it must move in a downward direction, and it must separate as it moves into discrete segments. If one or another of these conditions does not hold, the use of the word will be regarded as anomalous by fluent speakers. Of course, as Lyons (1968) points out, the referential boundaries of words are not always fully determinate, in that "it is not always clear whether a particular object or property falls within the scope of a given lexical item" (p. 426). Still, there is enough agreement among speakers that deviations from normal usage are readily recognized.

Not all words are referential in the sense that they "represent" or "stand for" some object, event, property, etc. For example, "hi," "goodnight," and "goody!" have no referents. Nevertheless, such words also are linked with governing concepts that specify the conditions under which they can be used appropriately. Thus, regardless of whether or not a word makes reference, a speaker's ability to use it productively and appropriately in a variety of nonidentical contexts depends ultimately on his ability to categorize—to perceive invariances across entities or situations that are superficially quite diverse.

The governing concept of a word—that is, the set of conditions that must obtain before the word can be used correctly—is not presented to the young child in any clear-cut way; it must be inferred. Even in the relatively straightforward case of ostensive definition, when, for example, an object is shown to the child and he is told "dog" or "that is a dog," much is left unexplained. What features are the critical ones that determine what new objects could or couldn't be called "dog"? The fur? The presence of four legs? The color? The size? The bark? People's reaction to it? (See Clark, 1974b, pp. 106–107, for more on this dilemma). As Olson (1970b) points out, "simply being shown an object does not indicate the set of alternatives from which it is differentiated. You might note a few features of the object without knowing if you'd noticed the critical ones on which recognition is to be based" (p. 265).

If even ostensive definitions leave the referent indeterminate, consider how much more ambiguity there is in the case of words whose "domain of application" (i.e., possible referents, if the word is used referentially, otherwise simply the situations in which the word is appropriate; cf., Lyons, 1968, p. 434) cannot be indicated by pointing out and labeling instances. It is not surprising, therefore, that children often show, by the way they use or understand given words in new situations, that they have misconstrued the meanings which adults intended in their prior uses of these same words. The *ways* in which they misconstrue give valuable insights into the nature of the processes by which word meanings are acquired.

In the following two subsections on the acquisition of word meaning we will consider the "syntax and semantics of equivalence" in the concepts governing children's use of words. These terms were suggested by Olver and Hornsby (1966) to designate, respectively, the *formal structure* of conceptual groupings and the *nature of the similarities* that link the various category members. By "formal structure" is meant, for example, whether the category is "superordinate"—i.e., whether all the instances are similar to one another by virtue of one or more shared features—or whether the category has one or another of several more loosely-knit forms of organization such that there are no features common to all instances.

The Syntax of Equivalence

Superordinate Concepts   According to a recent influential theory of the acquisition of word meaning proposed by Eve Clark (1973b, 1974a and b), the child learns the adult meanings of words gradually, but in such a way that he consistently associates certain meaning components with each word:

> ... the child begins by identifying the meaning of a word with only one or two of its semantic components or features of meaning, rather than with the complete combination of components used by the adult. ... Once the child has attached *some* meaning to a word, however incomplete, it obviously *has that meaning* for him and is used accordingly. Whatever components or features of meaning the child has picked out as the meaning of a word (its lexical entry) will be criterial in deciding whether it can be applied or not in a particular situation (1974b, p. 108).

Because the child has fewer features associated with the word than an adult, he uses it in a broader range of contexts than the adult would. For example, if the feature "four-legged" has been picked out as criterial for the meaning of "doggie," the child will use the word in connection with cats, cows, hippopotamuses, and so on. If the criterial features attached to the word "Mommy" are "adult, female," the child will use the word for women other than his mother. This use of words in contexts which adults would divide into two or more different categories has been called *overextension* (Clark, 1973b). Clark proposes that the child's tendency to overextend words gradually diminishes as he learns additional semantic features that from his point of view restrict the contexts in which the words can be appropriately used. It is important to recognize that Clark's hypothesis concerns only the acquisition of *word meanings*. She does not claim that overextensions necessarily reflect a failure to *discriminate* between, say, dogs and cows or Mommy and other women; she argues only that the child does not yet realize that the discrimination is relevant for the meanings of the words in question.

A difficulty with interpreting overextensions as a result of incomplete word meanings is that, as more recent research has shown, children who overextend words in production can often pick out the correct referents for these words from an array of competing "similar" stimuli when asked to do so (Huttenlocher, 1974; Thomson and Chapman, 1975; Labov and Labov, 1974). For example, a child whose spontaneous speech suggests that she knows no more about the meaning of "Mommy" than that it refers to a family member may consistently look only at her mother when asked "where is Mommy?" (Labov and Labov, 1974). To deal with this phenomenon, Clark (1974a, 1975) suggests a modification of her original account of overextensions: a child may have several features attached to a word but overextend to new referents on the basis of only one or some of these. Clark calls this "partial" overextension, to contrast it with overextension in which a child has very few features available for a word but uses them all when he refers to a new item by that word. (For a different account of the phenomenon of overextension in production but not in comprehension see Huttenlocher, 1974, p. 367).

Clark's research has focused much attention on overextension, but several researchers have noted that overextension is only one of several ways in which children can use words consistently (i.e., as if they have a stable set of features associated with them) and yet not in accordance with adult norms (Bloom, 1973; Nelson, 1974; Anglin, 1975). For example, children also sometimes *underextend* (or "underinclude" or "overrestrict") words, in that they use them only for a subset of those items which the corresponding adult concept would encompass. As Anglin (1975) notes, underextensions are hard to spot, since, unlike overextensions, they involve no overt errors of usage. However, underextensions can be ferreted out experimentally (Anglin, 1975) or by careful record-keeping. Bloom (1973, p. 72) provides an example obtained by the latter method from her daughter Allison: at 9 months, Allison used the word "car" to refer only to cars moving on the street below as she watched from the living room window, and not for cars standing still, for pictures of cars, or for cars that she was inside of. A similar example of underextended usage comes from my daughter Eva, who from 14¹/₂ to almost 19 months systematically used "off" only in the anticipated or actual context of clothes or other objects (life jackets, safety harnesses, sleep shades, pinned-on pacifiers, bibs, etc.) being removed from her own or someone else's body. This contrasts with the *over*extended use of "off" by Eva's older sister Christy at a corresponding age. Christy's single word "off" was used in connection not only with the removal of objects from the body and in other appropriate adult English "off" situations such as climbing off her rocking horse and taking lids off jars, but also in non-"off" situations involving separation, such as pulling cups *apart, opening* hinged or sliding boxes, *unfolding* newspapers, and so on.

In forming an underextended word meaning, a child appears to identify the word not only with contextual features that are critical to that concept from the adult point of view but also with some that are irrelevant. Allison, for example, included extraneous material about motion and location of observation (living room window) in the concept governing her use of "car." For Eva, "off" was a relationship of separation that required the participation of a restricted set of objects: bodies and objects that can be worn on them. Achieving adult knowledge of an initially underextended word involves freeing the word from its contextual constraints, i.e., learning that certain semantic features that were once intimately linked with the word are irrelevant, or at best only probabilistically associated with it.

Still another way in which children may use given words differently from adults has been pointed out by Schlesinger (1974), who calls it a mix of overextension and overrestriction, and Anglin (1975), who calls it *overlap*. In overlap, the word is used for some referents in accordance with adult norms, but it is also used for some referents for which an adult would use other words and it is *not* applied to all the referents for which an adult would consider it appropriate. For example, one 16-month-old used "cake" for any food that he could eat himself and "eat" for all other foods, including, presumably, cake eaten by others (Segerstedt, 1947, cited in Schlesinger, 1974). Here, the word is used appropriately only for the food the child eats which is actually cake, but in addition to this area of appropriate usage the word is both *overextended* with respect to other foods eaten by the child and *overrestricted* (i.e., underextended) with respect to cake eaten by others.

Complexive Groupings   Although much of the recent research on the acquisition of word meaning has been concerned with discovering contextual features that recur in all the situations in which a word is produced, earlier investigators instead stressed examples in which the child had apparently failed to identify the word with a stable feature or combination of features (e.g., Vygotsky, 1962; Werner, 1948). In the famous example cited by Vygotsky (1962, p. 70), for instance, a child used "quah" first for a duck swimming in a pond, then for water in a glass and milk in his bottle, then for a coin with an eagle on it, then for any round, coinlike object. Vygotsky called such usages *chain complexes,* noting that "each new element included has some attribute in common with another element, but the attributes undergo endless changes" (p. 70). Vygotsky argued that "complex formations make up the entire first chapter of the developmental history of children's words" (p. 70). Brown (1965) appears to concur, although cautiously stating only that "it is possible that children characteristically attempt to use words as names for chain complexes" (p. 327).

Bloom (1973) attributes complexive usage of words to the child's stage of cognitive growth. She points out that according to Piaget, children do not attain a clear concept of object permanence until the second half of the second year. Because until that time the child allegedly has no firm mental representations or images of objects, the meanings of his object words are unstable and can shift. The instability of early object words is reflected not only in complexive usages, but also, according to Bloom's analyses of her daughter Allison's speech, in the infrequent use of particular words for objects and in their high "mortality rate," or tendency to drop out of use. Bloom contrasts Allison's unstable use of object words with her frequent and consistent early use of "function" words such as "away," "more," and "up." Because these latter words referred not to objects themselves but rather to their recurrent *behaviors,* they presumably did not depend for their meaning on mental representations of objects.

In studying the acquisition of word meaning by my two daughters, Christy and Eva, I found, like Bloom, that certain function words such as "off" were used early, frequently, and consistently (i.e., noncomplexively) (Bowerman, in press a; cf. examples in the discussion of underextensions). However, unlike Bloom, I also found that many of the children's earliest words for objects (e.g., "dog," "ball," "bottle") were used frequently and stably over time for objects that shared one or more properties. This finding is inconsistent with the hypothesis that the child cannot acquire a stable meaning for object-words until he has reached the final stage in his development of the concept of object permanence in the last half of the second year. Huttenlocher (1974) presents data on word comprehension that are relevant here. She found that when she asked her young subjects "where is X?" (when X was an object with a permanent location in the house that was out of sight at the time of questioning), some children as young as 13 or 14 months were capable of responding by going to the spot. Huttenlocher argued on the basis of such data that "it certainly appears that children may possess a considerable capacity for mental representation of object properties in the period before they name many objects" (p. 365). In summary, we can only conclude that the relationship between the way in which children use their early object words and the time at which, according to Piaget's analyses, they attain the final stage of the concept of object permanence is unclear.

In analyzing data from Christy and Eva, I found evidence for a type of "complexive" usage which, unlike "chain complexes," did not reflect unstable, endlessly shifting meanings, nor was its occurrence limited to the very earliest period of the single-word stage; rather, it continued on for many months (Bowerman, in press a). In chain complexes as Vygotsky (1962) and Brown (1965) described them, the successive referents of a word are linked with each other in an end-to-end fashion such that the last referent does not necessarily have anything in common with the first. However, Vygotsky (1962) also described another kind of complex, the "associative complex," which is evidenced in the way children sometimes perform in block sorting experiments. In associative complexes, the successive blocks picked by a child to go with a first block provided by the experimenter do not necessarily share anything with each other, but all share at least one feature (e.g., size, color, shape) with the original block.

Some of Christy's and Eva's word usages were clearly associative complexes of this sort. A good example is provided by Eva's early use of "kick." She said "kick" 1) first (at 17 months, 3 weeks) in connection with herself kicking a stationary object, 2) then while looking at a picture of a cat with a ball near its paw, 3) for a fluttering moth, 4) for cartoon turtles on TV kicking their legs up, 5) as she threw an object, 6) as she bumped a ball with her trike wheel, making it roll, 7) as she pushed her chest up against a sink, and so on. These diverse situations were not related to each other through any constant shared features(s), nor were they linked end-to-end by a shifting series of similarities. Rather, all of the situations in which the word was used were characterized by one or some combination of three features *all* of which are present at the same time in what can be considered an original or *prototypical* "kick" situation, in which the word had most often been modeled: the kicking of a ball with a foot. For instance, examples 3 and 4 are characterized by "a waving limb", example 7 by "sudden sharp contact", example 1 by "sudden sharp contact" plus a "waving limb", example 6 by "sudden sharp contact" plus "an object propelled," and example 5 by a "waving limb" plus "an object propelled." (See Bowerman, in press a, for further examples similar to "kick".)

Complexive usages of this type, where several features are probabilistically associated with a word but not all must be present before the word can be used, are not limited to child speech. Maratsos (1976), for example, cites evidence that many words as they are used by adults have no single defining feature or set of features that characterizes all referents; instead, there is simply a set of relevant features that are present in various combinations in the referents to which the words are applied (see also Wittgenstein, 1953; Rosch, Mervis, 1975). Because this type of complexive usage is not limited to children, it cannot be considered a primitive mode of conceptual organization that fades out. The particular *words* that initially are treated in this way may later receive a more constrained interpretation but the process itself remains a viable way of organizing and storing word meaning.[8]

The Semantics of Equivalence

Expressive vs. Referential Language   Findings from several recent studies suggest that children may differ considerably in the kinds of similarities across experiences to which they are initially attuned for purposes of acquiring and using words. These differences may be reflected either in the particular words that they "select" to acquire

---

[8]The view that a word may be associated with a set of features not all of which need be present in the contexts in which a word is used is found in Clark's (1974a, 1975) concept of "partial overextension" (see p. 116, above). It gains support from data presented by Labov and Labov (1974), who observed that for one child the word "cat" appeared to be identified with a set of core features. Although the child used the word for animals that displayed only one or two of these features, she did so with hesitation, saving the more confident use of the word for animals in which many or all of the features were present. The notion that at least some words are initially learned in connection with "prototypical" exemplars is also in accord with an interpretation of word meaning offered by Fillmore (n.d.) as an alternative to theories that characterize word meanings as "checklists" of independent conditions to be satisfied. According to Fillmore, the meanings of many words even for adults are best explained by appeal to prototypes or best exemplars. Rosch (1973b) presents related arguments.

from those that are modeled or in the way in which they *use* the words that they have, or both.

In a study of how 18 children acquired their first fifty words, Nelson (1973b) found evidence that some children tend to specialize in learning general (as opposed to proper) names for objects, while others concentrate primarily on names for people and on "personal-social" words and phrases such as "no," "yes," "want," "please," "stop it," "go away," "hi," and "ouch" (pp. 21–22). The categories of experience that are tagged by words like "no," "ouch," "want," and "hi" differ from those labeled by words like "ball" and "doggie" in that they involve the recognition of similarities across particular internal states (e.g., of rejection, pain, desire) and social situations (e.g., "encounters with friendly people") as opposed to recognition of similar "objective " properties in diverse objects. Thus, to the extent that children "specialize" in learning either expressive ("personal-social") words or names of objects, they are attending to different kinds of invariances across their experiences as they acquire words.[9]

Nelson (1973b) accounted for these differences among her subjects in terms of differences in children's initial perception of the *function* of language. She hypothesized that some children see language primarily as a tool for reference while others see it as a means of expressing feelings and needs and of regulating social interactions (pp. 22–24). She proposed further that such differences in language use derive ultimately from differences in children's prelinguistic cognitive styles, or ways in which they typically organize their experience (pp. 101–102).

Rosenblatt (1975) performed an analysis similar to Nelson's on the first words of a group of English children and also found that some of the children seemed to be learning a "reference" language and others an "expressive" or "person oriented" language. She reported in addition that the children's tendency to learn words of one type or the other was correlated with the way in which they played with toys: the early learning of "general nominals" (common, as opposed to proper nouns) was "related to shorter latency to touch toys, high visual attention to toys, high task persistence, and negatively related

---

[9]The words a child uses cannot be taken as a direct guide to the concepts he may have, nor does the sequence in which his words come in necessarily reflect the order in which his concepts were formulated, for reasons discussed in Bloom, 1973, p. 140; Huttenlocher, 1974, p. 366; and Schlesinger, 1974, pp. 141–143.

to social attention and interaction." In contrast, learning "personal-social words" was "related to adult-oriented behaviour, and greater time spent 'not playing'." These correlations between linguistic and nonlinguistic behaviors accord well with Nelson's (1973b) interpretation of children's word selection strategies as reflecting their general cognitive style.

In an intensive study of two children, Dore (1974) came up with findings related to those of Nelson and Rosenblatt. According to his analyses, one of his subjects used language "primarily to declare things about her environment" while the other used it "mainly to manipulate other people" (p. 350). Dore called these the "code-oriented" and the "message-oriented" styles, respectively. The code-oriented child produced far more words than the message-oriented child, and most of these were used in acts which were not addressed to other people, such as labeling, repeating, and practicing. The message-oriented child produced fewer words but controlled a larger repertoire of prosodic features (intonation patterns), which he used instrumentally to influence other people, by, for example, calling, protesting, and requesting things.

In sum, the distinction between children who use language primarily to refer and those who use it primarily to interact with other people and influence their behaviors has received support from several sources and so may prove to be of some generality. Learning to refer to things appears to necessitate acquiring words, but learning linguistic ways to manipulate and interact with people can involve either learning words ("please," "want," "thank you," "bye bye") or learning intonation patterns that can be used "wordlessly" (Dore, 1974) or in conjunction with words.

It must be stressed that the "expressive" or "message-oriented" style and the "referential" or "code-oriented" style are not mutually exclusive. All of the children studied combined elements of both, but simply leaned in one direction or another. Ultimately, deciding which way a child leans must depend not only on classifying the early words he produces, as Nelson (1973b) and Rosenblatt (1975) did, but on observing closely *how* he uses these words in a variety of situations. Words that are initially used in an expressive way can develop referential properties as well. For example, my daughter Christy used "bye bye" expressively at 14 months, either when people left or when she was playing a game in which she announced her own intended departure. By 17 1/2 months, however, she was using it most often as a *comment*, equivalent to "allgone," on "departures" of all kinds: for example, as she closed a drawer after putting an object into it, as she put a lid on a teapot after filling it with peg dolls, after she stuffed dominoes under her legs as she sat on the couch. In a similar example of shift from expressive to referential meaning, Ferrier (1975) reports that her daughter used "phew!" first as a greeting when her mother entered her room in the morning (derived from her mother's reaction to the smell that met her), but later applied it to diapers, whether soiled or not. Just as words that appear to be expressive can also be used referentially, words that "look" purely referential (e.g., labels for objects) can be used exclusively in situations in which the child is trying to influence adult behavior (see Bates, this volume, for some examples). In short, then, distinguishing between referential and expressive usage is a complicated matter that requires close attention to the contexts in which words are used.

Categorizing Objects: Perceptual or Functional Similarities? When children learn words that refer to classes of objects, how do they classify the objects? Are some bases for categorizing objects for purposes of word use more available to them than others? That is, are children predisposed towards seeing certain kinds of similarities and not others among the objects they encounter? This question has aroused strong but conflicting opinions in the recent literature on the acquisition of word meaning.

After a careful examination of overextensions reported in diary studies from many countries, Clark (1973b, 1974b) concluded that the similarities children primarily respond to in applying words to new objects are *perceptual* properties, particularly shape, then size, sound, movement, texture, and, to a much lesser extent, taste. (Color was notable for its absence as a basis for extension). For example, a word such as "button" would be extended to anything small and round, such as a collar-stud, a door handle, and a light switch (Pavlovitch, 1920). Or a word for "cat" would be extended to cotton or any soft material (Shvachkin, 1973).

Nelson's (1974) position on how children form the categories that underlie their early use of words for objects contrasts sharply with Clark's. According to Nelson, perception plays a secondary rather than a primary role in concept formation, not only in childhood but throughout life. More basic than perception is *function*. Thus, she argues, children do not start out by analyzing the objects they encounter into perceptual components such as "round" or "four-legged" and using such components as a basis for classifying those objects with other objects. Rather, they experience objects as wholes, in terms of the sets of dynamic relationships and actions they can enter into. Objects are regarded as similar not because they look similar but because they enter into the same relationships, or, put more simply, because they function (act or can be acted upon) in the same way (Nelson, 1974, p. 274).

Perception is secondary, in this view, because it is used not as a basis for categorizing but simply to *identify* an object as a probable instance of a concept even when the object is experienced apart from the relationships and actions that are concept-defining. For example, a child forms a concept of "ball" on the basis of the kinds of activities he engages in with balls (e.g., rolling, bouncing). At any time after the concept is formed, he begins to analyze the individual exemplars of the concept to find recurrent perceptual attributes that will allow him to recognize new objects as balls even when they are not experienced in action. Perceptual features that help him identify instances of a concept are only probabilistically correlated with the concept. An object can still be considered an instance of the category even when one or more of the expected perceptual features is absent as long as the object satisfies the function-based defining criteria for the concept.[10]

The theories of Clark and Nelson make clear-cut but divergent predictions about how children initially use words for objects. Clark's theory predicts that a given word will be used to refer to objects that *look* (or, less frequently, sound, taste, or feel) alike, regardless of function, while Nelson's theory predicts that the word will be used to refer to objects that either function in the same way, regardless of looks, or that the child *predicts* would function in the same way on the basis of their appearance. Both the functional and the perceptual

---

[10]A difficulty with Nelson's function-based theory of concept formation is that the kinds of shared functions which she hypothesizes the child uses in classifying objects as equivalent are *themselves* categories, and Nelson does not account for how the child acquires *these*. For example, Nelson proposes that the child initially classifies as "balls" those objects that behave in a certain way characterizable as "bouncing" and "rolling." But bouncing and rolling are *categories* that sum across infinitely many slightly different events. That is, the ways in which different balls—e.g., ones that are big, little, textured, smooth, irregular, etc.—bounce and roll are *not identical*. If we assume, with Nelson, that the child's first basis for classifying objects is shared *function*, we must explain the acts of categorization that must take place prior to this—acts through which different behaviors, by different objects, of rolling, bouncing (or opening, barking, etc., to think of other behaviors or functions that could be used to classify objects) are rendered cognitively equivalent and so become available as cues for grouping the objects that perform them (see Brown, 1956, p. 288, for a discussion of this problem in a different context).

accounts of categorization are in agreement on the salience of *spontaneous motion* as a basis for classifying animate creatures, vehicles, etc. Thus, the conflict is primarily over the relative importance of static perceptual features like shape in classifying either animate or inanimate objects.

Which theory appears to account better for the data? Nelson (1973a) has provided some supporting experimental evidence for her function-based theory, but the bulk of evidence seems to favor Clark's perception-based theory. For example, in an explicit test of the two theories I analyzed previously collected data (both taped and hand-noted) on the way in which my two children extended each of their object-words to novel referents from the start of the one-word stage on (Bowerman, in press a). I looked only at usages that were erroneous from the adult point of view, since correct usages could have been learned through modeling. Many errors involved objects that were similar both perceptually *and* functionally (e.g., "cherry" for both cherries and grapes); for these, of course, either or both kinds of similarities may have contributed to the categorization. The only errors that were useful for comparing the accuracy of the two theories' predictions were those involving objects that are clearly perceptually dissimilar but functionally similar or *vice versa*. Among these, there was only a tiny handful in which the error was based on *shared function* in the absence of perceptual similarity, while there were scores involving perceptual similarities, particularly, shape, in the absence of functional similarities.[11]

What is particularly significant for purposes of evaluating the two theories is that the children's overextensions based on shared perceptual attributes often *cut across* functional differences among the objects involved which were *well known* to the child. In other words, known functional differences were overlooked in the interests of classifying on the basis of a perceptual similarity such as shape. For example, Eva used "moon" from 15;4 (15 months, 4 weeks) on to refer to the real moon, to half-grapefruits and slices of lemon she was looking at or handling, to tiny flat circular green leaves she had

---

[11]Examples of overextensions based purely on function in the absence of perceptual similarity are rarely reported in the literature, so two are given here to illustrate the genre. At 16 months, 3 weeks, Eva watched Christy blowing on a harmonica, then she herself picked up a tiny bead bracelet and blew on it, saying "balloon." At about 25 months Eva began to say "wastebasket" (usually in a sentence) to refer to any place she was dropping or putting scraps of waste paper (e.g., the floor, under a sofa cushion).

picked, to a ball of spinach she was about to eat, to a magnetic letter D she was putting on the refrigerator, to hangnails she was pulling off, to crescent-shaped bits of paper she had torn, etc.

Naming behavior of this kind obviously was not predictive in nature. That is, Eva was not using perceptual features (round, half-moon, or crescent-shaped) as a means of identifying probable instances of a concept "moon" which had a core meaning involving functional relationships. Use of perceptual similarities as a clue to probable function did occur at times (as when Eva at 17;1 said "barrette" while trying to fasten a small stapler into her hair), but it cannot account for the majority of perceptually based overextensions in the Christy and Eva data.

Experimental studies of somewhat older children also suggest that the early classification of objects is more often based on perceptual than on functional similarities, although the studies perhaps do not provide a fair test of the two theories because the "functional" similarities among the stimulus objects had to be inferred from pictures rather than experienced in action. In one study, Press (1974) asked children from 2 years, 8 months to 6 years to look at a picture of an object and then find "another one" or "another BORK" (or other word), depending on the condition, from an array of three pictured objects. The children's choices, especially those of the younger subjects, were based more on perceptual similarities such as shape and pattern than on inferrable functional similarities. Anglin (1975) reported that young children (exact ages not given) overextended words to pictured objects that were "perceptually similar" to the objects normally referred to by those words far more often than they overextended words to objects that were "functionally similar." (Perceptual and functional similarity had been determined previously by the ratings of judges). For example, errors such as calling a balloon "apple" predominated over errors like calling a sled "car"; in fact, there were almost no errors of the latter type.

The above discussion presented evidence indicating that perceptual similarities are stronger determinants than functional similarities of children's judgments of equivalence among objects. However, the potential that objects have for acting and being acted upon is evidently an important determinant of *which* objects children initially "select" to learn names for. Studies of children's first words have revealed that children tend to ignore names for items that are "just there" and do not do anything, like furniture, trees, and rooms, in favor of names for objects that act or which they can act on, like pets and other animals, cars, shoes, foods, and toys (Nelson, 1973b, 1974; Anglin, 1975). For example, Huttenlocher (1974) discusses a boy who, despite his emerging ability to understand other words, apparently did not learn the referents of "kitchen" and "refrigerator" even after extensive and persistent maternal modeling and demonstration. It seems, then, that children's attention is drawn to objects with potentials for acting or being acted on, and they will tend to learn names for such objects earlier than names for more static objects. However, classifying such objects as equivalent for purposes of word use appears to depend more upon their perceptual qualities than upon their functions.

Nonobject Concepts   Most investigators have made a sharp distinction between words that refer to objects and those that refer to actions, attributes, processes, etc. (e.g., Bloom, 1973, pp. 68–70; Nelson, 1974, p. 281). However, the grounds for determining which words refer to objects and which do not have never been made entirely clear. For example, when a child says "ball" only in connection with objects that he throws (or rolls, etc.), is he naming the object or the action he is performing on it? When one child (my daughter Eva) says "close" while closing a door or a barrette or while pushing a chair up to a table, and another (a friend named Rachel) says "door" in exactly these same contexts, should we assume that the former is naming the actions that she is performing while the latter is naming the objects, which she has classified together because they are acted upon in the same way? When a child says "allgone," are we to assume, with Bloom (1973), that she is referring to an event of disappearance, or could she perhaps be using disappearance as a "functional relationship" by means of which objects can be classified, such that she is really naming the departed object as a member of the category defined by the transitory function "allgoneness"? Before we can confidently determine whether a child's words refer to objects themselves or to the actions, behaviors, or attributes associated with them, we must determine the principles by which a child might be expected to decide that some actions, behaviors, and attributes (e.g., rolling, bouncing, opening, sitting on, being round, etc.) are useful for classifying objects as members of the same category while others (e.g., disappearance, upward motion, color, etc.) are not. Having registered this need for caution in classifying children's words according to the nature of their putative referents, however, I want to proceed to consider some types of words children use in the early stages of word acquisition that are most *plausibly* described in terms of concepts of action and the like rather than objects.

Bloom has highlighted children's early acquisition of words encoding the notions of *recurrence* ("more") and *disappearance, nonexistence,* and *cessation* ("allgone," "no more," "away," "no," "stop") with data from both her own daughter during the one-word stage (Bloom, 1973) and from three somewhat older subjects who were just beginning to combine words (Bloom, 1970). Data from my children at the one-word stage support the salience of these particular notions and confirm the early availability of other concepts that Bloom and/or others have discussed, such as various directional movements ("up," "down," "in," "out," "on," "off," "back," etc.), sharp or sudden impacts, often associated with falling ("bonk," "bump," "boom," "uh oh," "fall," etc.), and manipulations of objects ("open," "close," "break," "push," etc.). The concept of "existence" of an object is reflected in the deictic use of "this," "that," "there" (Leopold, 1939; Bloom, 1973, p. 71), and, for one of my children, in "find!" (when an unexpected object was suddenly encountered). Early labels for *properties* of objects primarily designate changeable and transitory states like "hot," "wet," and "dirty" rather than permanent qualities like "round" or "red" (MacNamara, 1972; Wells, 1974).

Some investigators (e.g., MacNamara, 1972) have hypothesized that names for objects are learned before names for actions, states, and properties, but there seems to be some variability among children in this regard. For example, as noted earlier, Bloom's (1973) daughter used a number of words referring to actions or behaviors (e.g., "away," "up," etc.) productively and consistently *before* she knew many object names, and she often used them in connection with the behaviors of objects for which she had no words. On the other hand, Huttenlocher (1974) found that the three children she studied both understood and produced object words before nonobject words. Such differences among children might be due to variations in cognitive style of the kind discussed earlier in connection with children's differential attentiveness to "personal-social" words vs. "referential" words.

Like words for objects, words for actions, behaviors, properties, etc. may initially be linked to a somewhat different configuration of nonlinguistic properties than they are later in a child's development. Sometimes they are overextended. For example, Christy's "off," described earlier, at first seemed to encode any kind of separation of two objects or two parts of the same object. Similarly, but for the reverse operation, Velten's (1943) daughter Joan had a word "ba" (from "bang") which applied to things which had "moveable parts that may be joined together, such as boxes with hinged covers, doors and books to be slammed shut, napkins and papers that can be folded over, and all kinds of fasteners like buckles, snaps, safety pins, and zippers" (p. 283). The breadth of application of such words is subsequently narrowed down as children acquire words that subcategorize the semantic domain, as when Joan Velten learned "shut," "snap," and [bat] ("button, buckle").

Initial restriction of a nonobject word to a limited range of contexts (underextension), which indicates that the child has identified the word with a set of rather specific contextual features, is possibly even more common than overextension. For example, Leopold's daughter Hildegard first used "up" only in connection with her own movements, and not until 2 months later in connection with movements upon inanimate objects (Ingram, 1971). Similarly, both Christy and Eva used "up" and "down" initially for their own activities (as requests and comments), then for those of other people, and finally for inanimate objects. Christy and Eva also used "more" in connection with a restricted set of objects at first—food and drink. Bloom's (1973) daughter Allison likewise first produced "up" in connection with herself and "more" as a request for an additional serving of food or drink, although within only a few days she began to use these words across a range of more varied contexts. It is not clear, of course, whether a child's underextended use of a word stems from his not having yet *formulated* the broader concept (e.g., the upward motion of any object, the recurrence of any object or action) or from his failure to *use* a concept that he has formulated on the nonlinguistic level as a linguistic category.

Unlike "more," "up," "down," and related words that adults can apply to the behaviors of almost any entity, many words in adult usage *must* be restricted to the activities of particular kinds of objects, e.g., animate beings. Christy and Eva treated some of these words exactly as they did "up" and "down," in that they initially used them only in connection with themselves and other animate beings and later extended them to inanimate objects (e.g., "walk" for slow-moving cars and airplanes, "night night" for normally vertical objects like bottles and Christmas trees seen in a horizontal position, "sit" when the child plopped a handful of toys on the floor). Changes over time in the use of these words was thus the same as for "up," "down," etc. However, notice that while "up" and "down" were initially *underextended* from the adult viewpoint and later used appropriately, "walk," "sit," etc. were initially used appropriately and later *overextended*.

To sum up, the data presented in the last two subsections ("The Syntax of Equivalence" and "The Semantics of Equivalence") indicate that getting a word hooked up to exactly the right set of contextual properties is an extremely complicated matter. Every setting in which a child hears a word is composed of a complex configuration of discriminable components. Some of these components have to do with directly observable phenomena (e.g., objects, actions, and their properties), others with the speaker's feelings, reactions, beliefs about the feelings of others, and intention or purpose in speaking (e.g., to command, register a reaction ("phew!"), interrogate, etc.). The child learning language is faced with the task of trying to discover which of the innumerable aspects of the contexts in which he hears words used are the relevant ones. It is hard to imagine how he ever arrives at the right solutions, and correspondingly easy to see how he might pick out components or combinations of components that are salient to him but incomplete or irrelevant from the adult's point of view.

Origins of Children's Word-Concepts

Cognition or Language First?   According to a traditional account of the acquisition of word meaning, a child learns the meaning of a word by hearing it paired with a number of different referents and gradually abstracting out a concept consisting of all of the attributes which the referents have in common (see Nelson, 1974, for a description of this account, which she terms "abstraction theory"). Many investigators currently studying the acquisition of word meaning take issue with this view, however. For example, Nelson (1974) argues that initially, at least, words are learned as labels for concepts that have already been formed on a nonlinguistic basis rather than themselves serving to introduce new concepts to the child. The evidence she advances for this hypothesis includes the child's "selectivity [of words to learn] from a larger set of parent words" (see the discussions of Nelson's (1973b) study in this regard in the section on "The Semantics of Equivalence") and the fact that children sometimes invent words for idiosyncratic concepts if they have not encountered suitable lexical items in the adult input to them (1974, p. 269).

Like Nelson, Huttenlocher (1974) stresses the language-independent origins of the early concepts to which words are attached: ''... the 'meanings' which became linked to word-sounds formed unitary cohesive elements of experience before that linkage occurred. ... The existence of salient unitary 'meanings' (schemas) may even have been a prerequisite for the child to attend to the accompanying word-sound'' (p. 356).

Clark (1974a) also theorizes that the meanings children initially attach to words depend upon nonlinguistic categorization processes.[12] Specifically, she proposes that children extend words to novel referents on the basis of perceptual categories that are formed prior to the learning of those words. Where do these perceptual categories come from? Clark (1974a) argues that at least some of them reflect a universal way of organizing experiences. In formulating this hypothesis, Clark notes that the properties which children use as a basis for extending words to new objects are very similar to the properties encoded by the obligatory classifiers found in many natural languages. Classifiers are words or particles used when objects are being counted (e.g., ''nine *round-things* balls'') or with verb stems (e.g., ''he caused-*round-solid-thing*-to-move upwards stone'' [he picked up the stone]). According to Clark, ''visual perception appears to play a central role both in children's overextensions and in the semantics of classifier systems. In both, objects are categorized on the basis of perceptible properties of shape which may be combined with other secondary characteristics. Furthermore, the same basic properties of shape appear to be selected as relevant to categorization in both the acquisition data and in classifier systems. Roundness and length ... appear to be the most salient of all.'' Clark concludes that children's emerging semantic distinctions and the classifier systems of natural languages are similar because both depend on a universal ''*a priori,* nonlinguistic categorization process'' (Clark, 1974a).

In a somewhat earlier era of research, Brown (1965) stressed the problem that cross-linguistic variation creates for a concept-precedes-word theory of cognitive development. He noted that certain concepts (e.g., object permanence, conservation) appear to de-

---

[12]Nelson criticizes Clark's theory as being ''no more or no less than a revised version of the abstraction of critical attributes plus hypothesis testing'' (1974, p. 272), but in fact the postulation of hypothesis-testing on the part of the child distinguishes Clark's view sharply from the one Nelson is challenging. According to Clark (1974a and b, 1975), the hypothesis the child forms about the meaning of a word in fact derives directly from his nonlinguistic conceptualization of the world. I cannot see an essential difference between Nelson and Clark on this point.

velop universally and therefore probably do not depend on language. However, he argued, "the ubiquity of linguistic nonequivalence suggests that reality can be variously construed and, therefore, that the child's manipulations and observations are not alone likely to yield the stock of conceptions that prevail in his society" (1965, p. 317). He concluded, therefore, that many concepts are introduced through language rather than acquired first on a nonlinguistic basis. In particular, he proposed that "the recurrent word [as heard by the child] . . . serves to attract relevant experiences, to sum them over time into a conception governing the use of the word" (1965, p. 311).

There is not necessarily a conflict between Brown's view and those of Nelson, Clark, and Huttenlocher. One way of reconciling the two positions would be to suppose that the latter three investigators are talking about the very earliest stage of word acquisition while Brown's arguments may be more relevant for a slightly later period. Not even staunch advocates of the cognition-first position argue that language *never* plays a role in introducing concepts. Nelson (1973b) specifically suggests, in fact, that "the child acquires his first *n* (productive) words by matching environmental labels to his own concepts (*n* is some unknown number between 10 and perhaps 100). . . . After the child has acquired *n* words that match his own concepts he may reverse the process and build a concept to match a word that others use to him" (pp. 114 and 115). There is another possibility, however, which is that linguistic input can play a part *from the start* in shaping children's conceptual development. Some lines of argument and evidence for this position will be reviewed.

Role of Linguistic Input   As noted in an earlier section entitled "Origin of Semantic Concepts," some researchers have begun to question whether the child's prelinguistic conceptual development is totally uninfluenced by the kind of language directed to him. Wells (1974), for example, argues that there are a number of different determinants of how children come to structure and interpret their experiences and that their conceptualizations undergo constant revision. In the early stages of development, suggests Wells, the child uses criteria for classification that "are derived directly from his actions upon and his perceptions of the people, objects, and events in his environment" (p. 254). However, the particular structuring of the environment, both physical and verbal, provided by the child's caretakers begins to have an increasing effect on what the child attends to and tries to make sense of. Thus, according to Wells, "language is an important means of discriminating and giving salience to those aspects of the environment that are considered important, but even before the child acquires language, the meanings that he constructs will be influenced by his attention being selectively directed by those around him" (p. 254). Wells concludes that "it would be surprising if the frequency of occurrence of different kinds of meanings in the adult linguistic input to the child did not have some influence on what the child attended to and sought to communicate about," over and above the effects of very general cognitive developments of the type of Piaget has investigated (p. 268).

Wells' comments about the role of social interaction in general and linguistic input in particular are in accord with Bruner's (1975) analyses of the roots of language in the shared activities and ritualized play interactions of the mother and child. Bruner studied the way in which 6 mothers interacted with their babies (who were initially approximately 7 months old) for a period of about 6 months. He found that a large proportion of the interactions involved the mothers' efforts to verbally *interpret* their child's actions by inferring his intentions or other "directive states" (p. 12). Moreover, each mother sought to " 'standardize' certain forms of joint action with the child" in such a way as to allow the child to bring his attention into line with her own, predict her intentions, and develop "more or less standard ways of signalling his intent" (p. 12). It seems highly unlikely that a child's developing cognitive understanding of the world would remain totally uninfluenced by such a barrage of repetitive interactions with caretakers who verbally label and describe his activities and intentions according to their own interpretations.

A second line of argument for the view that the verbal input to a child may influence his conceptual development can be made by drawing on a study by Brown (1958a, 1965) on the way in which parents *select* the words that they use with their offspring. Brown pointed out that every object or event can be referred to in a variety of ways, at different levels of generality. For example, "the dime in my pocket is not only a *dime*. It is also *money*, a *metal object*, a *thing*, and, moving to subordinates, it is a *1952 dime*, in fact a *particular 1952 dime* with a unique pattern of scratches, discolorations, and smooth places" (1958a, p. 4). How do parents decide on the level of generality at which to refer to things? Should they call the dime a *dime*, a *coin*, *money*, a *thing*, or what? Brown noted that parents do not always choose the same words they would use to other adults, but they tend to agree in the particular choices they make. What accounts for this phenomenon? According to Brown, parents name at the level of generality that categorizes objects and events at their "level of probable nonlinguistic equivalence" for the child (1965, p. 319). In other words, parents "anticipate the functional structure of the child's world" (1958a, p. 8) by providing names at the level of generality that categorizes objects or events in a way that they assume the child will find meaningful. For example, the mother selects "dog" instead of "collie" because she knows that as far as the child is concerned there is no sense in distinguishing between breeds of dogs; all are the "same" in terms of how the child is expected to behave toward them. Conversely, however, the mother does not choose "animal" as a label for a dog because it is too general: behaviors that are appropriate for the child to produce in response to dogs are not appropriate for lizards, horses, squirrels, etc.

Anglin (1975) reports some experimental confirmation of Brown's proposals both that parents tend to label things differently for children than for adults and that the objects classified together by the words they select are those towards which children are expected to behave in the same way ("behavioral equivalence"). Anglin asked mothers to name pictures of objects both for another adult and for their 2-year-olds. For the adults the mothers gave words like "Volkswagen," "collie," and "pigeon," but for the children they provided "car," "bird," "dog," etc. When other adults were asked to rate terms from a set of hierarchically nested category labels (e.g., vehicle, car, Volkswagen; animal, dog, collie) on the basis of the degree to which they name objects at a "behaviorally equivalent" level of generality for the 2-year-old, they rated as most behaviorally equivalent those words that mothers typically provide.

The same sort of parental selectivity of ways to refer to things undoubtedly occurs for words for attributes, actions, etc., as for words for objects, although it has not to my knowledge been documented. Have not most of us at some time or other, when speaking to a child, referred to a torn book or coming-apart teddy bear as "broken," or said of an object put away in a box that it was "going night night"—words which we would never use to an adult in these same situations? This kind of word selection anticipates what we suppose a child will be able to understand, which in turn reflects our assumptions about how he has classified events in his world.

The fact that parents modify their labels for referents in the direction of the level of abstraction at which children may already be predisposed towards categorizing experiences makes it difficult to assume with confidence that linguistic input plays no role in helping the child formulate his initial word-concepts. Children may indeed tune out words that correspond to none of their mental constructs, but the recurrence of the same words in contexts which they are already cognitively predisposed towards regarding as similar may well aid in their construction of the relevant concepts.

Data from Christy and Eva   One way to study the origin of children's word-concepts would be to examine children's use of particular words closely to assess the likelihood that the governing concepts could have been formulated totally independently of language input. In performing a preliminary analysis of this sort on data from Christy and Eva, I found evidence for several different relationships between linguistic input and concept formation (Bowerman, 1976).

In some cases there was evidence that the child had on her own firmly decided on the nature and boundaries of a concept underlying the use of a word, apparently resisting the interpretation that patterns of adult usage would call for. An example of this type is Eva's initial use of "off," mentioned earlier, which for some time was restricted to objects being removed from the body. The concept of "things coming off the body" was not implicit in the parental use of "off," as is substantiated by Christy's completely different initial interpretation of the word. When two children differ sharply in the way they first use a word despite having received similar verbal input, it seems likely that their interpretations of at least this word were determined primarily by how they had organized their experiences on the nonlinguistic level.[13]

In contrast to examples like "off," however, there were other

---

[13]Of course, Eva's input was somewhat different from Christy's because she had an older sibling, which Christy did not. However, there is a 2½-year age difference between them. By the time Eva was acquiring "off," Christy was close to 4 years old and her use of "off" was indistinguishable from that of an adult.

Since adult English usage classifies all actions resulting in removal of things from the body as "take off," one must ask whether Eva was not encouraged by linguistic input to regard at least all of *these* operations as similar. One way to test this hypothesis would be to investigate the classification system of Japanese-speaking children, who do *not* receive a homogeneous input with respect to acts of removal from the body (see p. 109). If they typically use different words for different subclasses of removal right from the start, then language probably influences the child's initial classification of this domain. If, however, Japanese children tend to overextend a word to all acts of removal from the body, it would be apparent that the classification can easily be made independently of language input. Even if language may have influenced Eva to regard acts of removal from the body as similar, her "decision" to include no other kinds of separations in this category was clearly made independently of language, given the much wider adult usage of "off."

patterns of word use that seemed to reflect an interaction between the adult input and the child's own efforts to impose structure on events. A good illustration comes from Christy's data. At 18 months she began to use "hi" in a peculiar way in addition to its normal use as a greeting. For example, she said it as she balanced tiny toys or drops of milk on the end of her finger, while sliding her hands under a blanket or the hood of her snowsuit and holding them up, as she stuck her fist into the silverware holder of the dish drainer and into a mitten-shaped potholder, when a washrag drifted across her foot in the tub, and when a shirt fell over her foot in her crib.

What would cause a child to develop a concept to do with something resting on or covering her hands or feet? The most plausible assumption is that language was influential in getting this concept started, but that the particular shape the concept assumed was Christy's own invention. When playing with her I would sometimes put a finger puppet or a tiny object like the cap of a pen on my finger and pretend that it was a little person, coming to say "hi." So she heard "hi" modeled in connection with seeing something stuck on the end of a finger. What is a child to make of this modeling? Rather than construing "hi" in its known sense as a greeting, she apparently concentrated on the connection between the word and the object on the finger, and from this start managed to account for the usage she had encountered by constructing a concept around the notion of things resting on or covering the hands, or, by analogy, the feet. In this example, then, adult usage appears to have provided the germ of a concept, perhaps, as Brown suggests, by "attract[ing] relevant experiences" (1965, p. 311), but the child herself supplied the structure of the concept from her own ingenuity at making sense of events.

I have not yet done the necessary analyses to determine whether word usages like Eva's "off" tended to be early phenomena while those like Christy's "hi" were relatively late in the one-word stage. This is what would be predicted by Nelson's (1974) hypothesis that the child acquires at least his *first* words by matching modeled forms to his own independently generated concepts, only beginning to build concepts to match words somewhat later. Even if this view should turn out to be correct, however, it is apparent that a complex interaction develops quite early, before the child's vocabulary is very large, between the child's own propensities for viewing things as similar to each other and the classification schemes imposed by the language to which he is exposed.

ACQUIRING RULES FOR WORD COMBINATION

Now let us move ahead in the child's development to explore the kinds of concepts he makes use of in formulating his earliest rules for word combination. Consider Kendall, a 23-month-old girl whom I studied when she had just begun to put two words together (mean length of utterance 1.10 morphemes) (Bowerman, 1973a). Over a period of 2 days she produced 102 different nonimitated word combinations such as "horse walk," "Kimmy read," "spider move," "Daddy sit," "find Mommy," "taste cereal," "close door," "Bill book," "more lights," and "Daddy here."

The diversity of Kendall's utterances and their appropriateness to novel situations (e.g., "Melissa 'way" as I left the room) suggest that she was not just repeating memorized phrases. Moreover, the fact that she used relatively consistent word order indicates that she was not simply combining two words randomly. Rather, she had some knowledge of sentence structure. But what knowledge? There are a number of theoretical possibilities.

In 1963, Braine proposed that the productivity of children's early syntactic systems derives from their knowledge of where to position *particular words* in a sentence. (Similar proposals were made by Miller and Ervin, 1964, and Brown and Fraser, 1963). Certain words belong in first position, other words belong in second position (a given child might have only a set of first- or second-position words, or both), and still other words are free to appear in either position. For example, Kendall might have learned that when she is making up a sentence with "more" in it, "more" should go in first place.

The proposal that children's early syntactic rule systems primarily reflect knowledge about the permitted positioning of words in sentences has been challenged on both theoretical and empirical grounds. Subsequent analyses of data from a variety of children learning English or other languages have indicated that the position in which a word appears in a sentence typically depends not on the word itself but on the functional relationship(s) it contracts with the other word(s) in the sentence. That is, the young child's use of consistent patterns of word order stems from his identification of these patterns with particular relational meanings that can hold between elements in sentences (Bloom, 1970; Schlesinger, 1971b; Bowerman, 1973a, Brown, 1973). For example, "more" might appear in first position when "moreness" is being attributed to some entity ("more cookie") but in final position when it represents the object of action or desire ("take more," "want more"). Similarly, "taste" might appear in first position if it is juxtaposed with a word for the item tasted, but in second position if it is accompanied by a name for the one who does the tasting.

Identifying regularities in sentence construction that are deeper than those manifested in consistencies in the positioning of particular words requires making interpretations of what children *mean* by what they say. This in turn requires analyses of the contexts in which the utterances are spoken. Brown (1973) has termed this approach the method of "rich interpretation." Rich interpretation has proved a fruitful approach to the study of child language in several respects. For example, it has led to the identification of basic similarities in the development of children learning a variety of native languages (Bowerman, 1973a; Brown, 1973), and it provides a much-needed route for linking children's linguistic development with their more general cognitive growth (Bloom, 1970; Schlesinger, 1971b; Brown, 1973; Bowerman, 1973a, Edwards, 1974; Wells, 1974). However, despite the usefulness of this approach and its power to explain the relevant body of data, there persists a nagging problem that is particularly resistant to investigation: to identify the *particular* relational meanings with which children's patterns of word combination are correlated.

Four aspects of this problem are considered in the subsections that follow. The first subsection discusses the very general cognitive concepts that are built up during the first 2 years of life. It is argued that while these concepts can be regarded as prerequisites for sentence construction, they cannot in themselves constitute the kinds of relational categories that are required for rules of word combination to operate upon. The second subsection illustrates a range of possible relational categories that children might hit upon. In the third subsection some empirical findings that bear on the problem are reported. And the fourth subsection considers the origins of children's relational categories.

General Cognitive Prerequisites for Sentence Construction

"If you ignore word order, and read through transcriptions of two-word utterances in the various languages we have studied, the utterances read like direct translations of one another. . . . There is a great similarity of basic vocabulary and basic meanings conveyed by the word combinations" (Slobin, 1970, p. 177). In samples from almost every language one finds sentences that point out or name ("this (that, it) doggie," "here (there) ball," "see man," etc.), constructions that deal with recurrence ("more cookie," "'nother car"), disappearance ("no more noise," "milk allgone," "doggie away"), rejection, denial ("no truck," "no dirty soap"), location ("duck water," "sit lap," "where dollie?"), possession ("Daddy coat," "Mommy nose"), and relationships among agents, actions and objects ("Mommy push," "man dance," "bite finger," "drive car," "spank me") (Brown, 1973; Bowerman, 1973a and b, 1975b).

Attempts to explain these commonalities among children have focused on the correspondence between the semantic content of the early sentences and the general cognitive understanding of the world which a child at the start of word combination can be expected to have achieved (Brown, 1973; Edwards, 1974; Wells, 1974). For example, Brown (1973, pp. 198–201), who draws on Piagetian theory (as do the other investigators just cited), points out that the meanings of the first sentences reflect rather directly the concepts that are established during the sensorimotor period of development (birth through 18–24 months): the continuing existence of objects in space and time (object permanence), the distinction between actors and actions on the one hand and between actions and objects-acted-upon on the other, causal relationships between objects (animate or inanimate) that can initiate actions and the spatial displacements or other changes that objects undergo as a result, and so on.

The universality of the early sentence meanings, their close connections to sensorimotor intelligence, and related evidence have led Slobin to propose that "language is used to express only what the child already knows" (1973, p. 184). Slobin hypothesizes that the child is aided in his efforts to find linguistic devices for expressing his cognitive understanding of the world by a number of "universal operating principles." For example, "a basic expectation which the child brings to the task of grammatical development is that the order of elements in an utterance can be related to underlying semantic relations" (1973, p. 197).

The recognition that there are close links between the meanings of children's early sentences and their more general cognitive capacities has constituted an important advance in the study of child language. However, it is essential to realize that what is still lacking in our knowledge of how children learn to construct sentences is an account of how a child's very general grasp of object permanence, causality, the location of objects in time and space, etc., becomes organized or transformed into the more specific sorts of relational categories which could constitute the conceptual building blocks for rules of world combinations to operate on (cf. Nelson, 1974, p. 273; Bloom, Lightbown, and Hood, 1975b, for similar observations). The questions that arise when this issue is not dealt with can be illustrated with a proposal by MacNamara (1972). Like Slobin (1973), MacNamara argues that the child's task is to relate semantic intentions that are worked out independently of language to syntactic structures and devices. He suggests that

> ... children initially take the main lexical items in the sentences they hear, determine referents for these items, and then use their knowledge of the referents to decide what the semantic structures intended by the speaker must be. ... Once the children have determined the semantic structures, their final task is to note the syntactic devices, such as word order, prepositions, number affixes, etc., which correlate with the semantic structures. Such a strategy will yield most of the main syntactic devices in the language (1972, p. 7).

What is missing here is an explanation of how the child determines the *scope* of the semantic category that goes with the syntactic device he has noted in a particular sentence. To *understand* sentences expressing events in the immediate context, a child need not have formulated any relational semantic categories at all, since, as Mac-Namara observes, he can simply identify the referents of the lexical items and see for himself how they are related (cf. Bloom, 1974, for discussion of this theme). But to be able to *produce* sentences other than those he has already heard, the child must link the syntactic devices of the input sentences with relational categories broad enough to include not only the specific relationships encoded in those sentences (e.g., between "Mommy" and "cut," "baby" and "mittens," "cup" and "table") but also the many particular *novel* relationships with which he will be confronted.

To how wide a range of "similar" situations will a child assume that he can extend a syntactic device he has registered in a particular input sentence? Suppose that the child has noticed that when Mommy said "Mommy is cutting the meat," Mommy was performing the action of cutting. Now he can perhaps conclude that when he wants to talk about Mommy cutting meat he should put the word "Mommy" first. But what if Mommy is cutting not meat but paper, and using scissors instead of a knife? Should the rule apply here too? Possibly he will assume that whenever he wants to talk about Mommy performing the variety of activities that he would categorize as "cutting," he should put the word "Mommy" first. But what if Daddy is doing the cutting? Can he assume that whenever one is talking about an act of cutting and a cutter, the name for the cutter should go first? And what about breaking? Is this similar enough to cutting that the child will decide that any syntactic device that applies to the relationship between cutter and cutting will also apply to that between breaker and breaking? How about kissing, running, eating, shouting, spilling, etc.? These activities are not very much like either cutting or breaking, but at a rather abstract level their meanings are similar because they all involve an *action* of some kind. Is the child aware of this similarity?

In trying to account for how children get from their understanding of sentences in concrete situations to more abstract relational categories, it is not possible to appeal directly to the child's general sensorimotor understanding of notions of causality, location, and the like. Having a practical knowledge that objects can be located in space in a variety of ways, or that the child himself or others are capable of initiating actions which have effects on other objects, or that people have territorial rights over certain objects does not directly translate into having *categories* like "location," "action," "agent" or "possessor" upon which rules for generating sentences can operate. As Schlesinger (1974) has pointed out, it is quite possible that the young child initially has only an understanding of the specific relationships involved in concrete situations of cutting, spilling, owning mittens, etc. He has not yet identified higher-order similarities across these experiences and coalesced them into the kinds of categories that are needed in a system of rules for sentence construction that allows for productivity, or the extension of existing information about patterns of word order and the like to new situations.

Possible Varieties of Relational Categories

What kinds of relational categories might a child formulate as the bases of his first productive rules for word combination? Little evidence bearing on this problem is yet available, so it is perhaps particularly important to envision as wide a range of possibilities as we can so that preconceptions will not limit the ways in which we approach the analysis of data either as investigators or as critics. This section of this chapter is primarily devoted to a discussion of possibilities that are semantically based, but first an alternate possibility is briefly noted.

Are the Relations Semantic or Syntactic?   Relationships between the words or phrases in a sentence can be specified either on the basis of the way in which the referents of these words are related to each other in the nonlinguistic situation or in terms of the way the words themselves function within the sentence, regardless of their referents. Relationships of the former kind are commonly called "semantic"; those of the latter kind, like "subject-predicate" and "verb-direct object," are called "grammatical" or "syntactic." Semantic categories tend to be correlated with syntactic categories—e.g., most relationships between agents and actions are encoded with a subject-predicate structure—but there is by no means a perfect correspondence between the two. For example, the subject-predicate relationship in English encodes not only relations between agents and their actions (e.g., "the boy is running") but also between experiencers and the states they experience ("Daddy wants that," "Mommy sees a doggie"), locations and events associated with them ("This boat sleeps five"), and so on. Thus, syntactic relations are more abstract than semantic ones because they subsume a number of semantic distinctions that could be made (see Brown, 1973, pp. 120–123; Bowerman, 1973a and b, 1975a, for further discussion).

Syntactic relations have often been invoked in accounts of children's early ability to position words consistently in sentences, even well before the method of "rich interpretation" (using context to interpret children's intentions) was accorded formal recognition. For example, McNeill (1966, 1970, 1971) argued that knowledge of the basic grammatical relations is innate and guides the child's understanding and production of utterances from the beginning of language development. Like McNeill, Bloom (1970) posited an early understanding of syntactic relations such as subject-predicate and verb-direct object, although she did not believe the knowledge to be innate.

A number of researchers have taken issue with the position that children's early two- and three-word utterances reflect knowledge of syntactic relations. For example, in Bowerman (1973a and b), I argued that the structural phenomena that motivate the description of adult speech in terms of syntactic relations are missing in child speech; hence, there is no clear evidence that children in fact have made these abstractions. I concluded that the characteristics of the early utterances are more compatible with an alternative hypothesis first proposed by Schlesinger (1971b): the knowledge underlying children's early two- and three-word utterances might be simple order rules for combining words that are understood as performing various semantic roles such as *agent, action, location,* etc., or perhaps other semantic roles that are even less abstract.

The debate about whether or not children have knowledge of syntactic relations during the early period of word combining is not yet resolved (see Schlesinger, 1974; Bloom, Lightbown, and Hood, 1975b, Bloom, Miller, and Hood, 1975; Bowerman, 1975a; and Braine, in press, for further arguments pro and con). However, in the meantime, research goes on that takes us further into the possible semantic underpinnings of children's early rule systems.

Relational Semantic Categories: Which Ones Are "Psychologically Real?" A given set of two- and three-word utterances can be classified semantically in a number of different ways. How can we know which way is "right," in the sense that it classifies according to semantic distinctions which are functional in the child's own system of rules for combining words and which therefore determine the kinds of novel constructions the child is able to make?

The problem of trying to identify the level of abstraction at which children might formulate semantic rules for sentence construction has been discussed by Brown (1973). He pointed out that although the sets of relational meanings that different investigators have selected for describing and classifying children's utterances overlap to an extent, they are not identical. For example, Bloom (1970) distinguished sentences with "more" (e.g., "more cookie") both from those with other attributives ("pretty," "hot," etc.) and from possessive constructions like "Mommy sock," while Schlesinger (1971b) lumped all of these together in a "modifier-head" relation. Similarly, Bloom subdivided negative constructions (negative word + X) into three semantic categories while Schlesinger's category of negative constructions did not differentiate these.

Differences such as these make it clear, observed Brown, "that the relations [which have been used] . . . are abstract taxonomies applied to child utterances. That it is not known how finely the abstractions should be sliced and that no proof exists that the semantic levels hit on by any theorist, whether Bloom, Schlesinger, Fillmore, or whomever, are psychologically functional" (1973, p. 146). In short, concluded Brown, "description in terms of a set of prevalent semantic relations may be little more than a technique of data reduction, a way of describing the meanings of early sentences short of listing them all" (1973, p. 173).

As studies aimed at identifying the semantic bases of word combination or at outlining the order in which children learn to produce sentences in various semantic categories proliferate, it is important to bear in mind that the problem of how best to classify sentences semantically has not yet been solved. Different investigators continue to divide up the utterances in corpora of children's speech in various noncongruent, overlapping ways, such that particular utterances that are grouped together as semantically similar in one study may appear in separate categories in another study (compare, for example, Bloom, Lightbown, and Hood, 1975b, and Wells, 1974).

The problem can be illustrated by showing some alternate ways of classifying a given set of data. Let us look at children's sentences with verbs, as these offer a particularly large number of possibilities for semantic groupings.

The verbs present in a typical 2-year-old's vocabulary each have their own lexical meaning and so at the most fundamental level are all unique. Suppose that the child initially sees no similarities at all among the events to which his verbs refer. That is, as far as he is concerned, carrying, opening, cutting, hitting, seeing, wanting, etc., are all discrete categories of events with no shared characteristics. In considering this possibility, Brown (1973, p. 122), pointed out that a child does not really need to form semantic categories at an inter-mediate level of abstraction like "agent," "action," "experiencer," "state," etc., at all. He could simply learn piecemeal the position associated with each semantic role of each verb. For example, he could learn that the name for the one who opens (*or* cuts, throws, sees, wants, etc.) goes first while the name for the object opened (*or* cut, thrown, seen, wanted, etc.) goes last. Each one of these rules could generate subject-verb or verb-object strings involving one par-ticular verb only (e.g., "Mommy/Daddy/monkey, etc. *throw,*" "*throw* ball/book/block, etc."). However, noted Brown, "there is a potential economy or advantage" in forming semantic abstractions like "agent" in that the child who does so is spared having to learn, one by one, the position for each particular semantic role associated with each verb. Instead, he can simply refer to the verb's semantic class membership. If the verb designates an *action,* for example, he can assume that the name for the one who performs the action will go in initial position, and he will usually be right (1973, p. 122).

The semantic category of "action" has an air of plausibility about it, and it has been used in a number of classification systems (e.g., Brown, 1973; Schlesinger, 1971b). But notice that "action" is only one possible feature shared by two or more verbs in a list of "action" verbs. It is theoretically quite possible that a child might not recognize any property linking *all* action verbs, but nevertheless would regard certain subsets of actions as similar on less abstract grounds. In this case he might formulate rules for expressing the relationships between particular classes of agents, actions, and objects but have no superordinate "action" concept subsuming them all.

For example, consider how one might divide up the following set of verbs on the basis of various kinds of similarities among them: "carry," "put," "throw," "give," "walk," "run," "go," "fly," "break," "open," "cut," "touch," "hit," "poke," "watch," "listen," "look at," "draw," "make," and "build." "Carry," "put," "throw," "give," "walk," "run," "go," and "fly" are all similar, and distinct from other verbs, in that they refer to actions that result in a *change of location*. "Carry," "put," "throw," and "give" can be differentiated from "walk," "run," "go," and "fly," however, because the former verbs involve an agent who changes the location of some other object while the latter verbs involve an agent who changes his *own* location. "Break," "open," and "cut" have ties to "carry," "put," "throw," "give," "walk," etc., in that they all refer to a *change of state* of some kind, whether the change is locational or attributive. And both change of location verbs involving an agent and another object and change of attributive state verbs are similar to "hit," "touch," and "poke" in that they all involve *physical action* upon an object. Yet "hit," "touch," and "poke" constitute a semantic subclass by virtue of the *kind* of physical action specified: *surface contact* (see Fillmore, 1970, for a discussion of syntactic as well as semantic differences between verbs like "hit," "touch," etc. and those like "break," and Wells, 1974, p. 251, for a discussion of difficulties involved in classifying children's sentences with "touch," "hit," etc.). "Watch," "listen," and "look at" form a subclass distinct from the other verbs because they all involve the direction of one's attention, while "draw," "make," and "build" designate actions that result in the creation of something, as opposed to actions on existing objects.

To undo all these hierarchically organized, mutually exclusive, or overlapping classes and start over again, we can classify the verbs according to whether they specify "momentary" or "continuative" actions (cf. Fillmore, 1969). For example, "carry," "walk," "run," "go," "fly," "watch," "listen," "look at," "draw," and "build" specify activities that continue over a span of time, while "put," "throw," "give," "break," "open," "cut," "hit," and "poke" cannot continue (unless they are repeated); rather, they are rapidly completed. "Touch" can be either momentary or continuative, while "make" seems indeterminate with regard to this semantic feature.

These examples have illustrated various ways of subclassifying verbs expressing actions, but the distinction that separates "actions" from the referents of other verbs is itself one that need not necessarily figure in any particular child's rule system. For example, rather than distinguishing between "actions" and what are often referred to as "states" (e.g., "want," "need," "see," "hear"), a child might attend to semantic features that are shared by certain "action" and certain "state" verbs, thereby creating categories that cut right across the distinction. An example of such a category would be "notice," which Bloom, Lightbown, and Hood (1975b) used in classifying utterances containing the "action" verbs "look at," "watch," and "listen," and the "state" verbs "see" and "hear."

This discussion of ways in which sentences can be classified and cross-classified was based on semantic similarities and differences among verbs, but the same exercise in classification can be carried out equally easily in other semantic domains, e.g., to determine possible subcategories of "possessive" or "locative" relationships between two sentence elements. The point is that it is possible to imagine almost an infinite variety of ways in which particular children might come to regard some relationships between objects or events in their experience as similar to other relationships, and to formulate rules for sentence construction that would apply only to situations qualifying as instances of those categories.

Although the various categories mentioned above suggest a rather static classification system whereby the child neatly enters each event into one or another pigeonhole, it is of course quite possible that even a very young child, like an adult, can conceptualize the same situation in a variety of ways. A child with a variety of classificational principles at his disposal might be able to encode the relationship he perceives between object, event, or property X and object, event, or property Y on the basis of rules for word combination at more than one level of abstraction. For example, the sentence "hit ball" might reflect knowledge not only of how to express a relationship between an act of hitting and the object hit, but also of how to deal syntactically with "verbs of surface contact," of which "hit" would be a member, and, at an even more abstract level, of how to talk about actions in relation to things acted upon. Alternatively, the child might start out forming rules for word combination at only one level of abstraction (i.e., each event would be conceptualized in only one way for purposes of sentence construction) but gradually begin to see a variety of links at different levels of abstraction among events. In this case, the child's earliest rules for combining words would be a set of discrete formulae, each one capable of encoding a particular kind of semantic content. But the rules would gradually lose their independence and begin to join up with each other in such a way that the child would end up with a flexible system of relational categories that are hierarchically organized or overlapping. This would then enable him to learn operations applying either to all of the members of a very abstract category (e.g., person and number agreement between sentence-subject and all verbs), or to only one or more subclasses within that category (e.g., -*ing* for "process" but not "state" verbs), and so on.

This rather theoretical discussion of varieties of semantic groupings was provided to illustrate the difficulty of making principled, nonarbitrary decisions about the semantic bases of children's rule systems. Let us now turn to some evidence bearing upon the problem of justifying one classification scheme over another.

Nature of Early Relational Categories: Some Empirical Evidence

Identifying the nature of the semantic categories underlying children's word combinations has been, as Brown pointed out, "an empirical question awaiting a technique of investigation" (1973, p. 146). In the most recent studies available, attention has been given to developing the needed analytical tools. A promising technique that several investigators have either suggested or actively employed is to discover natural divisions between groups of utterances by determining what kinds of utterances *emerge at about the same time* in the child's development (Brown, 1973, p. 142; Bowerman, 1973a, and b; Schlesinger, 1974; Bloom, Lightbown, and Hood, 1975b; Braine, in press; Greenfield and Smith, in press).[14] Schlesinger (1974) outlines the reasoning as follows: "If two items in a list of possible relations [relational categories, in the terminology of this chapter] begin to appear in children's speech simultaneously, and if they use the same syntactic patterns [e.g., word order] to express these, there

---

[14]See Brown, Cazden, and Bellugi (1969), Brown and Hanlon (1970), and Bowerman, (1975a) for comments on a methodological problem that can invalidate attempts to determine the order of emergence of various forms in child speech.

is good reason to regard them as belonging to one and the same underlying relational concept" (p. 136). Conversely, it follows that one has reason to suspect that a putative relational category has no psychological reality for the child if either a) utterances from the various subclasses of the category do not all begin to appear at the same time but instead come in sequentially, or b) utterances from the different subclasses are treated differently syntactically (e.g., display different patterns of word order) even if they come in at about the same time.

Three studies (Braine, in press; Bloom, Lightbown, and Hood, 1975b; Bowerman, this chapter) that have used simultaneous emergence (or lack of it) as a clue to children's relational categories are described below, along with relevant data from a fourth, related study by Wells (1974).

Braine's Study   Braine (in press) analyzed 16 corpora of speech from 11 children learning either English, Finnish, Samoan, Hebrew, or Swedish in an effort to determine the nature and scope of the rules children use in the earliest period of word combination. Data came from published sources or his own files. The mean length of utterance (MLU) of every sample was under 1.7 morphemes, so the children were in the developmental period that Brown (1973) has termed "Stage I" (MLU between 1.0 and 2.0). Two or more sequential samples were available for only a few of the children, so for most of the children Braine had to infer the order of emergence of various construction patterns from the characteristics of a single sample rather than by documenting change from one sample to the next.

Braine's method of analysis can be illustrated with an example from his son Jonathan's data. In Jonathan's first sample there was evidence that the child had acquired a productive way of constructing two-word sentences with *big* and *little,* using a consistent word order. Braine observed that utterances of both types might have been formed according to a single rule such as "size" + X, since they emerged at the same time, displayed the same word order, and are semantically closely related. Since other utterances with adjectives, such as *hot* + *X, old* + *X,* and *hurt* + *X,* emerged soon afterwards, Braine considered whether Jonathan might in fact have learned an even more abstract rule such as "property" + X which would account for all of them. However, argued Braine, there is one important bit of evidence against this hypothesis: if such a rule were present, it should govern the construction of all utterances with "property" words. But in fact there was a set of sentences with *wet* or *all wet* that did not display the consistent word order of the other utterances with "property" words. Instead they were characterized by what Braine termed a "groping" pattern: a pattern of unstable word order which, according to Braine's analyses, is associated with rules for sentence construction that are just coming in and are not yet well established. Braine concluded, therefore, that Jonathan had not formulated a superordinate concept like "property," of which *hot, big, wet,* etc. would be only instances. Rather, he argued, rules for producing sentences with these words appear to have been independent acquisitions. At most they might involve only small semantic groupings such that, for example, one rule might have been responsible for generating all the sentences with *big* and *little* and another rule all the sentences with *more* and *other.*

After analyzing each corpus separately in the detail that the above example suggests and then comparing them, Braine concluded that "the first productive structures are formulae of limited scope for realizing specific kinds of meaning. They define how a meaning is to be expressed by specifying where in the utterances the words expressing the meaning should be placed." Although the particular categories upon which the formulae operate are semantic rather than syntactic, according to Braine, they are narrower than the broad semantic categories such as "agent" posited in case grammer (cf., Fillmore, 1968, 1971).

Braine found that "children differ considerably in the kinds of contents expressed by their productive patterns ... Certain kinds of content seem to be popular and recur in many children. Others are less popular and appear in fewer children." Among the most common were patterns that draw attention to something *(see + X, here/there + X,* etc.), patterns that remark on specific properties of objects *(big/little + X),* patterns expressing possession, patterns that note plurality or iteration *(two + X, and + X),* patterns concerned with recurrence or alternate exemplars of a type *(more/other + X),* and patterns involving location *(X + (preposition) here/there, X + Y* ("X is in, on, has moved to Y")). Braine explicitly specified that he found no evidence for "narrow-scope patterns confined to particular actions" as far as the relationship between action and actor is concerned. In fact, a broad *actor-action* pattern was productive for many of the children. However Braine's data did *not* reveal an analogous broad pattern governing the construction of a range of verb-object sentences. Verb-object strings were relatively infrequent (an important difference between the children investigated here and Bloom's (1970) subjects). Many of those that did occur were quite variable with respect to word order; others reflected positional patterns involving either specific verbs (e.g., *see* + *X, want* + *X*) or small sets of verbs expressing a narrow range of semantic content such as "actions to do with oral consumption" (*eat/bite/drink* + *Y*), or "actions to do with movements of vehicles" (*drives/pulls/tows* + *X*).

Braine observed that despite the overall popularity of certain patterns, the children differed considerably in the *order* in which they acquired them. There was, in fact, so much variation in this respect that the productive patterns found in the corpora of two children early in the two-word stage did not overlap at all. Although Braine did not speculate on the determinants of such differences, it is tempting to hypothesize that variability in "cognitive style" may play a role, just as it appears to in determining the early words that children "select" to learn. This possibility was raised in 1964 by Miller and Ervin, who stated that "there are some suggestions in our data that linguistic patterns correlate with some nonlinguistic behavior" (p. 30). They observed that one subject who had productive patterns involving the words *off* and *on* "was a busy little girl who was always taking things off and putting them back on." A second subject, in contrast, always sat down to be entertained by the investigator, who brought a bag of toys, and her favorite construction patterns were *that* + *X* and *this* + *X,* used in identifying or labeling objects. However, despite these early intriguing suggestions on cognitive correlates of children's preferences in sentence-construction, little, if any, further work has been done on the subject.

In comparing his current proposal to his earlier (1963) work, Braine notes that it "echoes two important aspects" of his original hypothesis that children's early sentences reflect knowledge of how to position particular words in utterances: "the notions that limited formulae (rather than broad grammatical generalizations) are learned one after another during the early development, and that the formulae are positional" (i.e., make use of consistent word order). However, Braine argues that the current hypothesis amends some deficiencies of the earlier one. For example, it does not require that the positional formulae operate *only* upon specific words: categories like *actor, possessor,* or *location* can also be used. In addition, the present proposal deals explicitly with semantic relationships whereas the earlier one ignored meaning entirely.

Bloom, Lightbown, and Hood's Study; Wells' Study A recent study by Bloom and her colleagues (1975b) presents an interesting contrast to Braine's monograph. In a general way it addresses some of the same questions as his but the methods are different and certain of the findings are discrepant.

Bloom et al. examined the development over time of four children to discover, among other things, the order in which the children acquired the ability to combine words to express various kinds of relational meanings. They first inspected developmental changes in the children's data in a rough way and then set up a taxonomy of "semantic-syntactic" categories that appeared to encompass the vast majority of all the children's utterances and to reveal developmental trends. Following this, Bloom et al. attempted to determined the order in which the children demonstrated productive knowledge of how to construct utterances in the various categories by setting up a criterion for productivity based on frequency of production.[15]

The primary categories used in the study were seven categories of verb relations. Bloom et al. classified the children's utterances into one or another of these, regardless of whether an actual verb appeared in them, "according to whether or not relevant movement accompanied the utterance (action vs. state events), and whether or not place was relevant to either action or state (locative vs. nonlocative events)" (p. 10).

Utterances assigned to the *action* category included 1) those referring to "action that affected an object with movement by an agent" (e.g., "my open that," "Gia ride bike," "Gia bike," "I made," etc.) (p. 10) and 2) those referring to "movements by actors (persons or objects) in events where no object other than the actor was affected" (e.g., "Kathryn jumps," "tape go round") (p. 11). Utterances assigned to the *locative action* category included 1) those entailing at least two of the four components of an *agent-action-affected object or person-place or goal of motion* pattern (e.g., "put in box," "tape on there," "you put ə finger"), and 2) those in which the agent and affected person or object were identical (e.g., "Mommy stand up ə chair," "I get down") (p. 11). *Locative state* utterances "referred to relationship between a person or object and its location" (p. 11), where there was no movement in the time surrounding the child's utterance (e.g., "light hall", "I sitting"). *Notice* utterances

---

[15]Methodological difficulties with the study that render some of the findings equivocal are discussed in Bowerman (1975a). Bloom *et al.* (1975a) present further analyses to support the proposed developmental sequence in a reply. The interested reader is advised to examine the matter closely.

included those with verbs of attention such as "see," "hear," "watch," and "look at" (p. 12). *State* utterances referred either to 1) internal states with "want," "need," "like," "sick," etc., or 2) temporary ownership ("have") (p. 12). Two other verb categories involved *intention* and *causality*, with matrix verbs like "want to," "have to," and "make" (p. 12).

In addition to these verb categories, Bloom et al. set up categories involving *possession* ("reference to objects that were within the domains of particular persons by virtue of habitual use or association" (p. 10)), *existence* ("pointing out or naming an object" (p. 13)), *negation* ("nonexistence, disappearance, or rejection of objects or events" (p. 13)), *recurrence* ("reference to 'more' or another instance of an object or event" (p. 13)), *attribution* ("counting, specifying, or otherwise qualifying objects" (p. 13)), *Wh-questions*, *datives* ("specifying the recipient of an action that also involved an affected object" (p. 13)), *instruments* ("specifying the inanimate object that was used in an action to affect another object" (p. 13)), and *place* ("specify[ing] where an action event occurred, for example, 'baby swim bath' " (p. 13)).

According to Bloom et al.'s findings, the productive ability to make sentences in the various categories emerged in the following sequence: constructions expressing the existence, nonexistence, and recurrence of objects preceded those involving verb relations. Within verb relations, *action events* (actions and locative actions) preceded *state events* (locative states, notice, and states). For two of the children actions preceded locative actions, while for the other two both emerged at the same time. Constructions involving possession and attribution emerged in variable order, while those involving instruments, datives, Wh-questions, place of action, intention, and causality were late developments for all of the children.

Bloom et al.'s emphasis on the consistency of order of development in their subjects is in striking contrast to Braine's conclusion that children differ greatly in the order in which they learn to produce utterances of different patterns. Some of the discrepancies may be due to methodological differences. Bloom et al.'s relational categories were much broader than Braine's, which could have contributed to differences in the findings in at least three ways. First, many of Bloom et al.'s categories, being relatively broad, were potentially capable of encompassing a number of different formulae which the children they studied might have learned in variable order as independent acquisitions. For example, at a given time a child might be able to freely produce one variety of "locative state" utterances (e.g., "I sitting") but not the other (e.g., "light hall"). Second, many of Bloom et al.'s categories encompassed utterances with a variety of specific relationships holding between their constituents. For example, "I made" (agent-action) and "open drawer" (action-affected object) were both classified as *action* events. Braine, in contrast, distinguished carefully between such utterances and found that the productive ability to make constructions of one type (e.g., agent-action) was not necessarily accompanied by the ability to make constructions of another type (e.g., action-affected object). Third, Bloom et al. did not require that all utterances involving the same relationship between their constituents (e.g., all agent-action strings) exhibit the same word order in order to be classified into the same category, while identity of word order patterns was critical to Braine's analyses.

These differences in methods of analysis can account for some of the discrepancies between Braine's and Bloom et al.'s findings. Children can differ sharply from each other at the level at which Braine was looking, yet these differences can still be consistent with the more abstract regularities in order of emergence found by Bloom et al. Not all the differences can be resolved by reference to disparate methodologies, however; certain discrepancies remain. For example, Bloom et al. found that constructions expressing *locative actions* (X goes to Z, X moves Y to Z) consistently preceded those expressing *locative states* (X is located at Y), and they discuss possible cognitive factors that could account for this. Yet Braine discovered no such consistency. Some of the children in his study developed productive formulae for expressing locative actions before locative states, but others (for example, Braine's son Jonathan) began to produce utterances of both kinds at the same time. A second discrepancy between the findings of the two studies is that while Bloom et al. concluded that *state* events involving verbs like "want," "sick," "have," and "see" became productive only after action events, Braine's study included samples from several children who demonstrated a very early productive ability with constructions involving one or another "state" word, such as *want + X, have-it + X,* or *see +X.*[16,17]

---

[16]Edwards (1974, pp. 429–431) has argued that a close examination of the contexts in which children initially use what look like "state" or "experience" verbs reveals that these verbs are in fact really linked with *actions,* such that "see" is equivalent to "look at," "want" is a request for something to be given, etc. His discussion highlights the fact that identifying the relational semantic categories a child uses requires a

Findings reported in a recent study by Wells (1974) are related in a rather complex way to those of Braine (in press) and Bloom et al. (1975b). Like Bloom et al., Wells set up a semantically based taxonomic system, classified the utterances of his subjects (a total of 8 children) into one or another category according to inferences about the child's intentions that were based on the linguistic and nonlinguistic contexts in which the utterances were produced, and tried to determine the order in which utterances of various semantic types emerged. Wells' categories were similar to those of Bloom et al. in that they were indifferent to word order and did not distinguish between, e.g., agent-action and action-object strings of a given semantic type. However, Wells' categories distinguished much more finely than Bloom et al.'s among a variety of semantic notions, such that some utterances grouped together in the Bloom et al. study would have been placed in separate categories by Wells.

Wells' findings on order of acquisition are similar to those of Bloom et al. in a global sort of way. For example, both studies report that children learn how to talk about actions and locations before they begin to produce sentences with "experiential" verbs referring to feelings and perceptions. Like Bloom et al. and unlike Braine, Wells also found that *changes* of location are consistently talked about before locative states. All three studies agree that sentences involving function words like "this," "that," and "more" are among the earliest to be produced. Like Braine, Wells also found sentences such as *want* + X and *see* + X emerging early, which supports Wells' argument that these should not be classified (as in Bloom et al.'s study) with other later-appearing "states."

Despite these areas of agreement, Wells' findings differ from those of Bloom et al. in a number of details, due largely to the fact that certain utterances which would have been classed together in Bloom et al.'s study were distinguished by Wells and found to emerge at different times. For example, Wells reports that constructions specifying "functions of people" (e.g., sentences with "eat," "play," "kiss," and "sing") came in relatively late, along with states, while those involving "changes of physical attributive states" (e.g., sentences with "open," "close," "break," and "cut") were

---

detailed knowledge of how the child construes the meanings of the words in his sentences (cf. Bowerman, 1974a, p. 203, for more on this theme).

[17]See Bowerman (in press b) for further discussion of differences between the approaches of Braine and Bloom.

much earlier. Utterances of both these kinds were classified as *action* events by Bloom et al., and the action category became productive in their data well before the state category. Such discrepancies make it clear that the use of different classificational systems affects the apparent order in which the ability to produce utterances of various kinds emerges.

It is not clear whether the findings reported by Bloom et al. and by Wells can be directly applied to questions about the nature of the relational categories children use in their earliest rules for word combination. Wells makes no claims that his taxonomic system employs categories that were functional in his subjects' internalized grammars. Bloom et al.'s position on this matter is somewhat ambiguous, however. Early in the study they argue that their categories were not a "superimposed *a priori* system of analysis", but rather were "presumably derived from an individual child's own rule system and were, therefore, functional for the child" (p. 9). (The meaning of "functional" in this context is not explained). The impression that they are dealing with categories assumed to have psychological reality for the child is strengthened by their observation that utterances involving verbs belonging to particular semantic categories, such as those expressing movements of one's body ("go," "sit," "stand up," etc.), were regular and distinguishable from utterances with other kinds of verbs relations (p. 3). Later in the monograph, however, Bloom et al. caution that "the taxonomy of linguistic structures that has been presented here is a linguistic description of speech data that can represent the child's knowledge and changes in the child's knowledge only in a very gross way. There is no way of knowing, at the present time, the form in which such knowledge about linguistic structure is represented in the child's mental grammar" (p. 33). Further research will clearly be required before we can be certain whether semantic concepts like Bloom et al.'s *locative action* or Wells' *change of physical attributive state* play any role in children's rule systems, or whether instead they simply provide a convenient vocabulary for describing changes over time in the subject matter of children's conversations.

Evidence from Christy and Eva   An analysis I have performed on data collected from my children during the early stages of word combination is similar in spirit to the study by Braine discussed above and supplements his findings in certain ways. Like Braine, I was interested in exploring the nature and scope of children's early rules for sentence construction. The data I used, which were collected for the purpose of eventually performing such an analysis, consisted of weekly tapes and extensive daily notes on utterances and the contexts in which they occurred. My plan of data collection had been to get a detailed enough record that the history of every word each child used could be traced from the single-word stage on up through the early period of word combination. The wealth of data that was ultimately available allowed a very fine-grained analysis. Only certain aspects of the study are reported on here.[18]

The information of interest included what word combinations began to occur at about the same time, whether these could conceivably be related to each other as reflections of the same relational category on grounds of either semantic or syntactic similarity, and, if so, whether they employed the same word order. In addition, information on *single-word utterances*—a type of data not available to Braine in his study—was used to determine whether there were verbs, adjectives, and the like in the child's vocabulary that potentially could have been used in constructing sentences of a given semantic or syntactic type but that did not begin to enter into combination at the same time as semantically similar words.

Christy and Eva were obliging subjects in that they opted for strikingly different approaches to the business of word combination and so provide an interesting glimpse into the range of individual differences possible among children who receive a rather similar environmental and linguistic input. The differences between them are consonant with two strategies for acquiring grammar that Bloom (1970, pp. 222–227) has outlined, as will be discussed following a presentation of the children's data.

Let us consider Eva first. Eva's initial approach to word combination was clearly based on learning how to express the specific semantic relationships encoded by function or operator-like words which exerted a constant semantic effect on the words with which they were juxtaposed. That is, her early rules for combining words did not operate on *categories* of words, such as "action" or "modifier," that could include more than one exemplar. Rather, each word was treated as a semantic isolate, in the sense that the ability to combine it with other words was not accompanied by a parallel ability to make two-word utterances with semantically related words.

---

[18]A fuller report on the study was given in "Relationship of Early Cognitive Development to a Child's Early Rules for Word Combination and Semantic Knowledge," a miniseminar presented at The American Speech and Hearing Association Annual Meeting, Las Vegas, November, 1974, but a discussion of the material appears here in print for the first time.

For example, the first week of word combination at about 17½ months was characterized by the sudden production of a large number of constructions involving the word "want," in sentences like "want bottle," "want juice," "want see," and "want change." At the time that Eva began to combine "want" with other words she was using approximately 25 other verbs of adult English as single-word utterances. These included both names for actions, such as "wipe," "push," "pull," "open," "close," "bite," and "throw," and names for states such as "see" and "got" (in the sense of "have"). However, none of these verbs began to enter into combination for another month. Eva's ability to combine "want" with another word thus did not reflect a growing awareness of how to combine verbs with direct objects but rather was based simply on her knowledge of how to combine words to express a request for an object or an activity. This initial rule for word combining was thus very narrow, and did not permit generalization in sentence construction beyond the meaning of "want" itself, either to other states like "see" or "got," or, more generally, to verbs that take direct objects.

A second example of Eva's approach involves her treatment of noun modifiers. At 18 months, 1 week Eva began to combine "more" with other words. At this time she was using about seven adjectives as single-word utterances ("hot," "wet," etc.) as well as several other words with close semantic ties to "more," such as "again," "no more," and "allgone." Yet none of these began to enter into construction with other words for at least a month after combinations with "more" started, and when they did start to combine, they did so sequentially over a long period of time rather than all at once.

This type of lexically based rule learning prevailed for about 2½ months. During this period new function words like "no," "yukky," and "here" (while handing over an object) began to enter into combination, but each word was initially treated as semantically unique. Thus, Eva did not at first take advantage of the potential economy she could have introduced into her rule system by formulating rules on a more abstract level, such as "word for an action precedes word for an object acted upon," "quantifier precedes word for object quantified," or "modifier precedes word for object modified."

Nor was there evidence for the operation at a later time of rules at an intermediate semantic level, which would indicate that after a period of experience with the syntax of particular words Eva had reorganized her information about them according to simpler superordinate semantic categories like "agent" or "action" (cf. Schlesinger, 1971a, pp. 79–80, for mention of this kind of reorganization as a theoretical possibility). For example, she did not suddenly begin to produce great numbers of combinations involving all the words she knew of a particular semantic type (e.g., actions, quantifiers) after an initial period of learning to combine certain of these one by one. She went instead rather swiftly from an approach based on learning sequentially how to make constructions with particular lexical items to a much more mature system in which words of virtually all semantic subtypes were dealt with fluently. I do not know how she accomplished this transition, but there is no evidence that she achieved it with the aid of relational concepts at a level of abstraction intermediate between the semantics of particular words and syntactic notions that are independent of any particular semantic content, such as "subject" and "direct object."

Eva's lexically based approach to word combination was accompanied by a tendency to work a new construction pattern heavily (e.g., *more* + *X*) and then to virtually drop it in favor of one or more new patterns. Braine (in press) remarks on a similar behavior in his son Jonathan, who, like Eva, appeared to favor lexically based rules for word combination. This behavior contrasts strikingly with Christy's. Christy, as we shall see shortly, did not employ the lexically based method, and her syntactic progress was relatively smooth, with no abrupt shifts or discontinuities.

One possible explanation for the discontinuous behavior that tentatively seems to be correlated with the lexically based approach to word combination is that this approach is too restricting. There is little power in a syntactic system predicated on how to combine words that encode particular conceptual notions like "desire" or "moreness" with words representing the objects or events that are desired or of which there is "more." Each rule is so limited in the kinds of sentences it can generate that the child achieves relatively low returns for all his efforts. Eva seemed to be trying valiantly to crack into the syntactic system of English, taking one route after another, but she was not able to progress very far as long as she stuck to the method of learning how to combine individual words with other words to express restricted relational meanings. She did not begin to go quickly forward, losing her "try it, then drop it" behavior, until she apparently began to realize, at about 20 months, that word combination can be based on deeper abstractions than those manifested in the semantics of particular words.

The data from Christy illustrate quite a different approach. Christy did not rely heavily on the strategy of learning how to combine particular words with other words to express fixed semantic relationships (there were a few such patterns initially, however). Instead, she seemed to take a more abstract view of the problem of sentence construction, searching for patterns of some generality that could govern word combinations with many different lexical items.[19]

Christy's treatment of noun modifiers provides a good illustration of this. Recall that Eva began to use different modifiers in combination with other words at different times, apparently learning a position for a new modifier every couple of weeks while semantically similar words continued to occur only as single-word utterances. In contrast, Christy produced almost no modifier-modified constructions until about 2 months after word combination had started, despite the fact that she used many adjectives as single-word utterances and knew names for many of the objects in connection with which they were said. Then within a period of a few days she suddenly began to combine "hot," "wet," "allgone," and "alldone" with "that" or a word for an object, consistently placing the modifier in second position: e.g., "that wet," "Daddy hot," "bottle allgone."

The fact that Christy began to use several different modifiers in identically ordered sentences at about the same time indicates that she had learned something more abstract than the position of individual words. This supposition is supported by the fact that she first began to produce predicate nominative constructions like "that airplane" during the same week. Predicate adjective constructions like "swing wet" and "that hot" and predicate nominative constructions like "that airplane" can perhaps be considered semantically related in that both *attribute* something to an object: a property in one case and a name in the other. Syntactically they are clearly related in that in adult English they both are expressed by a copular sentence pattern. Whatever the nature of the similarity in Christy's mind, it seems clear that her production of these utterances was delayed until she had organized the structural information governing them at a fairly abstract level.

Christy's utterances with verbs, like those with modifiers, support the hypothesis that she was organizing structural information according to patterns based on abstractions subsuming more than one

---

[19]Christy did not begin to combine words quite as early as Eva. This provides some supporting evidence for Haselkorn's (1973) proposal that it may take longer for a child to develop abstract *categories* of relational notions such as agent-action and possessor-possessed than to discover the distributional properties of function or operator-like words such as "more."

lexical item. For example, the locative particles "up," "down," "on," "off," and "back" all began to combine at about the same time with a word for the person or object undergoing the indicated directional motion. Similarly, a wide spectrum of words naming actions of various sorts began to appear with agentive subjects at close to the same time, while verbs that do not take agents, like "fit" and "got," continued to occur only in isolation.

To summarize, the early utterances of Eva on the one hand and Christy on the other reflect different approaches to word combination. These approaches are consistent with two strategies for learning to combine words that Bloom (1970) has outlined. The distinction between the two strategies (which are not mutually exclusive) is based on the nature of the rules for word combination that the child appears to be formulating. Formulating one kind of rule, which Bloom termed "pivotal" (from Braine's (1963) notion of "pivot" words for which a position is learned), involves searching for constancies in the expression of relationships involving the semantic notions encoded by *particular words* such as "more," "no," "yukky," etc. Eva's earliest rules were virtually all of this nature; Bloom's subject Eric initially followed this strategy too.

The other strategy Bloom outlined involves formulating rules that specify how to position words performing relational functions like "possessor," "subject" or "agent," and "direct object" or "object affected." Bloom called this kind of rule "categorical." Christy's approach to word combination was certainly more "categorical" than it was "pivotal," and so in this respect she was more like Bloom's subjects Gia and Kathryn than like Eric. However, the characteristics of Christy's early utterances, together with those of some of Braine's (in press, discussed above) subjects, indicate that two kinds of categorical rules should be distinguished. The variety with which Bloom (1970) was concerned are quite abstract, being essentially independent of the lexical meanings of the words used to fulfill the relational categories. For example, the relationship between possessor and possessed, between subject and object, and between object located and location is not inherent in any way in the meanings of the particular words that can function in these roles. But some of Christy's rules for word combination appeared to operate upon relational categories that were *not* independent of lexical meaning in this way. For example, there was evidence for a rule having to do with directional motion, as expressed by a small set of locative particles ("up," "down," etc.). Similarly, Braine (in press) found evidence, as noted earlier, for rules involving the placement of words referring to size, to oral consumption, or to the movements of vehicles. Rules specifying how to deal with *groups* of words, all of which share a semantic feature, must be considered "categorical," like those involving notions such as "possessor" or "agent," because they make reference to *categories* of words rather than to single words. However, they are rather similar to "pivotal" rules in that they are not independent of lexical meaning and may involve as few as *two* words with a shared semantic feature (e.g., "big" and "little"). Formulating rules of this intermediate type requires a somewhat different kind of induction about linguistic structure than is needed either for rules based on the semantics of particular lexical items or for those involving categories like "possessor" or "object located" that do not necessitate recognition of similarities in word meaning. Some children may arrive at such rules easily, while other children may never use them. Further study of the process is clearly needed to determine how the language development of children who formulate these rules may differ from that of children who do not.

Origins of Children's Relational Concepts

How the child arrives at the relational concepts with which he constructs his first word combinations is perhaps even more mysterious than how he formulates the categories underlying his use of words. How much is contributed to the process by the child's nonlinguistic cognitive development, and how much by his analysis of sentence structure in the language to which he is exposed?

Prior Knowledge   One possibility, of course, is that the child's two-word utterances reflect relational concepts that are formulated independently of linguistic input.[20] Schlesinger (1971b) initially argued for this view, although his position has since altered somewhat as will be discussed shortly. According to Schlesinger's original proposal, the relational categories underlying sentence construction are concepts like "agent," "action," "object," and "location." These are innate in the sense that they are "part and parcel of our way of viewing the world" (1971b, p. 98); that is, they are determined by the basic cognitive capacity of the child. Acquiring grammar, according

---

[20]McNeill's (1966, 1970, 1971) hypothesis that knowledge of the basic grammatical relations is innate and guides children's language development even prior to word combination fits in here. In this chapter, however, we will be looking only at semantically based proposals of this nature.

to this view, simply involves learning the appropriate syntactic devices for expressing these concepts.

A related approach is taken by Nelson, who proposes that "the earliest sentences (as opposed to learned phrases) express the child's own conjunction of concepts" (1973b, p. 117). (This view is, of course, consistent with her position on the concepts underlying early word meanings that was outlined on p. 130). Nelson's stance on the initial relational concepts differs from Schlesinger's in one important respect, however. Unlike Schlesinger, Nelson does not consider the categories to be innate or predetermined to take certain forms. On the contrary, she argues that they are acquired on the basis of experience and may vary considerably from child to child.

The view that the categories children initially use in constructing sentences are formed independently of linguistic input receives some support from child language data. As Brown (1973) points out, "the productive acquisition of a syntactic construction seldom at first entails using it over the full semantic range to which it applies" (p. 196). For example, in the early period of word combining children's genitive constructions ("(the) X('s) Y") express only the semantic notions of "prior rights of access" ("Daddy chair") and part-whole relationships ("doggie tail," "Mommy nose"). The genitive in adult speech is not limited in this way, cf. "the ship's captain," "Germany's capital" (Brown, 1973, p. 196). Similarly, according to Horgan's (n.d.) analyses, children initially use the full passive construction in accordance with semantic constraints that are not found in the adult syntax of passivization. A plausible explanation of a child's usage of *any* form (whether it be a pattern for sentence construction, an inflection, a word, etc.) over a *semantically restricted* range is that the child has identified the form with a concept of his own devising. This concept thus serves as the child's hypothesis about the semantic range across which the linguistic form is applicable. An alternative explanation of the phenomenon, of course, is that adults may *model* forms primarily or exclusively in connection with a limited range of semantic content; little is yet known about this, however (but cf. Bowerman, 1973a, pp. 191–192, for one bit of evidence along these lines).

The Interactionist Position   Schlesinger (1974) has recently reappraised the role of linguistic input in the development of children's early relational categories. As noted above, he proposed earlier that relational categories reflect the child's innately determined way of viewing the world; they would develop in the same way whether the child acquired language or not. Schlesinger now suggests instead that the child "probably comes into a world which is a booming and buzzing confusion, rather than into one which is neatly parceled into agents, actions, and so on" (1974, p. 145). Relational concepts gradually develop *both* through nonlinguistic experience and through observations of the way in which various events are encoded linguistically. For example, "by hearing sentences in which all agents are treated the same way, [the child] acquires the agent concept with rules for realizing it in speech" (1974, p. 145). In sum, Schlesinger rejects "cognitive determinism," which "postulates a one-way influence from cognitive to linguistic development." He argues instead for an interactionist approach whereby the learning of sentence structure can contribute to the way in which the child "slices up" his experiences (1974, p. 145). Schlesinger's proposal that cognitive development is determined by many factors, linguistic input among them, is very similar to the position taken by Wells (1974, 1975), which was discussed above on pp. 132–133.

Bloom's (1973) views on the origin of the relational categories underlying early sentences appear to have some similarities to those of both Nelson (1973b) on the cognition-first side and Schlesinger (1974) on the interactionist side. The way Bloom differs from both of these investigators highlights some of the complexities involved in evaluating the opposing positions.

Unlike Schlesinger and like Nelson, Bloom tends to reject the possible influence of language on children's cognitive organization of their experiences: "The evidence presented thus far appears to indicate that the child's conceptual representation of events does not depend on or derive from a linguistic basis" (1973, p. 64). However, unlike Nelson, Bloom does not feel that the independently achieved understanding of the relationships among objects and events can themselves directly constitute the relational categories upon which rules for word combination can operate: "Cognitive categories do not develop in a one-to-one correspondence with eventual linguistic categories; that is, the cognitive categories that are formed in the last half of the second year are not directly mapped onto corresponding linguistic categories" (Bloom, 1973, p. 121). Rather, Bloom argues, the cognitive schemata by which children mentally represent the relationships among objects and events are global in that they do not distinguish specifically between the participants in the relations. That is, for example, "cognitive categories represent the *entire* relationship among, for example, agent, action, and object, or possessor and possessed" (Bloom, Lightbown, and Hood, 1975b, p. 30; emphasis added). What the child must do before he can start to combine words to express such relationships, according to Bloom, is to induce, from his experiences with language, information about the kinds of relationships that can hold between words. Bloom (1973) outlines this process as follows: "... the child hears words in combination that refer to the categories of events that he has come to represent conceptually. The child comes to discover the semantic relations that can exist between words by hearing such words in relation to each other, in relation to the events in which they occur, and using such words successively in the same kinds of situations" (p. 120). In short, "such differentiated semantic categories as agent, place, affected object, etc., are linguistic inductions that the child has made on the basis of his linguistic experience relative to existing relations in cognitive schemata" (Bloom et al., 1975b, p. 30).

While Bloom and Schlesinger (1974b) seem to agree that concepts like agent, action, etc., are formed by experience with sentence structure rather than developing autonomously, they differ sharply in their interpretation of the subsequent cognitive status of such categories. Whereas Schlesinger feels that the child's conceptualization of events is influenced by his awareness of how they are treated syntactically, Bloom emphatically denies that semantic categories also become cognitive categories: "The child does not have a cognitive notion AGENT or PERSON-AFFECTED; rather, his cognitive categories are mental representations of the entire relation in experience between agent-action-object or person affected-affecting state, etc." (1973, p. 121).

To summarize, Bloom apparently regards semantic categories like agent, etc., as exclusively linguistic inductions that neither directly reflect the child's presyntactic cognitive organization nor act back upon that organization to influence its subsequent development. Linguistic categories and cognitive categories thus lead independent lives: how the child represents events to himself is quite separate from the information he uses to express these events in sentences. This is a theoretical possibility, but it requires substantiation. While I fully agree with Bloom that conceptual and semantic categories must be distinguished (cf. Bowerman, 1974b, pp. 156–159) and that semantic categories may in principle be learned through language rather than necessarily reflecting prior cognitive distinctions, I hesitate to conclude either that cognitive categories can never be used as the basis for semantic categories or that semantic categories arrived at by the processing of linguistic data can have no influence on the child's conceptual structuring of experience. The matter is enormously complex, however, and only recently are some of the relevant theoretical distinctions and alternative possible views becoming differentiated. We can expect to see much future debate on these issues.

IMPLICATIONS FOR LANGUAGE TRAINING

The foregoing discussions of word meaning and sentence construction have emphasized that being able to use language in novel ways requires the speaker to recognize implicitly the *categorical* nature of language—that words and syntactic devices are linked not to unique experiences but to *classes* of events. The child learning language must operate with this basic assumption in order to work out even preliminary correspondences between his nonlinguistic experiences and linguistic forms and devices.

How can programs designed to help language-deficient children benefit from recent advances in our understanding of how normal children go about constructing the categories that enable them to use words in new situations and to create novel sentences? Some possibilities are considered below. The first subsection suggests some possible ways in which the language materials that are presented to the child can be tailored so as to take advantage of, rather than clash with, his natural classificational tendencies. This should facilitate ease and speed of learning. The final subsection of this chapter outlines a way in which the use of negative feedback to the child about his performance may have undesirable effects on his ability to formulate and test hypotheses about linguistic categories.

Choosing and Sequencing Language Training Materials

In order to link a word or a pattern of word combination with a category of objects, events, properties, or relationships, a child must be able to see similarities among the various situations in which the word or sentence pattern is modeled. If the child is presented with several exemplars for the object "dog" or the action "open" which do not seem at all alike to him, regardless of how similar they may seem to adults, he can do no more than memorize independent associations between word and exemplars. Similarly, if the clinician gives the child a number of sentences such as "the boy runs," "the baby eats," and "the doggie barks" in the hopes that the child will be able to abstract out a rule governing the production of other agent-action strings, but the child can see no similarity linking boys running with babies eating and doggies barking, the induction cannot be made.

Ideally, all of the exemplars with which a word or a pattern for combining words are taught would be ones that the child can perceive as similar in some way. The elimination of input that is nonsense from the child's point of view, in that it does not contribute to his grasp of a governing concept, would lead to greater speed and efficiency in the child's formulation of rules for word use and sentence construction. To the extent that this ideal can be approximated, moreover, the child is spared the frustration of having to respond in a trial-and-error fashion because he cannot "solve the puzzle"—cannot find ways to organize and make sense of the mass of individual words or sentences with which he is presented.

Of course, one can never know with certainty in advance how a particular child is already classifying things or what kinds of experiences he can learn to regard as similar with a little help. Nevertheless, information about processes in normal language acquisition can suggest some categories that are typically "easy" for children and hence help the clinician to minimize some of the noise in the linguistic input.

Teaching words   There is evidence, as was reported earlier, that children may differ systemantically in the kinds of similarities across situations to which they are sensitive in their attempts to link words with categories of experiences. Nelson (1973b) has been particularly interested in the ways in which the linguistic input to a child can harmonize or clash with his conceptual style. In her study of children's acquisition of their first 50 words, she found that children whose mothers use language in a way that is consonant with their cognitive style acquire vocabulary faster than those whose mothers use language in a contrasting way. In particular, "great difficulty seems to arise when the mother uses the language primarily in a R mode [for naming and describing objects and events] while the child has organized the world primarily in an active or social mode or the reverse" (1973b, p. 103).

These considerations suggest that a language-deficient child can be taught vocabulary more effectively if first words to be trained are selected on the basis of close observations of the child's way of interacting with his physical and social environment rather than taken directly from a standardized program. An additional source of information about the child's personal style of classifying experiences can be gained by analyzing the ways in which he misuses words. What classificational principles do the errors suggest that the child is using? Perceptual similarities like shape? Functional similarities like common behaviors or actions associated with different objects? Similarities across social settings or across internal reactions or intentions as opposed to similiarities among objects or events? If the child's classificational tendencies can be determined, words whose meanings *require* the speaker to make these sorts of classifications can be selected for initial training.

Some more specific recommendations about the selection and sequencing of words to be taught are listed below.

1. There is much evidence to suggest that children are cognitively predisposed toward classifying objects on the basis of perceptual similarities, particularly shape. The selection of initial words for objects and of exemplars for these words should take advantage of this natural tendency. That is, the words used should have as possible referents objects that *look* quite similar. According to this criterion, "shoe," "ball," and "cookie" would be good candidates while "toy" and "food" would not. Within the constraint imposed by maintaining perceptual similarity, first words should be tags for objects that are salient by virtue of their ability to *act* spontaneously or to be *acted upon* by the child.

2. The selection of words for nonobject concepts (verbs, adjectives, etc.) should be guided by information about the kinds of concepts acquired early by normal children, as judged by their word use. Words to do with existence, disappearance, recurrence, falls and bumps, directional motion, manipulations of objects, bodily activities, and transitory properties like "wet" and "hot" appear to be good candidates for easy acquisition.

3. Many normal children appear to associate words for directional motion ("up", "down", etc.) and bodily activities ("night night," "sit," "walk") first with activities of their own bodies, then with the bodies of other people, then (sometimes inappropriately) with actions of or upon inanimate objects. Words like "more" and "allgone" often appear first in connection with requests for additional food and drink, only later being extended to additional or alternate exemplars of other things. Following a similar sequence in presenting illustrative *referents* for such words may help certain language-deficient children—those who have difficulty seeing abstract similarities from one situation to the next—to gradually widen initially narrow categories until the categories encompass more diverse exemplars.

This kind of schedule could be quickly abandoned for children who readily recognize rather abstract similarities among experiences.

Teaching Patterns for Sentence Construction   Recent semantically oriented studies of early syntactic development have begun to influence the planning of programs to teach children how to make sentences. For example, Miller and Yoder (1974), who argue that "the content for language training for retarded children should be taken from the data available on language development in normal children" (p. 511), have concluded after review of the relevant literature that "that basis of early language development is the semantic concept. Semantic concepts or functions, then, are the basic elements to be taught in the teaching program" (p. 516). The specific concepts that their program employs in organizing and sequencing training materials are derived from studies by Bloom (1970, 1973), Brown (1973, elsewhere), and Schlesinger (1971a and b). They include such relational categories as existence, nonexistence, disappearance, recurrence, agent, action, object, possessive, locative, attributive, experiencer, state, and others.

While this general approach is well founded, it is important to recognize that the taxonomic systems by means of which normal children's "semantic intentions" have been described do not at this point provide a principled guide to the relational notions underlying their utterances, although they are useful as provisional hypotheses. As we saw earlier, it is quite uncertain whether children actually make use of concepts like "agent," "possessor," or "location" in constructing sentences. It is quite possible that the specific relational semantic categories underlying normal children's earliest patterns for word combination are somewhat idiosyncratic (Braine, in press) and that children may vary considerably in the preferred level of abstraction at which they formulate these categories (cf. the comparison of Christy and Eva in this connection, pp. 156–160 above). In summary, lack of knowledge about children's "natural" tendencies in classifying relationships among objects and events constitutes a lingering obstacle to programs like Miller and Yoder's that aim at helping the child discover links between syntactic devices like word order and underlying semantic relationships.

Despite these difficulties, our current state of knowledge could perhaps be used to improve syntax-teaching programs in at least two ways. First, the way in which modeled sentences are grouped and sequenced for presentation to the child could be refined somewhat on the basis of recent findings by Bloom, Lightbown, and Hood (1975b) and Wells (1974) on the order in which normal children acquire the ability to produce sentences of various semantic types (see pp. 150–155 above). (What to do in areas where the two studies do not agree is a problem, of course). Second, the existing evidence (see p. 160 above) that children tend to follow one of two (or possibly more) alternate strategies in forming relational categories for sentence construction could be used to develop alternative syntax-teaching programs. These would differ somewhat with respect to the way sentences are initially grouped and sequenced for the child. For example, one would implicitly stress abstract relational categories like agent-action, modifier-modified, possessor-possessed, etc., while another would stress distributional consistencies in the expression of *particular* relational semantic notions like *more + X, see + X,* and so on. A child who did poorly with one program could then be switched to another that might provide a better match for his cognitive style.

Role of Negative Feedback

Any successful language training program must aim not only at encouraging children to link linguistic forms and devices with categories of experiences but also at helping them to improve on their initial guesses about these categories when they are incorrect. The techniques that can promote this improvement most effectively will probably not be found until we learn more about the little-understood process to which Clark (quoted in Bowerman, 1974a, p. 200) has called our attention: how normal children who have adopted a given hypothesis go about determining whether or not it is correct.

At this point there seems to be more to say about how normal children apparently do *not* improve their hypotheses than about how they do. This information centers on the role of *negative feedback* (by which I mean here any explicit message to the child that his linguistic performance was imperfect, e.g., "No, say it *this* way . . . ," "That's not an X, it's a Y," etc. *No* feedback, i.e., ignoring the child's utterance, may also function rather like negative feedback). Because negative feedback is such a widely used clinical tool, it seems important to review briefly some evidence that at least for normal children it is not only unnecessary and ineffective but also may actually be detrimental to progress.

Learning theory accounts of language acquisition have generally assumed that a child's language development depends heavily upon his access to feedback, both positive and negative, about the adequacy of his utterances. In recent years, however, there have been several studies that question whether the language-learning mechanisms of normal children depend to any large extent upon feedback about their performance. Brown and Hanlon (1970), for example, found evidence that children in the early stages of language acquisition receive very little information about the grammaticality of their sentences either in the form of direct praise and criticism or in the form of parental comprehension contingent upon syntactic well-formedness. These authors tentatively conclude that "the only force toward grammaticality operating on the child is the occasional mismatch between his theory of the structure of the language and the data he receives" (p. 50).

Braine (1971) argues even more strongly that "negative information cannot be necessary for first language acquisition," pointing to the conspicuous lack of information about what is not a sentence in the speech of even education-conscious middle-class parents, to evidence that children are quite insensitive to explicit corrections, and to the "universality with which language is acquired at a fairly rapid rate . . . despite a wide variety of cultural conditions and child-rearing practices" (pp. 159–160). Braine proposes that the child acquiring language is "capable of learning—and typically learns—from positive instances [i.e., actual models of speech] only" (p. 168).[21]

Evidence of this sort suggests that feedback about inadequate performance is neither required for language learning nor does it particularly accelerate its pace. However, the focus in these studies has primarily been on the possible effects of feedback upon learning grammar rather than upon acquiring word meanings. Cazden (1968, pp. 135–136) suggests that parents typically provide more negative feedback for their children's errors of word choice than for grammatical mistakes, and proposes that learning the meanings of

---

[21]In arguing against the view that knowledge of language structure is innate, Braine (1971) contended that the lack of negative feedback to the child precludes a hypothesis-testing model of how the child acquires language. He pointed out that information about what is not a sentence is essential if a hypothesis-testing child is to avoid formulating an overinclusive grammar that would generate not only all well formed sentences but ungrammatical ones as well. However, Braine noted that the terms "hypothesis" and "hypothesis testing" have been used with meanings other than those which he was challenging (p. 154). I think that his view of a language acquisition device which proceeds by "registering and accumulating properties of verbal strings and correlations between properties of strings and other events" (p. 154) is compatible with the way in which the notion of "hypothesis testing" has been used in this chapter. Specifically, the "hypotheses" with which I have been concerned are precisely the child's provisional assumptions about the nature of the "correlations between properties of strings and other events."

words may benefit more from "active tuition" than does learning grammar. Brown (1958b), like Cazden, has emphasized the tutorial role played by the parent in the child's acquisition of vocabulary. In the operation of what Brown termed "the Original Word Game," "The tutor [parent] names things . . . The player [child] forms hypotheses about the categorical nature of the things named. He tests his hypotheses by trying to name new things correctly. The tutor . . . checks the accuracy of fit between his own categories and those of the player. He improves the fit by correction" (p. 194). Similarly, " . . . the child and his father can play [the Original Word Game] as they walk along the street, father naming, child trying, father correcting" (p. 223).

In view of these assumptions about how word meaning is acquired, some recent evidence that negative feedback on adequacy of word use may actually impede a child's progress is particularly arresting. In her study of the acquisition of vocabulary by 18 children, Nelson (1973b) found that "directive" mothers, who felt that they must " 'teach' the child the right words" (p. 103) by correcting his inaccurate efforts, had children who learned relatively slowly compared to children whose mothers accepted their utterances even when these utterances were phonologically ill-formed or semantically inappropriate. Nelson concluded that "rejection or nonacceptance inevitably slows the child's learning. Active control and premature differential reinforcement retards rather than advances progress. It is the generally accepting mother who appears to be the most facilitative; selective responding, for example, correcting early errors, is unproductive" (1973b, p. 113).

Bruner (1975), in discussing his own data on mother-child interactions, concurred with Nelson's view on the effects of negative feedback, noting that "it is often the case that mother's correction of a 'mismatch' inhibits the interchange" (p. 15). He theorized that the process of language acquisition is "made possible by the presence of an interpreting adult who operates not so much as a corrector or reinforcer but rather as a provider, an expander and idealizer of utterances while interacting with the child" (p. 17).

Why should correcting the child's errors, which in theory should give him the information he needs to adjust his hypotheses about the links between language forms and nonlinguistic events, actually work to slow his progress? Nelson (1973b) hypothesizes that a directive maternal style "impose[s] the mother's views and expectations and prevent[s] the child from effectively formulating and naming his own concepts'' (p. 94). She adds that "the process of parental education may persuade him that his own categories are not to be trusted and that he must rely upon parents... to define the world'' (p. 118). In short, the effect of negative feedback may be to discourage the child from taking an active role in acquiring language. Rather than gently directing his efforts to arrive at an adult-like understanding of the concepts that particular linguistic forms encode, the frequent receipt of corrections may put such a damper on the child's initial efforts to communicate that he is deterred from actively looking further for connections between concepts and language forms. Instead, he learns in effect to wait passively to be instructed on the requisite concepts.

That negative feedback may have undesirable consequences has not yet been conclusively demonstrated, of course. Further investigation is needed, especially on the consequences of correcting syntactic errors as opposed to inaccurate word choices and on the possible contribution of the child's stage of development to the effects of correction.

Despite the need for caution, however, the possibility that negative feedback may carry with it unexpected and unwelcomed side effects has important implications for language intervention. For some populations of language-disturbed children, the consequences may be minimal. For example, severely retarded children may be so deficient in the ability to form and test hypotheses about the categories governing the use of words and other linguistic devices that whatever knowledge of language they are to achieve must essentially be "built in" in a completely artificial manner. Corrective feedback, both positive and negative, perhaps plays an indispensable role in this type of teaching.

For other more able children with language disturbances, however, it might be more profitable in the long run to work on encouraging initial efforts with little concern for deviations from adult norms. The ability to make guesses, however inaccurate, about connections between linguistic and nonlinguistic categories may well be one of the child's most valuable tools in the language acquisition process. To press for accuracy from the start, by insisting in effect that the child make discriminations or abstractions which he is not yet ready to make, may therefore be to risk losing one of the clinician's most important potential allies.

In conclusion, it appears likely that at least for some children the clinical use of negative feedback may be less effective as a procedure for teaching language than techniques designed to uncritically support and encourage initial stumbling efforts. To the extent that negative feedback is not used, however, other methods of helping the child gradually improve his inaccurate hypotheses will have to be instituted. It seems likely that effective new methods of implementing this goal may ultimately be derived from the findings of recent studies (e.g., Broen, 1972; Snow, 1972; Cross, 1975; Newport, Gleitman, and Gleitman, 1975) on the way that mothers of normal children, especially those of children who are linguistically advanced, structure their linguistic input to the child at successive stages of his development.

REFERENCES

Anglin, J. 1975. The child's first terms of reference. *In* S. Erlich and E. Tulving (eds.), Special Issue of the Bulletin de Psychologie on Semantic Memory.

Antinucci, F., and D. Parisi. 1973. Early language acquisition: A model and some data. *In* C. A. Ferguson and D. I. Slobin (eds.), Studies of Child Language Development, pp. 607–619. Holt, Rinehart, and Winston, New York.

Binnick, R. I. 1971. Studies in the derivation of predicative structures. Papers in Linguistics, 3, nos. 2 and 3.

Bloom, L. 1970. Language Development: Form and Function in Emerging Grammars. M.I.T. Press, Cambridge.

Bloom, L. 1973. One Word at a Time: The Use of Single-word Utterances before Syntax. Mouton, The Hague.

Bloom, L. 1974. Talking, understanding, and thinking. *In* R. L. Schiefelbusch and L. L. Lloyd (eds.), Language Perspectives: Acquisition, Retardation, and Intervention, pp. 285–311. University Park Press, Baltimore.

Bloom, L., P. Lightbown, and L. Hood. 1975a. Reply to commentaries on their monograph "Structure and variation in child language" by M. Bowerman and M. Maratsos. Monographs of the Society for Research in Child Development, Vol. 40, No. 2, Serial No. 160.

Bloom, L., P. Lightbown, and L. Hood. 1975b. Structure and variation in child language. Monographs of the Society for Research in Child Development, Vol. 40, No. 2, Serial No. 160.

Bloom, L., P. Miller, and L. Hood. 1975. Variation and reduction as aspects of competence in language development. *In* A. Pick (ed.), Minnesota Symposium on Child Psychology, pp. 3–55. University of Minnesota Press, Minneapolis.

Bolinger, D. 1965. The atomization of meaning. Language 41:555–573.

Bourne, L. E. 1967. Learning and utilization of conceptual rules. *In* B. Kleinmutz (ed.), Concepts and the Structure of Memory. Wiley and Sons, New York.

Bowerman, M. 1973a. Early Syntactic Development: A Cross-linguistic Study with Special Reference to Finnish. Cambridge University Press, London.

Bowerman, M. 1973b. Structural relationships in children's utterances: Syntactic or semantic? *In* T. M. Moore (ed.), Cognitive Development and the Acquisition of Language, pp. 197–213. Academic Press, New York.

Bowerman, M. 1974a. Discussion summary: Development of concepts underlying language. *In* R. L. Schiefelbusch and L. L. Lloyd (eds.), Language Perspectives: Acquisition, Retardation, and Intervention, pp. 191–209. University Park Press, Baltimore.

Bowerman, M. 1974b. Learning the structure of causative verbs: A study in the relationship of cognitive, semantic, and syntactic development. Papers and Reports on Child Language Development, Stanford University Committee on Linguistics. 8:142–178.

Bowerman, M. 1975a. Commentary on "Structure and variation in child language" by L. Bloom, P. Lightbown, and L. Hood. Monographs of the Society for Research in Child Development, Vol. 40, No. 2, Serial No. 160.

Bowerman, M. 1975b. Cross-linguistic similarities at two stages of syntactic development. *In* E. H. Lenneberg and E. Lenneberg (eds.), Foundations of Language: A Multidisciplinary Approach, pp. 267–282. Academic Press, New York.

Bowerman, M. 1976. Cognitive vs. linguistic determinism: On the origins of the concepts underlying children's early use of words. Paper presented at the Western Regional Meeting of the Society for Research in Child Development, April, Emeryville, Cal.

Bowerman, M. The acquisition of word meaning: An investigation of some current conflicts. *In* N. Waterson and C. Snow (eds.), Proceedings of the Third International Child Language Symposium. Wiley, New York. In press a.

Bowerman, M. Commentary on "Children's first word combinations" by M. D. S. Braine. Monographs of the Society for Research in Child Development. In press b.

Braine, M. D. S. 1963. The ontogeny of English phrase structures: The first phase. Language. 39(1):1–14.

Braine, M. D. S. 1971. On two types of models of the internalization of grammars. *In* D. I. Slobin, (ed.), The Ontogenesis of Grammar, pp. 153–186. Academic Press, New York.

Braine, M. D. S. Children's first word combinations. Monographs of the Society for Research in Child Development. In press.

Broen, P. A. 1972. The verbal environment of the language learning child. American Speech and Hearing Monograph, No. 17.

Brown, R. 1956. Language and Categories. Appendix to J. S. Bruner, J. J. Goodnow, and G. A. Austin. A Study of Thinking, pp. 247–312. Wiley, New York.

Brown, R. 1958a. How shall a thing be called? Psychol. Rev. 65(1):14–21. Reprinted in Brown, R., 1970. Psycholinguistics: Selected Papers by Roger Brown. pp. 3–15. The Free Press, New York.

Brown, R. 1958b. Words and Things. The Free Press, New York.

Brown, R. 1965. Social Psychology. The Free Press, New York.

Brown, R. 1973. A First Language: The Early Stages. Harvard Press, Cambridge.

Brown, R., C. Cazden, and U. Bellugi. 1969. The child's grammar from I to III. *In* J. P. Hill (ed.), Minnesota Symposium on Child Psychology, Vol. 2. University of Minnesota Press, Minneapolis.

Brown, R., and C. Fraser. 1963. The acquisition of syntax. *In* C. N. Cofer and B. S. Musgrave (eds.), Verbal Behavior and Learning. McGraw-Hill, New York.

Brown, R. and C. Hanlon. 1970. Derivational complexity and order of acquisition in child speech. *In* J. R. Hayes (ed.), Cognition and the Development of Language, pp. 11–53, Wiley, New York.

Bruner, J. S. 1975. The ontogenesis of speech acts. J. Child Lang. 2(1):1–19.

Bruner, J. S., J. J. Goodnow, and G. A. Austin. 1956. A Study of Thinking. Wiley, New York.

Carroll, J. B. 1964. Language and Thought. Prentice-Hall, Englewood Cliffs, N.J.

Cazden, C. B. 1968. Some implications of research on language development for preschool education. *In* R. Hess and R. Baer (eds.), Early Education: Current Theory, Research and Action. Aldine, Chicago.

Chomsky, N. 1965. Aspects of the Theory of Syntax. M.I.T. Press, Cambridge.

Chomsky, N. 1968. Language and mind. Harcourt, Brace, and World, New York.

Clark, E. 1973a. Nonlinguistic strategies and the acquisition of word meaning. Cognition 2(2):161–182.

Clark, E. 1973b. What's in a word? On the child's acquisition of semantics in his first language. *In* T. M. Moore (ed.), Cognitive Development and the Acquisition of Language, pp. 65–110. Academic Press, New York.

Clark, E. 1974a. Classifiers and semantic acquisition: Universal categories? Presented at the 73rd Annual Meeting of the American Anthropological Association, November, Mexico City.

Clark, E. 1974b. Some aspects of the conceptual basis for first language acquisition. *In* R. L. Schiefelbusch and L. L. Lloyd (eds.), Language Perspectives: Acquisition, Retardation, and Intervention, pp. 105–128. University Park Press, Baltimore.

Clark, E. Knowledge, context, and strategy in the acquisition of meaning. 1975. *In* D. Dato (ed.), Proceedings of the 26th Annual Georgetown University Round Table: Developmental Psycholinguistics: Theory and Applications. Georgetown University Press, Washington, D.C.

Cromer, R. 1974a. The development of language and cognition: The cognition hypothesis. *In* B. Foss (ed.), New Perspectives in Child Development, pp. 184–252. Penguin, Baltimore.

Cromer, R. 1974b. Receptive language in the mentally retarded: Processes and diagnostic distinctions. *In* R. C. Schiefelbusch and L. L. Lloyd (eds.), Language Perspectives: Acquisition, Retardation, and Intervention, pp. 237–267. University Park Press, Baltimore.

Cross, T. G. 1975. Some relationships between selected features of motherese and levels of linguistic development in speech-accelerated children. Papers and Reports on Child Language Development, Stanford University Department of Linguistics, 10:117–135.

Donaldson, M., and J. McGarrigle. 1974. Some clues to the nature of semantic development. J. Child Lang. 1(2):185–194.

Dore, J. A. 1974. A pragmatic description of early language development. J. Psycholing. Res. 3(4):343–350.

Dore, J. 1975. Holophrases, speech acts, and language universals. J. Child Lang. 2(1):21–40.

Edwards, D. 1974. Sensory-motor intelligence and semantic relations in early child grammar. Cognition 2(4):395–434.

Ervin-Tripp, S. 1971. An overview of theories of grammatical development. In D. I. Slobin (ed.), The Ontogenesis of Grammar, pp. 189–212. Academic Press, New York.

Ferrier, L. J. 1975. Dependency and appropriateness in early language development. Paper presented at the Third International Child Language Symposium, September, London.

Fillmore, C. 1968. The case for case. In E. Bach and R. T. Harms (eds.), Universals in Linguistic Theory, pp. 1–88. Holt, Rinehart and Winston, New York.

Fillmore, C. 1969. Types of lexical information. In F. Kiefer (ed.), Studies in Syntax and Semantics. Dordrecht.

Fillmore, C. 1970. The grammar of hitting and breaking. In R. Jacobs and P. Rosenbaum (eds.), Readings in English Transformational Grammar, pp. 120–133. Ginn and Co., Waltham, Mass.

Fillmore, C. 1971. Some problems for case grammar. In R. J. O'Brien (ed.), Monograph Series on Languages and Linguistics. 22nd Annual Round Table. Georgetown University Press, Washington, D. C.

Fillmore, C. An alternative to checklist theories of meaning. Unpublished paper, n.d.

Flavell, J. 1970. Concept development. In P. H. Mussen (ed.), Carmichael's Manual of Child Psychology, Vol. 1, pp. 983–1059. Wiley, New York.

Fodor, J. A., T. G. Bever, and M. F. Garrett. 1974. The Psychology of Language. McGraw-Hill, New York.

Goodson, B. D., and P. M. Greenfield. 1975. The search for structural principles in children's play: A parallel with linguistic development. Child Dev. 46:734–746.

Greenfield, P. M., K. Nelson, and E. Saltzman. 1972. The development of rule-bound strategies for manipulating seriated cups: A parallel between action and grammar. Cog. Psychol. 3:291–310.

Greenfield, P. and J. H. Smith. Communication and the Beginnings of Language: The Development of Semantic Structure in One-Word Speech and Beyond. In press.

Haselkorn, S. L. 1973. Single-word utterances: What do they mean? Unpublished paper, Harvard University.

Horgan, D. Children's strategies for the production of passives. Unpublished paper, University of Michigan.

Huttenlocher, J. 1974. The origins of language comprehension. In R. L. Solso (ed.), Theories in Cognitive Psychology: The Loyola Symposium, pp. 331–368. Lawrence Erlbaum Associates, Potomac, Md.

Ingram, D. 1971. Transitivity in child language. Language 47:888–909.

Katz, J. T. 1966. The Philosophy of Language. Harper, New York.

Katz, J. T., and J. A. Fodor. 1963. The structure of a semantic theory. Language 39:170–210.

Kernan, K. T. 1969. The acquisition of language by Samoan children. Unpublished doctoral dissertation, University of California at Berkeley.

Labov, W., and T. Labov. 1974. The grammar of *cat* and *mama*. Presented at the 49th Annual Meeting of the Linguistic Society of America, New York.

Lakoff, G. 1971. Irregularity in Syntax. Holt, Rinehart and Winston, New York.

Lenneberg, E. H. 1967. Biological Foundations of Language. Wiley, New York.

Leopold, W. 1939. Speech Development of a Bilingual Child, Vol. 1. Northwestern University Press, Evanston, Ill.

Lyons, J. 1968. Introduction to Theoretical Linguistics. Cambridge University Press, London.

MacNamara, J. 1972. Cognitive basis of language learning in infants. Psychol. Rev. 79(1):1–13.

Maratsos, M. P. 1976. Disorganization in thought and word. *In* J. Bransford and R. Shaw (eds.), Acting, Perceiving, and Comprehending. Lawrence Erlbaum Associates, Potomac, Md.

McCawley, J. D. 1971. Prelexical syntax. *In* R. J. O'Brien (ed.), Monograph Series on Languages and Linguistics. 22nd Annual Round Table. Georgetown University Press, Washington, D.C.

McCawley, J. D. 1974. (Dialogue with) James McCawley. *In* H. Parret, Discussing Language. Mouton, The Hague.

McNeill, D. 1966. The creation of language by children. *In* J. Lyons and R. J. Wales (eds.), Psycholinguistic Papers, pp. 99–115. Edinburgh University Press, Edinburgh.

McNeill, D. 1970. The Acquisition of Language: The Study of Developmental Psycholinguistics. Harper and Row, New York.

McNeill, D. 1971. The capacity for the ontogenesis of language. *In* D. I. Slobin (ed.), The Ontogenesis of Language, pp. 17–40. Academic Press, New York.

Miller, J. F., and D. E. Yoder. 1974. An ontogenetic language teaching strategy for retarded children. *In* R. L. Schiefelbusch and L. L. Lloyd (eds.), Language Perspectives: Acquisition, Retardation, and Intervention, pp. 505–528. University Park Press, Baltimore.

Miller, W., and S. Ervin. 1964. The development of grammar in child language. *In* U. Bellugi and R. Brown (eds.), The Acquisition of Language. Monographs of the Society for Research in Child Development, Vol. 29, No. 1, Serial No. 92, pp. 9–34.

Morehead, D. M., and A. Morehead. 1974. From signal to sign: A Piagetian view of thought and language during the first two years. *In* R. L. Schiefelbusch and L. L. Lloyd (eds.), Language Perspectives: Acquisition, Retardation, and Intervention, pp. 153–190. University Park Press, Baltimore.

Nelson, K. 1973a. Some evidence for the cognitive primacy of categorization and its functional basis. Merrill-Palmer Quart. Behav. Dev. 19:21–39.

Nelson, K. 1973b. Structure and strategy in learning to talk. Monographs of the Society for Research in Child Development, Vol. 38, Nos. 1–2, Serial No. 149.

Nelson, K. 1974. Concept, word, and sentence: Interrelations in acquisition and development. Psychol. Rev. 81(4):267–285.

Newport, E., L. Gleitman, and H. Gleitman. 1975. A study of mothers' speech and child language acquisition. Papers and Reports on Child Language Development, Stanford University Department of Linguistics, 10:111–116.

Olson, D. 1970a. Cognitive Development: The Child's Acquisition of Diagonality. Academic Press, New York.

Olson, D. R. 1970b. Language and thought: Aspects of a cognitive theory of semantics. Psychol. Rev. 77(4):257–273.

Olver, P., and R. Hornsby. 1966. On equivalence. In J. S. Bruner and P. Olver (eds.), Studies in Cognitive Growth, pp. 68–85. Wiley, New York.

Parisi, D. 1974. What is behind child utterances? J. Child Lang. 1(1):97–105.

Pavlovitch, M. 1920. Le Langage Enfantin: Acquisition du Serbe et du Francais par un Enfant Serbe. Champion, Paris.

Postal, P. 1971. On the surface verb "remind". In C. J. Fillmore and T. D. Langendoen (eds.), Studies in Linguistic Semantics, pp. 180–270. Holt, Rinehart and Winston, New York.

Press, M. 1974. Semantic features in lexical acquisition. Papers and Reports on Child Language Development, Stanford University Committee on Linguistics. 8:129–141.

Reber, A. 1973. On psycho-linguistic paradigms. J. Psycholing. Res. 2: 289–320.

Rosch, E. H. 1973a. Natural categories. Cog. Psychol. 4:328–350.

Rosch, E. H. 1973b. On the internal structure of perceptual and semantic categories. In T. M. Moore (ed.), Cognitive Development and the Acquisition of Language, pp. 111–144. Academic Press, New York.

Rosch, E., and C. B. Mervis. 1975. Family resemblance: Studies in the internal structure of categories. Cog. Psychol. 7:573–605.

Rosenblatt, D. 1975. Learning how to mean: The development of representation in play and language. Paper presented at the Conference on the Biology of Play, June, Farnham, England.

Schlesinger, I. M. 1971a. Learning grammar: From pivot to realization rule. In R. Huxley and E. Ingram (eds.), Language Acquisition: Models and Methods, pp. 79–89. Academic Press, New York.

Schlesinger, I. M. 1971b. Production of utterances and language acquisition. In D. I. Slobin (ed.), The Ontogenesis of Grammar, pp. 63–101. Academic Press, New York.

Schlesinger, I. M. 1974. Relational concepts underlying language. In R. L. Schiefelbusch and L. L. Loyd (eds.), Language Perspectives: Acquisition, Retardation, and Intervention, pp. 129–151. University Park Press, Baltimore.

Segerstedt, T. T. 1947. Die macht des wortes: Eine sprachsoziologie. Pan Verlag, Zurich.

Shvachkin, N. 1973. The development of phonemic speech perception in early childhood. Translated from the Russian by Elena Dernbach and edited by D. I. Slobin. In C. A. Ferguson and D. I. Slobin (eds.), Studies of Child Language Development, pp. 91–127. Holt, Rinehart and Winston, New York.

Sinclair-deZwart, H. 1971. Sensorimotor action patterns as a condition for the acquisition of syntax. In R. Huxley and E. Ingram (eds.), Language

Acquisition: Models and Methods, pp. 121–130. Academic Press, New York.

Sinclair-deZwart, H. 1973a. Language acquisition and cognitive development. *In* T. M. Moore (ed.), Cognitive Development and the Acquisition of Language, pp. 9–25. Academic Press, New York.

Sinclair-deZwart, H. 1973b. Some remarks on the Genevan point of view on learning with special reference to language learning. *In* L. L. Hinde and H. C. Hinde (eds.), Constraints on Learning, pp. 397–413. Academic Press, New York.

Slobin, D. I. 1966. Comments on McNeill's Developmental psycholinguistics. *In* F. Smith and G. A. Miller (eds.), The Genesis of Language: A Psycholinguistic Approach, pp. 85–91. M.I.T. Press, Cambridge.

Slobin, D. I. 1970. Universals of grammatical development in children. *In* W. Levelt and G. B. Flores d'Arcais (eds.), Advances in Psycholinguistic Research, pp. 174–186. North Holland Publishing Co., Amsterdam.

Slobin, D. I. 1973. Cognitive prerequisites for the development of grammar. *In* C. A. Ferguson and D. I. Slobin (eds.), Studies of Child Language Development, pp. 175–208. Holt, Rinehart and Winston, New York.

Snow, C. E. 1972. Mothers' speech to children learning language. Child Dev. 43:549–565.

Thomson, J. R. and R. S. Chapman. 1975. Who is "Daddy?" (Revisited). The status of two-year-olds' over-extensions in production and comprehension. Papers and Reports on Child Language Development, Stanford University Department of Linguistics, 10:59–68.

Tyler, S. A. 1969. Cognitive Anthropology. Holt, Rinehart and Winston, New York.

Velten, H. V. 1943. The growth of phonemic and lexical patterns in child language. Language 19:281–292.

Vygotsky, L. S. 1962. Thought and Language. 1st Ed., 1934. M.I.T. Press, Cambridge and Wiley, New York.

Wells, G. 1974. Learning to code experience through language. J. Child Lang. 1(2):243–269.

Wells, G. 1975. Interpersonal communication and the development of language. Paper presented at the Third International Child Language Symposium, September, London.

Werner, H. 1948. Comparative Psychology of Mental Development. Science Editions, Inc., New York.

Whorf, B. L. 1956. Language, Thought and Reality: Selected Writings of Benjamin Lee Whorf. Edited by J. B. Carroll. M.I.T. Press, Cambridge.

Wittgenstein, L. 1953. Philosophical Investigations. MacMillan, New York.

Zwicky, A. M. 1968. Naturalness arguments in syntax. Papers from the Fourth Regional Meeting of the Chicago Linguistics Society. University of Chicago Linguistics Department.

A Developmental Study of Language Behavior in Retarded Children

JAMES R. LACKNER

In the study reprinted here, Lackner developed extremely useful methods for comparing the linguistic systems of normal and deficient populations. First, he collected large samples (1,000 utterances per child) for five retarded children and wrote a preliminary grammar for each sample from which he constructed imitation and comprehension tasks. These imitation and comprehension tasks were then used 1) to modify the original grammars of the retarded children so that they reflected not only production but also comprehension; and 2) to establish the linguistic level of the retarded children by presenting sentences from their grammars in these two tasks to normal children. As a result, he was able to include a number of significant experimental refinements usually unmanageable in matched designs—large language samples (by collecting production data on just the deficient population), more reliable assessment of competencies (by including comprehension and imitative data), and a matching of the two groups on specific linguistic criteria (by using both comprehension and imitation tasks and mean length of sentence). Using these methods, Lackner demonstrated that the linguistic systems of retarded children follow developmental trends similar to those of normal children—a finding that complemented the earlier work of Lenneberg, Nichols, and Rosenberger (1964).

—DMM

This research was supported in part by grants from the National Aeronautics and Space Administration (Contract No. NsG 496) and the National Institute of Mental Health (Contract No. MH 05673) to Professor Hans-Lukas Teuber. The author also holds an NDEA fellowship.

Originally published in *Neuropsychologia*, 1968, 6:301–320. Reprinted with permission from Pergamon Press.

Human languages are systems of tremendous complexity which until recently have defied adequate formal description (1, 2). And yet, on the basis of unprompted fragmentary exposure to the language, the child learns to understand and create a virtually infinite number of sentences that he has never heard before (4). It remains a complete mystery how he is able to do so.

It is now possible to characterize the language capability of adult speakers of English as a set of rules which generate all the sentences understandable or produceable within the language (1–4). In the present study an attempt was made to write "grammars" (sets of rules) for retarded children at different stages of language development. The assumption was made that retardation does not yield a different form of language behavior but simply a slowing of the normal developmental sequence and a termination of development at a stage below that attained by normal children. There is independent evidence to support this hypothesis (5–7).

By comparing the grammars of children at different levels of language development, insight into the acquisition and ordering of language rules could be obtained. Thus it could be determined whether an invariant ordering exists in the acquisition of syntax, for example, whether subject-verb number agreement precedes or follows correct use of pronouns, or whether a given child may learn either first. Such knowledge would provide insight into the actual dynamics of language acquisition and could be used in evaluating competing theories of language development. The latter is beyond the scope of the present discussion, but see Chomsky (4) and Fodor (8, 9).

Using the grammars developed to describe the speech of the retarded children, sentences were constructed for presentation to normal children. Knowing the age at which a normal child understood all the sentences generated from a particular retardate's grammar, it was possible to establish a rough correlation between a given grammar and a given chronological age in normal development.

METHODS

Subjects

Five mentally retarded children, three female and two male (R. P. and W.C.), were selected for intensive study. The primary basis for selection was mental age. An ascending order from approximately 2 to 9 was desired. Children with aphasia or dysarthria were not considered. At the time of the investigation four of the children were wards of the state and were living in state homes for the mentally retarded. W.C. lives at home and goes to a special ungraded school. The chronological ages (C.A.), mental ages (M.A.), and medical histories are summarized in Table 1.

Five normal control subjects, three boys and two girls, all from middle-class families, were selected on the basis of chronological age, normal physical and mental development, and average performance in school. These children were brought in by their mothers for a single test session which lasted approximately two hours.

Tape Recordings

Each retarded child was admitted to the M.I.T. Clinical Research Center for approximately eight weeks. L.L. and R.P. came together and shared a room, as did S.W. and M.F.; W.C. came alone. A microphone was suspended from the ceiling in the children's bedroom and tape recordings of their spontaneous speech were made when they got up in the morning, during their afternoon nap (during which they usually lay in bed and talked back and forth), and at bedtime.

In addition, recordings of each retarded child's speech were made while he performed naming tasks, sentence repetition and imitation tasks, and sentence comprehension tasks administered by the experimenter.

Tape recordings were made of the normal children's speech during the same naming, sentence repetition, and sentence comprehension tasks.

Sentence Length

One thousand sentences were selected randomly from the tape recordings of each of the retarded children's spontaneous speech. The sampling was divided equally among the morning, afternoon, and bedtime tapes. These sentences were analyzed according to sentence length, and average sentence length for each retardate was calculated.

Sentence Type

The one thousand sentences for each retardate were classified according to sentence type: declarative (D), question (Q), negative (N), passive (P), negative passive (NP), and negative passive question

Table 1. Medical data for the five retarded children whose language behavior was intensively studied

Subject	Diagnosis	Major findings	C.A.	M.A.
L.L.	Encephalopathy, congenital, secondary to prematurity	Infantile spastic diplegia, mental retardation	6–5	2–3
S.W.	Encephalopathy, probably congenital with arrested hydrocephalus	Mental retardation, kypho-scoliosis, multiple skeletal anomalies	13–1	2–11
R.P.	Encephalopathy, congenital, secondary to complicated prematurity	Spastic quadriparesis, mental retardation	7–10	3–3
M.F.	Encephalopathy, early acquired, secondary to influenzal meningitis age 6 months	Left hemiparesis, mental retardation	16–2	4–9
W.C.	Encephalopathy, early acquired, sagittal sinus thrombosis or meningo-encephalitis at 2 years 10 months	Right spastic hemiparesis, right attention hemianopia	14–4	8–10

(NPQ). A tabulation was made for each retardate giving the number of each sentence type out of the total one thousand sentences.

Phrase Structure Grammar

The concept of phrase structure grammar has been developed within contemporary linguistic theory. Chomsky (1–4) has shown that the grammar of a language may be represented as a system of rules. These rules "generate" or account for all of the sentences in a given corpus or language. Such a set of rules is called a "generative grammar." It consists of three components: a syntactic component, a semantic, and a phonologic one. Only the syntactic component is of concern in the present study. If it is a transformation syntax, it is divided into two subparts: a phrase structure grammar and a set of transformational rules. The phrase-structure subcomponent is a set of ordered rewriting rules that generates strings of formatives (minimal, syntactically functioning components). Each output string is a *phrase marker*; that is, a labeled bracketing indicating the syntactic category of each substring of formatives. The transformational subcomponent maps the phrase markers of terminal strings generated by the phrase structure subcomponent into *derived phrase markers* of *T terminal strings*. These complex mapping operations called transformations are partially ordered; some are obligatory such as tense and number, while others are optional. The structural description (specification of linguistic elements and their structural relationships) of a T terminal

Table 2. Representative example of a simplified phrase structure grammar

Sentence	$\rightarrow$	NP+VP
NP	$\rightarrow$	NP_{sing}
		NP_{pl}
VP	$\rightarrow$	aux.+VP_1
VP_1	$\rightarrow$	V+NP
aux.	$\rightarrow$	C(M)(have+en)(be+ing)
M	$\rightarrow$	can, will, may, shall, must
C	$\rightarrow$	past, present

"$\rightarrow$" means "rewritten as"; "NP" stands for noun phrase; "VP" stands for verb phrase; "aux" stands for auxiliary; "M" stands for modal; "C" stands for tense; "{ }" means obligatory selection of one of the items within the brackets; "( )" denotes optical selection.

string consists of the underlying phrase markers, the derived phrase marker of the entire string, and a "transformational history."

The "output" of the phrase structure subcomponent is not a sentence but an abstract underlying form. Obligatory and optional transformations operate on this underlying form to derive the structure of actual sentences. An underlying phrase marker on which only obligatory transformations have been applied becomes the derived phrase marker of a declarative sentence. Different types of sentences (questions, passives, or negatives, and so on) are derived by the application of different sets of optional transformations.

A simplified version of a phrase structure grammar is shown in Table 2.

The derivation of the sentence "The boy had watched the sunrise" up to the phrase marker level is shown in Figure 1. The full derivation of the sentence is completed with application of the auxiliary transformation which maps the phrase marker in Figure 1 according to the rule:

SD (Structural description): (X, AF, V, Y)
SC (Structural change): $(X_1-X_2-X_3-X_4 \quad X_1-X_3+X_2-\#-X_4)$
 where AF is en, ing, C. V is M, have, be, V.
Thus by   The boy—past+have—en watch the sunrise
T aux   The boy had watched the sunrise.

The one thousand sentences for each retardate were analyzed individually and a complete derivational history was written. Phrase structure grammars were then written for each corpus. Each phrase structure grammar could generate the phrase marker of any sentence in the corpus from which it was developed. Writing phrase structure grammars for each child permitted easy comparison of rule structures.

Transformations

The derivational histories of the sentences in each retardate's corpus were analyzed and information was tabulated on the incidence of different grammatic transformations employed. For each transformation, it was noted whether it was used in full generality or in a restricted form. The set of transformations used by each child in conjunction with his phrase structure grammar is necessary and sufficient to generate "correctly" and in its entirety each sentence used by each child.

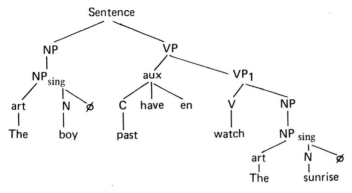

Figure 1. Phrase marker generated by phrase structure rules for the sentence "The boy had watched the sunrise."

Sentence Comprehension and Imitation Task

Novel sentences were devised for each retardate from vocabulary items and transformations present in his grammatic repertoire. In addition, sentences were constructed that were syntactically more complex than any the child had spontaneously used. Such sentences involved grammatic transformations or combinations of transformations which had not been used by the child.

These sentences were presented to the child who had been instructed so that either a verbal response, a pointing or retrieval movement, or a pantomime would demonstrate his interpretation of the syntax of the sentence. Systematic care was taken to ensure that the child could not give correct responses on the basis of key words or intonational patterns of the sentences.

The results of the sentence comprehension task were used to refine the phrase structure grammar and transformations for each retardate. If he understood a form which was not generable by his phrase structure grammar, then it was revised to include that form. Likewise if he understood a transformation or particular combination of transformations that he did not use himself, this was noted also. The phrase structure grammars and lists of transformations in the results section represent the sets of rules after modification to include forms the child understood but did not use spontaneously.

The same sentences used in the comprehension task were used in a sentence imitation (repetition) task. The sentence was read aloud to the child who had been instructed to repeat the sentence as soon as he heard it. Errors in repetition were scored according to whether the child (a) maintained the same syntactic form but dropped out non-content words (articles, conjunctions, etc.); (b) changed the syntactic form and dropped out non-content words; (c) lost the syntactic form and was just able to repeat a few disconnected words.

The sentence comprehension and imitation tasks using the same sets of sentences developed for the retardates were administered to normal subjects. It was then established for each normal child which set of rules developed for a retardate best described his own level of language attainment. This simple control was used to indicate whether there is an invariance in the ordering of rule structures in normal language behavior.

RESULTS

Sentence Length

The data on sentence length are presented in Table 3.

Sentence length, measured in words, increases with mental age. McCarthy (10) has summarized data on sentence length in children's speech. Table 4 represents data extracted from her comprehensive presentation.

There are no striking differences in sentence length for a retardate of a given mental age and a gifted child of that chronological age. However, by the age of four-and-a-half the gifted children have surpassed the most advanced retardate. It must be noted that if normal children and retarded children of the same chronological age were compared, the normal children would have longer sentences at all ages (10).

Sentence Types

The data on sentence types are summarized in Table 5. A regularity is apparent in the order of appearance of sentential types as mental age

Table 3. Average sentence length for a one thousand-sentence sample for each related child

	L.L.	S.W.	R.P.	M.F.	W.C.
Mental age (years, months)	(2–3)	(2–11)	(3–3)	(4–9)	(8–10)
Sentence length (words)	4.4	6.7	7.2	7.4	7.8

Table 4. Sentence length as a function of age in a group of gifted children studied by Fisher (information was extracted from McCarthy (10)

N	Chronological age							
	$1^1/_2$	2	$2^1/_2$	3	$3^1/_2$	4	$4^1/_2$	5
Boys	35	3.4	4.7	3.4	7.0	8.4	6.9	10.1
Girls	37	3.9	4.8	5.3	6.3	5.6	7.6	8.3
All	72	3.7	4.8	4.7	6.7	6.9	7.2	9.5

Sentence length (words)

increases. A given sentential type is found only if all sentential types of a lower order of complexity are also found. This regularity parallels the increasing complexity of the sentential types when complexity is defined in terms of the amount of structural change involved in the transformational histories of the sentence types. However, the number of transformations involved in the derivation of a sentence is not necessarily an index of its complexity. Syntactic complexity, for sentence recognition at least, seems to be a function of the degree to which surface structure cues are present to indicate the deep structure relations of the sentence (11). The present result may be considered a "natural history" approach to syntactic complexity.

Phrase Structure Grammars

The phrase structure grammars presented in Appendix A are based on an analysis of the children's recorded utterances and their performance on the sentence imitation and comprehension tasks. The rules are presented in the form developed by Chomsky (1, 2). An exami-

Table 5. Frequency of sentential types in the one thousand-sentence samples for each retarded child

M.A.	Sentence type						
	D	N	Q	NQ	P	NP	NPQ
2–3	563	275	162				
2–11	517	293	171	19			
3–3	516	337	99	37	11		
4–9	430	393	127	41	9		
8–10	438	351	119	45	24	18	5

nation of these grammars reveals that, with increasing mental age, phrase structure rules become more differentiated and specific. Omissions and redundancies of NP, VP, T, Prt, and Prep decrease as the grammars become more specific. The rules become increasingly context sensitive, and number agreement between subject and verb becomes firmly established. None of the structures generated by the rules is incompatible with adult usage; rather each phrase structure grammar seems a subset of the grammar at the next level of complexity.

These phrase structure grammars must be considered grammars of the children's competence rather than of their performance. That is, these grammars generate the underlying phrase markers of any sentence the children were able to understand and not just of sentences they spoke.

Transformations

Information is presented in Appendix B on sixteen grammatic transformations used by one or more of the retarded children. It is noteworthy that the number of transformations a child understood, as well as used, increased with mental age. Some transformations can apply to a number of different underlying phrase markers. A child may have one of these base structures, but not all of them, in his phrase structure rules. In that case he may use the transformation in a limited context only.

The combinations of transformations as well as the types of transformations understood increase as mental age increases. At earlier ages the understanding and usage of transformations singly does not imply comprehension of sentences involving multiple transformations. Only the child with a mental age of 8–10 showed full understanding and usage of all the transformations in all their possible combinations.

Sentence Comprehension and Imitation Task

It was systematically demonstrated that each retardate could understand any nonsemantically anomalous sentence constructed from vocabulary items and syntactic transformations present in his speech sample of one thousand sentences.

Test sentences were then presented with the same vocabulary items as the previous test sentences but of a more complex syntactic structure, thus involving transformations or combinations of transformations which had not been found in the child's spontaneous speech. The two children who had not used passive constructions could understand many passive constructions though not all of them. Of the two children who used passive constructions but not negative passive constructions, the older (in mental age) was able to understand all negative passive constructions in his test, but the younger was able to understand only a few (3 out of 10). The two children who did not spontaneously use passive constructions, but who could still understand some of them, were unable to understand any of the negative passive constructions used in the test.

These results received substantiation from a sentence imitation test using the sentences constructed for the comprehension task. The children were able to repeat with few errors sentences constructed from vocabulary items and of the syntactic types found in their spontaneous repertoire. This was true despite the fact that the length, in words, of the sentence exceeded the child's immediate memory span for a list of random words. It implies that if the child is able to detect structure; namely, syntactic structure, he will "chunk" the input into larger segments, thus effectively increasing his memory span (12).

The results obtained with sentences involving familiar vocabulary items but more complex syntactic structures are of interest. The children were unable to repeat correctly those sentences which they had been unable to understand. They would repeat two or three words from the sentence, usually function words, as substantives. Often these words were not repeated in the same order as they appeared in the test sentence, and their order of recall bore no relationship to syntactic structure.

With more complex sentences which they had been able to understand, the children's behavior was strikingly different. Often the child would be able to repeat the sentence correctly except for the omission of one or two function words, which were irrelevant to the syntactic structure of the sentence. These latter cases are particularly interesting. A typical example is illustrated by two sentences that were presented:

(1) John hit Mary with the ball.
(2) Mary was hit by the ball.

Each sentence has six words, and these were common to the children's speech; however, it was much easier for them to repeat sentence (1). Mistakes are also made in repeating sentence (1), but they show that the child understands the sentence structure and meaning. Some examples are:

"John hit Mary"
"John's ball hit Mary"
"John ball hit Mary"

Whereas for sentence (2):

"Mary ... the ... hit"
"Mary ... ah ... ball"
"Mary ... hit ... ah ... ball"
"The ball hit Mary"

The first three of these repetitions were produced by a child who did not understand the meaning of the sentence, while the fourth was by a child who did understand the meaning of the sentence. The differences in ease of repeatability of sentences (1) and (2) may be related to the differences in syntactic complexity of these sentences and the child's perception of the complexity. Sentence (1) is a simple declarative sentence with only obligatory transformations present in its derivation. Sentence (2), which is one of the most complicated types, is a passive construction. It is of interest to note that the last response to sentence (2), "the ball hit Mary," corresponds to the base form of (2) before the passive transformation has operated.

Many other examples of this "regression"[1] to a lower level of the grammar have been obtained. These "regressions" were made only on syntactic forms which were not part of the child's production constellation. They further illustrate the fact that production lags behind comprehension in the acquisition of language. They also constitute evidence for the psychological reality of abstract underlying structures and transformational operations.

Some preliminary results indicate that if a sentence with a transformational derivational history peculiar to the child's production capability is changed so that a particular grammatical transformation is incomplete (i.e., there is a structural element missing in the sentence), the child upon repeating the sentence may complete it. Thus the oldest child (in mental age) would complete the sentence

---

[1]Lenneberg et al. (7) found similar grammatical "regressions" during sentence repetition tests administered to Mongoloid children.

"Mary hit by the ball" as "Mary was hit by the ball." After this subject had successfully completed a number of passive transformations in this manner, sentences like the following were presented for repetition: "The ball was hit the boy." In this case many spontaneous corrections would be possible; the boy could be either the doer or the receiver of the action, i.e., it could be "The ball was hit by the boy" or "The ball was hit to (or near, past, etc.) the boy." The child always passivized this form to "The ball was hit by the boy," never noticing that this sentence is ambiguous—i.e., "by the boy" could mean "close to the boy" or the boy doing the hitting. The practice with a particular form, the passive transformation, temporarily limited the child's spontaneous corrections to passive corrections. If an ambiguous form similar to "the ball was hit the boy" was presented to the child for imitation prior to practice repetitions (which could only be spontaneously corrected as passive), then the child would respond seemingly indifferently with "The ball was hit to the boy" or "The ball was hit by the boy," i.e., he did not seem to have any bias.

Spontaneous corrections constitute further evidence for the psychological internalization of grammar. The nature of the child's spontaneous corrections should be investigated systematically since they yield valuable information about grammatic competence. If semantically deviant sentences were also "corrected" by the child, this technique might serve as a tool for investigating the nature of concept formation in young children.

The sentences used in the comprehension and imitation tasks with the retardates were also presented to normal children of different chronological ages in similar test situations. All the effects found with the retardates were also found with the normal children. They were unable to repeat correctly any sentence which they were unable to understand; they, too, showed what have been referred to above as "grammatic regressions"; they showed completion effects in grammatically incomplete sentences which they had been asked to repeat; and they showed perseveration in the types of grammatic completions after prior practice with a given form. No qualitative differences were apparent between the language behavior of the normal children and the retarded children in the sentence comprehension and imitation tasks.

The normal children were evaluated in comparison to each of the five grammars describing the language behavior of the retarded children. The results of this evaluation are presented in Table 6. An

Table 6. Shows for each normal child the grammars which he was able to understand. The grammars were written to describe the language behavior of the retarded children studied. Each grammar is identified by the initials of the retarded child and his mental age

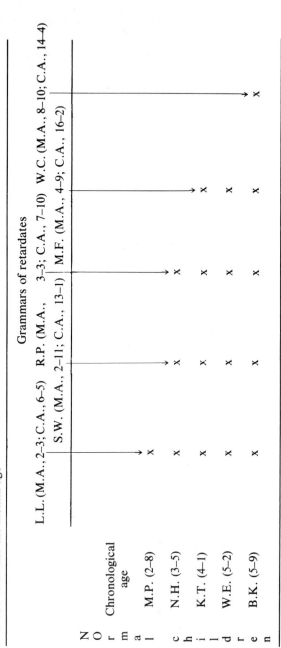

	Grammars of retardates				
Normal Chronological age	L.L. (M.A., 2–3; C.A., 6–5)	S.W. (M.A., 2–11; C.A., 13–1)	R.P. (M.A., 3–3; C.A., 7–10)	M.F. (M.A., 4–9; C.A., 16–2)	W.C. (M.A., 8–10; C.A., 14–4)
M.P. (2–8)	x				
N.H. (3–5)	x	x	x		
K.T. (4–1)	x	x	x	x	
W.E. (5–2)	x	x	x	x	
B.K. (5–9)	x	x	x	x	x

"x" indicates that the normal child understood all the sentences generated with that grammar.

These results are noteworthy in that an ordering is maintained between the complexity of the grammars and the mental ages of the retarded children, and the chronological ages of the normal children. This result should not be interpreted as meaning that the language behavior of a retarded child of a given mental age is equivalent to that of a normal child of a particular chronological age. Rather, these findings suggest that the language behaviors of normal and retarded children are not qualitatively different, that both groups follow similar developmental trends, but that the most severely retarded children become arrested in their development and remain at a lower level of normal language acquisition.

DISCUSSION

The primary concern of most studies of language acquisition has been to describe overt aspects of language behavior. This vocabulary size, sentence length, and sentence complexity (defined in terms of compound and coordinate sentence structures) have been shown to increase as the child grows older (10). Unfortunately, such measures yield little insight into the dynamics of language acquisition. Some recent studies (13, 14) utilizing the concept of a transformational grammar have attempted to write "grammars" for normal children at different stages of language development. This is a difficult task; the child's acquisition of language progresses rapidly and his grammar changes continually, so that a stable perspective of a particular level of development is virtually impossible to attain.

It has been assumed by some writers (13) that the grammar of a young child learning his native language is more primitive than that of the adult. If this were so, writing "child grammars" would give insight into the framework of a fully ramified adult grammar. But this may not in fact be true. It is possible to write more than one grammar to account for a child's recorded utterances, and there is often no way of choosing one over another. In choosing the grammar for an adult, much more is required. The grammar has to assign degrees of grammaticality or well formedness to linguistic sequences. It must also account for the creative aspect of linguistic capability—the ability to understand and produce sentences which have never been encountered before. Chomsky (4) has pointed out that most of what the child, as well as the adult, hears and produces is of such low likelihood of occurrence as to approach zero probability. In effect this means that, except for a few stereotyped phrases and social greetings, most of what is said and heard is new. This, of course, only refers to the structuring and ordering of sentences, not their vocabulary.

Until the last decade, studies of language acquisition have been based largely upon analyses of tape-recordings of children's speech. These studies are assessments of the child's language *performance* rather than his language competence, where *performance* is taken to mean the child's actual linguistic productions, and *competence* the child's ability to understand more constructions than he actually uses and his knowledge of grammatical relations (3). It is true that language competence can be studied only through language performance, but other more subtle techniques are needed in addition to tape-recordings, as many nonlinguistic factors such as mood and attention-span may influence speech. In order to assess the child's full linguistic capabilities, it is necessary to take the creative aspects of language usage into account and develop techniques for elucidating them. A variety of evidence must be brought to bear in exacting the child's full language competence.

The present study was based on the hypothesis that retarded children develop language functions in the same sequence as normal children but with increased spacing between major developmental landmarks. Retarded children were selected who had either already reached the apex of their linguistic development or who were progressing so slowly that a stable perspective of their language development was attained. With such a population of retarded children it was possible to investigate systematically the child's use and comprehension of sentences, his ability to detect and correct grammatic deviance, and his application of grammatic rules in new situations.

Individual grammars were developed for each of the five retarded children. The grammar of each child could "generate" sentences that the child spontaneously used and, in addition, forms understood by the child. The basic structures generated by the grammars of these children were presented to normal children in comprehension and imitation tasks. An ordering between complexity of the grammar and chronological age of the normal child was found. The youngest normal child could understand all forms generated with the lowest level grammar and the oldest normal child all forms generated by the most advanced grammar.

The grammars of the retarded children appear to be subsets of an adult grammar. The lower-level grammars are very general, nonspecific, and lack context sensitivity. The same is true of their transformational levels. It is only in the grammars of the children with higher mental age that the specificity and wider range of applicability, so characteristic of the adult grammar, come to the fore.

ACKNOWLEDGMENTS

I should like to thank Dr. H.-L. Teuber for the enthusiasm, encouragement, and advice he gave me during this study. I am grateful to Drs. Suzanne Corkin, Jerry Fodor, Merrill Garrett, and Thomas Twitchell for helpful discussions of the procedures and implications of this study. Dr. Corkin administered the intelligence tests and Dr. Twitchell performed the neurological examinations on the retarded children.

REFERENCES

1. Chomsky, N. 1957. Syntactic Structures. Mouton, The Hague.
2. Chomsky, N. 1964. A transformational approach to syntax. *In* J. Fodor and J. Katz (eds.), The Structure of Language: Readings in the Philosophy of Language. Prentice-Hall, Englewood Cliffs, N.J.
3. Chomsky, N. 1965. Aspects of the Theory of Syntax. M.I.T. Press, Cambridge.
4. Chomsky, N. 1959. A review of B. F. Skinner's *Verbal Behavior*. Language 35:26–58.
5. Lenneberg, E. 1962. Understanding language without ability to speak: A case report. J. Abnorm. Soc. Psychol. 65:419–425.
6. Lenneberg, E. 1964. New Directions in the Study of Language. M.I.T. Press, Cambridge.
7. Lenneberg, E., Nichols, I., and Rosenberger, E. 1964. Primitive stages of language development in mongolism. Proc. Assoc. Res. Nerv. Ment. Dis. 42:119–137.
8. Fodor, J. A. 1965. Could meaning be an r_m? J. Verb. Learn Verb. Behav. 4:73–81.
9. Fodor, J. A. 1966. How to learn to talk: Some simple ways. *In* F. Smith and G. Miller (eds.), The Genesis of Language. M.I.T. Press, Cambridge.
10. McCarthy, D. 1954. Language development in children. *In* L. Carmichael (ed.), A Manual of Child Psychology, 2nd Ed. Wiley, New York.
11. Fodor, J. A., and M. Garrett. 1967. Some determinants of sentential complexity. Perception and Psychophysics 2:289–296.
12. Miller, G. A. 1956. The magical number seven. Psychol. Rev. 63:81–97.
13. Brown, R., and C. Fraser. 1963. The acquisition of syntax. *In* N. Cofer and B. S. Musgrave (eds.), Verbal Learning and Behavior. McGraw-Hill, New York.
14. Fraser, C., U. Bellugi, and R. Brown. 1963. Control of grammar in imitation, comprehension and production. J. Verb. Learn. Verb. Behav. 2:121–135.

APPENDIX A

Phrase structure grammars of the five retarded children.

Case L.L. (C.A.=6−5, M.A.=2−3)

1. $S \rightarrow (NP)+(VP)(adv.)$

2. $VP \rightarrow aux. \left\{ \begin{matrix} be & \left\{ \begin{matrix} adj. \\ adv. \end{matrix} \right\} \\ VP_1 \end{matrix} \right\}$

3. $VP_1 \rightarrow \left\{ \begin{matrix} V \; (\left\{ \begin{matrix} (NP) \\ adj. \end{matrix} \right\}) \\ (V) \left\{ \begin{matrix} (NP) \\ adj. \end{matrix} \right\} \end{matrix} \right\}$

4. $V \rightarrow \left\{ \begin{matrix} V_s \text{ in env.} - (adj.) \\ V_t \text{ in env.} - (NP) \\ V_i \text{ in env.} - \left\{ \begin{matrix} \# \\ adv. \end{matrix} \right\} \end{matrix} \right\}$

5. $Adv. \rightarrow \left\{ \begin{matrix} \text{Prep. phrase of time} \\ \text{Prep. phrase of place} \\ \text{Adv. of time} \\ \text{Adv. of place} \end{matrix} \right\}$

6. $NP \rightarrow \left\{ \begin{matrix} NP_{sing} \\ NP_{pl} \end{matrix} \right\} \text{ in env.} \left\{ \begin{matrix} NP_{sing} \\ NP_{pl} \end{matrix} \right\} +aux.+be\text{---}.$

7. $\left\{ \begin{matrix} NP_{sing} \rightarrow (T)+N+\emptyset \\ NP_{pl} \rightarrow (T)+N+S \end{matrix} \right\}$

8. $N \rightarrow \left\{ \begin{matrix} N_h \\ N_c \end{matrix} \right\}$

9. $V_t \rightarrow \left\{ \begin{matrix} V_{t1} \text{ in env. } N_h \ldots - \\ V_{t2} \text{ in env.} \ldots - \ldots N_h \\ \left\{ \begin{matrix} V_{t31} \\ V_{t32} \end{matrix} \right\} \text{ in env. } N_h \ldots - \ldots N_c \\ V_{tx} \text{ in env.} \ldots -Prt. \end{matrix} \right\}$

10. $Prt. \rightarrow (prt.)(prt.)$
    $Prt. \rightarrow in, on, \ldots$

11. $T \rightarrow (T) \; (T)$
    $T \rightarrow a, the, \ldots$

12. $aux. \rightarrow C(M) \; (have+en) \; (be+ing)$

13. $C \rightarrow present, past$

14. $M \rightarrow can, will$

15. $\left\{ \begin{matrix} N_h \rightarrow I, me, girl \\ N_c \rightarrow it, doll, \ldots \end{matrix} \right\}$

16. $V_i \rightarrow$ come, ...

17. $V_s \rightarrow$ hurt, ...

18. $\begin{aligned} &V_{t1} \rightarrow \text{hate}, \ldots \\ &V_{t2} \rightarrow \text{scare}, \ldots \\ &V_{t31} \rightarrow \text{find, lose}, \ldots \\ &V_{t32} \rightarrow \text{eat}, \ldots \\ &V_{tx} \rightarrow \text{take}, \ldots \end{aligned}$

19. Adj. $\rightarrow$ tiny, ...

Case SW (C.A. = 13–1, M.A. = 2–11)

1. $S \rightarrow (NP)(NP) + (VP)(VP)(adv.)$

2. $VP \rightarrow aux. \begin{Bmatrix} be & \begin{Bmatrix} adj. \\ adv. \end{Bmatrix} \\ VP_1 \end{Bmatrix}$

3. $VP_1 \rightarrow V \begin{Bmatrix} (NP) \\ adj. \end{Bmatrix}$

4. $V \rightarrow \begin{Bmatrix} V_s \text{ in env.} \ldots \text{ (adj.)} \\ V_t \text{ in env.} \ldots \text{ (NP)} \\ V_i \text{ in env.} \ldots \begin{Bmatrix} \# \\ adv. \end{Bmatrix} \end{Bmatrix}$

5. $Adv. \rightarrow \begin{Bmatrix} \text{Prep. phrase of time} \\ \text{Prep. phrase of place} \\ \text{Adv. of time} \\ \text{Adv. of place} \end{Bmatrix}$

6. $NP \rightarrow \begin{Bmatrix} NP_{sing} \\ NP_{pl} \end{Bmatrix} \text{ in env. } \begin{Bmatrix} NP_{sing} \\ NP_{pl} \end{Bmatrix} + aux. + be—$

7. $\begin{Bmatrix} NP_{sing} \rightarrow (T)(T) + N + \emptyset \\ NP_{pl} \rightarrow (T)(T) + N + S \end{Bmatrix}$

8. $N \rightarrow \begin{Bmatrix} N_h \\ N_c \end{Bmatrix}$

9. $V_t \rightarrow \begin{Bmatrix} V_{t1} \text{ in env. } N_h \ldots — \\ V_{t2} \text{ in env.} \ldots — \ldots N_h \\ \begin{Bmatrix} V_{t31} \\ V_{t32} \end{Bmatrix} \text{ in env. } N_h \ldots — \ldots N_e \\ \begin{Bmatrix} V_{ta} \text{ in env. } N_h \ldots —NP \\ V_{tx} \text{ in env.} \ldots —Prt. \end{Bmatrix} \end{Bmatrix}$

10. $\begin{aligned} &Prt. \rightarrow (Prt.)(Prt.) \\ &Prt. \rightarrow in, on \end{aligned}$

11. $\begin{aligned} &T \rightarrow (T)(T) \\ &T \rightarrow a, the \end{aligned}$

12. $aux. \rightarrow C(M)(have + en)(be + ing)$

13. C→Present, Past

14. M→Can, will, may

15. $\begin{cases} N_h \to \text{I, you, boy} \\ N_c \to \text{dog, doll, it} \end{cases}$

16. $V_i \to$ come,...

17. $V_s \to$ hurt, burn,...

18. $\begin{aligned} &V_{t1} \to \text{like,}\ldots \\ &V_{t2} \to \text{scare, surprise,}\ldots \\ &V_{t31} \to \text{find,}\ldots \\ &V_{t32} \to \text{eat, drink,}\ldots \\ &V_{ta} \to \text{want,}\ldots \\ &V_{tx} \to \text{take, put,}\ldots \end{aligned}$

19. adj.→little, big,...

Case R.P. (C.A.=7−10, M.A.=3−3)

1. S→(NP)(NP)+VP(adv.)

2. $\text{VP} \to \text{aux.} \begin{Bmatrix} \text{be} \begin{Bmatrix} \text{adj.} \\ \text{adv.}_{.1} \end{Bmatrix} \\ \text{VP}_1 \end{Bmatrix}$

3. $\text{VP}_1 \to \text{V} \begin{Bmatrix} \text{(NP)(NP)} \\ \text{adj.} \end{Bmatrix}$

4. $\text{V} \to \begin{Bmatrix} V_s \text{ in env.} \ldots \text{ adj.} \\ V_t \text{ in env.} \ldots \text{ NP(NP)} \\ V_i \text{ in env.} \ldots \begin{Bmatrix} \# \\ \text{adv.} \end{Bmatrix} \end{Bmatrix}$

5. $\text{Adv.} \to \begin{Bmatrix} \text{Prep. phrase of time} \\ \text{Prep. phrase of place} \\ \text{Adv. of time} \\ \text{Adv. of place} \end{Bmatrix}$

6. $\text{Adv}_1 \to \begin{Bmatrix} \text{Prep. phrase of place} \\ \text{Adv. of place} \end{Bmatrix}$

7. $\text{NP} \to \begin{Bmatrix} \text{NP}_{\text{sing}} \text{ in env. NP}_{\text{sing}} + \text{aux. be—} \\ \text{NP}_{\text{pl}} \text{ in env. NP}_{\text{pl}} + \text{aux. b—} \end{Bmatrix}$

8. $\begin{Bmatrix} \text{NP}_{\text{sing}} \to \text{(T)T} + \text{N} + \emptyset \\ \text{NP}_{\text{pl}} \to \text{(T)T} + \text{N} + \text{S} \end{Bmatrix}$

9. $\text{N} \ldots \begin{Bmatrix} N_h \\ N_c \\ N_{ab} \text{ in env.} \begin{Bmatrix} \# \\ V_t \end{Bmatrix} \text{(T)T} \ldots \emptyset \end{Bmatrix}$

10. $V_t \rightarrow \left\{ \begin{array}{l} V_{t1} \text{ in env. } N_h \dots - \\ V_{t2} \text{ in env. } - \dots N_h \\ \left\{ \begin{array}{l} V_{t31} \\ V_{t32} \end{array} \right\} \text{ in env. } N_h \dots - \dots N_h \\ \left\{ \begin{array}{l} V_{ta} \text{ in env. } N_h \dots -\text{Comp.} \\ V_{tx} \text{ in env.} \dots -\text{Prt.} \end{array} \right. \end{array} \right\}$

11. Prt.→Prt.(Prt.)
    Prt.→in, on, . . .

12. T→T(T)
    T→a, the, . . .

13. aux.→C(M)(have+en)(be+ing)

14. C→Present, Past

15. M→Can, will, must

16. $\left\{ \begin{array}{l} N_h \rightarrow \text{boy, girl, me} \dots \\ N_c \rightarrow \text{it, truck, toy,} \dots \\ N_{ab} \rightarrow \text{love,} \dots \end{array} \right\}$

17. $V_i \rightarrow$ come, . . .

18. $V_s \rightarrow$ tickle, hurt, . . .

19. $V_{t1} \rightarrow$ love, like, . . .
    $V_{t2} \rightarrow$ scare, . . .
    $V_{t31} \rightarrow$ find, . . .
    $V_{t32} \rightarrow$ smoke, eat, drink, . . .
    $V_{ta} \rightarrow$ want, believe, . . .
    $V_{tx} \rightarrow$ take, bring, put, . . .

20. adj.→happy, little, . . .

Case M.F. (C.A.=16-2, M.A.=4-9)

1. S→NP(NP)+VP(adv.)

2. $VP \rightarrow \text{aux.} \left\{ \begin{array}{l} \text{be} \left\{ \begin{array}{l} \text{adj.} \\ \text{adv.}_1 \end{array} \right\} \\ VP_1 \end{array} \right\}$

3. $VP_1 \rightarrow V \left(\left\{ \begin{array}{l} NP(NP) \\ \text{adj.} \end{array} \right\} \right.$

4. $V \rightarrow \left\{ \begin{array}{l} V_s \text{ in env.} \dots \text{ adj.} \\ V_t \text{ in env.} \dots \text{ NP} \\ V_i \text{ in env.} \dots \left. \right\} \begin{array}{l} \# \\ \text{adv.} \end{array} \right\}$

5. $\text{Adv.} \rightarrow \left\{ \begin{array}{l} \text{Prep. phrase of time} \\ \text{Prep. phrase of place} \\ \text{Adv. of time} \\ \text{Adv. of place} \end{array} \right.$

6. $Adv._1 \begin{cases} \text{Prep. phrase of place} \\ \text{Adv. of place} \end{cases}$

7. $NP \rightarrow \begin{cases} NP_{sing} \text{ in env. } NP_{sing} + aux. + \begin{cases} \text{be} \\ \text{become} \end{cases} \{ — \} \\ NP_{pl} \text{ in env. } NP_{pl} + aux. + \begin{cases} \text{be} \\ \text{become} \end{cases} \{ — \} \end{cases}$

8. $\begin{cases} NP_{sing} \rightarrow T(T) + N + \emptyset \\ NP_{pl} \rightarrow T(T) + N + S \end{cases}$

9. $N \rightarrow \begin{cases} N_h \\ N_c \\ N_{ab} \text{ in env. } \begin{Bmatrix} \# \\ V_t \end{Bmatrix} \{ T(T) — \emptyset \} \end{cases}$

10. $\begin{cases} NP_{sing} \rightarrow T + N + \emptyset \\ NP_{pl} \rightarrow T + N + S \end{cases}$

11. $N \rightarrow \begin{cases} N_h \\ N_c \\ N_{ab} \text{ in env. } \begin{Bmatrix} \# \\ V_t \end{Bmatrix} \{ T — \emptyset \} \end{cases}$

12. $V_t \rightarrow \begin{cases} V_{t1} \text{ in env. } N_h \ldots — \\ V_{t2} \text{ in env. } — \ldots N_h \\ \begin{Bmatrix} V_{t31} \\ V_{t32} \end{Bmatrix} \text{ in env. } N_h \ldots — \ldots N_c \\ V_{ta} \text{ in env. } N_h \ldots — Comp. \\ V_{tx} \text{ in env.} — Prt. \end{cases}$

13. $Prt. \rightarrow$ out, in, up . . .

14. $T \rightarrow$ a, an, the

15. $aux. \rightarrow C(M)(have + en)(be + ing)$

16. $C \rightarrow$ Present, past

17. $M \rightarrow$ can, will, . . .

18. $\begin{cases} N_h \rightarrow \text{I, you, he, etc.} \\ N_c \rightarrow \text{it, table, book, etc.} \\ N_{ab} \rightarrow \text{it, truth, sincerity, etc.} \end{cases}$

19. $V_i \rightarrow$ arrive, depart, . . .

20. $V_s \rightarrow$ feel, hurt, . . .

21. $\begin{aligned} &V_{t1} \rightarrow \text{like, . . .} \\ &V_{t2} \rightarrow \text{scare, . . .} \\ &V_{t31} \rightarrow \text{find, . . .} \\ &V_{t32} \rightarrow \text{eat, smoke, . . .} \\ &V_{ta} \rightarrow \text{catch, want, keep, . . .} \\ &V_{tx} \rightarrow \text{take, bring, . . .} \end{aligned}$

22. $adj. \rightarrow$ little, old, . . .

Case W.C. (C.A.=14−4, M.A.=8−10)

1. S→NP+VP(adv.)

2. $VP→aux. \left\{ \begin{array}{l} be \quad \left\{ \begin{array}{l} Pred. \\ adv._{\cdot 1} \end{array} \right\} \\ VP_1 \end{array} \right\}$

3. $VP_1→V \; (\left\{ \begin{array}{l} NP \\ Pred. \end{array} \right\}$

4. $V \left\{ \begin{array}{l} V_t \text{ in env.—NP} \\ V_s \text{ in env.—Pred.} \\ V_i \text{ in env.—} \left\{ \begin{array}{l} \# \\ adv. \end{array} \right\} \end{array} \right\}$

5. $Adv.→ \left\{ \begin{array}{l} \text{Prep. phrase of time} \\ \text{Prep. phrase of place} \\ \text{Adv. of time} \\ \text{adv. of place} \end{array} \right\}$

6. $Adv._{\cdot 1}→ \left\{ \begin{array}{l} \text{Prep. phrase of place} \\ \text{Adv. of place} \end{array} \right\}$

7. $NP→ \left\{ \begin{array}{l} NP_{sing} \\ NP_{pl} \end{array} \right\}$

8. $Pred.→ \left\{ \begin{array}{l} NP_{sing} \text{ in env. } NP_{sing}+aux. \left\{ \begin{array}{l} be \\ become \end{array} \right\} — \\ NP_{pl} \text{ in env. } NP_{pl}+aux. \quad \left\{ \begin{array}{l} be \\ become \end{array} \right\} — \\ Adj. \end{array} \right\}$

9. Adj.→(very)+adj.

10. $V_t→ \left\{ \begin{array}{l} V_{t1} \text{ in env. } N_h \ldots — \\ V_{t2} \text{ in env. } — \ldots N_h \\ \left\{ \begin{array}{l} V_{t31} \\ V_{t32} \end{array} \right\} \text{ in env. } N_h \ldots — \ldots N_c \\ \left\{ \begin{array}{l} V_{ta} \text{ in env. } N_h \ldots —comp. \\ V_{tx} \text{ in env.} \ldots —prt. \end{array} \right. \end{array} \right\}$

11. Prt.→in, on, down . . .

12. T→a, the . . .

13. Aux.→C(M)(have+en)(be+ing)

14. C→present, past

15. M→can, will, . . .

16. $\left\{ \begin{array}{l} N_h→\text{I, you, he} \ldots \\ N_c→\text{it, chair, bird, book} \ldots \\ N_{ab}→\text{it, truth} \end{array} \right\}$

17. $V_i→$come, leave . . .

18. $V_s \rightarrow$ feel, hurt ...

$V_{t1} \rightarrow$ hate, like ...
$V_{t2} \rightarrow$ scare, ...

19. $V_{t31} \rightarrow$ find, ...
$V_{t32} \rightarrow$ smoke, eat, ...
$V_{ta} \rightarrow$ catch, want ...
$V_{tx} \rightarrow$ take, put, ..

20. adj. $\rightarrow$ tiny, mean ...

APPENDIX B

Syntactic transformations used by the five retarded children.

1. *Number*

   a. Structural Description: $(NP_{sing}, Present, X)$
       Structural Change: $X_1 - X_2 - X_3 \rightarrow X_1 - S - X_3$
   b. S.D. $(NP_{pl}, Present, X)$
       S.C. $X_1 - X_2 - X_3 \rightarrow X_1 - \emptyset - X_3$

Four of the children S.W. (C.A.=13-1, M.A.=2-11), R.P. (C.A.=7-10, M.A.=3-3), M.F. (C.A.=16-2, M.A.=4-9), and W.C. (C.A.=14-4, M.A.=8-10) understood and used both parts of the number transformation. L.L. (C.A.=6-5, M.A.=2-3) confused them; for example, in (a) and (b) "X_2" went to either "S" or "$\emptyset$."

2. *Auxiliary*

   S.D. (X, Af, v, Y)

   S.C. $X_1 - X_2 - X_3 - X_4 \rightarrow X_1 - X_3 + X_2 - \# - X_4$

   where Af is en, ing, or C. v is M, have, be, V.

L.L. and S.W. understood and used this transformation with Af$\rightarrow$C, and v$\rightarrow$V. R.P. understood the full form but did not always use it consistently. M.F. and W.C. understood and used the full form.

3. *Object*

   S.D. $(X, V_t$ or Prep, $T + \left\{ \begin{array}{c} he \\ I \end{array} \right\}, Y)$

S.C. $X_1-X_2-X_3-X_4 \rightarrow X_1-X_2-X_3+M-X_4$

The application of this transformation yields "I hurt him" instead of "I hurt he." It applies to the second NP in the pretransformed stage of $NP+V_t+Comp$ he, thus resulting in "him" not "he" in these sentences.

L.L. and S.W. understood and used this transformation for S.D.:

$$X, V_t, T+ \left\{ \begin{matrix} he \\ I \end{matrix} \right\}, Y$$

but not for the frame $NP+V_t+Comp$ he. The latter frame cannot be generated by their phrase structure grammars. R.P., M.F., and W.C. understood and used this transformation for both frames.

4. *Word boundary*

S.D. (X, Y), where $X=v$ or $Y=Af$

S.C. $X_1-X_2- \rightarrow X_1-\#-X_2$

All of the children understood and used this transformation correctly.

5. *Do*

S.D.(X, #, Af, Y)

S.C. $X_1-X_2-X_3-X_4 \rightarrow X_1-X_2-do+X_3-X_4$

All five children understood a restricted form of this transformation with $Af \rightarrow C$, but only R.P., M.F., and W.C. understood and used it in full generality with $Af \rightarrow en$, ing C.

6. *Negation*

S.D. (a) NP, C, VP_1
     (b) NP, C+M, X
     (c) NP, C+have, X
     (d) NP, C+be, X
S.C. $X_1-X_2-X_3 \rightarrow X_1-X_2+n't-X_3$

L.L. and S.W. understood and used part (a). R.P. understood all four forms and used (a) often and (b), (c), and (d) infrequently. M.F. and W.C. understood and used all four forms.

7. *Interrogative*

S.D. (a) NP, C, VP$_1$
     (b) NP, C+M, X
     (c) NP, C+have, X
     (d) NP, C+be, X
S.C. $X_1-X_2-X_3 \rightarrow X_2-X_1-X_3$

L.L. and S.W. understood and used part (a), and they also understood part (b). R.P. understood all four forms though he had some trouble in using (b), (c), and (d) correctly. M.F. and W.C. understood and used all four forms correctly.

8. *Wh-*

$$\text{S.D. } (X, \text{ T}+ \begin{bmatrix} \text{he} \\ \text{it} \end{bmatrix} (M)+ \begin{bmatrix} \o \\ S \end{bmatrix}, Y)$$

S.C. $X_1-X_2-X_3 \rightarrow \text{Wh-}+X_2-X_1-X_3$

L.L., S.W., and R.F. used stereotyped questions of this form; however, they did not understand the generalized "Wh-" question transformation. M.F. and W.C. understood and used the form correctly.

9. *Affirmation*

S.D. (a) NP, C, VP$_1$
     (b) NP, C+M, X
     (c) NP, C+have, X
     (d) NP, C+be, X
S.C. $X_1-X_2-X_3 \rightarrow X_1-X_2+A-X_3$

L.L. and S.W. understood and used part (a); they also understood part (b). R.P. used forms (a) and (b) and understood all four forms. M.F. and W.C. understood and used all four forms.

10. *Contraction*

S.D. (a) NP, X, VP$_1$
     (b) NP, X+M, Y
     (c) NP, X+have, Y
     (d) NP, X+be, Y
S.C. $X_1-X_2-X_3 \rightarrow X_1-X_2+\text{cntr.}-X_3$

L.L. and S.W. understood and used part (a). R.P. understood all four forms but only used (a) and (b). M.F. and W.C. understood and used all four forms.

11. *Inversion*

S.D. (S, C+V_t, Y)

S.C. $X_1-X_2-X_3 \rightarrow X_3-X_2-$(easily . . .)

R.P., M.F., and W.C. understood this transformation, but only W.C. used it.

12. *Elliptic*

S.D. (a) NP, C, VP_1
    (b) NP, C+M, X
    (c) NP, C+have, X
    (d) NP, C+be, X
S.C. $X.-X_2-X_3 \rightarrow X_1-X_2$

L.L., S.W., and R.P. understood and used part (a). R.P. also used part (b). M.F. and W.C. understood and used all four forms.

13. *Separation*

(a) S.D. (X, V_t, Prt., NP)
    S.C. $X_1-X_2-X_3-X_4 \rightarrow X_1-X_2-X_4-X_3$

(This transformation is obligatory if X_4 is a pronoun.)

(b) *S.D. (X, V_t, Comp., NP)
    S.C. $X_1-X_2-X_3-X_4 \rightarrow X_1-X_2-X_4-X_3$

All five children understood and used both forms of the transformation, except L.L. and S.W. who did not use part (b).

14. *So*

S.D. (a) NP, C, VP
    (b) NP, C+M, X
    (c) NP, C+have, X
    (d) NP, C+be, X
S.C. $X_1-X_2-X_3 \rightarrow$ so$-X_2-X_1$

Only W.C. understood and used this transformation. R.P. and M.F. understood it but did not use it.

15. *Deletion*

　　S.D. (X, V_{t32}, Y)

　　S.C. $X_1 - X_2 - X_3 \rightarrow X_1 - X_2$

All five children understood and used this transformation.

16. *Passive*

$$\text{S.D. (NP, aux., } V_t, \text{ NP} \begin{Bmatrix} \text{adv} \\ - \end{Bmatrix})$$

　　S.C. $X_1 - X_2 - X_3 - X_4 - X_5 \rightarrow X_4 - X_2 + be + en + X_3 - by + X_1 - X_5$

Only R.P., M.F., and W.C. understood and used passives. Occasionally L.L. and S.W. understood a passive but they appeared to have memorized that specific sentence rather than the generalized "frame."

The Development of Base Syntax in Normal and Linguistically Deviant Children

DONALD M. MOREHEAD and DAVID INGRAM

There have been contradictory reports in the literature comparing the structure of the linguistic systems of normal and deficient children: Lenneberg, Nichols, and Rosenberger (1964) and Lackner (1968, reprinted this volume) suggested similar linguistic development, while Menyuk (1964) and Lee (1966) reported dissimilar development. Morehead and Ingram attempted to resolve this controversy by matching normal and deficient populations on linguistic criteria (mean morphemes per utterance) rather than on the standard criteria of age, IQ, and socioeconomic level. Their comparative study gives a detailed linguistic analysis of a rather large population of children (15 subjects per group) from which a number of specific linguistic measures were derived to compare aspects of productive use. Morehead and Ingram reported highly similar linguistic systems in the two groups for the early period of language acquisition corresponding to Brown's (1973) five levels of linguistic development. An important difference found, however, was that despite similar linguistic systems the deficient children were not able to use their systems with the same degree of efficiency. Since the two groups of children were compared at levels where the utterances were of similar length, Morehead and Ingram concluded that deficient children, at least at the levels studied, add words to their existing constructions but fail to develop the combinatorial potential that is inherent in

This research was supported by the National Institute of Neurological Diseases and Stroke Research Grant NS-07514 to the Institute for Childhood Aphasia, Stanford University School of Medicine.

Originally published in the *Journal of Speech and Hearing Research*, 1973, 16:330–352. Reprinted with permission from the American Speech and Hearing Association.

their grammars—a failure evidenced by less frequent use rather than absence of more complex structures within a given level of linguistic development. A recent review of grammatical studies and their relationship to assessment and habilitation of language-deficient children can be found in Crystal, Fletcher, and Garman (1976).

—AEM

Recent evidence suggests that early stages in first language acquisition are difficult to impede, save extensive brain dysfunction. Even with serious brain dysfunction, the prognosis for acquiring a base linguistic system is good due to the plasticity of the developing brain (Lenneberg, 1967). Despite this apparent strong biological component for language development, some children (including those without any detectable brain dysfunction) experience extreme difficulty in acquiring language. Children with language learning deficits are generally felt to demonstrate a linguistic system which is, in certain significant aspects, quite different from that of the normal child. Recently this "qualitative" difference has become the central focus for studying linguistically deviant children (Menyuk, 1964; Lee, 1966).

Menyuk's (1964) early work represents the first systematic attempt to compare normal and deviant children using descriptive techniques based on Chomsky's early transformational grammar. She matched both groups according to the criteria of age, IQ, and socioeconomic level and found that the utterances sampled from linguistically deviant children were qualitatively different from those of normal children. The deviant group used fewer transformations and produced more restricted or ungrammatical forms than did the normal group. More forms were also omitted by the deviant group in constructions representing the phrase structure, transformational, and morphological levels of the grammar. Since few statistically significant differences were found, these results were projected to indicate possible trends of differences between normal and deviant children. Menyuk (1964) did include a comparison between a normal 2-year-old child and a deviant 3-year-old child. The dissimilarities were again found to be more predominant than the similarities. Unfortunately, only two subjects were compared and they were not matched on any specific criteria.

Lee (1966) has designed four levels of developmental sentence types for comparing syntactic progress in normal and deviant children. In constructing the sentence types which postulate different linguistic levels, she followed closely the review of early work in syntactic development by McNeill (1966). As a pilot test of the utility of the sentence types and linguistic levels, a language sample of a normal 3-year-old was compared with that of a deviant 4¹/₂-year-old. The normal child's utterances more closely approximated the sentence types at all four levels than did the utterances of the deviant child. The deviant child also omitted constructions that were not omitted by the normal child. From these findings, Lee concluded that there were qualitative differences between the two children.

The research involving rule-based behavior indicates that all level or stage changes appear to be qualitative (Piaget, 1970; Kohlberg, 1968). Therefore, unless subjects are matched according to criteria which reflect a specific level or stage of development, qualitative differences can be predicted on the basis that each level or stage of development is radically different from the preceding or following stage of development. Moreover, recent work in language acquisition suggests that finding qualitative differences may not be unique to deviant and normal subjects but may reflect linguistic level differences indicating individual differences in cognitive function and linguistic experience (Bloom, 1970; Brown, Cazden, and Bellugi, 1968).

During the past decade, research on language acquisition has focused primarily on the development of syntax. It appears that the most active period for learning base syntax is between 18 months and 4 years and that this period reflects distinct levels of linguistic development (McNeill, 1970; Brown, 1973). Thus, it is of considerable heuristic value to compare linguistically deviant children with normal children actively engaged in acquiring base syntax at a similar level of linguistic development.

In addition, recent methods for writing children's grammars vary considerably from the early notions of "pivot" grammars which do not include the important distinction between deep (semantic) and surface (phonetic) structure (Bloom, 1970; Brown, 1973). Moreover, if deep and surface structure relations are to be adequately described, it is necessary to collect contextual information for each utterance in a language sample. For example, noun + noun constructions, such as *Daddy bike,* may require two or more deep or semantic interpretations to separate the possessive form from such forms as the subject-object. Grammar writing for young children now includes analysis of both aspects of grammatical relations (Bloom, 1970; Brown, 1973).

This study compared language samples that included contextual information of young normal children (18–36 months of age) actively engaged in learning syntax with those of deviant children of a comparable level of linguistic development.

METHOD

Subjects

The subjects were 15 normal and 15 linguistically deviant children, selected to represent as nearly as possible the five linguistic levels previously determined by Brown (1973) (Table 1). Mean morpheme per utterance was used as the criterion for establishing linguistic level and, thus, for matching the two groups. This measure appears to be a more reliable indicator of linguistic development than is chronological age up to 3 years of age (Menyuk, 1969; Bloom, 1970; Brown, 1973). The normal group, representing the age when children acquire a base syntactic system, was selected from the population of the Bing Nursery School at Stanford University and within the Stanford community. The deviant group was selected from the deviant population of children currently seen at the Institute for Childhood Aphasia, Stanford University School of Medicine.

Three children from each group were assigned to each of Brown's five linguistic levels of development on the basis of the mean number of morphemes per utterance. Level I utterances were slightly over two morphemes in length while level V utterances had slightly under six morphemes per utterance (Table 1). The age range for the normal group was 1 year, 7 months to 3 years, 1 month, with a mean age of 2 years, 4 months. The deviant group had an age range of 3 years, 6 months to 9 years, 6 months, with a mean age of 6 years, 7 months (Table 1). The normal group was screened for speech and hearing pathologies. The linguistically deviant group was restricted to children who lacked sufficient intellectual or physiological impairment to account for their difficulties in acquiring language.

An adaptation of Chomsky's (1965) transformational grammar by Rosenbaum (1967) was modified (Ingram, 1970) and grammars were written for the language sample of each child. Rosenbaum's (1967) system was selected because it incorporates many of the recent advances on Chomsky's (1965) transformational grammar. The grammars accounted for all but 8 to 10% of the utterances in the samples of both groups. The two groups representing five linguistic levels of development were compared according to 1) phrase structure rules,

Table 1. Description of normal and deviant language-development groups in terms of mean number of morphemes per utterance (MM/U), mean sample size (number of relational utterances), and mean age (months) [a]

Linguistic level	Brown MM/U	Normal			Deviant		
		MM/U	Sample size	Age	MM/U	Sample size	Age
I	2.00 (1.75–2.25)	2.23 (2.11–2.26)	76.7	20.0	2.33 (2.10–2.43)	79.7	62.3
II	2.50 (2.26–2.75)	2.72 (2.51–2.66)	100.7	21.0	2.83 (2.69–2.98)	155.3	71.3
III	3.13 (2.76–3.50)	3.70 (3.41–3.92)	223.3	33.0	3.80 (3.31–4.05)	161.0	70.0
IV	3.75 (3.51–4.00)	4.67 (4.62–4.86)	242.7	34.3	4.53 (4.33–4.73)	200.0	88.0
V	4.63 (4.01–5.25)	5.61 (5.36–5.88)	234.0	33.7	5.83 (5.21–6.50)	147.7	104.6

[a]For comparison, the five levels of linguistic development defined by Brown (1973) are presented. The ranges on which the mean for each group was based are given immediately below the MM/U in parentheses.

2) transformations, 3) construction types or surface realization of major syntactic categories and their relations, 4) inflectional morphology, and 5) select lexical items representing minor syntactic categories.

The five linguistic aspects were chosen because they reflect a broad assessment of base syntactic development. Phrase structure and transformational analysis presumably characterize some important aspects of the child's knowledge about sentence organization. From the characterization of the child's grammars, certain criterion measures were developed for comparing type and occurrence of phrase structures and transformations. In addition, construction types, inflectional morphology, and minor lexical items were selected to represent important aspects of the realization of the child's knowledge of sentences. However, the grammars were written from production data and therefore, in any strict sense, assess only language performance.

Language Samples

The language samples were collected under three conditions: free play with the experimenter or parent, elicitation while playing with toys, and elicitation while viewing a standard children's book. It was generally possible to collect samples under all three conditions, except for the younger normal children and the lower-level deviant children. In cases where it was not possible to collect the samples under all three conditions, samples were collected only under the first two conditions. The utterances of each sample were divided into spontaneous and response utterances to determine whether the conditions under which the samples were collected had differential effects for the two groups. The proportion of spontaneous to response utterances was nearly identical in both groups. In addition, separate grammars were written for the two types of utterances in each sample to determine any differences which might be attributed to performance variables or to the conditions used in collecting the samples. Since few differences were found, the spontaneous and response utterances were pooled for group comparison.

A high-fidelity tape recorder was used to record the linguistic interaction between the adult and the child. In addition, an observer recorded the initial adult utterance, if any, the child's utterance, and the adult expansion of the child's utterance. The expansion of the child's utterance was determined by the contextual information collected when the language sample was taken. In this way, the child's intended grammatical and semantic relations were more closely approximated than by tape recordings or by observational records alone. The utterances were then transcribed, generally on the same day, and compared with the observer's records before a final decision was made.

The mean number of utterances for the normal group was 175.5, while the mean number of utterances for the deviant group was 148.7. One-word utterances were not included in the samples of either group so that each utterance would involve base syntactic relations. In addition, each linguistic structure had to occur two or more times in order to be considered part of the child's productive system.

Established criteria do not exist for determining what is an adequate sample size for linguistic analysis. The number of utterances used in analysis varies considerably from less than 100 (Menyuk, 1964) to over 1500 utterances (Bloom, 1970). Brown (1973) collected nearly 700 utterances, including one-word utterances, for each time sample. We attempted to collect 100 relational utterances for the two lower levels of linguistic development and 200 relational utterances for the three upper levels of linguistic development (Table 1).

RESULTS

The phrase structure grammars necessary to account for the utterances of the normal and deviant groups were nearly identical for each of the five linguistic levels. Minor differences did appear in the grammars for the two groups at each of the five levels, but these differences were no greater than the differences between subjects within the same group at a given linguistic level. Two examples of the phrase structure grammars taken from one normal and one deviant child are presented in the list below. (A detailed description of the grammars is available in Ingram (1972). In the list, S = sentence, NP = noun phrase, VP = verb phrase, N= noun, VB = verb, ( ) = optional element, # = sentence boundary, and → = "is rewritten as."

Normal–MM/U-2.66
S → # (NP) (VP) #
VP → VB (NP)
NP → N (S)

Deviant–MM/U-2.69
S → # (NP) (VP) #
VP → VB (NP)
NP → N (S)

Conditions:
1. (S) is either an adjective or possessive
2. (S) only occurs when S → NP

Conditions:
1. (S) is a possessive

2. (S) only occurs when S → NP

The two grammars are equally capable of generating or accounting for the utterances of either the deviant or the normal child, with the single restriction that the deviant child does not include adjective modifiers in constructions taking the form N (S).

The two groups also did not differ significantly in the proportion of utterances reflecting only phrase structure relations across the five linguistic levels. The proportion of phrase structure utterances, however, decreased with linguistic level for both the normal and the deviant groups. Nearly half the utterances at level II were without transformations, while fewer than 10% of the utterances were without transformations at level III. This rather dramatic change in phrase-structure-transformations ratio between levels II and III held for both groups. Despite these similarities, when chronological age rather than linguistic level was considered, the deviant group showed a marked delay as compared to normals in both onset and acquisition time. The age disparity between the two groups, although the data are cross-sectional, suggests that the onset time for base syntax or two-word utterances may be delayed as much as $3^1/_2$ years in the deviant child. Moreover, acquisition time, or the time required to go from level I to V, is nearly $2^1/_2$ years longer for the deviant children. This delay in onset and acquisition time also holds for transformations, construction types, inflections, and minor lexical categories. Given that normal children initiate and acquire base syntax between approximately 18 and 40 months, it appears that deviant children take on the average three times as long to initiate and to acquire base syntax.

Forty different transformations were identified in the language samples of both groups. The transformations of each group were assigned absolute ranks based on their frequency of occurrence. Listed in Appendix A are the transformations in order of their frequency of occurrence and examples of each. The examples provide the base form and its corresponding transformation. A Spearman rank order correlation was significant ($r = 0.96, t = 21.30, p < 0.01$), indicating a high degree of similarity between the two groups (Figure 1). In addition, the 40 transformations were compared individually for the two groups using the Mann-Whitney U Test (Siegel, 1956). Four of the 40 transformations showed significantly greater occurrence for the normal group (question *do* segment, locative segment, demonstrative segment, and noun deletion), while two showed significantly greater occurrence for the deviant group (progressive affix segment and plural affix segment).

To determine any differences between the two groups on infrequently occurring transformations, the 40 transformations were divided into frequently occurring and infrequently occurring transformations. Figure 1 shows that a convenient boundary exists between the frequent and infrequent transformations near the twentieth transformation for both groups. In order that an equal number of transformations could be compared, they were divided between the 20 most frequent and the 20 least frequent transformations. A sign test (Siegel, 1956) revealed no significant difference for the frequent transformations, while the infrequent transformations revealed a significant difference ($p < 0.06$). This finding suggests that while no overall significance exists between the two groups on the frequency of transformation types, the least frequent transformations, and those presumably more difficult as a group, were used significantly less by the deviant group. The infrequent transformations occurred 5% or less of the time (Figure 2).

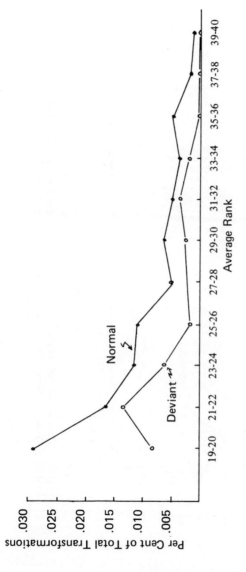

Figure 1. The average rank of the 40 transformations and their frequency of occurrence for the normal and deviant groups.

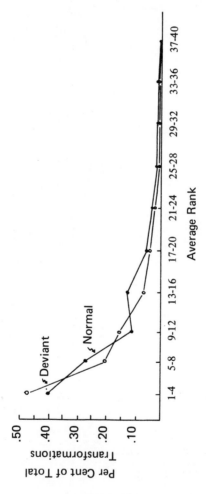

Figure 2. The average rank of the infrequently occurring transformations and their frequency of occurrence for the normal and deviant groups.

An additional check was made to determine if more specific differential use of the transformations could be found between the two groups. The 40 transformations were divided into four general categories: 1) sentence transformations, 2) noun transformations, 3) verb transformations, and 4) question transformations. Significant linguistic level effects were found for sentence transformations (F = 8.70; df = 4,20; $p<0.01$), noun transformations (F = 48.62; df = 4,20; $p<0.01$), verb transformations (F = 10.90; df = 4,20; $p<0.01$), and question transformations (F = 9.32; df = 4,20; $p<0.01$). However, significant group differences were only found for question transformations (F = 27.17; df = 1,20; $p>0.01$). In addition, a significant interaction was found between linguistic level and the two groups (F = 5.53; df = 4,20; $p<0.01$) as a result of one deviant child having more questions marked at level I, namely, marking questions by wh forms. The normal group had significantly more question transformations at the four remaining linguistic levels (Figure 3).

As noted previously, significant level differences were found for the transformation types across the five linguistic levels of development. Appendices B and C present the transformations showing their frequency of occurrence at each of the five linguistic levels for the normal and deviant groups, respectively. The lists indicate that both the number and type of transformations change with each advancing level of development, and that there is considerable

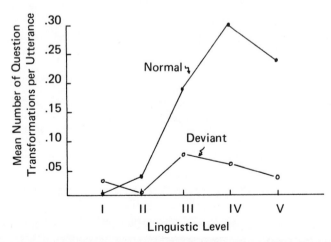

Figure 3. The mean number of question transformations per utterance plotted across five linguistic levels for the normal and deviant groups.

similarity in the transformational development of both groups across the five levels of linguistic development.

Finally, the mean number of transformations used per utterance was compared across the five linguistic levels for the normal and the deviant groups. No significant group differences were found; however, a significant level effect was found ($F = 66.12$; $df = 4,20$; $p<0.001$), and the differences were significant for both groups across all five levels (Figure 4). When the mean number of transformations per utterance was correlated with age, the normal group had high positive correlation ($r = 0.905$; $p<0.01$), while the deviant group did not ($r = 0.161$). Again, a major finding is the marked delay in onset time and acquisition period for acquiring transformations.

The construction types depict major lexical categories (that is, noun, verb, and noun$_{\text{object}}$) and their syntactic frames or possible relations (noun-verb and noun-verb-noun). Appendix D provides a list of the construction types and their corresponding examples. Two measures were derived from the construction types and compared for the two groups. The mean number of major lexical categories per construction type was used to determine the occurrence of major categories in a variety of contexts for the language samples of both groups. Significant differences were obtained between the two groups

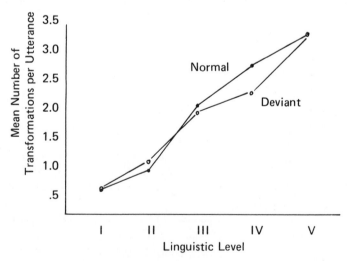

Figure 4. The mean number of transformations per utterance plotted across five linguistic levels for the normal and deviant groups.

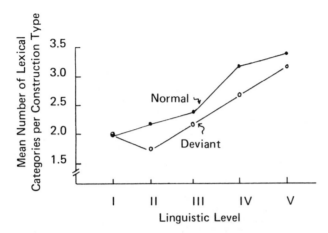

Figure 5. The mean number of lexical categories per construction type plotted across five linguistic levels for the normal and deviant groups.

($F = 5.51$; $df = 1,20$; $p<0.05$) and across the five linguistic levels ($F = 23.81$; $df = 4,20$; $p<0.01$) (Figure 5). In addition, each syntactic relation or construction type was compared for the two groups on the basis of their frequency of occurrence. A low positive correlation was found when the construction types of the two groups were compared ($r = 0.435$). When age was correlated with mean number of lexical categories per construction type, the normals showed a high correlation with age ($r = 0.762$; $p<0.01$), while the deviant group showed a low correlation with age ($r = 0.136$). The deviant group again manifested the marked delay in onset and acquisition time.

Linguistic level was found to be significant for both groups on the number of lexical categories per construction type. Appendices E and F provide a list of the construction types in order of their frequency of occurrence for both groups at each of the five linguistic levels. The tables show that the type and number of constructions change for both groups with advancing levels of linguistic development. However, as the tables clearly indicate, the deviant group did not use major linguistic categories in as many different contexts or syntactic frames as did the normal group.

To determine the relative increase in the occurrence of inflections such as plurals, past tense, and possessives across the five linguistic levels, word-morpheme ratios were computed for the two groups. Utterances had either no inflections (that is, two words, two morphemes) or two inflections (that is, five words, seven mor-

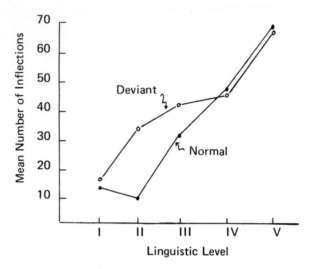

Figure 6. The mean number of inflections plotted across five linguistic levels for normal and deviant groups.

phemes). The findings were not significant for the two groups, although a significant level effect was again found ($F = 71.81$; $df = 4,20$; $p > 0.01$). The deviant group did, however, have more inflections at the first three linguistic levels than did the normal group (Figure 6).

Select lexical items that represent minor lexical categories were also compared for the two groups. The lexical items used for comparison were pronouns, demonstratives, wh forms, prepositions, and modals. The primary concern in this comparison was to determine at what level and in what order the various items appeared for the two groups. Thus, two or more children at each linguistic level had to use a given lexical category two or more times in order for that category to be included. With the exception of pronouns, only minor variance was found in the level or order of appearance of the lexical items. The deviant group by level III had 16 pronouns, while the normal group had nine pronouns (Tables 2 and 3).

DISCUSSION

Clearly, the major differences between normal and linguistically deviant children of comparable linguistic level were not in the organization or occurrence of specific subcomponents of their base syntac-

Table 2. Linguistic level and order of appearance of minor lexical categories for the normal group

Linguistic category level	Normal				
	I	II	III	IV	V
Pronouns	I	my	you	we	her
		it	your	he	its
		it	she	they	her
		me	them	us	our
				you	
				him	
Demonstratives	that	this	these	those	
Wh forms		where	what	why	when
Prepositions		in	to	up	down
		on	with	at	of
				for	off
					like
					through
					over
					by
					under
					near
Modals	want		gonna	can	won't
			hafta	will	don't
				could	can't
				shall	gotta
					would
					may
					might
					should
					better

tic systems. Rather, the significant differences were found in the onset and acquisition time necessary for learning base syntax and the use of aspects of that system, once acquired, for producing major lexical items in a variety of utterances.

Phase structure development showed similar rule systems as well as similar occurrences of phrase structure utterances for both groups across five distinct levels of linguistic development. No overall differences were found in the frequency or type of transformational rules produced in the language samples of the two groups. Of

Table 3. Linguistic level and order of appearance of minor lexical categories for the deviant group

Linguistic category level	Deviant				
	I	II	III	IV	V
Pronouns	it I my	him	you it he them they she we you us your his	her their	its our
Demonstratives	that	these	this	those	
Wh forms		what		where why	how when who
Prepositions	in		on at to down	with like	up of off out of for over by after into about except
Modals			gonna	can't can want	don't won't gotta would hadda will could didn't hafta

the 40 transformations compared, only six were significantly different in their frequency of occurrence. Four occurred more frequently in the normal group (question *do* segment, locative, demonstrative, and noun deletion), while two occurred more frequently in the deviant group (progressive affix and plural affix). Moreover, the mean number of transformations per utterance used by the two groups across the five levels was not significantly different, indicating no severe limitation in the deviant group in the number of transformations used in a particular utterance.

The two groups were also compared on frequently occurring and infrequently occurring transformations and four general categories of transformations. Significant differences were found between the two groups on infrequently occurring transformations and the general category of questions. The findings for differences in infrequently occurring transformations are similar to those of Menyuk (1964). Of the 28 transformations compared according to the number of subjects using a given transformation, she found that 16 were used less often by the deviant group. However, only one of the 16 transformations was used significantly less often by the deviant group. The relative absence of questions in the language samples of our deviant group could reflect either a general sampling problem inherent to children with productive liabilities or a general sociolinguistic posture which is antithetical to seeking information by linguistic code. It would be difficult to assume that question transformations are psychologically more difficult than many of the transformations acquired by the deviant group.

The development of inflections and minor lexical items (pronouns, demonstratives, wh forms, prepositions, and modals) was also compared in the two groups. In the case of minor lexical items only minor variance was found in the level or the order of appearance of these items, save pronouns. The deviant group at level III had 16 pronouns as compared to nine for the normal group at the same level. The amount of time the deviant group spent between levels II and III seemed to allow them to make more distinctions between self and others and for those distinctions to be linguistically marked.

There were no significant differences in the development of inflections as determined by word-morpheme ratio. The deviant group, however, did have more inflections at the first three levels of linguistic development than did the normal group. This difference was also reflected in the comparison of transformation types where both the progressive and plural affix were used significantly more often by the deviant group. These differences may reflect both the increased time the deviant group spends at each linguistic level and the fact that, since inflections are not introduced by major transformations, they are easily detected in the surface structure. Where cognitive distinctions such as number are easily marked linguistically, as in the case of plural forms, deviant children appear to be somewhat less delayed in acquiring these forms.

Though few differences were found in phrase structure or transformational development, save infrequently occurring transformations and questions and including the mean number of transformations used per utterance, significant differences were found in the number of major lexical categories per construction type. Since the two groups were matched on essentially mean number of major lexical categories per utterance, the finding suggests a specific restriction in the variety of construction types produced by the deviant group. This finding is further supported by the low correlation found when types of constructions were compared between the two groups. Transformations also affect the variety of construction types produced, and a significant difference was found between the two groups on the infrequently occurring transformations.

These results suggest that deviant children, when studied at their particular level of linguistic development, are not seriously deficient in the organization of phrase structure rules, types of transformations, number of transformations used in a given utterance, minor lexical items, or inflectional morphology. However, deviant children appear to be significantly restricted in their ability to develop and select grammatical and semantic features which allow existent and new major lexical categories to be assigned to larger sets of syntactic frames. To clarify the specific deficit these results indicate, it is useful to discuss the findings in terms of Chomsky's transformational grammar.

In Chomsky's (1965) linguistic system, the base component of transformational grammar is composed of a categorical component and a lexicon. The categorical component handles general properties of the deep structure, such as defining grammatical relations and determining base syntactic order. The lexicon handles less general properties, including 1) properties relevant to the function of transformational rules, 2) information regarding the varied placement of lexical items in a sentence, and 3) properties relevant to semantic interpretation. Thus, grammatical relations and order are determined by the categorical component, while contextual restrictions are determined by the lexicon.

The utterances produced by the deviant group manifested grammatical relations and base syntactic order not unlike those of the normal group. The finding of similar phrase structure rules indicates that the two groups were not different in their base organization for the categorical component. However, the members of the deviant group were restricted in their ability to handle less general properties specified by the lexicon as indicated by the finding of differences on infrequently occurring transformations and major lexical categories per construction type. When compared with normals they also showed a low correlation on types of constructions. Specifically, these restrictions would involve the function of transformational rules and information regarding varied placement of lexical items in a sentence. In addition, the delay in both onset and acquisition time for base syntax is, no doubt, closely related to the deviant group's ability to assign an adequate semantic interpretation to an utterance in comprehension as well as production. The properties of the lexicon are also closely related to how well formed an utterance is. Our observations of the language samples and those of Menyuk (1969) suggest that the utterances produced by deviant children are on the whole less well formed than those of normal children.

Other research has also found that linguistically deviant children have a specific deficit that is quantitatively different from normal children rather than a general qualitative deficit. Studies in both language and cognitive development have reported similar findings on the nature of the difference between normal and deviant children. Lackner (1968) reported that retarded children of different mental ages do not develop language behavior differently from normal children, but rather reflect a delayed developmental sequence with lower terminal development.

Inhelder (1966) and de Ajuriaguerra (1966) have studied the cognitive development of linguistically deviant children. Using Piagetian-type tasks, they found that children with a slow rate of linguistic development frequently had normal operative or base intellectual development. However, the deviant children did show a specific deficit in the figurative or representational aspect of cognition. According to Piaget's (1970) cognitive developmental theory, the child develops a general capacity for representation which includes aspects of perception, deferred imitation, imagery, symbolic play, drawing, and dreaming, as well as language.

The importance of these findings is that they suggest a possible relationship between delayed language acquisition and an underlying aspect of cognitive development. For example, perceptual deficiencies, which in Piaget's theory are related to general representational development, have long been suspect in children who fail to develop language at a normal rate. Such deficits have been demonstrated in both vision and audition (Mackworth, Grandstaff, and Pribram, 1973; Rosenthal and Eisenson[1]). Moreover, Grandstaff et al.[2] have shown that the performance of linguistically deviant children on a simple match to sample task is not different from that of normal children in terms of the number of matching errors. However, the deviant children take nearly twice as long, once the correct symbol is located, to indicate their choice. These findings are consistent with those of Inhelder (1966) and de Ajuriaguerra (1966), who also found that deviant children are deficient in their ability to evoke reproductive images necessary for solving simple matching tasks. Lovell, Hoyle, and Siddall (1968) report a significant correlation between mean morpheme per utterance length and the amount of time spent in symbolic play by linguistically deviant children, that is, the fewer the number of morphemes per utterance, the less time spent in symbolic play.

    In summary, linguistically deviant children do not develop bizarre linguistic systems that are qualitatively different from normal children. Rather, they develop quite similar linguistic systems with a marked delay in the onset and acquisition time. Moreover, once the linguistic systems are developed, deviant children do not use them as creatively as normal children for producing highly varied utterances. Other research suggests that these children may have a specific cognitive deficit in all aspects of representational behavior which, according to Piaget, includes language.

ACKNOWLEDGMENTS

We want to express our appreciation to Jon Eisenson, project director, and to Dorothy Tyack, Judith Johnston, and Geoffrey Loftus for their assistance in the collection and analysis of the data. The authors also wish to extend special gratitude to Mark Solomon whose general competencies were invaluable to the study.

---

[1]W. Rosenthal and J. Eisenson, unpublished study on auditory temporal order in aphasic children as a function of selected stimulus features, personal communication.

[2]N. Grandstaff, N. Mackworth, A. de la Pena, and K. Pribram, unpublished study on model formation and use by aphasic and normal children during visual matching to sample, personal communication.

REFERENCES

Ajuriaguerra, J. de., 1966. Speech disorders in childhood. *In* C. Carterette (ed.), Brain Function: Speech, Language and Communication, Vol. III. Univ. of California Press, Los Angeles, Cal.

Bloom, L. 1970. Language Development: Form and Function in Emerging Grammars. M.I.T. Press, Cambridge, Mass.

Brown, R. 1973. A First Language. Harvard Univ. Press, Cambridge, Mass.

Brown, R., C. Cazden, and U. Bellugi. 1968. The child's grammar from I to III. *In* S. P. Hill (ed.), The 1967 Minnesota Symposium on Child Psychology. Univ. of Minnesota Press, Minneapolis.

Chomsky, N. 1965. Aspects of the Theory of Syntax. M.I.T. Press, Cambridge, Mass.

Ingram, D. 1970. IBM Grammar II: An adaptation for child language. *In* Papers and Reports on Child Language Development. Stanford University, December.

Ingram, D. 1972. The development of phrase structure rules. Lang. Learn. 22:23–33.

Inhelder, B. 1966. Cognitive development and its contribution to the diagnosis of some phenomena of mental deficiency. Merrill-Palmer Quart. 12:299–319.

Kohlberg, L. 1968. Early education: A cognitive developmental view. Child Devel. 39:1013–1062.

Lackner, J. 1968. A developmental study of language behavior in retarded children. Neuropsychol. 6:301–320.

Lee, L. 1966. Developmental sentence types: A method for comparing normal and deviant syntactic development. J. Speech Hearing Dis. 31:311–330.

Lenneberg, E. H. 1967. Biological Foundations of Language. John Wiley, New York.

Lovell, K., H. Hoyle, and M. Siddall. 1968. A study of some aspects of the play and language of young children with delayed speech. J. Child Psychol. Psychiat. 9:41–50.

Mackworth, N., N. Grandstaff, and K. Pribram. 1973. Prolonged orientation to pictorial novelty in severely speech-disordered children. Neuropsychol. 11:443–450.

McNeill, D. 1966. Developmental psycholinguistics. *In* F. Smith and G. A. Miller (eds.), The Genesis of Language: A Psycholinguistic Approach. M.I.T. Press, Cambridge, Mass.

McNeill, D. 1970. The Acquisition of Language: The Study of Developmental Psycholinguistics. Harper and Row, New York.

Menyuk, P. 1964. Comparison of grammar of children with functionally deviant and normal speech. J. Speech Hearing Res. 7:109–121.

Menyuk, P. 1969. Sentences Children Use. M.I.T. Press, Cambridge, Mass.

Piaget, J. 1970. Piaget's theory. *In* P. H. Mussen (ed.), Carmichael's Manual of Child Psychology, Vol. I. John Wiley, New York.

Rosenbaum, P. 1967. IBM Grammar II, IBM Research Report.

Siegel, S. 1956. Non-parametic Statistics. McGraw-Hill, New York.

APPENDIX A

Forty transformations listed in order of their combined frequency of occurrence for the normal and deviant groups. The examples provide the base form and its corresponding transformation.

Frequent types	*Examples*
Pronoun segment	Ball ... it
Article segment	Ball ... a ball
Demonstrative segment	Ball ... that ball
Preposition segment	Table ... on table
Adjective genitive placement	Ball red ... red ball
Verb particle segment	I go ... I go up
Type placement	Not I go ... I not go
Locative segment	Table ... there
Plural affix segment	Ball ... balls
Progressive affix segment	He go ... he going
Copula contraction	It is red ... it's red
Number segment	Ball ... two ball
Wh question	That ball ... what ball
Noun deletion	That ball ... that
	John's ball ... John's
Progressive auxiliary segment	He running ... he is running
Present affix segment	He run ... he runs
Conjunction segment	Boy girl ... boy and girl
Question tone	Ball ... ball?
Infinitive segment	I want go ... I want to go
Question *do* segment	I go ... do I go?

Infrequent types	*Examples*
Copula segment	It red ... I make it red
Negative *do* segment	I not go ... I do not go
Tag question	I go ... don't I?
Past affix segment	I bat ... I batted
Question copula shift	He is going ... is he going?
Pronoun number segment	Them ... two of them
Complete all segment	It gone ... it all gone
Genitive affix segment	John ball ... John's ball
Vocative segment	I go home ... Daddy, I go home
Verb deletion	I pick up ball ... I up ball
Verb qualifier statement	I run ... I (really) run
	(just)
Inchoative segment	It red ... it got red
Particle intensive segment	I go up ... I go (way) up
	(back)
	(right)
Verb particle shift	I pick ball up ... I pick up ball
Question modal shift	He will go ... will he go?

Noun object shift	Hit ball ... ball hit
Stative verb particle shift	Ball up ... up ball
Object noun retention	Hit ball ... hit it ball
Repetition segment	I go ... I go again
Demonstrative copula	That there ... that's there

APPENDIX B

Transformation types pooled in order of their frequency of occurrence across five linguistic levels of development for the normal group.

Linguistic Level I

Locative segment
Pronoun number segment
Adjective genitive placement
Complete all segment
Pronoun segment
Vocative segment
Preposition segment
Stative verb particle shift
Demonstrative segment
Verb qualifier segment
Plural affix segment

Linguistic Level II

Adjective genitive placement
Article segment
Verb particle segment
Plural affix segment
Demonstrative segment
Pronoun segment
Locative segment
Noun object shift
Question tone
Noun deletion
Wh question
Pronoun number segment
Verb deletion
Object noun retention
Noun retention

Linguistic Level III

Demonstrative segment
Verb particle segment
Pronoun segment

Preposition segment
Article segment
Locative segment
Noun deletion
Pronoun number segment
Adjective genitive placement
Wh question
Type placement
Present affix segment
Question tone
Progressive affix segment
Plural affix segment
Infinitive segment
Copula contraction
Progressive auxiliary segment
Conjunction segment
Question do segment
Inchoative segment
Tag question
Question copula shift
Copula segment
Past affix segment
Verb particle shift
Verb deletion

Linguistic Level IV

Pronoun segment
Demonstrative segment
Type placement
Preposition segment
Adjective genitive placement
Article segment
Wh question
Verb particle segment

Copula contraction
Pronoun number segment
Locative segment
Noun deletion
Progressive affix segment
Plural affix segment
Question *do* segment
Progressive auxiliary segment
Present affix segment
Question tone
Conjunction segment
Tag question
Copula segment
Infinitive segment
Genitive affix segment
Question copula shift
Negative *do* segment
Question modal shift
Verb particle shift
Past affix segment

Linguistic Level V

Demonstrative segment
Pronoun segment
Article segment

Preposition segment
Type placement
Adjective genitive placement
Verb particle segment
Locative segment
Present affix segment
Copula contraction
Wh question
Noun deletion
Pronoun number segment
Plural affix segment
Question *do* segment
Infinitive segment
Conjunction segment
Negative *do* segment
Copula segment
Past affix segment
Question copula shift
Pronoun number segment
Progressive affix segment
Question tone
Tag question
Progressive auxiliary segment
Question modal shift
Verb qualifier segment
Repetition segment
Genitive affix segment

APPENDIX C

Transformation types pooled in order of their frequency of occurrence across five linguistic levels of development for the deviant group.

Linguistic Level I

Adjective genitive placement
Plural affix segment
Number segment
Locative segment
Wh question
Verb particle segment
Pronoun segment
Progressive affix segment
Demonstrative segment
Preposition segment
Copula contraction
Noun object shift

Linguistic Level II

Article segment
Preposition segment
Progressive affix segment
Adjective genitive placement
Verb particle segment
Pronoun segment
Demonstrative segment
Plural affix segment
Verb deletion
Genitive affix segment
Locative segment
Number segment

Noun deletion
Demonstrative copula

Linguistic Level III

Article segment
Pronoun segment
Preposition segment
Demonstrative segment
Progressive affix segment
Plural affix segment
Adjective genitive placement
Locative segment
Verb particle segment
Type placement
Wh question
Noun deletion
Conjunction segment
Copula contraction
Number segment
Question tone
Progressive auxiliary segment
Copula segment
Demonstrative copula
Pronoun number segment
Past affix segment
Verb particle shift
Present affix segment

Linguistic Level IV

Article segment
Pronoun segment
Preposition segment
Adjective genitive placement
Verb particle segment
Demonstrative segment
Plural affix segment
Progressive affix segment
Progressive auxiliary segment
Type placement
Question tone

Locative segment
Wh question
Conjunction segment
Number segment
Noun deletion
Infinitive segment
Copula contraction
Negative *do* segment
Past affix segment
Copula segment
Inchoative segment
Present affix segment
Demonstrative copula

Linguistic Level V

Pronoun segment
Article segment
Preposition segment
Adjective genitive placement
Type placement
Progressive auxiliary segment
Progressive affix segment
Copula contraction
Plural affix segment
Demonstrative segment
Verb particle segment
Conjunction segment
Number segment
Present affix segment
Infinitive segment
Past affix segment
Negative *do* segment
Locative segment
Wh question
Genitive affix segment
Verb qualifier segment
Copula segment
Question *do* segment
Question tone
Complete all segment

APPENDIX D

Construction types listed in order of their combined frequency of occurrence for the normal and deviant groups. Key: N = noun, VB = verb, V = copula, T

=type, N_o = object noun (used only with copula), N_{loc} = locative noun, Q = question, S = sentence, and Tag_Q = tag question.

Construction Types	Examples
N-VB-N	Me find a hotdog
VB-N	Open the gate
N-VB	Ducks are quacking
N	Another hamburger
N-V-N_o	That's a ladder
N-T-VB-N	We will take this out
N-V-N_{loc}	Here's an owl
VB	Go up
N-S	Pretty shoe
Q-N-VB-N	Do you got a hurt?
N-T-VB	I hafta go
Q-N-V-N_{loc}	Where the dolls?
Q-N-V-N_o	Is this a hot dog?
N-VB-N-N	We have the bear for dinner
N-V-N_o-S	Here's my knee
Q-N-VB	Are you going?
VB-N-N	Put truck in garage
N-VB-N-S	I have blue box
Q-N-T-VB-N	Would you do this?
N-T-VB-N-N	I'm gonna put playdough on it
T-VB-N	Gonna take this
Q-N-T-VB	Why doesn't this stay up?
VB-N-VB-N	Let's take this off
VB-N-S	Fix Jim's car
N-VB-VB-N	He went to fix the baby
T-VB	Gonna go
N-T	It isn't
N-S-V-N_{loc}	Round balls in there
Q-N-T-VB-N-N	Where the people gon drive on it?
Q-N-S-V-N_{loc}	Where's his dinner?
VB-N-VB	Make this one stand up
Q-VB-N	Go here?
Q-N-S-V-N_o	What is the name of this color?
VB-N-VB-N-N	Let's put these back in here
N-T-VB-N-S	I can't ride a big bike
N-VB-N-Tag_Q	You put these back, okay?
Greeting N	Hi daddy
N-S-VB-N	My mommy put them on
N-S-VB	Poor snail cry
Q-N	Right here?
N-T-VB-N-Tag_Q	I have to put this away, okay?
Q-N-VB-N-N	What do you put in there?
N-T-V-N_o	There's no water
N-VB-S	I think it is
Q-N-T	It can?

$Q-N-V-N_o-N_{loc}$	What's that in there?
$Q-N-V-N_o-S$	That mommy' bear?
Adverb-S-S	When you have your mask on, it scares you
$N-V-N_{loc}-Tag_Q$	It was in here, wasn't it?
S-what-S	Look what he taked from you
VB-VB	Want go
N-S-S	A big big bear
VB-VB-N	Gonna put these away
VB-N-VB	Make this one stand up
$N-V-N_o-Tag_Q$	There a train, right?
Q-N-VB-N-S	When do we had the marble game?
Q-N-VB-VB	Who mommy want hit?
N-VB-N-VB	You make it stand up
N-VB-N-VB-N	I want you stay there
N-VB-VB	I want talk
S-because-S	This doesn't open because it's too little
N-VB-N-N-S	I have this in my program
$N-V-N_o-N$	There's more in it
N-N	Elephants and giraffes
T-VB-N-N	Gonna take this one home
N-say-S	My mom said I can't go
N-VB-VB-N-S	I want to go to the marble game
$N-S-V-N_o$	Dog name's Jippy
N-VB-N-S-N	It's got my thumb in this
N-T-VB-N-N-S	He will throw ball in his eyes

APPENDIX E

Construction types pooled in order of their frequency of occurrence across five linguistic levels of development for the normal group.

Linguistic Level I	*Linguistic Level II*
N-VB	VB-N
VB-N	N-VB-N
N	N-S
VB	N-VB
$N-V-N_{loc}$	VB
$N-V-N_o$	N
N-S	$N-V-N_{loc}$
T-VB	VB-N-S
N-VB-N	VB-N-N
N-T	Q-N-VB
Greeting-N	N-S-VB
$N-S-V-N_{loc}$	N-VB-N-S
VB-N-S	Greeting-N
$Q-N-V-N_o$	VB-VB
	N-S-S

Linguistic Level III

VB-N
N-VB-N
N-VB
VB
N
N-V-N$_o$
N-V-N$_{loc}$
Q-N-V-N$_{loc}$
VB-N-N
N-S
N-T-VB-N
N-VB-N-N
Q-N-VB-N
T-VB-N
N-T-VB
Q-N-VB
Q-N-V-N$_o$
N-V-N$_o$-S
N-VB-VB-N
N-VB-VB
N-S-VB-N
N-VB-S
Q-N-T-VB-N
VB-N-S
VB-VB-N
T-VB
VB-N-VB
N-T
N-VB-N-S-N

T-VB-N
Q-N-T-VB-N
VB-N-VB-N
VB
Q-VB-N
N-VB-N-S
N-V-N-N
N-VB-VB-N
N-T-VB-N-N
Q-N-S-V-N$_{loc}$
Q-N-V-N$_{loc}$
Q-N
VB-N-VB
Q-N-S-V-N$_o$
Q-N-T
N-T
Q-N-VB-N$_o$-N$_{loc}$
Q-N-VB-N$_o$-S
VB-N-S
Q-N-T-VB-N-N
N-S-VB
VB-N-VB-N-N
N-T-VB-N-Tag Q
N-V-N$_o$-Tag Q
Q-N-VB-N-S
Q-N-VB-N-N
Q-N-VB-VB
N-VB-N-Tag Q

Linguistic Level IV

N-VB-N
N-VB
N-T-VB-N
Q-N-VB-N
N-V-N$_o$
VB-N
N
Q-N-V-N$_o$
N-T-VB
N-V-N$_{loc}$
Q-N-T-VB
N-S
Q-N-V-N
Q-N-VB
N-V-N$_o$-S
VB-N-N

Linguistic Level V

N-VB-N
N-T-VB-N
N-VB
N-T-VB
N-V-N$_{loc}$
VB-N
Q-N-VB-N
N-VB-N-N
N-V-N$_o$-S
N-V-N$_o$
Q-N-V-N$_o$
N
N-T-VB-N-N
N-VB-N-S
Adverb + S + S
Q-N-V-N
VB-N-VB-N

N-T-VB-N-S
N-S-V-N_{loc}
Q-N-T-VB-N
Q-N-T-VB-N-N
N-T-V-N_o
VB-N-VB-N-N
Q-N-VB
N-V-N_{loc}-Tag Q
N-VB-N-Tag Q
S-what-S
Q-N-S-V-N_{loc}
Q-N-T-VB
T-VB-N

VB-N-S
N-says S
N-S-VB-N
N-VB-VB
S-because-S
N-VB-S
N-VB-N-N-S
N-VB-VB-N
VB-N-VB
Q-N-S-V-N_o
Q-N-VB-N-N
N-T-VB-N-Tag Q
V-VB-N-VB-N

APPENDIX F

Construction types pooled in order of their frequency of occurrence across five linguistic levels of development for the deviant group.

Linguistic Level I

VB-N
N-S
N-VB
N
VB
N-V-N_{loc}
Q-N-V-N_{loc}
N-VB-N
N-V-N_o-S
VB-N-S
T-VB
T-VB-N
N-S-V-N_{loc}

Linguistic Level II

VB-N
N
VB
N-S
N-VB
N-VB-N
N-V-N_{loc}
VB-N-S
N-V-N_o
N-VB-N-S

N-S-VB-N
N-N
VB-N-N
N-T-VB
N-S-VB

Linguistic Level III

N
VB-N
N-VB-N
N-VB
VB
N-V-N_o
N-V-N_{loc}
N-S
Q-N-V-N_o
Q-N
N-VB-N_o-S
N-VB-N-N
N-T-VB-N
N-S-V-N_{loc}
Q-N-V-N_o
Q-N-T-VB-N
Q-N-VB-N
T-V-N-N

T-VB-N
VB-N-N
N-T-VB-N-N
VB-N-S
N-T-VB-N-S
Q-N-T-VB-N-N
Q-N-V-N_{loc}
N-T-VB

Linguistic Level IV

N-VB-N
N-VB
N
VB-N
N-VB-N-S
N-T-VB-N
N-S
VB
N-VB-N-N
N-T-VB-N-S
Q-N-VB-N
N-T-VB
N-S-VB
T-VB-N
Q-N
N-V-N_o
N-VB-VB-N
N-S-VB-N
N-T-VB-N-N
N-V-N_{loc}
VB-N-S
N-says-S
N-VB-S
N-T
S-because-S
Q-N-VB
VB-VB-N
N-N

N-VB-VB-N-S
Adverb-S-S
N-VB-N-N-S
N-VB-S

Linguistic Level V

N-VB-N
N-T-VB-N
N-VB
N-VB-N-N
N-VB-N-S
N-T-VB
N
N-T-VB-N-N
VB-N
N-V-N_o
N-S
N-V-N_o-N_{loc}
N-VB-N-N-S
N-T-VB-N-S
N-VB-N-S-N
N-V-N_{loc}
VB
N-VB-N-VB
N-VB-VB-N-S
Q-N-VB-N
N-S-VB-N
N-V-N_o-S
N-says-S
VB-N-S
N-S-V-N_o
N-T
Q-N-V-N_{loc}
N-VB-N-S
N-T-VB-N-N-S
N-says-S
Adverb-S-S

The Use of Grammatical Morphemes by Children with Communication Disorders

JUDITH R. JOHNSTON and TERIS KIM SCHERY

Methods for studying morphology in linguistically deficient children have, with the exception of this study by Johnston and Schery, been adopted from Berko's (1958) early research. Lovell and Bradbury (1967) and Newfield and Schlanger (1968) are two excellent examples of early studies using Berko's techniques with retarded children as subjects. It was not until Brown (1973) reported a detailed description of the acquisition of 14 grammatical morphemes in three young normal children studied longitudinally that the elicitation technique introduced by Berko was replaced by detailed structural and semantic analysis. Brown found that the order of acquisition was nearly invariant for the 14 morphemes across the three children. de Villiers and de Villiers (1973) studied the spontaneous speech samples of 21 normal children of various ages and found a high correlation in the acquisition order of the same grammatical morphemes studied by Brown. The de Villiers' study suggests that cross-sectional data can be an efficient method for validating results found in laborious and time-consuming longitudinal analysis. This research strategy is also a very effective way to apply the extensive data on normal language development to linguistically deficient populations. Based on a preliminary study of a large group of children, Johnston and Schery report here data for eight of the grammatical morphemes showing a similar invariant but delayed order of acquisition to that reported by Brown and de Villiers and de Villiers.

—DMM

This report was completed while J. Johnston held a predoctoral traineeship (2-TOL-HD-00153-06A1) in Developmental Psychology in the Department of Psychology, University of California, Berkeley.

Over the past 2 decades, developments in linguistic theory have led to a wealth of theory and observation in language acquisition. Studies of normal child language have inspired new looks at atypical development. Early studies by Menyuk (1964) and Lee (1966) suggested that there might be differences between the syntactic patterns of normal and language "deviant" children. In these studies, however, the normal and deficient children were chronologically matched. More recent studies have matched groups according to language development stage and have found deficient language patterns to be normal in most respects (Lackner, 1968; Graham and Graham, 1971; Morehead and Ingram, 1970; Ingram, 1972a). These reports have shown that the development of phrase structure rules, transformational rules, imitation/comprehension behavior, and question forms is qualitatively similar for normal and linguistically deficient children.

No previous research on the acquisition of specific grammatical morphemes by atypical populations has been reported, though Morehead and Ingram (1970) have found that aphasic children use a higher proportion of inflections at the end of the two-word stage than do normal children. Normal acquisition of grammatical morphemes has been investigated longitudinally by Brown (1973) and cross-sectionally by deVilliers and deVilliers (1973). These two studies found that grammatical morphemes were acquired in a consistent order and at specific language stages, i.e., with specific relationship to mean utterance length. Rates of acquisition for different morphemes were found to be similar across individual children by deVilliers and deVilliers (1973) but varied by Brown (1973).

The research to be reported here, then, was motivated by descriptive, comparative, and methodological goals. We wished to observe the use of grammatical morphemes by linguistically deficient children, to compare their performance to that reported for normal children, and to explore the use of language sample analysis as an index of language change.

METHOD

Subjects

Subjects for this study were 287 children, aged 3.0–16.2, enrolled in the special day classes of the Los Angeles County Program for severe oral language disorders/aphasia. Seventeen percent of the children were from minority backgrounds, a percentage which also reflected the County enrollment. In order to qualify for placement in this program, each child had to exhibit normal range performance on a standardized IQ measure (defined as two standard deviations from the test mean plus the standard error of measurement), and a performance on at least two auditory-verbal language scales that fell two standard deviations or more below expected mental age performance levels. A wide variety of atypical learning, behavioral, neurological, and emotional problems was represented among these children. However, in the judgments of the evaluation psychologist, language specialist, and teacher, each child's primary disability was difficulty with oral language.

Teachers

The 64 teachers in this program held currently valid California State Speech and Hearing Credentials. Approximately 80% of them also had Master's degrees in speech pathology. Most were selected in part for their familiarity with and interest in clinical application of current language development theory.

Testing Procedures and Measurement Categories

During the Fall of 1972, teachers were asked to collect and analyze a 100-utterance conversational sample from each child in their classes, using a guidebook prepared by the authors.[1] Samples were taped during individualized play sessions, using a variety of stimulus materials. The importance of adequate contextual information was stressed and teachers were encouraged to make contextual notes during their interviews. The teachers then transcribed the tapes, analyzed them, and reported the following measures:

1. Mean number of words per utterance
2. Mean number of morphemes per utterance
3. Language level as determined by mean words per utterance
   Level 1: 2–2.5 words
   Level 2: 2.5–3 words

---

[1]The language sample analysis guidebook used in this study is unfortunately not available for circulation. It consists primarily of conventions for determining sentence length and descriptions of specific grammatical morphemes. The morpheme-counting conventions essentially follow those of Brown (1973) except that we exclude single-word utterances and responses to questions. The description of grammatical morphemes, their functions, and typical contents are based directly upon Brown's (1973) analysis. Additional methodological information may be obtained by specific request from the authors.

Level 3: 3–4 words
Level 4: 4–5 words
Level 5: 5 or more words

4. Percentage of occurrence in obligatory contexts for 14 grammatical morphemes:

Progressive inflection - *ing*
Preposition *in*
Preposition *on*
Regular noun plural -*s*
Irregular past tense
Possessive noun -*s*
Copula in uncontractible context
Articles *a, the*
Regular past tense -*ed*
Regular third person singular present indicative -*s*
Irregular third person singular present indicative *does, has*
Auxiliary BE in contractible contexts

5. A listing of any of the above grammatical morphemes which had been directly taught during the preceding 2 years.

Six months later, the teachers took a second sample from each child and again reported mean length of utterance measures. Grammatical morpheme data from the 27 children who first tested at levels 1–2 were also collected at this time.

Manual Reliability

Since a team of some 75 people was involved in the collection of these data, we were obviously concerned about reliability. As a check on the clarity of the guidebook, 13 teachers were asked to score a single sample and their analyses were compared with one prepared by the authors. The teachers averaged 84% agreement with the master score sheet; this average increased to 92% after some additional training. As a field check on the reliability of each teacher-coder, the program specialists were asked to re-score the first sample prepared by each teacher. The percentage agreement averaged 86%. Presumably this figure rose with feedback and experience.

Analysis

Data submitted by the teachers were examined for developmental trends and other patterns of usage of grammatical morphemes. This descriptive analysis centered on five hypotheses:

1. that the ratio between mean-words-per-utterance and mean-morphemes-per-utterance decreases at level 2;

2. that the percentage of children using a particular grammatical morpehem increases with language level;

3. that the mean percentage-use-in-obligatory-contexts for a given grammatical morpheme increases with language level;

4. that the slope of the acquisition curve, as indexed by mean percentage-occurrence-in-obligatory-contexts at successive language levels, differs from morpheme to morpheme; and

5. that different grammatical morphemes are acquired (at 90%-use-in-obligatory-contexts) at different language levels.

Two additional hypotheses which compared the performance of linguistically deficient and normal children were:

6. that children with communication disorders acquire grammatical morphemes in the same order as do normal children; and

7. that children with communication disorders acquire grammatical morphemes at the same language levels as do normal children.

Finally, our last group of hypotheses explored changes in language performance over a 6-month interval. It was predicted:

8. that utterance length as measured by mean-morphemes-per-utterance increases over time;

9. that the amount of increase in mean-morphemes-per-utterance varies with language level; and

10. that percentage-occurrence-in-obligatory-contexts for individual morphemes increases over time.

RESULTS

**Use of Grammatical Morphemes
by Children with Communication Disorders**

Table 1 summarizes mean-length-of-utterance measures for children at all language levels. The apparent rise in the mean-word/mean-morpheme ratio at level 2 was tested using ANOVA and Scheffe's method of multiple comparisons. The ANOVA test indicated a significant difference between group means ($F = 2.92; v = 4,282; \alpha = 0.05$); in the post hoc explorations, the contrast between the mean of level 2 and the weighted combination of the remaining means was significant ($S = 3.08; v = 4,282; \alpha = 0.05$), but none of the other means differed

Table 1. Mean values for summary language measures by level

Level	N	Mean-words-per-utterance	Mean-morphemes-per-utterance	Mean-words/mean-morphemes
1	10	2.29	2.58	0.890
2	17	2.78	2.95	0.944
3	51	3.67	4.05	0.907
4	76	4.59	5.12	0.895
5	133	6.19	6.97	0.894

significantly from each other. In other words, the proportion of inflectional morphemes in each utterance was constant across levels, except at level 2 where relatively fewer inflectional morphemes were used.

Table 2 indicates the percentage of children at each language level who used a given grammatical morpheme. For all morphemes except the article, those children using the morpheme tended to be at higher language levels (Chi square, $v=4$, $\alpha=0.14$ for 14 tests combined). Articles were used by similar percentages of children at all language levels. Although significant, the actual Chi square values represent only weak associations. The probability of error in predicting whether a child will use a particular morpheme was only

Table 2. Percentage of samples in which a morpheme was present at each language level

Morpheme	1	2	3	4	5	Total
-ing	90.0	82.4	98.0	100	97.0	96.9
in	70.0	76.5	96.1	93.4	97.7	94.1
on	30.0	52.9	78.4	88.2	92.5	84.3
Plural -s	70.0	64.7	96.1	94.7	98.5	94.1
Irreg. past	70.0	23.5	82.4	88.2	92.5	84.7
Copula contr.	50.0	35.3	82.4	89.5	96.2	86.8
Aux.BE contr.	40.0	29.4	80.4	80.3	87.2	79.1
Article	90.0	94.1	96.1	100	99.2	98.3
Possessive -s	30.0	17.6	33.3	42.1	56.4	45.3
Copula uncontr.	10.0	23.5	51.0	65.8	76.7	63.8
Past -ed	10.0	0.0	39.2	63.2	77.4	59.9
3PS -s	20.0	23.5	41.2	57.9	78.2	61.0
Irreg. 3PS	30.0	5.9	39.2	40.8	61.7	47.7
Aux.BE uncontr.	10.0	5.9	27.5	52.6	66.2	50.2

Table 3. Mean and standard deviation of percentage-use-in-obligatory-contexts for grammatical morphemes by language level

Morpheme/level	1	2	3	4	5	Total
-ing						
M	41.1	58.8	71.7	81.1	85.0	78.5
SD	28.8	37.3	26.0	22.2	23.7	26.7
In						
M	44.8	70.8	81.5	83.5	91.8	84.9
SD	41.8	42.3	29.6	27.1	17.3	27.1
On						
M	27.3	46.0	66.4	79.4	85.5	76.1
SD	44.4	46.7	39.3	33.9	27.6	36.1
Plural -s						
M	50.1	52.7	75.2	79.5	90.9	81.4
SD	42.3	47.0	31.1	28.2	17.0	28.7
Irreg. past						
M	64.4	14.8	49.1	64.6	78.2	65.2
SD	46.9	33.2	38.7	36.5	28.7	37.4
Article						
M	24.9	40.3	57.2	80.2	92.5	77.5
SD	28.6	34.8	30.3	21.8	12.6	28.5
Copula contr.						
M	11.8	18.7	44.2	58.0	79.2	61.4
SD	23.7	36.1	33.6	35.3	27.1	36.8
Aux.BE contr.						
M	17.8	12.8	30.3	46.3	65.0	49.1
SD	34.0	28.8	32.5	38.9	34.5	38.8
Possessive -s						
M	29.7	17.5	24.3	33.8	50.6	38.8
SD	47.8	38.9	40.7	44.2	46.7	45.9
Copula uncontr.						
M	2.5	11.2	26.4	48.6	64.4	48.1
SD	7.9	23.2	34.7	42.0	40.3	42.6
Past -ed						
M	0.0	0.0	23.2	47.0	64.1	46.3
SD	0.0	0.0	34.1	42.4	40.1	43.2
3PS -s						
M	2.0	11.6	19.7	33.3	63.6	42.5
SD	6.3	25.6	34.7	38.4	40.0	42.5
Irreg. 3PS						
M	14.9	5.8	20.3	24.8	49.5	34.0
SD	33.5	24.0	32.1	36.5	44.8	41.8
Aux.BE uncontr.						
M	1.0	5.8	20.3	34.8	57.3	39.8
SD	3.2	24.0	36.8	41.5	44.5	44.5

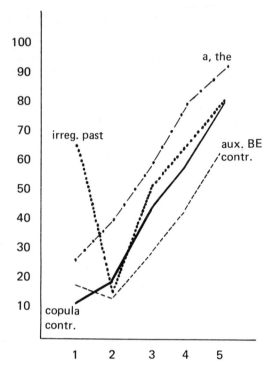

Figure 1. Mean percentage-use-in-obligatory-contexts at each language level.

slightly decreased by knowledge of his language level (mean Lambda$_B$=0.09).[2]

However, when we looked at percentage-occurrence-in-obligatory-contexts rather than mere use, the relationship between language levels and performance on grammatical morphemes seemed stronger. Means and standard deviations for this measure appear in Table 3. Direct statistical tests of the differences between stages were not possible due to heterogeneity of variance. Examination of the data, however, revealed only four points at which language level and morpheme performance lacked correspondence: irregular past, possessive -s, does/has, and auxiliary BE in contractible contexts show decreases in level of occurrence from level 1 to level 2.

Growth curves for the eight morphemes with the lowest variance

---

[2]Goodman and Kruskal index of predictive association (Hays, 1963, p. 608). Lambda$_B$ values represent the percentage reduction in error of prediction.

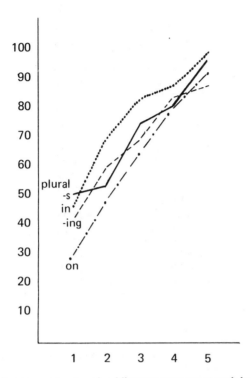

Figure 2. Mean percentage-use-in-obligatory-contexts at each language level.

are displayed in Figures 1 and 2. These graphs suggest that rate of acquisition may differ from morpheme to morpheme. This possibility of difference in slope was tested with a multivariate linear regression analysis. The null hypothesis of equal slopes for 14 dependent variables was rejected at $p < 0.01$ ($F = 6.20$; $v = 13,273$). A significant difference among the slopes did occur. The actual value of the slopes appears in Table 4. Those morphemes which show a slower rise in percentage usage with increase in mean-morphemes-per-utterance are listed at the top.

Table 5 lists the language level at which a given morpheme was used by at least 50% of the subjects at that level in at least 90% of its obligatory contexts. As can be seen, the 14 grammatical morphemes were found to meet this criterion of acquisition at different language levels.

To summarize this descriptive analysis for our sample of linguistically deficient children, these 14 grammatical morphemes dif-

Table 4. Multivariate linear regression slopes for grammatical morphemes

Morpheme	Slope
In	4.69
-ing	5.60
Plural -s	7.66
Possessive	8.07
On	8.27
Irreg. past	9.02
Irreg. 3PS	9.14
Aux.BE contr.	11.00
Article	11.14
Aux.BE contr.	12.06
Copula uncontr.	12.21
Copula contr.	12.86
Reg. 3PS	13.09
Reg. past -ed	13.85

Table 5. Language level (Johnston and Schery criteria) at which each morpheme was used at all and acquired (90%) by 50% of the subjects at that level in three research studies

	Use at all	90% Use in obligatory contexts		
	J&S	J&S	deVilliers	Brown
Plural -s	1	2	1	1
In	1	2	2	1
On	2	3	2	1
-ing	1	3	2	2
Irreg. past	1	1,4	—[a]	2
Article	1	4	4	3
Copula uncontr.	3	5	4	2
Possessive -s	5	+[b]	—	3
Aux.BE uncontr.	4	5	—	3
Past -ed	4	5	4	3
3PS -s	4	5	4	3
Aux.BE contr.	3	5	—	(4)[c]
Copula contr.	1	+[b]	3	(4)
Irreg. 3PS	5	5	—	(4)

[a]Dashes indicate insufficient data.
[b]Did not reach criteria at any level.
[c]Numbers in parentheses are probable.

fered in the language level and rate at which they were acquired. There was no meaningful difference between language levels in the percentage of children *using* a particular grammatical morpheme, but *consistency* of usage did improve as mean-utterance-length increased.

Comparison with Normal Data

In comparing the performance of our atypical children with that of normal children, we looked at both order and level of acquisition for the 14 grammatical morphemes. Table 5 indicates the language levels at which normal children acquire these grammatical morphemes (Brown, 1973; deVilliers and deVilliers, 1973). Since arbitrary mean-length-of-utterance values for language levels or stages—as well as specific morpheme-counting conventions—vary widely among child language research studies, we have tried to adjust for procedural and labeling differences whenever we compare research results. (Tables that summarize this attempt to establish equivalences can be found in Appendix A). We can see that children in our study who had reached the 90% usage-in-obligatory-contexts criterion tended to be at higher language levels than the normal children. Despite this higher acquisition level, however, the order of acquisition of the morphemes appears to be much the same across the three samples.

Kendall's tau for grouped data (Hays, 1963, p. 652) was used to test this apparent similarity in order of acquisition, as detailed in Table 5. The degree of agreement was 0.74 between our data and the Brown (1973) data, and 0.61 between our data and the deVilliers and deVilliers (1973) data. Assuming accurate translation of the normal data into the categories of our project, there was a moderately strong probability that any random pair of morphemes would show the same relative order of acquisition in both normal and deficient rankings.

A different analysis of order agreement was then conducted, taking each study on its own terms rather than translating it into our project categories, and looking only at the eight morphemes for which there was the best available cross-sectional data: *-ing, in, on,* plural *-s,* irregular past, copula in contractible contexts, auxiliary *BE* in contractible contexts, and articles. The other six morphemes exhibited high variance or occurred too infrequently in our data to justify detailed ordering. Brown's (1973) criterion for acquisition was 90% occurrence-in-obligatory-contexts in three successive samples. He studied three children longitudinally and each sample contained about 700 utterances. The deVilliers' (1973) samples, from 21 children

Table 6. Spearman rank order correlations, corrected for ties, between three orders of acquisition for eight grammatical morphemes

	de Villiers	Brown
Johnston & Schery	0.99	0.72
Brown	0.75	

studied cross-sectionally, averaged 360 utterances. For each morpheme, they analyzed only those samples containing five or more obligatory contexts. Order of acquisition was based on the mean percentage occurrence across all children for each morpheme. In our study, ordering for this comparison was achieved by plotting a series of linear regressions with mean-morphemes-per-utterance as the dependent variable and percentage usage of the specific morpheme as the independent variable. The morphemes were then ordered according to the predicted mean morpheme value at which each would be acquired at the 90% level. The criteria for identifying morphemes and obligatory contexts were approximately the same in all three studies. Table 6 indicates the Spearman rank order correlations for order of acquisition of morphemes among the three studies, using each author's own judgment of ordering. To summarize, we found that, using a 90% occurrence-in-obligatory-contexts criterion, our atypical children acquired these grammatical morphemes in much the same order as the normal children, but at later language levels.

Measurement of Language Change

Two hundred seventy-three children from the original group of 287 were scored for mean-length-of-utterance on a second language sample approximately 6 months following the first. During this period the children participated in their special classroom programs, which included individualized language therapy as well as grade-appropriate general curriculum. The content of and approach to language training varied from classroom to classroom. The mean-morpheme counts from the two language samples were compared to see whether there were any changes in mean-length-of-utterance. An analysis of covariance was used to control for the effect of age. The assumption of equal slopes was met, but the relationship between age and gain score was nonsignificant (regression coefficient = -0.002;

SE=0.002; t=0.89; p=0.05, two tailed). Bartlett's test for homogeneity of variance was significant (B=14.84; v=4; α=0.05, two tailed), indicating that the assumption of equal variance was not met. Therefore, no F test was done. However, the adjusted mean-morpheme gain score for each group was tested using its own variance. The original and adjusted mean gain scores for each group, as well as the SE_m, t values and degrees of freedom, are listed in Table 7. Error for the five tests combined was controlled at α=0.10. All five tests were significant. Each group showed an increase in mean-morphemes-per-utterance over a 6-month interval. The magnitude of the gain scores varied inversely with language level with level 5 showing the least gain. Children at each level showed language growth as indexed by increased sentence length, but there was less change in this index at higher language levels.

For a small subsample of the longitudinal group, N = 27 (children with initial mean-morpheme counts from 2–4, the range in which morphological growth was expected), differences in percentage-occurrence-in-obligatory-contexts over 6 months for the grammatical morphemes were also measured. Contextual frequency for 7 of the 14 morphemes was too low to allow for reliable longitudinal comparison. Mean difference scores for the remaining seven morphemes appear in Table 8. The size of the samples varies; any subjects with initial 100% ratings were dropped since they could show no further gains. As can be seen from the SD, the gain scores fluctuated widely. Tests for significance were made for each of the morphemes, and, with a combined α of 0.35, five of the tests proved significant.

As a further exploratory measure, these difference scores in percentage occurrence for the seven selected morphemes were

Table 7. Original and adjusted means for difference in mean-morphemes-per-utterance over 6 months at each language level (covariate = age; X = time 2 − time 1)

	Original	Adjusted	SE_M	df	t
1	1.2111	1.2514	0.372	8	3.3[a]
2	1.2059	1.2548	0.272	16	4.5[a]
3	0.8319	0.8640	0.170	46	5.4[a]
4	0.5849	0.5927	0.134	72	4.5[a]
5	0.2898	0.2640	0.105	126	2.6[a]

[a]Significant at p <0.02, two-tailed.

Table 8. Mean gain in percentage-occurrence-in-obligatory-contexts for selected grammatical morphemes for children at levels 1 and 2

Morpheme	Mean difference	SD	df	t
-ing	19	28.76	24	3.24[a]
In	32.7	45.84	16	2.86[a]
On	19.9	48.41	17	1.70
Plural -s	22.7	43.79	20	2.32[a]
Article	6.46	20.5	25	1.58
Contr. Copula	14.9	33.59	25	2.17[a]
Contr. Aux. BE	20.25	37.45	26	2.75[a]

[a]Significant at $p < 0.05$.

grouped according to whether the teacher had attempted to teach those items during the 6-month interval (Table 9). Unequal sample sizes and wide and unequal variances seemed to preclude statistical validation. By inspection, however, two of the seven morphemes showed a clear difference between the training and no training groups: auxiliary *BE* in contractible contexts, and noun plural -s.

To summarize the longitudinal analysis, a significant increase in mean-morphemes-per-utterance was found for all groups. The

Table 9. Mean change in percentage-occurrence-in-obligatory contexts over 6 months for seven grammatical morphemes, grouped according to whether student had received training on that item during interval

	Training			No training		
	N	X_D	SD	N	X_D	SD
-ing	8	28.25	34.2	17	14.64	25.78
In	12	30.33	50.15	5	38.40	37.80
On	10	19.2	62.0	8	20.87	27.31
Plural -s	4	78.0	34.47	17	9.71	35.08
Article	5	.60	19.33	21	9.76	20.16
Contr. Copula	15	17.47	38.83	11	11.45	26.21
Contr. Aux. BE	6	58.67	45.71	21	9.29	27.06

magnitude of the gain was not related to age, but did seem to decrease at higher language levels. Inadequate sample sizes mitigated the value of our analyses of progress in usage of specific grammatical morphemes. There was some suggestion, however, that change in percentage-occurrence-in-obligatory-contexts is a viable measure; it is sensitive to differences over a 6-month interval and can register the effects of training.

Nature of Deficient Language

Our results have bearing on the debate over the relative normalcy of "deviant" language development patterns. Of course, the most obvious difference between normal children and our research sample is age. When we use mean-length-of-utterance to match the Brown (1973) children with our children at levels 1 and 2, the contrast in age is dramatic: means of 28 months vs. 81 months. But what about other differences? Our results add to the list of remarkable similarities between the language of normal and language "deviant" groups. Our children acquired 14 grammatical morphemes in much the same order as the Brown (1973) and deVilliers' (1973) samples, and evidenced the same developmental relationship between mean utterance length and use of structural morphology as is reported throughout the normal acquisition literature.

But there were also indications of possible differences between normal and language "deviant" groups. Our children reached the 90% acquisition criterion one or two levels later than normal children, despite the fact that they first used many morphemes at the earliest levels. This suggests that the course of acquisition of grammatical morphemes might be abnormally protracted in this atypical population. More research into normal and deficient acquisition curves for individual morphemes is needed to explore this possibility. In particular, we need to re-examine the question of equality of slopes.

The variables that might contribute to differences in the acquisition curves for any two morphemes are numerous and complex: heterogeneity of morpheme categories; age at first appearance, with implied concomitant effects of neurological maturity and overall language complexity; degree of dependence upon specific conceptual and auditory perceptual prerequisites (Johnston, 1973; Slobin, 1973). Brown (1973) notes, for example, that acquisition curves for prepositions different from those for copula, inflections, or articles. He attributes this difference to the relative semantic and syntactic homogeneity of the prepositions.

We might expect that there would be greater diversity among acquisition curves for grammatical morphemes in the language "deviant" group, since they exhibit some intellectual abilities in advance of normal children at comparable language levels. This might mean that the entire range of certain morpheme categories would be more immediately available to them than to the normal child who must await intellectual growth before being able to assimilate more conceptually demanding contexts. On the other hand, attentional and memory difficulties might limit the language deficient child's performance level on the forms he knows.

In any case, if rates of acquisition for morphemes differ—i.e., if the order of appearance of specific morphemes differs from the eventual order of criterial acquisition—we must decide which of these two measures is more relevant to our research or clinical goals. In addition, most of the normal acquisition data concerns criterial acquisition points.

A third area of possible difference between deficient and normal populations is that of mean-word/mean-morpheme-per-utterance ratio. Morehead and Ingram's (1970) finding that aphasic children use an abnormally high proportion of inflections towards the end of the two-word stage does not at first seem congruent with the drop in proportion of inflectional morphemes observed in our samples at level 2. However, the two findings are not necessarily in conflict if the normal population exhibits an even greater drop in proportion of inflections at level 2 relative to other levels. This might be true if the normal child at this point in development expands his utterances by expressing more of the underlying semantic relations in uninflected forms, and the language-deficient child does this to a lesser degree.

Interpretation of Language Sample Data

The results reported in this paper highlight the importance of a continual refinement of the linguistic analytic approach (Lee, 1974; Tyack, 1973). Our cross-sectional data, as well as Brown's (1973) normal longitudinal data, clearly demonstrate that a given grammatical morpheme is acquired over time. Ten years ago researchers focused on the "rule-governed" nature of language behavior, but recently there has been a shift in emphasis to performance models (Ervinn-Tripp, 1971), and a concomitant recognition of the transitional phase during which a "rule" gains generalized and consistent usage. It may be this transitional phase which is most critical or language-deficient children. To chart these transitional phases, we need a fine-grained analytic tool rather than one which merely notes the presence or absence of a given form in the sample. Percentage-of-occurrence-in-obligatory-contexts is one measure which is sensitive to varying degrees of usage and allows comparison between morphemes with differing contextual frequencies.

Even with detailed analyses, however, the interpretation of scores for a single child remains problematic, particularly if the data are longitudinal. Wide fluctuations in percentage-occurrence-in-obligatory-contexts, in both directions, were frequent in our longitudinal data. Part of the fluctuation undoubtedly reflected day-to-day performance variability, particularly in a population noted for inconsistency. Unfortunately, we do not have test-retest reliability measures for this variable. Another portion of the fluctuation was probably linked to accidental differences in the frequencies of occurrence of a particular morpheme. Fluctuation could also reflect differences in the overall complexity of the two samples. For example, there seems to be some interaction between transformational complexity and the use of inflections at one stage of language learning. Earlier learned forms may be omitted under the performance pressures created by new transformations (Bellugi-Klima, 1968). Finally, fluctuations in morpheme performance must have reflected the fact that each of our grammatical morphemes is really a collapsed category of morphemes which are learned over time (Brown, 1973). For example, the four morphemes involving *BE* are collapsed across distinctions of number and person. Children seem to learn "is" before learning "am" or "are." A lowered performance on the *BE* morphemes could reflect an increased number of contexts requiring "am" or "are" rather than any change in the level of performance on "is" (Ingram, 1972b). Similar arguments can be drawn for many of the morphemes.

The clinician or researcher is actually caught between the need to use analytic categories that occur at measurably high frequencies and the fact that these categories may obscure the very development he desires to chart. It seems clear that any quantified results for an individual child should be augmented with careful qualitative analysis. Such a detailed qualitative analysis might reveal, for example, that a child used only the singular forms of *BE*; that he used past tense for changes of state but not activities; that the -*ing* suffix never occurred in embedded clauses; or, that the only plurals appeared as frozen forms. The normal acquisition literature provides many such analytic parameters and can guide us in planning appropriately sequenced learning programs, or in describing language acquisition, even within a single morphemic category.

To summarize, changes in percentage-occurrence-in-obligatory-contexts can reflect sampling variation, overall language complexity, accidental frequency of contexts, and the nature of the categorizing system, as well as reliable differences in performance on a given form. Such fluctuations were found in normal children (Brown, 1973), but may be accentuated in this population. Any single percentage score should be interpreted cautiously, in light of the particular sample from which it was derived and in conjunction with qualitative judgments.

Measurement of Language Change

Our results show that the children at each language level made a significant gain in mean-morphemes-per-utterance over a 6-month period, though the size of the gain decreased at higher levels. Similarly, when we looked at the performance of levels 1 and 2 children on the grammatical morphemes, percentage-occurrence-in-obligatory-contexts rose significantly over the 6-month interval in 5 out of 7 cases. In fact, the data provide an additional optimistic note. In our exploration of the effect of therapy on performance on grammatical morphemes, only two of the morphemes showed any obvious effect. This was not surprising since the samples were small, the morpheme performance scores variable, the teachers' reports incomplete, and the nature or extent of training completely uncontrolled. What was intriguing was this: the two morphemes evidencing a possible training effect were the two inflections then being taught by many teachers via a prepackaged, highly structured language instructional program. This suggests that our results were not artifacts, but reflected the influence of this teaching program. This in turn suggests that percentage-occurrence-in-obligatory-contexts is an index which can be sensitive to the effects of training and could be used in future research.

CONCLUSION

The focus of normal child language research has recently broadened to include investigations of semantics, conceptual development, and cognitive process variables. Our research suggests that similar studies in deficient language development are necessary. Our language-deficient subjects did not seem to differ from normal children in the structural aspects of grammatical morphology: they learned the same forms, in much the same order, and with the same general relationships to overall language development level as indexed by sentence length. However, they were found to differ from normal children in the rate at which they moved from the first use of a morphological rule to its consistent general application. Further research is now needed to discover the semantic, conceptual, and cognitive processing factors that may determine this difference in rate.

ACKNOWLEDGMENTS

This project was initiated under the auspices of the Office of the Los Angeles County Superintendent of Schools, Division of Special Education, Nadine Coates, Consultant. The authors wish to thank her, as well as the teachers and program specialists who made this report possible. Computing assistance was obtained from the Health Sciences Computing Facility, UCLA, sponsored by NIH Special Research Resources Grant RR-3.

REFERENCES

Bellugi-Klima, U. 1968. Linguistic mechanisms underlying child speech. *In* E. M. Zale (ed.), Proceedings of the Conference on Language and Language Behavior. Appleton-Century-Crofts, New York.

Brown, R. 1973. A First Language. Harvard University Press, Cambridge.

deVilliers, J., and P. deVilliers. 1973. A cross-sectional study of the acquisition of grammatical morphemes in child speech. J. Psycholing. Res. 2:267–278.

Ervin-Tripp, S. 1971. An overview of theories of grammatical development. *In* D. I. Slobin (ed.), The Ontogenesis of Grammar, pp. 189–212. Academic Press, New York.

Graham, J., and L. Graham. 1971. Language behavior of the mentally retarded: Syntactic characteristics. Am. J. Ment. Defic. 75:623–629.

Hays, W. 1963. Statistics. Holt, Rinehart and Winston, New York.

Ingram, D. 1972a. The acquisition of questions and its relation to cognitive development in normal and linguistically deviant children: A pilot study. Stanford University Committee on Linguistics Papers and Reports on Child Language Development 4:13–18.

Ingram, D. 1972b. The acquisition of the English verbal auxiliary and copula in normal and linguistically deviant children. Stanford University Committee on Linguistics Papers and Reports on Child Language Development. 4:79–92.

Johnston, J. 1973. Spatial notions and the child's use of locatives in an elicitation task. Presented at the Stanford Child Language Research Forum, April, Stanford, Calif.

Kirk, R. 1968. Experimental Design: Procedures for the Behavioral Sciences. Brooks/Cole Co., Belmont, Calif.

Lackner, J. 1968. A developmental study of language behavior in retarded children. Neuropsychologia 6:301–320.

Lee, L. 1966. Developmental sentence types: A method for comparing normal and deviant syntactic development. J. Speech Hear. Disord. 31:311–330.

Lee, L. 1974. Developmental Sentence Analysis. Northwestern University Press, Evanston, Ill.

Menyuk, P. 1964. Comparison of grammar of children with functionally deviant and normal speech. J. Speech Hear. Res. 7:109–121.

Morehead, D., and D. Ingram. 1970. The development of base syntax in normal and linguistically deviant children. Stanford University Committee on Linguistics Papers and Reports on Child Language Development 2: 55–75.

Sharf, D. 1972. Some relationships between measures of early language development. J. Speech Hear. Disord. 37:64–70.

Slobin, D. 1973. Cognitive prerequisites for the development of grammar. *In* C. A. Ferguson and D. I. Slobin (eds.), Studies of Child Language Development, pp. 175–208. Holt, Rinehart and Winston, New York.

Tyack, D. 1973. The use of language samples in clinical settings. J. Learn. Disabil. 6:213–216.

APPENDIX A

Stage or level	Johnson & Schery		Brown, 1973	Morehead & Ingram, 1970	
	MW	MM	MM	Normal MM	Deviant MM
1	2.29	2.58	1.75	2.23	2.33
2	2.78	2.95	2.25	2.72	2.83
3	3.67	4.05	2.75	3.70	3.80
4	4.59	5.12	3.50	4.67	4.53
5	6.19	6.97	4.00	5.61	5.83

Language stages or levels and corresponding mean number of words (MW) or morphemes (MM) per utterance for three research studies. The Brown values are theoretical "targets," the others are observed sample values.

```
| 1  ] 2  ] 3  ] 4  ] 5  ]      Brown, 1973, adjusted
|    1  ] 2  ]   3       ]  4   ] 5    Johnston and Schery
| 1  ] 2  ]   3      ]   4   ]   5    ] Morehead and Ingram, 1970
|
|    Mean-Morphemes-per-Utterance
2        3          4          5        6          7
```

Approximate range of mean morphemes per utterance at each language stage or level for three research studies. The Brown values have been tentatively adjusted for differences in morpheme counting conventions.

A Problem of
Language Disorder:
Length versus Structure

PAULA MENYUK and PATRICIA L. LOONEY

Elicited imitation has often been used as an independent means for assessing underlying competence for both normal (Brown and Fraser, 1963; Scholes, 1970) and deficient children (Lenneberg, Nichols, and Rosenberger, 1964; Menyuk, 1964, 1969; Lackner, 1968, reprinted this volume). Slobin and Welsh (1973) describe the use of elicited imitation and discuss its shortcomings and advantages, including that children in repetition tasks filter any linguistic sequence through their internalized language systems, allowing the researcher, through systematic construction of stimulus materials, to analyze productive strategies. In this study, Menyuk and Looney used just such an approach to explore the effects of varied sentence length and complexity on linguistic processing in normal and deficient children. Lenneberg et al. (1964) and Lackner (1968, reprinted this volume) both described a "regression" strategy which predicts that children confronted in elicited imitation with a form that is not part of their productive capacity will use a lower level of the grammar to process that form. Menyuk and Looney detailed these regressions by describing the relative levels of syntactic information used by the two groups in imitating sentences. What have not been reported in the deficient literature are data on comprehension or the relationship between imitation, comprehension, and production.

—DMM

The senior author's work is supported in part by NINDS Grant 5 R01 NS 04332-09. Research in the Hearing and Speech Division at Children's Hospital Medical Center is supported in part by the Children's Hospital Medical Center Mental Retardation and Human Development Research Program (HD-03-0773). Requests for reprints should be directed to Paula Menyuk, Research Laboratory of Electronics, Room 20 B-145, Massachusetts Institute of Technology, Cambridge, Massachusetts 02139.

Originally published in the *Journal of Speech and Hearing Research*, 1972, 15:264–279. Reprinted with permission from the American Speech and Hearing Association.

There is a population of children who develop language in a deviant manner, but medical and psychological examinations of these children do not clearly indicate why this occurs. The children show no evidence of damage to the peripheral auditory or vocal mechanisms obviously necessary for the acquisition and production of language. Their hearing thresholds are usually normal for pure tones and speech, and motor development is normal, including activities of the tongue, lips, and jaw. Neurological examinations and electroencephalographic measures, when available, reveal no obvious central nervous system dysfunctions. Psychological tests indicate that intelligence is average or above average. There is no evidence that these children suffer from gross mental illness although, clearly, the fact that these children cannot communicate easily with their parents, peers, and other members of the community can create emotional problems. These children have been variously labeled as having delayed speech, infantile speech, a functional language disorder, a specific language disorder, and as being minimally brain damaged. They do, indeed, vary in their language performance, so that intuitive judgments of the degree of their language deviancy range from labeling them mildly language-disordered to severely language-disordered.

Because these children do not suffer from any peripheral damage or from gross lesions in the central nervous system, they give us an opportunity to study and compare central encoding and decoding in language acquisition and development when these processes alone appear to be awry and when they are normal. We can ask these children with language disorders and children who are acquiring language normally to engage in various kinds of linguistic tasks and observe which aspects of language perception and production are affected by the language disorder. Such studies could lead to determining more effective ways to modify the language behavior of children with language disorders, because these studies provide more adequate descriptions of the language-processing differences between these children and normal-speaking children.

Children who are developing language normally do not merely imitate when given the task of repeating sentences (Menyuk, 1963). Their repetitions reflect their level of grammatical competence. Systematic changes in the structure of these repetitions occur between ages 3 and 7. These are significantly correlated with changes that occur in the structure of spontaneously uttered sentences. There are also significant differences in the performance of this task by children who have been diagnosed as using infantile speech or delayed speech when compared to children who are developing language normally (Menyuk, 1964, 1969). These results indicate that a repetition technique can be useful in determining and comparing aspects of the syntactic competence of the two groups.

In the studies cited, each sentence presented for repetition contained a different structure, and all varied in length. The sentences were selcted from the language samples of children who were acquiring language normally and were chosen to represent all the different types of structures used at various ages. Children who had been diagnosed as using infantile speech or as being language-delayed repeated some sentences with changes in the syntactic structure of the sentence, whereas other sentences were repeated with many omissions. In these latter instances, only the last word or words were repeated. The sentences that were repeated with gross omissions were more complex in underlying structure than those which were repeated with changes in their syntactic structure. They were also, for the most part, longer. Indeed, although sentence length did not correlate significantly with repetition performance for normal-speaking children, it did for deviant-speaking children. It was not entirely clear whether the length of the sentence or its structure had a greater effect on the deviant-speaking children's ability to repeat.

Probably the most valid way to examine the comparative effect of the structure of an utterance versus its length on children's ability to repeat it is to present utterances derived from two underlying sentences in their full and truncated forms. For example, conjoined, relative clause, and indirect object sentences might be presented for repetition in two forms. The conjoined sentence "Paul is a Boy Scout and knows how to tie knots" is shorter but presumably more complex than "Paul is a Boy Scout, and Paul knows how to tie knots." The relative clause sentence "Paul, a Boy Scout, knows how to tie knots" is shorter but presumably more complex than "Paul, who is a Boy Scout, knows how to tie knots." The indirect object sentence "Paul gave Tom the rope" is shorter but presumably more complex than "Paul gave the rope to Tom." Unfortunately, although these are the right types of structures to use to compare the effect of length versus complexity on sentence repetition accuracy, these were just the types of sentences that elicited only last word or last phrase responses from children with a language problem (Menyuk, 1969).

These children did attempt to repeat sentences derived from the transformational operations of negation, question, imperative, and active-declarative, but with modifications. Therefore, to test the varying contribution of length versus structure on the sentence repetition ability of the language-disordered children, sentence types which these children would at least attempt to repeat should be used. Only these sentence types and two others, which children with a language disorder had attempted to repeat in previous studies, were given for repetition in this study. However, unlike the previous examples, increasing the length of these sentence types also increases the complexity of their base structure. To increase length without changing transformational structure, the noun phrase is expanded with determiners (for example, "some apples" versus "apples") and the verb phrase is expanded with adverbs (for example, "runs here" versus "runs"). The question, then, must be: Are there differences in the accuracy with which these various transformed sentence types are repeated regardless of length, or are there differences in the accuracy with which various sentence lengths are repeated regardless of structure? A further question is: What is the nature of these differences? The two aims of this study are: 1) to begin to examine and compare the effect of length versus structure on the repetition of these sentence types by deviant-speaking and normal-speaking children, and 2) to examine what aspects of these sentences are either repeated or modified.

METHOD

The population in this study consisted of 13 language-disordered children (the experimental group) and 13 normal-speaking children (the control group). There were seven boys and six girls in each group. The children in the experimental group had been brought to a hospital for evaluation because of a speech and language problem. Medical, neurological, and psychological tests of 12 of these children showed that their development was normal and that their intelligence was average or above average. The birth history of one of the children indicated that he was 4 weeks over term, suffered fetal distress, and did not breathe spontaneously at birth. His medical history indicated slow growth and development, and the neurological evaluation stated "probable developmental aphasia." However, his neurological examination indicated normal functioning at the time of the examination. This child was the only one in the group whose sensory-motor development as well as language development had been termed delayed, and his language development was far from the most deviant in the group.

The function of the peripheral auditory and vocal mechanisms of all the children in the experimental group was normal when they were seen by a speech clinician for language testing. The language testing included the Peabody Picture Vocabulary Test (PPVT) (Dunn, 1959), segments of the Illinois Test of Psycholinguistic Abilities (ITPA) (Kirk, McCarthy, and Kirk, 1968), and the Hejna Developmental Articulation Test (Hejna, 1959). At the initial testing, the mean PPVT score for the experimental group was 0.3 years below their chronological age. On the visual-motor segments of the ITPA, they were functioning at or above age level, and on the auditory vocal segments (auditory-vocal automatic and auditory-vocal association), they were functioning 0.4 years below their chronological age level. Seventy-six items on the Hejna were given, and error rates ranged from 8% to 53%. The clinicians' evaluations of the children's overall language performance categorized their language problem as primarily "expressive" in nature, and mild to moderate or moderate to severe in deviancy.

The mean chronological age of the experimental group at the time of the sentence repetition task was 6.2 years and the age range was 4 years, 5 months to 7 years, 9 months. The children had been enrolled in a regular program of speech and language therapy in a hospital hearing and speech center for an average of 1.4 years. The PPVT was administered to these children at the time of their initial speech and language evaluation (before they entered therapy), during therapy, and shortly after they were given the sentence repetition task. At the time of initial evaluation, their mean chronological age was 4.8 years and their mean PPVT score was 4.5 years. At the later testing their mean chronological age was 4.9 years and their mean PPVT score was 4.6 years, and at the final testing their mean chronological age was 6.3 years, their mean PPVT score 6.1 years. Their PPVT scores were, therefore, generally 0.3 years below their chronological age. The children in the control group were attending a daily nursery school program at a college. None of these children was enrolled in a speech or language therapy program and none had ever been diagnosed as having a speech or language problem. The mean chronological age of this group at the time the repetition tasks and the PPVT were administered was 4.6 years, and their age range was 4 years, 2 months to 5 years, 1 month. The mean PPVT score they achieved was 5.9 years,

Table 1. Number, sex, mean age, and mean PPVT test
scores of children for the sentence repetition task. CA
stands for chronological age

	Experimental group	Control group
Number	13	13
Male	7	7
Female	6	6
Mean CA (Time of repetition testing)	6.2 years	4.6 years
Mean CA for PPVT (Time of administration)	6.3 years	4.6 years
Mean PPVT score	6.1 years	5.9 years

1.3 years above their chronological age. Thus, one might roughly
calculate that although the groups were widely different in chronological age, their language scores on this language test were similar.
However, no attempt was made to match groups according to test
scores. Table 1 indicates the number, sex, mean age, and mean PPVT
scores of the children in the study.

The sentences given in this study for repetition were active-
declarative, imperative, negative, and question sentences. Two variations, which language-disordered children had attempted to repeat
in a previous study, were included in addition to the other types. One
sentence was a truncated passive and the other an active-declarative
sentence with a negative subject. Some do not consider these two
sentence types to be derived from the transformational operations of
passivization and negative attachment, respectively, but rather to be
forms of the active-declarative. All active-declarative sentences and
the two other sentences described were five words long, including
modifiers and adverbs. Thus, it was possible to examine the comparative effect of base structure and transformational complexity.
The imperative, negative, and question sentences varied in length
from three to five words, and there were two instances of each
sentence length within these syntactic categories. Twenty-four
sentences were arranged in random order in the list.

A second set of sentences was given to these children to test their
ability to repeat the phonological sequences which make up words in
sentences (Menyuk and Looney, 1972). The words in these sentences

contained all the consonants in the English language in initial, medial, and final position. Although the primary purpose of this latter set was to test repetition of speech sounds, the repetition of syntactic structures in these sentences was also analyzed, and the results revealed further and interesting differences between the two populations. Eighteen of the sentences in this set (Set B sentences) were active-declarative. Seven contained the following structures: imperative, negative imperative, imperative with conjoined verbs, relative clause, negative subject, and active-declarative with conjoined objects. The sentences were five or six words long except for one four-word sentence.

Each child's clinician presented the sentence repetition task to the language-disordered children during a regular therapy session. The control group children were given the repetition task individually by one of the experimenters in an isolated room adjoining the nursery school play room. All responses were tape-recorded on a Wollensack Model T-1500 magnetic tape recorder with a special lavalier microphone attachment (Electro-Voice Model 624, high impedance, -56 dB output, 100–7000 Hz response). The tester instructed each child to "say what I say." Repetition trials with nontest stimuli were given before the test stimuli were presented and taping was begun. None of the children had any difficulty in understanding the task, and all attempted to carry out the instruction to "say what I say." If a child did not respond immediately to a particular sentence when it was first given, the stimulus was repeated, but only two presentations of any stimulus were given. The children were encouraged during the testing sessions by the experimenter's remarks and were rewarded at the end of the testing sessions.

The repetition of both sets of sentences was analyzed, and any deviation from complete and accurate repetition was scored as an error. Errors were then subdivided into modifications, substitutions, and omissions. An error was classified as a modification when it changed the transformational operation in the structure of the sentence, as a substitution when one member of a syntactic class was substituted for another, and an omission when a word was omitted in a sentence without altering the transformational structure. Examples of each classification are:

Modification: How will he get there?   (a) How he will get there?
                                            (b) How he get there?
Substitution: They won't play with me.   (a) He won't play with me.
                                            (b) They can't play with me.

Omission: Throw the ball very fast.   (a) Throw ball very fast.
                                             (b) Throw the ball fast.

Many of the errors that were produced by the children with a language disorder and classified as modifications were Type (b) modifications where a modal (can or will) or auxiliary marker (be or past) was omitted. The exact nature of the errors made will be described in greater detail in the discussion section.

RESULTS

Striking differences existed in the sentence repetition abilities of the normal-speaking (control group) and the deviant-speaking (experimental group) children. None of the children in the experimental group repeated Set A or Set B sentences entirely correctly, whereas 46% of the children in the control group repeated Set A entirely correctly and 23% repeated Set B entirely correctly. Significantly more errors occurred in the sentence repetitions of the experimental group than occurred in the repetitions of the control group with both Set A and Set B sentences. The percentage of children making errors, the number of errors made by both groups of children, and the significance of the differences between percentages and numbers for both groups calculated as chi-square evaluations are shown in Table 2. The proportion of number of errors was calculated in terms of the total number of words in each set and as will be observed later, in each sentence category.

In addition to the sharp differences in the number of errors made, the pattern of errors was somewhat different for both groups. Table 3 presents the percentage of subjects making errors and the number of errors made with each sentence type in Set A by the children in each group.

A chi-square evaluation was carried out comparing the percent-

Table 2. Percentage of children making errors, and number of errors

	Percentage of children			Number of errors		
Sentence sets	Experimental	p Value	Control	Experimental	p Value	Control
Set A	100	0.01	54	172	0.01	14
Set B	100	0.10	77	242	0.01	43

Table 3. Percentage of children making errors and number of errors in Set A sentences

Sentence type	Number	Percentage of subjects		Number of errors	
		Experi-mental	Control	Experi-mental	Control
Imperative	6	28	4	24	3
Negative	6	59	1	47	1
Question	6	67	4	53	3
Active-declarative	4	37	4	18	2
Negative subject and passive	2	81	19	30	5

age of subjects making errors and the number of errors made with each sentence type. In the control group there were no significant differences between the percentage of subjects repeating various sentence types with errors, except between the negative subject and the passive sentence (which were put together into one category) and all other sentence types. A greater percentage of normal-speaking children repeated these two sentence types with errors than they did all the other sentence types. In the experimental group, a greater percentage of subjects repeated the negative, question, and negative subject and the passive sentence with errors than they did the imperative or active-declarative sentences. The percentage of subjects making errors in the repetition of sentences was smallest with imperative sentences and largest with negative subject and the passive sentence, but there was no significant difference between the percentage of subjects making errors with imperative and active-declarative sentences or between the percentage of subjects making errors with negative, question, and negative subject and the passive sentence.

In summary, the normal-speaking children had almost no difficulty in repeating imperative, active-declarative, negative, and question sentences, and only relatively greater difficulty with a negative subject and a passive sentence. The deviant-speaking children had much greater difficulty than the normal-speaking children in repeating all sentence types. In addition, the degree of difficulty they encountered was a function of the sentence type. A greater percentage of subjects had difficulty in repeating the negative, question, and negative subject and the passive sentence than the active-declarative and imperative sentences.

Much the same picture emerges when number of errors per

Table 4. Chi-square evaluations of differences in percentage of children making errors and numbers of errors between sentence types

| Sentence types | Percentage of subjects | | Number of errors | |
	Experimental χ^2	Control χ^2	Experimental χ^2	Control χ^2
Imperative vs. active-declarative	1.25	—	—	—
Imperative vs. negative	10.59^a	—	7.45^a	—
Imperative vs. question	16.01^a	—	10.92^a	—
Imperative vs. negative subject and passive	25.84^a	8.52^a	16.74^a	2.59
Active-declarative vs. negative	5.04^a	—	4.10^b	—
Active-declarative vs. question	8.65^a	—	6.35^b	—
Active-declarative vs. negative subject and passive	16.41^a	8.52^a	17.38^a	2.44
Negative vs. question	—	—	—	—
Negative vs. negative subject and passive	3.46	14.44^a	2.98	5.80^b
Question v. negative subject and passive	1.32	8.52^a	1.49	2.59

[a]Significantly different at 0.01 level.
[b]Significantly different at 0.05 level.

sentence type is determined and comparisons are made. Sentence type caused the number of errors in repetition to vary markedly for the experimental group. More errors in repetition occurred with negative, question, and negative subject and the passive sentence than occurred with active-declarative and with imperative sentences. There were, however, no major differences between the number of errors occurring with negative subject and the passive, question, and negative sentences. Thus, when both frequency of errors and percentage of subjects repeating with errors were evaluated, the same pattern was found. The sentence types fell into two categories: the less difficult (imperative and active-declarative) and the more difficult (negative, question, and negative subject and passive). Question sentences were repeated with more errors than negative sentences, and negative subject and passive sentences were repeated with more errors than question sentences. In the control group there were no important differences between the number of errors occurring with sentence types except that more errors occurred in the repetition of the negative subject and the passive sentence than in the repetition of negative sentences (in fact, five errors versus one error). The re-

Table 5. Percentage of children repeating different sentence lengths with errors, and number of errors

Sentence lengths	Number	Percentage of subjects		Number of errors	
		Experimental	Control	Experimental	Control
3	6	28	4	23	3
4	6	59	1	45	1
5	12	60	6	104	10

sults of the chi-square evaluations of differences in percentage of subjects repeating various sentence types with errors and the number of errors that occurred in the various sentence types in each group are presented in Table 4. Chi squares that were less than one are not listed.

One of the questions this study attempted to answer was which aspect of the sentence structure affected sentence repetition accuracy most for children with and without language disorders—its length or its syntax. In the experimental group, the percentage of subjects repeating both four- and five-word sentences with errors was greater than the percentage of subjects repeating three-word sentences with errors, but there was no significant difference between the percentage of subjects having difficulty with four- and five-word sentences. Increasing the length from four to five words did not increase the number of subjects who repeated with errors. In the control group there were no major differences between the percentage of subjects

Table 6. Chi-square evaluations of the significance of the difference in percentage and numbers of children repeating sentences of different lengths

Sentence lengths	Chi-square evaluations			
	Percentage of subjects		Number of errors	
	Experimental χ^2	Control χ^2	Experimental χ^2	Control χ^2
3 vs. 4	10.59^a	—	2.83	—
3 vs. 5	11.64^a	—	2.18	—
4.vs.5	—	2.29	1.85	1.27

[a]Significantly different at 0.01 level.

repeating three- and four-word sentences, three- and five-word sentences, and four- and five-word sentences. In fact, the percentage of subjects having some difficulty was less for four-word than for three-word sentences. When chi-square evaluations were calculated for frequency of errors found between the sentences of varying length, all significant differences disappeared. This is true although the five-word sentences included the negative subject and passive sentences which caused the greatest difficulty in repetition for both groups of children. The syntactic structure of the other five-word sentences—that is, those that are active-declarative and imperative—appears to counteract this source of difficulty. Table 5 indicates the percentage of subjects repeating three-, four-, and five-word sentences with errors, and the number of errors occurring. Table 6 shows the significance of the difference between these percentages and numbers as calculated by chi-square evaluations. Chi squares that were less than one are not listed.

The syntactic structure of the sentence appeared to have a greater effect on ease of repetition than did sentence length. Perhaps, however, the three-word sentence is an exception for the experimental group. A greater percentage of the children with language disorders could repeat this length of sentence without error as compared to the percentages repeating four- and five-word sentences without errors. Three words may be within the immediate memory span of this group of children and, therefore, their repetition of three-word sentences may be rote imitation unaffected by the particular structure of the sentences.

There was an important difference in the ability of the two groups of children to repeat the sentences in Set B as well as those in Set A. A greater percentage of children in the experimental group than in the control group repeated Set B sentences with errors, and the children in the experimental group made more errors than the children in the control group. These results were previously shown in Table 2. Another interesting finding was that in the experimental group there was no significant difference in the percentage of subjects making errors on Set A and Set B sentences, nor in the total number of errors in repeating the two sets of sentences. The children in the control group repeated Set B sentences with a greater percentage of errors than Set A sentences, and made more errors with Set B sentences than with Set A sentences.

The control group's substitutions of lexical items in the repetition of the sentences accounted for most of the difference. Whereas the

Table 7. Percentages of children making errors and number of errors made with Set A and Set B sentences. The *p* value was calculated by chi-square analysis

Groups	Percentage of subjects			Number of errors		
	Set A	*p* Value	Set B	Set A	*p* Value	Set B
Experimental	100	—	100	172	—	242
Control	54	0.01	77	13	0.01	43

number of modification and omission errors the control group made with the two sets of sentences did not differ significantly, they made more substitution errors with Set B sentences. Of the 28 substitution errors the control group made, 13 were noun substitutions. Since Set B sentences were formulated to include as many American English sounds as possible in all three positions in words, some of the sentences contained fairly extraordinary lexical items and combinations of items.

No major differences were found between the number of modification and substitution errors the experimental group made with the two sets, but they made more omission errors with Set B, and most of this difference could be accounted for by article omission. In Set A they omitted articles in 14 instances, and in Set B in 41 instances. In this case the results are affected by the comparative number of articles in the two sets: 15 in Set B versus three in Set A. However, frequency of occurrence alone cannot account for the difference in the types of deviations from complete repetition that occurred with the two sets. Auxiliary and copula verbs occurred with equal frequency in both sets (14 and 14), but these verbs were omitted in 53 instances in Set A, where negative and question sentences were numerous, and were only omitted in 33 instances in Set B. Table 7 gives the percentages of children making errors and number of errors that occurred in the repetition of both sets of sentences by both groups. Table 8 shows the types of errors made.

Given these results, apparently the primary problem for the control group was not the syntactic structure of Set A and Set B, but the properties of some of the lexical items in Set B sentences. They were repeated as items more familiar or phonetically similar (for example, "grazed" for "gazed," and "mupp" for "muff"). The experimental group, on the other hand, simply repeated some of the

Table 8. Types of errors made on sentences in Set A and Set B. The p value was calculated by chi-square analysis

Groups	Modifications			Substitutions			Omissions		
	Set A	p Value	Set B	Set A	p Value	Set B	Set A	p Value	Set B
Experimental	115	—	120	41	—	73	16	0.01	49
Control	9	—	13	4	0.01	28	1	—	2

Table 9. Number of modifications, substitutions, and omissions produced by the experimental group with each sentence type

Sentence type	Modifications	Substitutions	Omissions
Imperative	2	15	7
Negative	31	12	4
Question	46	3	4
Active-declarative	10	7	1
Negative subject	12	2	0
Passive	14	2	0

exotic lexical items (perhaps without understanding) or omitted them, but they continued to find their greatest difficulty in reproducing the syntactic structure of the sentence.

DISCUSSION

The reasons for the degree of difficulty encountered by the language-disordered children in repeating the various sentence types can best be explained by looking at the kinds of errors that occurred. In the repetition of imperative sentences the most frequent errors were the substitution of members of a class in the original sentence ("my" for "your"). In the repetition of active-declarative sentences, the most frequent errors were not marking nouns as plural ("lot" for "lots"), and changing the verb number ("have" and "haves" for "has"). However, in the repetition of negative, question, negative subject, and passive sentences, the most frequent errors were those which either involved expansion of the verb phrase into auxiliary and modal verbs or those which involved the transformational operations necessary to the generation of the sentence type. The number of modifications, substitutions, and omissions that occurred in the repetition of each sentence type is shown in Table 9.

The most frequent error that occurred with negative sentences was modification of the negative construction to "not" or "no" with or without the auxiliary or modal verb as in the following examples:

They won't play with me	They no/not play with me
I can't sing	I no can sing
He doesn't have money	He no have money
She isn't very old	She not very old
The children can't run fast	The children no can run fast

The most frequent errors in the question sentences were omission of the auxiliary or modal verb or no permutation as in the following examples:

What is that	What that
How will he get there	How he will get there
Where is he going	Where he going
When will he come	When he will come

The most frequent error with the negative subject sentence was omission of the auxiliary. "Nobody is going downtown" was repeated as "Nobody going down town." There were two instances in which "nobody" was repeated as "onebody" and "is" was repeated as "isn't." This may indicate that these children were having difficulty with the negative attachment rule and could only apply it in one way, that is, to the verb. In repeating the passive sentence the most frequent types of errors were omission of the auxiliary or the passive marker. "That boy is named Tommy" was repeated as "That boy named Tommy," "That boy name Tommy," or "That boy is name Tommy." Less frequently the verb was not permuted, as in "That boy name is Tommy." A large proportion of the repetition errors of the experimental group were modification (67% of the errors). Most of the modification errors were of the kinds described previously: 46% of these errors were nonexpansions of the verb phrase and 36% were nonapplication of the entire set of rules needed to generate a sentence type.

It might be hypothesized that the children in the experimental group were simply having more difficulty than the children in the control group in remembering every item in a string. Several pieces of evidence indicate that this explanation cannot account for the behavior observed in the repetition of the simple but important sentence types tested in this study, even in those instances in which omissions occurred. First, the length of the sentence was not the factor which most severely affected sentence repetition. More errors did not occur with the longest sentences than occurred with all other shorter sentences. Clearly, this can only be said about the kinds of sentences used in this study. The repetition accuracy of a group of children with language disorders was severely affected by the length of a sentence when different structures than the sentence types used in this study were presented for repetition (Menyuk, 1969). One might hypothesize from these results that if the structure of a sentence is not understood, then repetition accuracy can be severely affected by length in the way that recall of meaningless verbal material is affected by length (Menyuk, 1971, Chapter 5).

Despite the fact that omissions of items in a string occurred, they occurred selectively. For example, when the sentences "Does the boy like milk?" and "That boy is named Tommy" are repeated, the first word is omitted in the first sentence and the third word is omitted in the second. Stress alone cannot account for both these items being omitted, since "does" in the first sentence receives some stress, while "is" in the second sentence receives no stress. The feature that both these items have in common is the fact that both are expansions of the verb phrase. Further, some of the errors observed had the effect of increasing the absolute length of the sentence, such as "I no can sing" for "I can't sing." Apparently, the factor creating the greatest difficulty in repetition for the experimental group is not difficulty in remembering all the items in the sentence but, rather, difficulty in understanding the transformational structure of these sentences.

Members of the group exhibited various degrees of difficulty in regenerating these sentences. The simplest reencoding of the sentence types produced by these children was the addition of the transformational marker to the underlying sentences as in negative + sentence ("He no have money") and question + sentence ("The boy have milk?" or "What that?"). This might be termed a Level I performance. A more complicated reencoding, or a Level II performance, includes the expansion of the verb phrase ("I no can sing" and "When he will come"). The next step in negation development, Level III, is the attachment of the negative element to the auxiliary or modal verb ("I can't sing"), and the next step in question development, Level III, is the permutation of the auxiliary or modal verb ("Does the boy like milk?" and "Where is he going?"). In the case of the passive sentence, a Level I analysis would result in either "That boy name Tommy" or "That boy named Tommy." Given the usual performance of the experimental group, the attachment of "ed" to "name" seems to be a result of rote performance rather than real comprehension and, therefore, "name" and "named" seem to reflect the same level of performance. A Level II analysis of the passive is "That boy is name Tommy." A Level III analysis is "That boy is named Tommy." One should remember that the passive construction requires the attachment of the passive marker to the verb. Figure 1 shows a graphic representation of the three levels.

Many of the children with language disorders were functioning

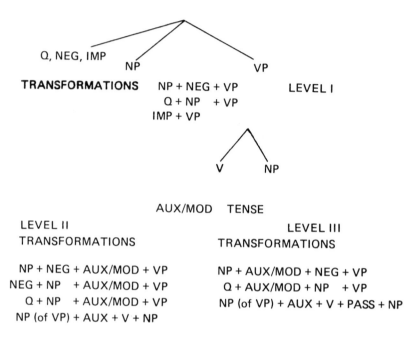

Figure 1. A graphic representation of the various levels of syntactic knowledge found in the sentence repetitions of the deviant-speaking and normal-speaking children.

on Level I. Their analyses of sentences had only reached the depth of determining the sentence type and applying a marker of that type. Other children in the group were capable of the deeper analyses involved in Level II and in some instances in the analyses involved in Level III. These latter children could reproduce the negative structure accurately but not the question. This is probably because question formation requires permutation of the subject and auxiliary and modal verbs. This transformational operation is a comparatively late acquisition by normal-speaking children (Menyuk, 1969). The difficulty with the negative subject and truncated passive sentences for those children who had achieved Level III in the repetition of the negative structure appears to be the attachment of the negative marker to the subject and the attachment of the passive marker to the verb. Whether or not these operations are also comparatively late acquisitions for normal-speaking children needs to be explored.

In contrast to the performance of the children in the experimental group, the most frequent error of the children in the control group with Set A sentences was changing the structure of a sentence by, theoretically at least, adding a transformational operation. That is, four children repeated "Nobody..." as "Nobody's..." and, thus, added the operation of deletion to generate a contracted structure. The performance of the two groups indicates that information about the underlying structure of sentences is stored by both deviant-speaking and normal-speaking children and used in sentence repetition, but the nature of the information stored varies. The children with language disorders as well as the children without do not generate sentences randomly.

The differences in the type of information stored can be described as differences in the level of analysis of sentence structures with different levels representing degrees of complexity of the analysis. Most of the children with language disorders analyze the sentence types tested at the simplest level (Level I), whereas the children without language disorders analyze these sentences at the most complex level (Level III). Each level of complexity appears to indicate a change in the form of the information about structures that is stored in memory, but information about the simpler form of a structure is retained since fluctuations occur in repetition. For example, some children reproduce negative sentences with both Level I and II forms and other children with Level II and III forms. However, no child produced negative sentences with I and III forms.

This description does not explain how these differences between the groups in sentence repetition abilities occur nor why they occur, but only what does occur. We can speculate about the how in a fairly logical manner. Although Level I is the simplest level of analysis, it does satisfactorily convey the information intended by the various structures. The negative of a declarative is expressed and a question is asked simply by marking the sentence as negative or question in some way. In the regeneration of these sentence types children who are functioning at Level I reproduce important information-bearing elements, although some aspects of information are lost. Information about time, for example, is completely lost, since tense is rarely marked. However, if there are limitations on the structural decoding capacities of these children, even though the meanings of these sentence types are understood, then elements which convey these meanings would be preserved and other aspects lost. In other words, these children retain representations of the semantic aspects of these sentence types, how to express them, and little more. Elsewhere

(Menyuk, 1969) it has been hypothesized that this distorted decoding capacity is the result of limits on immediate memory. These limits do not allow time for storage of the complete phrase or sentence and a deeper analysis than that required to derive meaning-bearing elements. Therefore, these children come up with the simple forms of rules that are reflected in their repetitions. These rules are now part of the children's grammars, and they use them to reproduce sentences. One cannot even logically speculate about why these differences in language processing exist between the two groups of children, but can only state that the differences must lie in their central nervous system functioning, and speculate that this functioning is specifically related to language, given their usual performance in other cognitive areas. The basis of this difference appears to be the functioning of memory in these children, but no evidence has been obtained about the possible anatomical and physiological reasons for this difference.

Even though we do not understand why linguistic functioning is awry for these children with language disorders, clearly they can be helped by therapeutic programs which take into account the level and content of their linguistic functioning in the generation of sentences. For example, in generating negative sentences, the child may be having difficulty because he hasn't learned to expand the verb phrase, because he doesn't know how to apply the negative attachment rule in any context, or because he doesn't know how to apply the attachment rule except in the case of modal verbs. Descriptions of his linguistic functioning, such as these examples, can reveal the important facts of what needs to be taught to these children. Teaching them to apply a grammatical operation in the generation of a sentence type may, in turn, give them the ability to apply this operation in all other contexts, and it is this kind of ability that is the basis of grammatical competence. What is needed, therefore, is more research on the level and content of linguistic functioning in the sentence generation of language-disordered children.

REFERENCES

Dunn, L. M. 1959. Peabody Picture Vocabulary Test. American Guidance Service, Circle Pines, Minn.
Hejna, R. F. 1959. Developmental Articulation Test. Typing and Printing, Madison, Wisc.
Kirk, S. L., J. J. McCarthy, and W. D. Kirk. 1968. Illinois Test of Psycholinguistic Abilities. University of Illinois Press, Urbana, Ill.

Menyuk, P. 1963. A preliminary evaluation of grammatical capacity of children. J. Verb. Learn. Verb. Behav. 2:429–439.

Menyuk, P. 1964. Comparison of grammar of children with functionally deviant and normal speech. J. Speech Hearing Res. 7:109–121.

Menyuk, P. 1969. Sentences Children Use. M.I.T. Press, Cambridge, Mass.

Menyuk, P. 1971. The Acquisition and Development of Language. Prentice-Hall, Englewood Cliffs, N.J.

Menyuk, P., and P. L. Looney. 1972. Relationships among components of the grammar in language disorder. J. Speech Hearing Res. 15:395–406.

COGNITION/
PRAGMATICS

The Cognitive Hypothesis of Language Acquisition and Its Implications for Child Language Deficiency

RICHARD F. CROMER

Cromer is one of the few child language researchers whose work concerns both normal and deficient populations and, consequently, covers a broad spectrum of research. In this paper, he provides a general framework for constructing the complex relationships between language and thought. To clarify these relationships, he draws an analogy between linguistic deep and surface structures (and the operations or transformations that connect them) and cognitive "deep" and "surface" structures (and the cognitive operations that map one onto the other). Moreover, Cromer proposes that it is not the cognitive *structures* described by Piaget that have the most immediate link to the linguistic system. Rather, intentions and meanings or the "surface" aspect of cognition underlies and forms the most immediate connection with linguistic developments. In addition, certain developments in language acquisition—both early and late—appear to evolve quite independently of cognition. The further study of these independent linguistic developments using a population of dysphasic children might well demonstrate whether independent aspects of language appear later than those aspects which are more closely tied to intellectual growth or whether some of them fail to develop at all.

—DMM

"Thought has its own structure, and the transition from it to speech is no easy matter." *Vygotsky*

The interrelationship of thought and language is a topic that has interested philosophers and scientists for centuries. For the past 50

years or more, psychologists have usually emphasized the importance of language in forming and shaping thought. There are historical
reasons for this.

TRADITIONAL BEHAVIORISTIC APPROACH TO LANGUAGE

In the attempt to make the practice of psychology more scientific, an
increasing emphasis was placed on observable behavioral phenomena. One cannot observe thoughts, but one can treat the descriptions of thoughts in a verbal medium as observable phenomena.
Moreover, considered experimentally, it is possible to measure and
quantify the acquisition of particular words or word classes, and it is
thus more tidy, theoretically, to conceptualize the influence of such
external phenomena as affecting thought (as measured by behavior)
than the other way around. Developmentally this is also true. In this
tradition, the child was conceived of as a passive organism that was
exposed to various stimuli, including verbal stimuli. Since language
was believed to be acquired as a series of habits, it was easy to explain
the origin of thought: it was nothing more than the accumulation of
various combinations of verbal stimuli—of words and language structure. This point of view reached its most extreme form in the theoretical writings of John B. Watson, the founder of the psychological
school of behaviorism. He claimed that thought was really a form of
subvocal speech, and that all thought would be observable as tiny
movements of the larynx when equipment sophisticated enough to
detect such movements was eventually developed. Although these
movements are now observable and can be seen to occur, the real
question is whether they are necessary in order for thought to take
place. One experiment by a highly motivated scientist suggests that
they are not. The subject was injected with a dose of d-tubocurarine
chloride sufficient for complete paralysis of his skeletal musculature.
As this paralyzes the respiratory system, he was kept breathing by
artificial means. In this state, with the speech musculature completely immobilized, the subject was still capable of thought and was
later able to report his thoughts and perceptions (Smith et al., 1947).
It is not necessary to engage in such an extreme experimental demonstration in order to make the point that not all thought is dependent on
language. Common observation suggests that the deaf, even those
who have had no language training in another sensory modality, are
capable of thinking (see James, 1890, pp. 266–269), and Furth (1966)

has provided experimental evidence of the abilities of the deaf to engage in complex thought processes.

INFLUENCE OF LANGUAGE ON THOUGHT

A second major influence emphasizing the importance of language on the thought processes came from anthropological linguistics. Edward Sapir and Benjamin Lee Whorf independently put forward the thesis which carries their names. The Sapir-Whorf hypothesis basically asserts that the language that one speaks directly determines major aspects of thought. For example, the "Standard Average European" languages, as Whorf called them, code their verbs into tenses roughly equivalent to temporal entities such as past, present, and future. By so doing, these languages objectify time as if it were a ribbon with various spaces marked off. By contrast, some American Indian languages such as Hopi do not use tenses for their verbs. Consequently, the Hopi speaker's conception of the notion of time or duration is very different from that of the speakers of Standard Average European languages. Since Whorf believed that language and language habits determine the thought processes, he would expect Hopi speakers to find concepts such as simultaneity difficult while we do not; but we find concepts of relativity difficult, while Hopi speakers understand these with ease. Reviews of the Sapir-Whorf hypothesis can be found in Henle (1958), Hoijer (1954), and Slobin (1971b). A number of studies on this topic have been reprinted by Adams (1972). Sapir's writings have been collected by Mandelbaum (1949, 1961), and Whorf's essays have been brought together by Carroll (1956).

It has been noted, however, that the speakers of one language *can* understand the concepts which are easily expressed and taken for granted by speakers of another language. In translation, it may be necessary to use long phrases where the original language uses a single word, but it can be done. Even when the language we speak is "resistant" to certain concepts, we can learn about these ideas, although they may not come to us as "naturally" as they might to speakers of another language. Roger Brown (1956), in an essay on language and thought, developed this idea in a way which somewhat undermines the extreme form of linguistic determinism found in the Sapir-Whorf hypothesis. Brown suggested that languages differ in the ease with which they code various concepts. The ease of codability of a concept in turn affects the availability of that concept for use by a speaker of that language. The Eskimo has several different words for differing kinds of snow, and this is important in his environment. But we too can learn to recognize hard-packed snow, soft-packed snow, etc., and to speak about them—even though it takes more than one word for us to do so—when circumstances make it important for us to take note of these differences. In other words, since these concepts are not as easily coded in our language as they are in Eskimo, we are less disposed to think in terms of them, although we can do so when necessary. Brown argues, then, that language does not *determine* our thoughts as the Sapir-Whorf hypothesis asserts; rather, our language only *predisposes* us to think in particular ways. This view has come to be known as the weak form of the Sapir-Whorf hypothesis, and a number of studies have given experimental support to it (e.g., Brown and Lenneberg, 1954, 1958; Lantz and Stefflre, 1964). Miller and McNeill (1969) have provided a good review of the whole issue.

The idea of the language we speak predisposing us to think in particular ways is closely related to another current of interest in psychology: the importance of language in facilitating thought through its use as a mediating function (see, e.g., Kendler, 1963; Spiker, 1963). This is a very interesting and important area of research, and has received attention from those dealing with mental retardation. For example, it has been claimed that in recognition experiments subnormal children may be relatively handicapped by their lack of spontaneously forming verbal connections (Bryant, 1965, 1967; see also review by Bryant, 1970). However, when they are *forced* to verbalize, the differences between normals and subnormals disappear. Bryant has argued that the severely subnormal suffer from a restriction of attention unless they are made to form verbal labels. Of course, the benefit of verbalization may not be due to mediating properties as such, but instead may result solely from increased attention which the verbal label induces. (See in this connection the carefully designed experiments on severely subnormal children by Morris, 1972, 1975). For varying theoretical reasons, then, verbalization and language are said to facilitate performance on some tasks. Anyone seriously studying the interconnections between thought and language will be concerned with research in this field. A good review of research and theory on this topic is to be found in Blank (1974).

In this chapter, a slightly different issue is being raised. Our central concern for the moment is not whether or how verbal materials facilitate thinking, but whether certain cognitive abilities are actually *dependent* on language. One of these is the ability to transfer information learned in one sensory modality to use in another sensory modality, a process which has come to be called crossmodal transfer. At one time, this ability was thought to be limited to human beings, and that language was the mechanism that served to link the modalities. However, Hermelin and O'Connor (1964) have found that normal, subnormal, and autistic children did not differ in their ability to transfer from vision to touch on some tasks, even though their verbal abilities differed markedly. They thus rejected the view that crossmodal effects were due to verbal coding. One can also approach the problem from the other way around. Training children to use particular verbal labels in a crossmodal task should lead to solution of the task. But O'Connor and Hermelin (1971) have found in other experiments that normal, subnormal, and deaf children were unable to transfer a touch discrimination to another modality even when most subjects were able to verbalize the solution.

There are still other reasons for suspecting that crossmodal transfer effects may not be entirely dependent on language. The importance of language as the causative agent in the solution of these tasks was initially based on the observation that animals cannot be trained to perform them. It was assumed that the reason that they could not transfer information from one modality to another was that they lacked language. But recently, crossmodal transfer has in fact been demonstrated in other species including apes (Davenport and Rogers, 1970; Davenport, Rogers, and Russell, 1973), rhesus monkeys (Cowley and Weiskrantz, 1975), and even in rats (Over and Mackintosh, 1969) and rabbits (Yehle and Ward, 1969).

A LINGUISTIC VIEWPOINT

A third source of increased emphasis on the importance of language has been the revolution in linguistics sparked by Chomsky (1957, 1959, 1965). His views on language are well known to most students in the field, and an excellent review of his basic ideas is to be had in Lyons (1970). The most important effect of his theory for psychologists has been to challenge some of the basic assumptions concerning methods by which human beings acquire language. Such principles as practice, frequency, imitation, and reinforcement have been called into question and are seen as being inadequate by themselves to explain the language acquisition process. The theoretical reasoning backed by empirical evidence for this position can be found in reviews by Bellugi (1967, 1971), Bever, Fodor, and Weksel (1965a, 1965b), Brown, Cazden, and Bellugi-Klima (1969), Ervin-Tripp (1966), McNeill (1966, 1970a, 1970b), Miller and McNeill (1969), Sachs (1971), and Slobin (1971b).

The claim which is of central importance for this paper has to do with how much the child brings with him to the language acquisition task. Chomsky's viewpoint (1962, 1965, 1966, 1968) is that the child has, innately, a number of formal and substantive linguistic mechanisms which are part of what is called his "language acquisition device" (LAD). Since these mechanisms are innate, they will be found universally in the structure of the languages of the world. Notice that the claim for innateness is not predicated on the observation of linguistic universals. Rather, it is based on a number of observations—the ease and rapidity with which a child acquires his language, the similarity of stages of acquisition in unrelated children and even across different languages, the observation of what appears to be a critical period, etc.—which suggest that children bring some specifically linguistic information and strategies to the job of learning language. It is only because these features are said to be innate that they will be found universally. And it should be noted that although more general cognitive and perceptual strategies may also play an important part in this acquisition process, at least some mechanisms are thought to be of a purely "linguistic" sort. There is a sense in which this is related to a view which Vygotsky (1962) put forward in the 1930's. He felt that language and thought came from separate roots and hypothesized the existence at a very young age of both a prelinguistic phase of thought and a preintellectual phase in the development of speech. It is this latter aspect which is emphasized by whose who study the acquisition of the structure of language with relatively little attention paid to thought and meaning. Many scientists feel uneasy about the idea of innate linguistic mechanisms. However, a few years ago they similarly felt uneasy about the idea of innate perceptual mechanisms. But the discovery by Hubel and Wiesel (1962) of specific perceptual receptors in the cortex of the cat for horizontal and vertical orientation has challenged the older beliefs and made speculation about innate perceptual analyzers respectable. Bower (1971) and Bower and Wishart (1972) in a number of cleverly designed experiments have demonstrated that the concept of object permanency is already present in infants only a few weeks old, which contradicts the Piagetian view that object permanence is much more slowly acquired during the sensorimotor period. In the field of language, recent experiments by Eimas (reviewed in Eimas, 1974) have shown that perception of speech differs from the perception of nonspeech acoustic signals in infants as young as 1 month of age. It is thus no longer unacceptable to hypothesize innate mechanisms for language and language structure, although these still remain to be more narrowly specified and experimentally demonstrated.

The three influences so far mentioned here—the traditional behavioristic approach to thought and language, anthropological linguistics with its emphasis on cultural relativity and the Sapir-Whorf hypothesis, and the linguistic school of generative grammar—have all emphasized the importance or priority of language. Whether believed to be learned by traditional learning theory methods or whether acquired by other means, language is seen as either a very important determiner of one's thoughts and cognitions or to be at least partially independent of those cognitions. More recently, however, psychologists studying language have begun to adhere to the opposite point of view. They are now emphasizing the importance of the underlying thoughts, meanings, or intentions, as significant in the development of language. Rather than a purely structural approach to the language acquisition process, they prefer to study the *functions* of language, and some claims have been made that this functional approach with greater attention paid to these underlying meanings and their communication is necessary to understand language at all. A few of these theorists even seem to imply that these functions are sufficient to *explain* the language acquisition process, an assumption that I will question further on in this chapter.

COGNITIVE PROCESSES UNDERLYING LANGUAGE

There are really two separate issues involved when one talks about cognitive processes underlying language. First, there are the thoughts, intentions, and meanings themselves, which can be called "cognitions." Some experimental evidence will be reviewed which lends support to the claim that language development depends to a great extent on these developing cognitions. Second, a related type of notion, which goes to a "deeper level," so to speak, and emphasizes the underpinnings of these thoughts or cognitions, is discussed. These mechanisms can be termed "cognitive structures." As is pointed out, Piagetian theory is essentially concerned with these cognitive structures and the ways in which various "cognitive operations" result in particular cognitions at different developmental stages. The

Piagetian view is that cognitive structures and operations make language acquisition possible. After reviewing these Piagetian claims, other mechanisms of cognitive structure will be discussed. These include, for example, short-term memory capacity and "production span capacity," and some attempt will be made to link these to child language deficiency.

In order to clarify this terminology, these various levels are illustrated in Figure 1. This representation shows the terms just mentioned. Those terms enclosed in round boxes represent structures. Those enclosed in square boxes denote rules and operations which link the various structural levels. Not all language-related phenomena are illustrated, nor are all the complex interconnections shown. For example, the graphological and phonological components are undoubtedly linked in complicated ways which would be of interest to those studying the processes involved in learning to read. There are important influences acting between surface structure and the semantic component, and these too are not shown. Indeed, not even

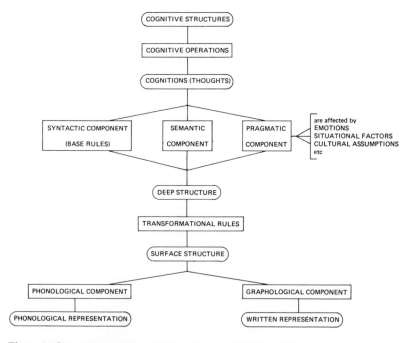

Figure 1. Structures and operations relevant to language. (*Round boxes* represent structures; *square boxes* denote rules and operations linking the structural levels.)

all of the phenomena which are shown are discussed. The purposes of illustrating some of the rules and structures in this way are, first, to draw attention to the differences between cognitive structures, cognitive operations, and cognitions (thoughts), and, second, to highlight the fact that thoughts and meanings are not identical with semantic meanings. Several psychologists unfortunately appear to have fallen into the habit of equating these quite different entities. A third point that is illustrated is the claim that is supported at the end of this article, that semantic operations and syntactic operations are at some level at least partially independent processes. This is true also of still another set of rules which have been labeled the pragmatic component. A good deal of research on mother-child interaction relevant to this pragmatic component is now being carried out (e.g., Bates, this volume; Bruner, 1975, in press; Ryan, 1974) but these are not dealt with in this chapter.

We are mainly concerned here with the interrelations between the various cognitive levels (cognitive structures, operations, and cognitions) and language itself (the syntactic, semantic, and pragmatic components). Having first reviewed some evidence for the importance of these cognitive processes in determining various aspects of language acquisition, I nevertheless question the explanatory adequacy of a purely "cognitive" approach in the sense just outlined. Although the cognitive viewpoint accounts for a great deal of the observed facts of language acquisition, I suggest that by itself it is insufficient to explain that acquisition, and I review some evidence to support the claim that there may be some purely "linguistic" processes which are also necessary in order to account for the encoding of thought into language. These purely linguistic processes are also of importance in dealing with some types of child language deficiency.

INFLUENCE OF COGNITIONS ON LANGUAGE ACQUISITION

The current emphasis in child language acquisition studies is on the fact that the child appears to be attempting to communicate meanings. He is not simply passively acquiring a number of language structures that he hears in his environment. This appears to be true even at the very earliest stages.

Cognitions in Infants

Recent studies suggest the possibility that meaning is present in the cries of the newborn infant. Lind (1965) has reviewed some studies of the cries of babies, and Wolff (1969) has demonstrated that different cries in the newborn communicate different meanings. Ricks (1972) has conducted an interesting experiment which suggests not only that infants express meanings in their cries, but that very young children who are diagnosed as being autistic do not share this same meaning-linked system. The normal infants in his study were aged 8–12 months. The autistic children were 3–5 years of age. Ricks observed that a child appeared to give similar cries in similar situations. He operationalized this by setting up a number of standardized situations and recording the child's cries in that condition. For example, to elicit the cry of "pleased surprise" he either blew up a balloon in front of the child or lit a sparkler in front of him. He similarly designed other standardized situations which elicited the three other cries he studied: a request cry, a frustrated cry, and a greeting. These four types of message were recorded on tapes. In the next part of the experiment, six parents of normal babies and six parents of autistic children listened to the sounds of four babies in the four types of situations, on tapes which had been re-spliced so that the cries occurred randomly. Parents of normal babies heard the cries of their own baby, two other babies of English-speaking parents, and one baby with non-English-speaking parents. The parents of autistic children heard the sounds made by their own autistic child, two other autistic children, and one nonautistic subnormal child matched for age. The task for the parents was very similar. They all had to label the 16 sounds they heard as to the four meanings. In addition, they were asked to pick out their own child. At the same time, parents of normal babies were asked to identify the baby of non-English-speaking parents, and parents of autistic children were asked to identify the nonautistic child. Finally, both groups heard the request sounds of six babies, and they were asked to pick out their own child.

The results showed that parents hearing the cries of normal babies had no difficulty in identifying the 16 cries. But much to their astonishment, they could not pick out their own baby. Furthermore, they could not identify which baby was the non-English baby. In other words, it is as if normal babies share a set of cries which are tied to specific meanings and which occur regardless of the language the parents speak. By contrast, the parents of autistic children easily identified their own child and its distinctive cries. But they could not identify the idiosyncratic cries of the other two autistic children. They were, however, able to identify the meanings of the cries of the nonautistic subnormal child. In other words, the subnormal child shared the intonated signals of normal babies, and these could be identified by the parents of autistic children. The autistic children, however, do not seem to share this vocabulary of intonated signals. Although these findings can also be cited as support for the position that in normal children, there is a specifically linguistic-like process which is independent of the exposure to particular languages, it is also of note that these earliest cries are directly tied to particular meanings.

Kaplan and Kaplan (1971) have suggested that the child's semantic system develops out of early distinctions that are present in his communication system. They hope eventually to be able to chart the developmental order of their emergence. For example, when the child is able to make the early distinction between human and nonhuman sounds, then he is credited with the feature ± human. When he differentiates himself from others, the feature ± ego is said to be operative. As the child acquires his knowledge of the properties of objects, he adds such features as ± existence and ± presence. Other later acquisitions include ± agent, ± past, etc. These semantic features are said by the Kaplans to place constraints on the child's language acquisition. Although the theory has been formulated with reference to the infant's first sounds, a similar kind of analysis could be extended to grammatical acquisitions at later ages.

Acquisition of First Words

Studies on the acquisition of first words by the child have recently provided some interesting evidence on the language/thought controversy. It used to be believed that children acquired the words they heard around them and thereby learned the associated concepts and ideas. Having more words would lead to having more concepts. A form of this theory is still generally believed as can be observed in the frantic study of lists of vocabulary items by students about to take scholastic aptitude tests, or in programs aimed at increasing the intelligence of some particular groups by giving intensive vocabulary and language training. However, another study by Ricks (1972, 1975) suggests that the child is a very active organism in acquiring his first words and seems to attempt to use words to express only those concepts that he is cognitively able to handle. Furthermore, only words that refer to these concepts are likely to be imitated. Ricks noticed that the child's first words, at about age 11–18 months, were of two basic types. One type, which he called "dada words," had very loose referents or were used in babble without any referents at all.

These included such common words as "mama" and "dada." At some point, however, the children began to use a second type of word which has very different characteristics. Ricks called these "label words" and noted a number of features by which they differed from the "dada words." For example, the label words are not found in the babbling as the dada words are. The label word only occurs along with the event for which it is a label. When the word is repeated the child does not modify it to resemble the more conventional term. Indeed, as Ricks points out, the parents often begin using the child's term. Other features of these label words are that they are repeated by the child with great excitement, and mention of these words usually captures the child's attention as if it alerts him to look for the object which it signifies. Finally, these words frequently generalize so that, for example, "bow wow" used for a dog is soon used for any four-legged animal. In a controlled experiment Ricks recorded three types of words on tapes for each individual child. The tapes included adults saying the child's own label words, dada words, and meaningless combinations such as "dibby," which the child was capable of producing but had not been heard to utter. The child's imitations of the words on the tapes were carefully recorded and revealed that most imitations were of his own label words. There was some imitation of the dada words, but imitation of the meaningless combinations was very low. It appears, then, that the child has a number of concepts that he attempts to use and to generalize to other situations. This is a very different conception from the older theories which saw the child as essentially a passive organism that was merely exposed to words which were then acquired by imitation. What seems to be nearer to the truth is that the child does not *learn* words; rather, he *invents* them for the things he wants to communicate.

It may be somewhat inaccurate to characterize these first inventions as "label words," for there is evidence that they are not used like labels at all. Many investigators have noticed that these first words are more like complete sentences or thoughts, and they have often been termed "mot-phrases," "sentence words," and "holophrases." For example, in 1927, Grace deLaguna noted that the proper names that the child uttered were not merely used to designate or label the individual. Instead, they were used to make various comments about that person. The child might point at a pair of slippers, but instead of labeling them he might say "Papa," whose slippers they happened to be. McNeill (1970a, 1970b) has argued that this holophrastic speech is evidence that the child possesses the basic grammatical relations such as predication, direct and indirect object relationships, and modification. If this is so, then it indicates that children are able to express meaning from the outset of language acquisition. In other words, the child is not learning a set of linguistic categories which then restructure his thinking. Instead, he brings certain meanings to the task of language acquisition, and these meanings affect even his very first words.

This prior understanding or intent to express meaning has also been emphasized by Ervin-Tripp (1971). She has suggested that the child would be unable to master language unless the meanings were obvious to him when he heard sentences expressing them. It is thus crucially important to study the various categories, features, and relations that are available to the child during his language acquisition, and to chart their developmental progression. One would then be able to specify which properties of the input are incomprehensible to children at various stages. Although Ervin-Tripp was making her claim in relation to normal children, it is obviously of even greater importance for language programs with educationally subnormal children or with children with other cognitive disabilities.

What then are some of the earliest meanings young children are said to be aware of before they have the linguistic means for expressing them, and how do they affect the language acquisition process? It is very difficult to assess what the young child intends, but one can rely to some extent on a combination of the situational cues, linguistic context, and parental interpretations to form some idea of what the child appears to be trying to communicate. In the well known studies by Roger Brown and his associates on the detailed acquisition of language by three children, there are a number of observations which bear on this important question. The children were recorded in their natural home situations for 2 hours at 2-week intervals for several years. Adult speech was also noted as were pertinent situational cues. Detailed descriptions of portions of the structural analysis of the children's utterances have been reported in a number of papers (Brown and Bellugi, 1964; Brown and Fraser, 1964; Brown and Hanlon, 1970; Brown, Cazden, and Bellugi-Klima, 1969; Brown, Fraser, and Bellugi, 1964) and most of these papers have been reprinted in Brown (1970).

Recently, Brown (1973) has turned his attention to the analysis of the expression of meaning in these utterances. In the earliest stage of their language acquisition, as defined not by age but by a mean utterance length of 1¹/₂–2 morphemes, the children used the verb in an unmarked, generic form; it did not have any inflectional endings. Nevertheless, such a verb was understood by the parents of the children in one of four ways, depending on the situation in which the utterance occurred. One of these was the *imperative,* as when the child said "Get book" as a kind of command. A second meaning was reference to the *past.* Thus, the child might say "Book drop" in a situation in which he had in fact just dropped the book. A third meaning ascribed to the child was that of *intention* or *prediction.* For example, the child once said "Mommy read" when the mother was getting ready to read to the child. Finally, there was the expression of what is called *present temporary duration,* where the adult would use a progressive form such as "The fish is swimming." By contrast, the child's unmarked form would be merely, "Fish swim."

During this stage, the children gradually began to modify the unmarked verb in three ways. They began using a past tense form using either "-ed" or an irregular allomorph, producing such utterances as "It dropped" and "It fell." These were at first limited to a very immediate past. A second way they began to modify the verb was to use it in conjunction with a semi-auxiliary or catenative such as "gonna," "wanna," and "hafta." It is impossible to judge when these forms are required by a context. Nevertheless, Brown notes that their meaning can be mainly characterized as expressing some kind of intentionality or imminence, a kind of immediate future about the child's own intentions or of actions about to occur. Utterances categorized as expressing this intent, as based on situational cues, include "I wanna go" and "It's gonna fall." The third modification that the child began to use was a primitive progressive form. This consisted of using "-ing" endings on the verb even though the auxiliary was still being omitted, as in, for example, "He swimming." Now what is startling is that these first three inflections that the child begins to use encode three of the four meaningful intentions attributed by adults to the child—the immediate past, intention or prediction, and present temporary duration. Furthermore, the fourth meaning, the imperative, has no specific grammatical marker in English, but Brown notes that children begin to use the word "Please" at just this time along with the three other markers. It appears, then, that the first grammatical distinctions that the child makes with his verbs are precisely those which encode the types of meaning he has been credited with trying to express just prior to the acquisition of those linguistic forms.

There are a number of other examples where the child apparently begins to express particular meanings just before acquiring the linguistic means for their proper expression. One of these is the possessive inflection, as, for example, the "'s" in "Adam's bike." Brown noted that the children in his study did not reach a criterion of 90% use in situations where this inflection was obligatory until what he called stage III—a stage at which their mean utterance length was above 2½ morphemes. Yet they had clearly been making reference to possession for some time before this. The children evidenced many constructions such as "Adam chair" in contexts where possession was indicated. In one case, Eve went around the room pointing and appropriately saying "That Eve nose," "That Mommy nose right there," "That Papa nose right there." These are not likely to have been rote learned. A clear indication that they are not occurred the very first time Colin Fraser was served coffee by the mother; Eve pointed and said "Fraser coffee." Bloom (1970) also presents evidence from three other children acquiring language which clearly shows that they used the concept of possession well before they began to use the grammatical inflection proper for its linguistic expression. It is from this same study by Bloom that some very interesting observations concerning the development of the expression of negation are made.

Development of Expression of Negation

Bloom's study paid particular attention to situational factors during language acquisition and thus focused on meaning. In looking at the syntactic development of negation, she approached the data in two ways. In one type of analysis, she noted all utterances which included some kind of negative element, such as "no," "not," "don't," etc. But, in addition, she also looked at the child's utterances from the standpoint of meaning. In doing this, she listed all utterances which carried a negative intent even though they contained no negative linguistic element. This negative intent was interpreted from various situational cues such as the child shaking his head, pushing an object away, or refusing to follow directions. Bloom found three basic types of negation—nonexistence, rejection, and denial. Nonexistence was used by the child in situations where, as the term indicates, the referent was nonexistent. For example, when the child said "no pocket" when in fact there was no pocket, this was listed as an example of nonexistence. Rejection was signaled by actions by which the child appeared to be registering that meaning, for example, by pushing an offered object away. The third type of negation, denial, asserts that some predication is not the case. If we say, "That's not an apple" when someone has said that it is, we are using this third type of negation. The intentions of the child are interpreted by a combination of cues. A good illustration of the way particular utterances are analyzed is the child's "No dirty soap" which is listed as an example of rejection. The child made the utterance while being given a bath, and as he did so he pushed away the soap which was being offered. The researcher did not rely on that cue alone, however; in addition, the existence of the soap and the fact that it was dirty were noted. In context, then, "No dirty soap" was not being used to indicate that there was no soap (nonexistence), nor that there was no *dirty* soap. It was through a combination of cues—the pushing away, the presence of a dirty piece of soap—that the utterance could be reasonably classified as an instance of rejection.

Bloom found that there was a fairly constant order of development of these three types of negation in the three children. The first to emerge syntactically was nonexistence. It was usually syntactically elaborated with the words "no more" as in "no more lights," "no more people." Rejection was the next category to be used and it eventually came to be signaled mainly by "don't" as in "I don't need pants off," "Don't eat it." Denial was the last of the three categories to be used, and it came to be marked mainly by the use of "not" as in "That not lollipop," and "It's not cold out." It should be noted, however, that Bloom was concerned solely with the development of *syntactic* negative reference. She does not make clear in her report whether the child was able to refer to all three types of negation at the earliest stage when only the nonsyntactically elaborated "No" was used. We are told that when the child's syntactic expression was limited to nonexistence, he used "No" to indicate both rejection and denial, and this would seem to imply that all three types of negative meaning were already available, at least at the stage that nonexistence was syntactically elaborated. There is another aspect to the acquisition of these negative forms which can be of help in unraveling the thought/language controversy.

It should be recalled that the three children in Bloom's study came to express nonexistence mainly by the use of "no more," rejection by the use of "don't," and denial by "not." Adult English does not make this distinction. Yet the children imposed this progressive differentiation in the forms used to express negation and these forms were directly linked to three different meanings. The way this differentiation occurred is of some importance. Bloom notes that when the children first began to use a new type of negative reference, such as rejection or denial, they did so by using the more primitive structure that previously had expressed the earlier acquired concept, nonexistence. For example, when rejection was first syntactically elaborated, use was made of the form "no more." As it developed as a category, it began to be expressed with other forms and came mainly to be expressed by "don't." Then, denial emerged, and it too was first formed by the use of "no more," only later coming to be signaled by "not." In other words, it is not the case that children learn some new vocabulary items like "don't" or "not" which then lead to the emergence of new meanings. Rather, when one looks at context and intended meaning, it is the cognitive category which is seen to emerge first. The child makes use of the linguistic forms he has already mastered in order to express the differentiation of these meanings.

Acquisition of Concepts of Time

A few years ago, when I made a study of the development of time concepts during the acquisition of language by two of the children in the Roger Brown study, Adam and Sarah, I observed the same phenomenon (Cromer, 1968). In fact, there are really two interrelated aspects to the observation that cognition plays a crucial role during the language acquisition process. Not only do children use primitive forms to express new meanings, but it is also observed that they fail to acquire common forms, some of which appear to be structurally simple, until they possess the cognitive capacity to understand the concepts to which these forms refer. For example, Slobin (1966) has called attention to the fact that for children acquiring Russian the conditional is a late acquisition in spite of it being a structurally easy category in that language. It appears that the reason for their failure to use this form is the relatively late emergence of the understanding of hypotheticalness. This was also observed in the children acquiring English (Cromer, 1968, 1974a). For example, there was a delay in the use of certain structures using "if." Young children were observed to use such structures, but only when they referred to "uncertainty of conditions" as in "See if Mommy wants some more grain." Only at a later age did children use these structures to refer to true hypothetical conditions, and thus begin to make utterances like "What you think would happen if I put a stick?" A still clearer illustration of these points is to be found in the child's acquisition of the perfect tense in English.

The perfect tense is said by linguists generally to encode a rather complex temporal relationship which they call "current relevance." Use of relevance indicates that the speaker is calling attention to the importance of the referred-to event to the time being indicated by the utterance being made. For example, a statement such as "The lamp fell" tells us nothing about the current state of the lamp. It may still be in a fallen position or it may have been righted by someone. On the other hand, if we say "The lamp has fallen," we are indicating that the lamp is still in a fallen position at the time of the utterance or that the consequences engendered by its falling are relevant to the utterance we are making. This notion of relevance can be extended beyond the use encoded in English to a psychologically similar process whereby one considers the relevance from likely future consequences to the actions one is currently engaged in. Some examples of this are given in Cromer (1968), but we will consider here only the more usual meaning of relevance.

One can approach the acquisition of a concept and its expression in two different ways. On the one hand, one can trace the development of the linguistic expression of the concept—the acquisition of the elements that make up the perfect tense, for example. On the other hand, one can trace the development of the cognition itself—for example, the ability to use the concept of relevance regardless of the linguistic devices normally employed to express it. Taking first the linguistic expression, it is not difficult to trace the development of its use in Adam and Sarah; it is an exceedingly rare form. In Adam's records, the first meaningful use of the perfect tense occurred at age 4:6 (4 years, 6 months). But Sarah never once used the perfect tense through age 5:5 in the protocols examined. The reason for the late emergence of the perfect tense is difficult to understand in purely linguistic terms. To illustrate the elements in the perfect tense, we can examine the sentence "I have seen it." The essential features include the use of "have" as an auxiliary verb. The main verb is used in its past participle form, in this case "seen." For many verbs in English, the past participle has the same form as the past tense, as with "tell" becoming "told" and "have told." But a number of common verbs have their own distinct past participle, as with "see" becoming "saw" and "has seen." In linguistic terminology, the formation of the perfect tense depends on the grammatical feature "have -en" which requires a rule of affix movement.

Now what is intriguing, when one looks at the language data from Adam and Sarah, is that both children possessed all of the necessary elements to produce the perfect tense before the age of 3 years. Yet, it was not until 1½ years later that Adam began to use this form, and Sarah was not observed to do so even 2½ years later. For example, both children were using "have" as a type of auxiliary by the age of 2:11. At that age, Adam produced such utterances as "Cromer have . . . eat pie" and "I have . . . be little," and by age 3:6 he was producing the entire quasi-auxiliary verb "have to" in such statements as "We have to keep dis for something" and "We have to . . . we has to get out our trucks." At that same age, Sarah too was saying, "I had do it" and "I have to go to the bathroom." Another thing that is obvious from these utterances is that both children had the "production span capacity" to produce the perfect tense. This is also observable from their mean utterance length at those younger ages. Furthermore, grammatical features like "Be -ing" which involve affix movement like "have -en" were occurring before the age of 3. The children also possessed, at an early age, some specific past participles like "seen" and "gone." It appears, then, that Adam and Sarah possessed all of the necessary elements to produce the perfect tense as well as the capacity to produce utterances of a sufficient length to combine them at a very early age. Furthermore, an analysis of the speech of the parents reveals that they were producing the perfect tense, although with a somewhat lower frequency than other grammatical forms. So both children were exposed to these forms. It is therefore rather difficult to understand why the children were not producing this form at an earlier age—difficult, that is, until the *meaning* of the perfect tense is examined. When one analyzes the data from this other point of view, it becomes apparent that the ability to use the perfect tense rests on a late-developing ability to consider the relevance of one timed sequence to another.

In examining the data, one is again faced with the difficulty of inferring the meaning or intention of the child. However, there are certain situations in which relevance would appear to be important. If we can observe a point in the child's development before which he ignores the relation between past events and present consequences, and after which he begins to relate the two, by whatever linguistic means he has at his disposal, then we may be able to account for the late emergence of the perfect tense in English-speaking children. In the samples of Adam's language between the ages of 2:3 and 4:0, there were no attempts to make such a relation. At 4:0 there was one utterance which appears to be the first use of relevance as a concept. It was at 4:6 that Adam first used the perfect tense, and it was at this time and thereafter that he made several utterances that included this category, even though in many of these he employed other linguistic forms which were available at a much younger age but which were not previously used to encode relevance. They included such utterances as:

> Hey, what else you bring the pajamas for?
> How come you didn't bring your car today?
> This one is the mostest tight you ever saw.
> You finished me lots of rings.

Since Sarah never used the perfect tense form in the data examined, the evidence from her development is even more striking. She began to use the concept of relevance at age 4:6, and to do this she developed slightly odd uses of the words "now" and "yet." For example, to the adult question concerning what had just happened to her, Sarah replied "Now, hit myself" (where it appeared that an adult might have replied, "I just hit myself," or "I have just hit myself"). There are a number of similar examples in her data. What is interesting is that although Sarah used utterances like these at an earlier age, she did not use them to indicate relevance. Similarly, both children, as noted earlier, had past participles in their language, and this is one of the very components used to express relevance by adults. One might suppose that the children used only this portion of the perfect tense to express relevance at the earlier age, and that all that later developed was the full grammatical form including the auxiliary verb "have." But again, when one examines the uses of these early participles, it appears that they were never used to express relevance. Examples of the early uses all seem to indicate a present condition: "Kitty gone," "All done," "Light broken."

One final bit of evidence concerning the acquisition of the perfect tense in English as being dependent on the development of the notion of relevance at about age 4:0 or 4:6 comes from the observation of a similar tense in German and Dutch. In these latter languages, however, the perfect tense is used to indicate simple past time, while the simpler past forms are more literary and not often used in speech. Some observations suggest that children in Germany and in Holland acquire the perfect tense very early but are not observed to use the past tense until a later age. While it is true that the past tense is a rather rare form in the adult spoken language, it must have been being produced since some young American children living in Holland were observed to try to use those forms to express the simple past

(Catherine Snow, personal communication). It would appear, then, that as long as children are capable of some minimal level of complexity that allows them to acquire particular linguistic forms, they will nevertheless acquire only those that encode the meanings they are capable of understanding. If relevance is a comparatively late-acquired concept, then English-speaking children will be delayed in acquiring the perfect tense form but not because of its grammatical complexity, and German and Dutch children will acquire such forms early but will be delayed in acquiring the past tense form in spite of its relatively simple structure.

The late acquisition of these various structures can nevertheless be imputed by some investigators to be due to differential frequencies with which the various forms are heard or to their structural complexity (which does in some cases impede acquisition as we will see). However, there is another line of evidence that the underlying cognitions play an essential role in language acquisition. This evidence comes from an analysis of the very *words* children acquire which are related to particular concepts. Here, there is no reasonable argument that the late acquisitions are due to structural complexities. In the same study of the development of time concepts in Adam and Sarah, an analysis was also made of the acquisition of particular time words. All of the various words were categorized into the types of time relationships they expressed. These included notions such as points in time, repetition, ordering and sequence, relevance, timelessness, and duration, among others. It should be noted that the use of a particular time word by a child does not indicate that the child understands the concept involved. If a child uses the word "tomorrow" in a spontaneous and not a rote-learned way, it still cannot be taken as evidence that the child understands that word in the way that an adult does. However, it can be taken as evidence that he is engaging in naming a "point in time," which is one of the categories used. In this way it is possible to classify the time words spontaneously used into categories of the temporal relationships which were being expressed.

Some of the categories find expression relatively early—naming of points in time, reference to simultaneity, and some types of ordering and sequence. However, some categories are very late to emerge, even though the words for these are very common in the mothers' speech. The category of relevance may be expressed prospectively by such words as "until," "about to," "ready to," and "start to." These are not used by the child until after age 4:0–4:6. Those expressing relevance from the past, like "remember," and "just" as in

"You just messed mine," occur at the same period. Words expressing a type of complex timelessness (as defined in Cromer, 1968),
such as "never," "always," and "sometimes," similarly are not
used until after age 4:0–4:6. This is also true of words expressing
duration and other cognitively difficult categories. Again, it is difficult
to understand why children are failing to use productively such common words if one ignores their meaning. The children were definitely
being exposed to the words expressing these concepts. In the speech
samples taken up to 2 years before Adam and Sarah began to make
use of these words, the mothers were saying such things as "Do it
before you go," "You *always* win," "Pull the one that's *already*
hangin'," "You can't put them on *until* next week *after* we get them
all sewed," etc. Indeed, Sarah's mother bombards her with time
words at a frequency of greater than one per minute in some of the
speech samples. Thus, neither structural complexity nor lack of exposure can be the reasons why words associated with some of these
categories are so delayed in acquisition. What is startling is that whole
categories of time words begin to be used at the point in development
when grammatical structures also begin to be used to express the
same ideas, and this is suggestive that çertain cognitions are necessary for the acquisition both of the words and the grammatical forms.
So far, the particular cognitions or ideas have been treated as separate
entities. In the study of the acquisition of time concepts, several
different types of cognitions appeared to emerge at about the same
age (4:0–4:6 in these two children). It is possible that what is developing is not a number of separate ideas, but a new structure of the mind
or a new set of cognitive operations that allow the emergence of these
concepts. That is basically what Piaget's equilibration theory claims,
and it is to the effects of these hypothesized structures and operations
on language acquisition that we will now turn our attention.

INFLUENCE OF COGNITIVE STRUCTURES
AND OPERATIONS ON LANGUAGE

Piagetian Theory

It is not easy to summarize Piaget's view of development. However,
there are a number of good reviews of his theory (Flavell, 1963; Furth,
1969) and Piaget has himself written several overviews (Piaget, 1970a,
1970b; Piaget and Inhelder, 1969). According to Piaget, the child
represents the world to himself through his interactions with the

environment during the first 18 months to 2 years of life. This stage is called the period of sensorimotor intelligence. During this time, the child acquires a number of important cognitive skills such as the achievement of object permanence (but see Bower, 1971, mentioned earlier), imitations of previously seen actions, and the anticipation of future positions of an object before its movement is completed. The Piagetian view on language itself is a very complex one. It is said to build on the cognitive abilities which arise in the sensorimotor period. That is why it does not begin to emerge until about 18 months of age. Hermina Sinclair, a linguist working in the Piagetian framework, has put the theory clearly. It is not until the end of the sensorimotor period that the child has reached the stage where he realizes that he is an active person distinct from the objects he acts upon. This allows for a differentiation between himself and others and therefore calls for communication. (But see Bruner, 1975a, 1975b, for example, for the child's earlier attempts at communication.) It is also said that it is only at about 18 months of age that a child comes to possess the ability to represent reality mentally, and this representation first begins to occur in a nonverbal form as in motor representations. Sinclair (1971) calls attention to a number of sensorimotor schemata that underlie or account for corresponding linguistic abilities observed in language acquisition. For example, the child's ability to put things in a spatial or temporal order has as its linguistic equivalent the concatenation of linguistic elements. The child's ability to classify things in action, as where he uses a whole category of objects for the same action, or alternatively applies a whole category of action schemata to one object, has as its linguistic counterpart the categorization of linguistic elements into major categories like noun phrase and verb phrase. The ability to relate objects and actions to one another is the underlying ability that allows for the functional grammatical relations of "subject of" and "object of." The ability to embed action schemata into one another allows the linguistic recursive property of inserting phrase markers into other phrase markers. In other words, action schemata and their coordinations which are available at the end of the sensorimotor period have certain structural properties that make it possible for the child to start comprehending and producing language.

There are a number of linguists and psycholinguists who are exploring the relationship between underlying meanings and how these affect language. Fillmore's case grammar (1968) and McCawley's semantic deep structures (1968), for example, place great emphasis on meaning—although they are concerned with a specifically linguistic meaning which is quite different from the kind of underlying meaning imputed to their theories by many psychologists. Schlesinger (1971a, 1971b, 1974, in press) has proposed a more psychological theory taking into account the speaker's intentions. Sinclair's Piagetian analysis differs from these theories in two ways. First, she is concerned primarily with the underlying cognitive operations and structures rather than static meanings per se. Second, and more important, Sinclair attempts to specify some *developmental* features of these cognitive abilities. Her analysis of sensorimotor schemata and the attempt to relate these to particular linguistic features is very interesting, and the underlying abilities which she has outlined may very well be *necessary* for language acquisition to occur. But we will also have to pose the question whether they are *sufficient* to explain that acquisition, a point to be raised in the next section of this chapter.

The Piagetian position, then, is that language acquisition cannot begin until certain operations of the sensorimotor period have been acquired. Piaget notes that, once language does emerge, it obviously plays a major part in the person's representation of the world. It permits, for example, the interiorization of action into thought. But he also points out that language is only one type of symbolic function. Other types are deferred imitation, mental imagery, symbolic games, and drawing. It is the whole symbolic function in its many manifestations which is seen to be important. When this symbolic or semiotic function begins to be operative, it has the advantage of being able to detach thought from action. Language is especially important in that it allows three developments to occur. One of these is the speeding up of representation over that made possible by pure sensorimotor representation. A second development that language allows is the ability to transcend immediate space and time. The third development is the ability to represent a number of elements simultaneously rather than by means of successive, step-by-step thought. The overall importance of the semiotic function, then, is that it allows thought to be detached from action, and language plays a particularly important role in this process (see Piaget and Inhelder, 1969). But the significant point in terms of the language/thought controversy, is that language builds on and affects a number of cognitive abilities that have already arisen in the sensorimotor period.

Conservation Studies   At later periods too, thought structures are seen to affect language rather than the other way around. Take, for example, the well known conservation experiments. In these studies, a child is shown equal amounts of liquid being poured from one of two equal-sized containers into a tall but narrow container. If he claims that now there is more water in the second container because its level is higher, he is classified as a nonconserver. After the achievement of operational thought structures, however, the older child, like the adult, knows that the amount of liquid has remained the same. The controversy has centered on the mechanisms by which this change takes place. Piaget emphasizes the development of the structures of the mind. For him, the conservation studies are merely one of many ways of illustrating that the child is capable of particular kinds of thought. Many researchers, however, have preferred to see the achievement of conservation as a particular ability which they conceive of as being directly learned. They have concentrated their energies on a number of studies attempting to show that nonconserving children can be taught to conserve (almost invariably ignoring the far more intriguing question of why all normal *noninstructed* children nevertheless become conservers and at about the same age). Among the theories advanced, some have centered on language. It has been proposed that the reason a child is a nonconserver at a certain stage is that he is seduced by the perception of the situation. The sight of the liquid in the second container being so much higher than the first one overcomes his more natural tendency to believe in the preservation of the identity of the quantity when he has seen that nothing has been added or taken away. Conservation is achieved, according to this view, through the mediation of the symbolic properties of language, which eventually override the apparent perceptual differences. It is not entirely clear exactly what these language properties are, but differences between the language used for describing the material by conserving and nonconserving children have been noted.

Sinclair (1969) has studied these language differences directly. She presented children with materials which differed in two dimensions which they were asked to describe. For example, the child was shown two pencils, one of which was short and thick and the other long and thin. What Sinclair noted was that children who were nonconservers tended to use undifferentiated terminology to describe the materials. For example, they might say one was big (indicating its width) and the other was big (indicating its length); whereas conserving children would use two different words for the two dimensions. Second, nonconserving children used absolute rather than comparative terminology. They were likely to say things of the form "One is big and the other is little." A third difference between the language of nonconserving and conserving children was found in the types of sentences they used to coordinate the two dimensions. The non-conserving children either described only one dimension or used four separate sentences. By contrast, conserving children would coordinate the dimensions in phrases such as "This is tall but it's thin; this is short but it's wide." Given these three basic differences in the language children use for their descriptions, one is still faced with the problem of causality. That is, one does not have sufficient grounds on which to base a judgment as to the relation between language and operational thought. Whether new linguistic structures and differentiated terminology *cause* operational thought to come about, or whether the new thought structures make it easier for the child to use more advanced language patterns, cannot be determined from Sinclair's data. For example, a few nonconservers nevertheless used the more advanced language forms. This could be taken as evidence that these children are acquiring language structures which will make conservation possible. But it is also possible to argue from the opposite point of view, that some nonconserving children have more complex linguistic structures without these giving rise to conservation ability. It is this latter interpretation that Sinclair supports with evidence from a further study she undertook.

Sinclair attempted to teach the nonconservers the more advanced language. She found it fairly easy to teach the young children to use differentiated terminology. Comparative terms like "more" and "less" were more difficult to teach. Most difficult of all to get the young children to use were the coordinated sentence structures. What she found was that even among the children who successfully learned the most complex expressions, only 10% acquired conservation. Most of the children who were language-taught did not become conservers, but they did begin to notice and make reference to the differing dimensions. Sinclair thus concluded that language training may lead children to pay attention to important features in the conservation task, but that such training does not of itself lead to conservation and operational thinking.

Reversibility   Another aspect of operational thought is "reversibility." This is often shown in an experimental procedure where a child is asked to place a series of sticks in order of increasing size, i.e., to seriate them. This is only made possible, like conservation, by thought structures available to the child who has reached the level of operational thinking. When a child is able to seriate the sticks and to insert new intermediate size sticks correctly into their proper places in an ascending or descending series, it is said that he has the ability to conceptualize a particular stick as being at the same time both longer than some sticks and shorter than others in the series. It also appears that verbal descriptions of the materials parallel the stages on this task. For example, Inhelder (1969) reports in a study that she and Sinclair undertook, that the youngest children used only two descriptive terms, "long" and "short," to describe successive pairs of sticks. The intermediate children used three descriptive terms. Still older children who were at a stage just prior to solution of the seriation problem would use comparative terms. They would describe the sticks, for example, as being "Short, longer, longer, longer..." However, when asked to describe the series again, beginning at the other end, they were unable to do so. They couldn't describe a stick they had just referred to as "longer" as being "shorter." In other words, the lack of reversibility seems to extend to the verbal descriptions as well.

In a study on another aspect of reversibility, Ferreiro and Sinclair (1971) found that nonoperational children were unable to reverse linguistically the order of two events in time. In their study, the child was presented with some actions carried out on two dolls. He was then asked to describe the actions, but to talk about the second action first. In one situation, for example, first a girl doll washed a boy doll and then the boy doll went upstairs. When asked to describe this in inverse order, the youngest children (aged about 4½ years) either gave a description that retained temporal order, thereby not complying with the instructions in the task, or else they made a description of the type asked for but omitting any temporal indicators. For example, they might say "He went upstairs and she washed him."

Children at the next stage of development (5½ years of age) were able to comply with the instructions to begin their verbal description with the second event, but they couldn't use the temporal indicators necessary for describing the actual order correctly. Some found it impossible, and would say, "The boy... the boy... No. You've got to start with the girl." Other children at this stage attempted a variety of solutions to this problem. Some simply inverted the order in their description: "The boy went to the top of the stairs and afterwards the girl cleaned him." Others went so far as to invert the action: "He goes downstairs again and the girl washes his arms." Still others inverted the actors and the events so that the action performed in the second event was attributed to the actor in the first: "The boy goes and washes her face and then it's her that goes upstairs.'' Other solutions included attributing a neutral action to the actor in the second event: "The boy came, she washed his face and then he left." It should be noted that Ferreiro and Sinclair also questioned the children about what they had seen. This questioning revealed that the children knew perfectly well which event had occurred first and which had come second. The difficulty lay solely in their inability to encode a temporal reversal linguistically. Ferreiro and Sinclair conclude that this aspect of the linguistic transformational system only becomes possible when the child has attained the stage of operational thinking, for the structures necessary for reversibility are not available until that stage of thought is reached.

Formal Operational Thought   According to the Piagetian view, there is still another stage of thought and it does not arise until about adolescence. This is the period of formal operational thinking. Formal operations are manifested in propositional thinking. That is, formal operations consist of a combinatorial system that allows the construction of hypothetical possibilities. This enables the individual, for example, to envisage all of the relationships that could hold true in a set of data, even if these are not specifically revealed. Studies on formal operational thought are found in Inhelder and Piaget (1958). This type of thinking, since it consists of manipulating propositions about objects and actions rather than the objects and actions themselves, would seem to be very dependent on language. Those who have studied the thinking processes of the deaf believe that at the stage of formal operational thought, language is of crucial importance. Furth and Youniss in a recent review of their studies (1971, reprinted in this volume) assert that while language may have only an indirect facilitating effect on concrete operational thought, it may directly facilitate certain formal operations. But while Piaget notes that propositional operations are closely related to manipulations of language, he also warns that it is a mistake to equate advances at that stage with advances in language. The formal operational structures that Piaget envisages, allow a kind of formal thinking that goes well beyond a mere linguistic ability to manipulate propositions, and he makes this clear in his writings on that topic (Inhelder and Piaget, 1958, Chapters 16 and 17). One could probably best characterize Piaget's position by saying that he believes that while language may be necessary for the propositional manipulations of formal thought, language itself is not a *sufficient* condition for that type of thinking. Indeed, it is rather difficult to see in what way the language of an individual at the formal operational level is significantly different from the language of those who have not quite reached this stage of thought (and Piaget claims that many adults do not reach this stage) except in the use which is made of the linguistic structures.

It can be seen that at all stages Piaget's view is that cognition affects language and not the reverse. At the most advanced stages, language may be a necessary prerequisite for the development of formal operational thinking, but even then the developing cognitive processes only make use of language; they are not determined by it.

Effects of Other Cognitive Mechanisms on Language Acquisition

Piaget's theory attempts to be a very comprehensive one, but many of its assumptions are subject to dispute. However, one need not view cognitive functioning in a Piagetian framework at all. There are many investigators who have studied specific limitations of cognitive ability at different developmental periods in normal children and in children who suffer from varying cognitive deficit, without reference to a particular encompassing framework such as Piaget's. It is possible to examine some of these more particular cognitive mechanisms and their effect on language acquisition. One such mechanism is short-term memory capacity.

Short-Term Memory Capacity   Menyuk (1964; 1969; this volume), in studying a group of children whose language was labeled as "infantile," hypothesized that a cognitive limitation on their short-term memory might be responsible for their deficit. The children in her study were aged 3:0–5:11. She examined both their spontaneous language and their responses to sentences in a repetition task which was also administered to young normal-speaking children. Her productive language results showed that at all levels throughout the age range the syntactic structures used by the language-deviant group were different from those used by the young normal speakers. In other words, although they were said to evidence infantile language, Menyuk's study showed that in fact their language was not merely delayed but quite deviant. The repetition task also revealed significant differences between the groups. In imitation, for example, normal-speaking children were constrained in their repetition by syntactic structure, not by the length of the utterance. Children as young as 3 years of age were able to handle some sequences up to nine words long. In fact, the correlation between sentence length and inability to repeat sentences was only 0.04, i.e., at chance level. The repetitions by the deviant group were quite different. The correlation for these children between length and inability to imitate was 0.53. Furthermore, an analysis of the types of mistakes these children made in their imitations revealed that sentence length was an important factor. The omissions that were made were almost invariably from the first part of the sentence, whereas the last things heard were the most frequently recalled. This was very different from the errors and omissions made by normal speaking children which consisted mainly of modifications of transformational structure. Menyuk also noted the especially poor auditory memory of the language-deviant children. Short-term memory even for utterances as short as 3–5 morphemes in length was impaired as indicated by omissions and modifications. Menyuk speculated that if a child is able to keep in memory no more than 2 or 3 morphemes, he would be severely limited in being able to carry out a deepening linguistic analysis on the incoming data. This would result in his producing utterances which would be not only impoverished and limited, but based in some cases even on different hypotheses and rules concerning language.

A similar hypothesis concerning the effects of a short-term memory limitation on language has been put forward by Graham (1968, 1974; Graham and Gulliford, 1968). He found that in his sample both repetition and comprehension scores on various types of sentences increased regularly with short-term memory as measured by random words and digits. By relating the notion of short-term memory to the amount of computation required by sentences of varying syntactic complexity, Graham was able to interpret his results as evidence that children are unable to process sentences that make demands on short-term memory which are beyond their capacity.

Short-term memory has been implicated by some investigators in developmental aphasic problems. Aphasia is generally defined as a disturbance or loss of ability to comprehend, elaborate, or express language concepts. "Developmental aphasia" is broadly definable as any failure of the normal growth of language function when deafness, mental deficiency, motor disability, or severe personality disorder can be excluded (Griffiths, 1972). Rosenthal (1972) has suggested that a cognitive deficit which results in limited short-term auditory storage may underlie the difficulty in perceiving speech signals. Thus, the language impairment in these children may result, like Menyuk's deviant language group, from a cognitive deficit that prevents them from making a linguistic analysis on the incoming data—in this case even preventing them from acquiring even very small speech units.

Sequencing and Temporal Order   Other investigators have proposed hypotheses which account for similar effects in aphasia but which see the cognitive limitation to be of a slightly different nature. One of these proposals is that the basic problem is one of sequencing and temporal order. For example, Efron (1963) has found that adult aphasics were seriously impaired in their ability to judge which of two sounds occurred first unless they were separated by a gap of as much as 575 msec. This is contrasted with the claim that in normal speech phonemes occur approximately every 80 msec. The suggestion, then, is that aphasics are unable to process normal speech because they cannot sort out the temporal order of the phonemes. Lowe and Campbell (1965) have extended this observation to aphasoid children. They found that whereas their normal-speaking control group needed two sounds to be separated by about 30 msec to be able to specify their order, the aphasoid children required gaps of 350 msec. There is some evidence, then, that the inability to sequence material rapidly may be the cognitive deficit which underlies some types of aphasia. This sequencing may be important at the level of the phoneme. Confirmatory evidence for this comes from a study by Sheehan, Aseltine, and Edwards (1973). In their work on adult aphasics, they found that the insertion of silent intervals between phonemes aided comprehension, while the insertion of silence between words did not.

If impairment of a sequencing ability is indeed the cause of some types of aphasic disorder, it is nevertheless unclear whether this is a failure of a general type, or whether it is specifically auditory. Doehring (1960), Stark (1966), and Withrow (1964) have found both visual and auditory impairments in aphasic patients. Poppen et al. (1969) propose a general sequencing disability not limited to auditory stimuli. By contrast, Tallal and Piercy (1973, 1974) have found no impairment in aphasic children on the visual tasks they presented. In their studies, they have noted that the aphasic child is unable to sequence auditory stimuli when the rate of presentation is too rapid. However, they do not conclude that the impairment is due to a sequencing inability as such. Rather, they believe that the deficit involves rate of auditory processing. For example, they have found that aphasic children have difficulty discriminating between stop consonants which have rapidly changing spectrums provided by the second and third formant transitions. These are of a relatively short duration (50 msec). By contrast, vowels have steady state frequencies of the first three formants which remain constant over the entire length of the stimulus (approximately 250 msec). Tallal and Piercy found that aphasic children did as well as matched nonaphasic normal children on the vowels but did significantly worse on the stop consonants.

The various studies on language-impaired children would seem to implicate some underlying cognitive dysfunction as the cause of the slow or deviant development of language in some children. Such ideas as short-term memory limitations, however, would also be applicable to mentally deficient individuals or even to younger normal children.

Production Span Capacity   There are other cognitive limitations too, which are the result merely of earlier stages during the course of normal development. For example, Bloom (1970) has made a very convincing case for a cognitive limitation on the number of elements young normal children can produce in a single utterance—a kind of "production span capacity." In order to account for the differences between the underlying structure necessary for the assumed meaningful interpretation of an utterance and the reduced form of the utterance which the child actually produces, she postulates that some kind of reduction transformation must be occurring. The support for her view comes from the consecutive utterances of a child which exhibit the expansion of some elements at the apparent expense of others which are then deleted. Bloom gives the following sequence uttered by Kathryn, a child she recorded:

Raisin there.
Buy more grocery store.
Raisins.
Buy more grocery store.
Grocery store.
Raisin ə grocery store.

Notice that when the child produced both nouns in the last utterance, she was apparently constrained to delete the verb "buy." Yet, the presence of the verb is obligatory in the underlying representation in order to account for the semantic interpretation—i.e., the grammatical relationship between "raisin" and "grocery store."

The interpretations that Bloom makes are supported by an analysis of the situation at the time of the utterance. The utterances themselves are not necessarily produced in a continuous sequence. For example, while playing with a toy car, Kathryn produced the following utterances which, although not uttered consecutively, all occurred within the same context over a short period of time:

Kathryn under bridge.
Kathryn ə make ə under bridge.
Make ə more under bridge.
Make ə car under bridge.

In the observed situation, Kathryn herself is not under the bridge, and the only way one can account for the relationship between "Kathryn" and "bridge" in the first utterance of the set is by assuming that the child is employing a reduction transformation. Bloom argues that the child must have the linguistic categories organized in a hierarchical structure which gives her the ability to add categories without increasing sentence length. This is done by the deletion of certain categories when others either occur or are expanded. It should also be noted that this production limitation is not on sentence length as such. Rather, Bloom believes it to be a cognitive limitation in handling structured complexity. For example, it may be that the number of syntactic operations within a sentence increases the "cognitive weight" of the sentence. The further problem of explaining which categories the child eliminates when she must eliminate something is unresolved, although Bloom notes that the grammatical forms most recently acquired by the child were the ones most likely to be deleted.

So far, the evidence that has been presented has been in support of a cognitive hypothesis about language acquisition—that is, that the underlying cognitions or meanings and the mechanisms which underlie them (cognitive structures and operations) determine or at least limit the language acquisition process. However, this is only a part of the picture. One needs to examine the way these cognitive processes are linked to language, for there is no necessary connection between having certain abilities and using these abilities linguistically. Take, for example, Sinclair's claim (1969) that the developing cognitive processes are necessary in order to acquire language. She put forward the view that the reason language acquisition does not take place until the age of $1^{1}/_{2}$–2 years is due specifically to the need for the processes of sensorimotor intelligence to be complete. She attacks Chomsky's view of an innate language acquisition device on the grounds of this time lag between the first manifestations of practical intelligence and the first verbal productions. There may be, of course, other reasons for this time lag, but one must also speculate whether those cognitive processes, even if necessary, are nevertheless *sufficient* to account for the language acquisition process. One source of evidence that they are not, comes from the observation that there are linguistic developments which occur at both the earlier and later stages of language acquisition which seem to be little related either to the maturing cognitive processes or to meaning. It is not a difficult matter to find many such developments, but, given the requirement of a short review chapter, I will cite only a few examples.

INDEPENDENT DEVELOPMENT OF LANGUAGE

One of the major unsolved problems of language acquisition concerns the growth and change of linguistic structures at different stages during the child's language development. Why do children, initially using a simple form to convey a meaning, begin to elaborate more complex forms to express the same concept? There are a number of "simple" answers to this question—e.g., in order to be able to communicate when the more primitive forms fail to do so; or to ease some sort of cognitive complexity by using global rules; or to match more closely the adult models to which the child is exposed—but unfortunately these answers are based only on theoretical notions and are not always supported by the language data from empirical studies. Let us examine some data bearing on the linguistic encoding of negation and self-reference by very young children, as well as a few more complex structures by older children.

Negation

Ursula Bellugi (1967) made an analysis of the structures that were used to express negation by the children of the Roger Brown study. She found several stages in the expression of this concept. At first, the child merely attached a negative morpheme such as "no" or "not" to the beginning of utterances. Thus, he would say "No wipe finger" and "Not fit." In a second stage, the negative appeared in five unrelated grammatical settings, but with no transformation relating them. At this second stage, the kinds of utterances found in the first stage still were occurring (e.g., "No Rusty hat"), but there were also some negatives being used with demonstrative pronouns (e.g., "That no fish school"). In addition, "don't" and "can't" were used as vocabulary items either in demonstrative sentences (e.g., "I don't sit on Cromer coffee") or in imperatives (e.g., "Don't eat daisy"). Finally, some utterances occurred with the element "why not" prefixed to negative sentences (e.g., "Why not cracker can't talk?"). In a third stage, auxiliary transformations had begun to be used. At this stage, the negative was truly attached to the auxiliary verb. Thus, sentences like "Why not cracker can't talk?" no longer occurred since "don't" and "can't" were now treated as being transformed from a negative element and an auxiliary instead of being used as vocabulary items with negative meaning. Parents responded to the messages as indicating negative intent, and arguments that the changes over time are due to attempts to improve communicative competence in the face of negative feedback receive little support. Furthermore, since all of these changes over the various stages of development encode the same basic meaning, it is difficult to see how meaning per se can account for this linguistic growth.

Of course, these forms may not really have the same meaning. Bloom's study (1970) of negation in which she paid particular attention to meaning and context has already been cited. Although the negative sentences she observed matched the surface structures that Bellugi found, Bloom specified some of these as making particular subtypes of negative reference. It will be recalled that rejection came mainly to be signaled by the use of the "don't"; denial was mainly signaled by "not"; and nonexistence was expressed either by "no" plus an element or by "can't." Earlier, it was argued that this was an example where the meaning determined to some extent the very structure that was used by the child. However, there was another aspect to this development which should be recalled. As each new category was acquired, it was expressed by a form which was already being used to convey the developmentally earlier meaning. For example, nonexistence was the first concept of negation to be expressed grammatically. Eventually it came to be the most complex form grammatically. That is, while reference to rejection and denial was made with the simpler forms which had initially been used to indicate nonexistence, reference to nonexistence took more grammatically complex forms. The point here is that if to express the meaning of a concept the child comes to use more and more complex forms over time, then these new complex structures cannot be being acquired due to advances in meaning.

Of course, rather than meaning, one might argue that the constraint is one of some kind of limited cognitive structure which is preventing the child from being able either to process more complex utterances or to produce them. The arguments for the effects of a limited memory span (cf. Menyuk, 1964, 1969) and a limited "production span" (cf. Bloom, 1970) have already been mentioned. However, there are some linguistic progressions that appear to depend neither on these kinds of changes in the cognitive capacities of the child nor on changes in meaning. One of these may be the development of self-reference during the acquisition of pronominalization or the formation of pronouns by the child.

Self-Reference

Bellugi (Bellugi-Klima, 1969; Bellugi, 1971) traced the progression of self-reference through several stages. At the earliest stage, the child used his name instead of a pronoun regardless of its position in the utterance—as his mother did about half the time when talking to him. Thus, the child would utter such sentences as:

Adam home.
Adam go hill.
Like Adam book shelf.
Pick Adam up.

In the second stage, he began to use the pronoun "I" for his name, but only if it occurred in the first position in the utterance:

I like drink it
I making coffee.

He would occasionally produce both his name and the "I" pronoun together:

I Adam driving.
I Adam do that.

At this stage, he substituted the pronoun "me" for his name if it occurred in any position other than the first position in the sentence (with the exception of vocatives and greetings). This strategy produced some sentences which sounded very adult-like:

One for me.
Wake me up.
Why laughing at me?

But it also caused him to produce a regular pattern of errors when judged against the adult grammar:

Why me spilled it?
What me doing?

Notice that these errors are not likely to be imitations, and that they are evidence that the child is not merely matching an adult model.

At the third stage, the child changed his rules and produced "I" for his name if it served a nominative function in the sentence, and used "me" if it served an object function, regardless of sentence position:

That what I do.
Can I put them on when I go outside?
You watch me be busy.
You want me help you?

There are even further stages in the development of self-reference, having to do, for example, with possessive pronouns like "mine," and reflexive pronouns like "myself," but this is enough to illustrate the main point. The child is developing his grammar in a regular and systematic manner. His productions can be described by certain rules which can account for the discrepancies between the child's utterances and the adult models. These stages change over time, but in ways that do not necessarily more closely match the adult models.

The reason why children go through such stages during their acquisition of language is unclear, but here is a case where changes are not based solely on meaning or reference. In these examples, the reference has remained the same—reference to self. It is also difficult to see how cognitive constraints could have played a part. Utterances like "Why me spilled it?" and "What me doing?" (stage 2) would not appear to be simpler in their structure than "Why I spilled it?" and "What I doing?" which conceivably could have been produced at stage 2 but which were not. In other words, neither meaning nor a simple measure of cognitive complexity (such as number of elements) suffices to account for developments of this type.

Ask and Tell

There is even some evidence, at later ages, that the linguistic structure in which a word is used can lead to its misinterpretation as compared to the adult meaning. Carol Chomsky (1969) studied a number of structures that children acquire rather late, between the ages of 5 and 10 years. One of these had to do with the words "ask" and "tell." At first she attempted to study a rather different but related problem having to do with the interpretation of sentences containing words such as "promise" and "ask," which violate a general grammatical principle. Take the following examples:

John told Bill to leave.
John wanted Bill to leave.

Both of these sentences are of the form: $NP_1 + V + NP_2 +$ to Inf.V. In these, the subject of the infinitive verb is "Bill"; it is he who is to be leaving. Some verbs, like "told," take a mandatory object ("Bill") which is the subject of the infinitive verb. But other verbs do not have to have an object. For example, with "want," one can also form the sentence "John wanted to leave." In this case, the subject of the infinitive verb becomes "John." Where the second NP is optional, one can write the description: $NP_1 + V + (NP_2) +$ to Inf.V. When the second NP occurs, it is the subject of the infinitive. Where it is omitted, the first NP becomes the subject. Chomsky described this as "the minimum distance principle" for it is the NP closest to the infinitive verb that is taken as the subject. It works for most verbs in English. However, some verbs violate this principle. One of these is "promise." In the sentence "John promised Bill to leave," it is John who will be leaving.

In her study, Chomsky found that children had great difficulty with sentences using "promise," for they had to learn that it was an exception to a general grammatical principle in the language. Even more complicated is the word "ask." It not only violates the minimum distance principle, but it does so inconsistently. When "ask" is used as a question, it consistently violates the minimum distance principle. In "John asked Bill what to sing," it is John who is going to be doing the singing. When "ask" is used as a request, however, as in "John asked Bill to sing," the interpretation conforms to the minimum distance principle, for it is Bill who will be singing. To add to the complications with the verb "ask," the interpretation when it is used as a request is itself inconsistent, at least in American English. Thus, while the sentence "The teacher asked the boy to leave the room" follows the principle, "The boy asked the teacher to leave the room" (a sentence not acceptable, however, in the permission-seeking sense in British English) violates it; it is the boy who will be leaving the room in both sentences, and the second is interpreted as his asking for permission. In any case we have the following situation. In both British and American English, "ask" as a question violates the minimum distance principle. "Ask" as a request conforms to the minimum distance principle, consistently in British English and inconsistently in American English. Chomsky predicted that because of the added complication of at least two meanings of "ask" with differing structural consequences, children will be even more delayed in comprehending structures of this type than they were with "promise."

When she tested a number of children with sentences using "ask," however, she was surprised by an unexpected result: Many of the children treated "ask" as if it meant "tell." In the situation, two children were seated at a table with various toys and objects in front of them. When the first child was told, "Ask Laura (the other child) what to feed the doll," instead of asking Laura, the first child might say, "Feed her lettuce"—i.e., imposing a "tell" interpretation of the sentence, just as if the experimenter had said "Tell Laura what to feed the doll." So Chomsky changed her experiment to explore just the problem of the interpretations of "ask" and "tell." She found that there were three structures of increasing difficulty for the child, which she labeled cases 1, 2, and 3. Examples of the three types are:

Case 1. Ask Laura what color this is.
Case 2. Ask Laura the color of this book.
Case 3. Ask Laura what color to make the square.

In case 1, the simplest case, in order to form the question the child does not have to supply any deleted material. All that is needed is a change from "what color this is" to "what color is that?" By contrast, case 2 forces the child to supply a question word and a verb in order to form the appropriate question: "The color of the book" must be changed to, "*What's* the color of the book?" In Case 3, the child must supply an auxiliary verb and must also specify a subject. Thus, "what color to make the square" must become, "What color *should I* make the square?" In doing this, the child must refer outside the complement clause to retrieve the subject and must essentially choose between NP_1 and NP_2. (It is not appropriate to say, "What color should *you* make the square?")

Chomsky found that children could be classified into five developmental stages. Hidden in these results is something no one has noticed before and which has a special significance for the argument that is presented in this chapter. Children at the most primitive developmental level on this type of structure (stage A) impose a "tell" interpretation on "ask" no matter in which of the three cases it is used. At the second stage (stage B), however, children treat "ask" as meaning "ask" when it is given in the structure of case 1, but impose a "tell" interpretation when used in cases 2 and 3. Stage C children treat "ask" in its adult interpretation when found in cases 1 and 2, treating it as meaning "tell" only when used in case 3 forms. At stage D, children finally treat "ask" correctly for all three cases, but assign the subject incorrectly in case 3 structures (e.g., using the inappropriate, "What color should *you* make the square?"). The most advanced children, stage E, give adult interpretations. This can be summarized,

Stage A: Failure on cases 1, 2, and 3
Stage B: Success on case 1; failure on cases 2 and 3
Stage C: Success on cases 1 and 2; failure on case 3
Stage D: Success on cases 1, 2, and 3; wrong subject assignment for case 3
Stage E: Success on cases 1, 2, and 3; correct subject assignment for case 3

where "failure" signifies the imposition of a "tell" interpretation on the word "ask."

The problem for a theory of language acquisition which only takes account of meaning is to explain the performance of children in stages B and C. Even by stage B, children can be said to know the "meaning" of "ask," but *only when it is used in specific grammatical structures*. Used in the same situation, but in a slightly different structure, the child falls back on a different interpretation of the meaning. Here is an example of an interview with a stage C child, taken from Chomsky's work:

Experimenter: Ask Joanne what color this book is. (Case 1)
Laura: What color's that book?
Experimenter: Ask Joanne her last name. (Case 2)
Laura: What's your last name?
Experimenter: Tell Joanne what color this tray is.
Laura: Tan
Experimenter: Ask Joanne what's in the box (Case 1)
Laura: What's in the box?
Experimenter: Ask Joanne what to feed the doll. (Case 3)
Laura: The hot dog
Experimenter: Now I want you to *ask* Joanne something. *Ask* her what to feed the doll. (Case 3)
Laura: The piece of bread
Experimenter: Ask Joanne what *you* should feed the doll. (Case 1)
Laura: What should I feed the doll?

This is startling. And it is not an isolated example. Of 39 children who participated in the experiment, nine evidenced this kind of behavior and were classified as being in stage C. As Chomsky put it, "Clearly they knew the correct interpretation of *ask* in simple constructions, but could not process it correctly in the more complicated constructions of case 3. Ability to interpret it in simple constructions was somehow not enough."

First Morphemes

It is clear that there are a number of grammatical developments that do not depend on meaning. The beginning of children's language acquisition may lie in meaning, but that is not a complete *explanation* of what occurs. For that, a more complex theory is needed, and one of the complexities is the addition of purely grammatical elements during the language acquisition process. Earlier, Brown's work (1973) was cited in conjunction with the argument that certain aspects of cognition preceded language. It will be recalled, for example, that he found evidence that the three earliest grammatical operations on verbs encoded the earliest semantic meanings attributed to the child. But Brown was not merely looking at the way cognition affected language. In fact, he viewed his data from various points of view. For example, one major part of his work examined the development of 14 early morphemes. These included the "-ing" of the present progressive, regular ("-ed") and irregular past tense, regular and irregular third person singular, plurals, possessives, the prepositions "in" and "on," the articles "a" and "the," and the copula and auxiliary "be." The acquisition of these forms across children was very similar. Brown compared this order of acquisition both to the degree of semantic complexity (the more complex defined as containing elements of the less complex) and to the degree of grammatical complexity (based on the transformational grammar of Jacobs and Rosenbaum, 1968). His findings indicated that both of these notions about equally well predicted the order of acquisition. That is, there was evidence that semantic complexity was a determinant of the order of acquisition, but the evidence was alternatively interpretable as demonstrating that transformational complexity was a determinant of the order of acquisition. Since both semantic and grammatical complexity seem to be confounded in the acquisition of the first morphemes acquired by the child, it would appear to be difficult to render a judgment on their differential effects. However, it may be that there is a method to disentangle the effects of meaning and grammar in some cases.

Bilingual Children

Slobin (1973) has proposed that one may be able to study the differential grammatical complexities of language by observing language acquisition in bilingual children. It has already been noted that children appear to acquire particular meanings before they have the ability to express such meanings grammatically. It is possible to judge these intentions to some extent from the situational context. Indeed, the whole study of intended reference discussed in an earlier section was devoted to pointing out how cognition preceded language acquisition. There is similar evidence for this proposal across languages as well. Burling (1959) reported on the acquisition of language by his bilingual son who, for a time beginning at the age of 1:4, was brought up speaking both English and Garo. Garo is a language of the Tibeto-Burman group spoken in an area of India where Burling lived while making an anthropological study. He noticed that often his son would learn simultaneously certain English and Garo words which expressed approximately the same meaning. It was as if once his understanding had reached the point of being able to grasp a concept, he was able to use the appropriate words in both languages. For example, when he began to name colors, he did so in both languages. Similarly, when he began to use English words indicating time such as "last night" and "yesterday morning," he also began using the corresponding Garo terms.

Slobin suggests, however, that certain concepts use difficult grammatical forms in some languages and that this will delay their acquisition. If it can be shown that children understand certain meanings at particular stages of their development, then one may observe whether some languages resist the encoding of these concepts into the adult forms. Slobin gives an example of a bilingual child acquiring both Hungarian and Serbo-Croatian. The child gave evidence of understanding certain aspects of spatial location. These are expressed by a number of case endings in Hungarian. The child had acquired these in Hungarian, but at the same time had practically no locative expressions in Serbo-Croatian. Locative expressions in Serbo-Croatian are grammatically more complex than in Hungarian in that they require both a locative preposition before the noun and case endings attached to the noun. It would appear, then, that the reason for the delay in the acquisition of this aspect of Serbo-Croatian is its grammatical complexity. Slobin gives an even more dramatic example from Egyptian Arabic. We know that young children are able to understand and use plural forms in English and other languages. But Slobin reports that in Egyptian Arabic the complete set of plurals is not acquired until nearly 15 years of age! It happens that this is an especially difficult grammatical form in Arabic. In addition to many special irregular forms, there are differences depending on whether a counted or collected noun is being used. Furthermore, things numbering 3 through 10 take the plural, while 11 or more revert to the singular. It would appear that the late acquisition of this part of the grammar is due to its complexity.

WEAK FORM OF THE COGNITION HYPOTHESIS

It has been suggested that there is a good deal of evidence that cognitions and the particular cognitive structures and operations that give rise to them direct the language acquisition process. Before the child has certain "meanings" at his disposal, he does not use the grammatical forms which normally express these meanings, and he uses other forms which could be so used only in a limited way. For example, before the age of about 4 years the perfect tense is not used at all, and past participles like "gone" or "broken" are used only in circumstances describing present conditions. Certain constructions with "if," which could be used to express hypothetical meanings, are used only to express "uncertainty of conditions" at an age prior to understanding the concept of hypotheticalness. Once the child has acquired certain meanings, however, he begins to use the forms he has at his disposal to express these new meanings, and he begins to learn new forms which are used by adults to encode these newly acquired concepts. This can be called the "cognition hypothesis" of language acquisition.

Increasingly, attention is turning to the underlying structures and processes which make certain meanings possible. This would appear to be a field of special interest to those dealing with the acquisition of language by special groups of children, for example the mentally retarded. In addition, there is the problem of understanding how the concepts, once achieved, are encoded into linguistic forms. One aspect of this encoding concerns the underlying cognitive structures which make such encoding possible. Here, studies on short-term memory limitations, "production span capacity," problems of sequencing the temporal order of language, rate of auditory processing, and other cognitive operations are vital. Finally, there is the problem of grammatical capacity and growth itself. Examples have been given in the previous section of this paper which seem to indicate that some aspects of language acquisition cannot be accounted for either by an overcoming of cognitive constraints or by the acquisition of particular meanings or cognitions. It was for these reasons that I suggested (Cromer, 1974a) a "weak form" of the cognitive hypothesis. It asserts essentially that although the study of cognitive structures and operations and the cognitions to which they give rise are of central importance in understanding the language acquisition process, these cognitive entities by themselves are not sufficient to *explain* that process. Our abilities "make available," so to speak, certain meanings to be encoded, but we must also possess certain specifically linguistic capabilities in order to express these meanings in language. Such linguistic capacity may be lacking in certain pathological conditions. For example, an alternative hypothesis for the difficulties in acquiring language by some developmentally aphasic children may be that they lack certain linguistic mechanisms said by some theorists to be innate.

It may also be that the mechanisms and strategies of learning are different for language acquisition from those used for other types of cognitive attainments. Here, for example, one is interested in whether there is such a thing as a critical period for language acquisition, which makes that learning very different from the acquisition of other processes. If there is a critical period, what would be its effect on language learning by older children? (See Cromer, 1974b, 1975, for speculation on this issue as regards educationally subnormal children.) What would be the effect of such a critical period on designing programs for older language-deviant individuals?

There is also the related issue of the grammatical and semantic aspects of language. Many psychologists have confused studies of semantics with concepts of cognitive meanings. It should be emphasized that the competing theories of an autonomous grammar (Chomsky) and the various proposals for case grammars (Fillmore, 1968, 1971) and generative semantics (e.g., McCawley, 1968, 1973; Seuren, 1974) are linguistic theories. Indeed, a close reading of the papers of the generative semanticists suggests an increased need to look at the grammatical aspects of language (which are seen as identical with the semantic rules), and not a decreased interest, as some psychologists appear to have inferred. But on this last issue there is also some evidence to suggest that from a psychological point of view the rules of semantics and the rules of syntax may be best kept conceptually distinct despite their many interrelationships. This is true whether one is studying the language difficulties that result from brain damage during adulthood—in which some types of aphasia appear to affect the grammatical system to a greater extent, while injuries in other areas of the brain lead to a greater impairment of the semantic system—or studying the acquisition of particular structures by normal children acquiring their language, as examples in the previous section pointed out.

We know little enough about the development of cognitive structures, cognitive operations, and thoughts. We know even less about the acquisition of language. It would be unfortunate if psychological thinking on these problems is swept away by the current wave of emphasis on "meaning" alone, for that, taken by itself, too easily leads back to an associationistic explanation—linking thoughts and meanings merely to the way the child hears them encoded in the language around him. And that kind of explanation has been found to be sorely deficient.

REFERENCES

Adams, P. (ed.) 1972. Language in Thinking. Penguin Books, Harmondsworth, Middlesex.

Bates, E. 1976. Pragmatics and sociolinguistics in child language. This volume.

Bellugi, U. 1967. The acquisition of the system of negation in children's speech. Unpublished doctoral dissertation, Harvard University.

Bellugi, U. 1971. Simplification in children's language. In R. Huxley and E. Ingram (eds.), Language Acquisition: Models and Methods, pp. 95–115. Academic Press, London.

Bellugi-Klima, U. 1969. Language acquisition. Presented at the Symposium on Cognitive Studies and Artificial Intelligence Research, Wenner-Gren Foundation for Anthropological Research, March 2–8, Chicago.

Bever, T. G., J. A. Fodor, and W. Weksel. 1965a. Is linguistics empirical? Psychol. Rev. 72:493–500.

Bever, T. G., J. A. Fodor, and W. Weksel. 1965b. Theoretical notes on the acquisition of syntax: a critique of "context generalization." Psychol. Rev. 72:467–482.

Blank, M. 1974. Cognitive functions of language in the preschool years. Dev. Psychol. 10:229–245.

Bloom, L. 1970. Language Development: Form and Function in Emerging Grammars. M.I.T. Press, Cambridge, Mass.

Bower, T. G. R. 1971. The object in the world of the infant. Sci. Am. 225:30–38.

Bower, T. G. R., and J. G. Wishart. 1972. The effects of motor skill on object permanence. Cognition 1:165–172.

Brown, R. W. 1956. Language and categories. In J. S. Bruner, J. J. Goodnow, and G. A. Austin (eds.), A Study of Thinking. John Wiley & Sons Inc., New York.

Brown, R. 1970. Psycholinguistics: Selected Papers by Roger Brown. The Free Press, New York.

Brown, R. 1973. A First Language. Harvard University Press, Cambridge, Massachusetts.

Brown, R., and U. Bellugi. 1964. Three processes in the child's acquisition of syntax. Harv. Edu. Rev. 34:133–151.

Brown, R., C. Cazden, and U. Bellugi-Klima. 1969. The child's grammar from I to III. *In* J. P. Hill (ed.), Minnesota Symposia on Child Psychology, Vol. 2, pp. 28–73. University of Minnesota Press, Minneapolis.

Brown, R., and C. Fraser. 1964. The acquisition of syntax. *In* U. Bellugi and R. Brown (eds.), The Acquisition of Language. Monographs of the Society for Research in Child Development. 29(1),43–79.

Brown, R., C. Fraser, and U. Bellugi. 1964. Explorations in grammar evaluation. *In* U. Bellugi and R. Brown (eds.), The Acquisition of Language. Monographs of the Society for Research in Child Development. 29(1):79–92.

Brown, R., and C. Hanlon. 1970. Derivational complexity and order of acquisition in child speech. *In* J. R. Hayes (ed.), Condition and the Development of Language, pp. 11–53. John Wiley & Sons, New York.

Brown, R. W., and E. H. Lenneberg. 1954. A study in language and cognition. J. Abnorm. Soc. Psychol. 49:454–462.

Brown, R. W., and E. H. Lenneberg. 1958. Studies in linguistic relativity. *In* E. E. Maccoby, T. M. Newcomb, and E. L. Hartley (eds.), Readings in Social Psychology, 3rd Ed., pp. 9–18. Holt, Rinehart and Winston, New York.

Bruner, J. S. 1975a. From communication to language—a psychological perspective. Cognition 3:255–288.

Bruner, J. S. 1975b. The ontogenesis of speech acts. J. Child Lang. 2:1–19.

Bryant, P. E. 1965. The effects of verbal labelling on recall and recognition in severely subnormal and normal children. J. Ment. Defic. Res. 9:229–236.

Bryant, P. E. 1967. Verbalization and immediate memory of complex stimuli in normal and severely subnormal children. Br. J. Soc. Clin. Psychol. 6:212–219.

Bryant, P. E. 1970. Language and learning in severely subnormal and normal children. *In* B. W. Richards (ed.), Mental Subnormality: Modern Trends in Research, pp. 150–163. Pitman Medical and Scientific Publishing Co., London.

Burling, R. 1959. Language development of a Garo and English speaking child. Word 15:45–68.

Carroll, J. B. (ed.) 1956. Language, Thought and Reality: Selected Writings of Benjamin Lee Whorf. M.I.T. Press and John Wiley & Sons, Inc., Cambridge, Mass.

Chomsky, C. 1969. The Acquisition of Syntax in Children from 5 to 10. M.I.T. Press, Cambridge, Mass.

Chomsky, N. 1957. Syntactic Structures. Mouton, the Hague.

Chomsky, N. 1959. A review of verbal behavior, by B. F. Skinner. Language 35:26–58.

Chomsky, N. 1962. Explanatory models in linguistics. *In* E. Nagel, P. Suppes, and A. Tarski (eds.), Logic, Methodology, and Philosophy of Science, pp. 528–550. Stanford University Press, Stanford.

Chomsky, N. 1965. Aspects of the Theory of Syntax. M.I.T. Press, Cambridge, Mass.

Chomsky, N. 1966. Cartesian Linguistics. Harper & Row, New York.

Chomsky, N. 1968. Language and Mind. Harcourt, Brace & World, Inc., New York.

Cowley, A., and L. Weiskrantz. 1975. Demonstration of cross-modal matching in Rhesus monkeys, *Macaca mulatta*. Neuropsychologia 13:117–120.

Cromer, R. F. 1968. The development of temporal reference during the acquisition of language. Unpublished doctoral dissertation, Harvard University.

Cromer, R. F. 1974a. The development of language and cognition: The cognition hypothesis. *In* B. Foss (ed.), New Perspectives in Child Development, pp. 184–252. Penguin Books, Harmondsworth, Middlesex.

Cromer, R. F. 1974b. Receptive language in the mentally retarded: Processes and diagnostic distinctions. *In* R. L. Schiefelbusch and L. L. Lloyd (eds.), Language Perspectives—Acquisition, Retardation, and Intervention, pp. 237–267. University Park Press, Baltimore.

Cromer, R. F. 1975. Are subnormals linguistic adults? *In* N. O'Connor (ed.), Language, Cognitive Deficits, and Retardation, pp. 169–187. Butterworths, London.

Davenport, R. K., and C. M. Rogers. 1970. Intermodal equivalence of stimuli in apes. Science 168:279–280.

Davenport, T. R. K., C. M. Rogers, and I. S. Russell. 1973. Cross-modal perception in apes. Neuropsychologia 11:21–28.

de Laguna, G. A. 1963. Speech: Its Function and Development. Indiana University Press, Bloomington, Indiana. (Originally published in 1927.)

Doehring, D. G. 1960. Visual spatial memory in aphasic children. J. Speech Hear. Res. 3:138–149.

Efron, R. 1963. Temporal perception, aphasia, and deja vu. Brain 86:403–424.

Eimas, P. D. 1974. Linguistic processing of speech by young infants. *In* R. L. Schiefelbusch and L. L. Lloyd (eds.), Language Perspectives—Acquisition, Retardation, and Intervention, pp. 55–73. University Park Press, Baltimore.

Ervin-Tripp, S. 1966. Language development. *In* M. Hoffman and L. Hoffman (eds.), Review of Child Development Research, Vol. 2, pp. 55–105. University of Michigan Press, Ann Arbor, Michigan.

Ervin-Tripp, S. 1971. An overview of theories of grammatical development. *In* D. I. Slobin (ed.), The Ontogenesis of Grammar: A Theoretical Symposium, pp. 189–223. Academic Press, New York.

Ferreiro, E., and H. Sinclair. 1971. Temporal relations in language. Int. J. Psychol. 6:39–47.

Fillmore, C. J. 1968. The case for case. *In* E. Bach and R. T. Harms (eds.), Universals in Linguistic Theory, pp. 1–88, Holt, Rinehart and Winston, New York.

Fillmore, C. J. 1971. Some problems for case grammar. *In* R. J. O'Brien (ed.), Report of the Twenty-Second Annual Round Table Meeting on Linguistics and Language Studies, pp. 35–56. Georgetown University Press, Washington, D.C.

Flavell, J. H. 1963. The Developmental Psychology of Jean Piaget. D. Van Nostrand Company, Princeton, N.J.

Furth, H. G. 1966. Thinking Without Language: Psychological Implications of Deafness. The Free Press, New York.

Furth, H. G. 1969. Piaget and Knowledge. Prentice-Hall, Englewood Cliffs, N.J.

Furth, H. G., and J. Youniss. 1971. Formal operations and language: a comparison of deaf and hearing adolescents. Int. J. Psychol. 6:49–64. (Reprinted this volume.)

Graham, N. C. 1968. Short term memory and syntactic structure in educationally subnormal children. Lang. Speech 11:209–219.

Graham, N. C. 1974. Response strategies in the partial comprehension of sentences. Lang. Speech 17:205–221.

Graham, N. C., and R. A. Gulliford. 1968. A psychological approach to the language deficiencies of educationally subnormal children. Educ. Rev. 20:136–145.

Griffiths, P. 1972. Developmental Aphasia: An Introduction. Invalid Children's Aid Association, London.

Henle, P. (ed.) 1958. Language, Thought, and Culture. The University of Michigan Press, Ann Arbor.

Hermelin, B., and N. O'Connor. 1964. Crossmodal transfer in normal, subnormal, and autistic children. Neuropsychologia 2:229–235.

Hoijer, H. (ed.) 1954. Language in Culture. The University of Chicago Press, Chicago.

Hubel, D. H., and T. N. Wiesel. 1962. Receptive fields, binocular interaction, and functional architecture in the cat's visual cortex. J. Physiol. 160:106–154.

Inhelder, B. 1969. Memory and intelligence in the child. In D. Elkind and J. H. Flavell (eds.), Studies in Cognitive Development, pp. 337–364. Oxford University Press, New York.

Inhelder, B., and J. Piaget. 1958. The Growth of Logical Thinking from Childhood to Adolescence. Basic Books, New York. (Originally published in 1955.)

Jacobs, R. A., and P. S. Rosenbaum. 1968. English Transformational Grammar. Blaisdell, Waltham, Mass.

James, W. 1890. The Principles of Psychology, Vol. 1. (Authorized, unabridged edition, Dover Publications, Inc., New York, 1950.)

Kaplan, E., and G. Kaplan. 1971. The prelinguistic child. In J. Eliot (ed.), Human Development and Cognitive Processes. Holt, Rinehart and Winston, New York.

Kendler, T. S. 1963. Development of mediating responses in children. In J. C. Wright and J. Kagan (eds.), Basic Cognitive Processes in Children. Monographs of the Society for Research in Child Development 28:33–47.

Lantz, D. L., and V. Stefflre. 1964. Language and cognition revisited. J. Abnorm. Soc. Psychol. 69:472–481.

Lind, J. (ed.) 1965. Newborn infant cry. Acta Paediatr. Scand. supplement 163.

Lowe, A. D., and R. A. Campbell. 1965. Temporal discrimination in aphasoid and normal children. J. Speech Hear. Res. 8:313–314.

Lyons, J. 1970. Chomsky. Fontana/Collins, London.

Mandelbaum, D. G. (ed.) 1949. Selected Writings of Edward Sapir in Language, Culture, and Personality. University of California Press, Berkeley.

Mandelbaum, D. G. (ed.) 1961. Edward Sapir, Culture, Language, and Personality: Selected Essays. University of California Press, Berkeley.

McCawley, J. D. 1968. The role of semantics in a grammar. In E. Bach and R. T. Harms (eds.), Universals in Linguistic Theory, pp. 124–169. Holt, Rinehart and Winston, New York.

McCawley, J. D. 1973. A review of Noam A. Chomsky, Studies on Semantics in Generative Grammar. Mimeographed paper, Indiana University Linguistics Club, Bloomington, Ind. November 1973.

McNeill, D. 1966. Developmental psycholinguistics. In F. Smith and G. A. Miller (eds.), The Genesis of Language, pp. 15–84. M.I.T. Press, Cambridge, Mass.

McNeill, D. 1970a. The Acquisition of Language. Harper & Row, New York.

McNeill, D. 1970b. The development of language. In P. H. Mussen (ed.), Carmichael's Manual of Child Psychology, Vol. 1, pp. 1061–1161. John Wiley & Sons, New York.

Menyuk, P. 1964. Comparison of grammar of children with functionally deviant and normal speech. J. Speech Hear. Res. 7:109–121.

Menyuk, P. 1969. Sentences Children Use. M.I.T. Press, Cambridge, Mass.

Menyuk, P., and P. L. Looney. 1976. A problem of language disorder: Length versus structure. This volume.

Miller, G. A., and D. McNeill. 1969. Psycholinguistics. In G. Lindzey and E. Aronson (eds.), The Handbook of Social Psychology, 2nd Ed., Vol. 3, pp. 666–794. Addison-Wesley, Reading, Mass.

Morris, G. P. 1972. Verbalisation and memory in the mentally subnormal. Unpublished doctoral dissertation, University of London.

Morris, G. P. 1975. Verbalisation and memory in the severely subnormal. In N. O'Connor (ed.), Language, Cognitive Deficits, and Retardation, pp. 143–150. Butterworths, London.

O'Connor, N., and B. Hermelin. 1971. Inter- and intra-modal transfer in children with modality specific and general handicaps. Br. J. Soc. Clin. Psychol. 10:346–354.

Over, R., and N. J. Mackintosh. 1969. Cross-modal transfer of intensity discrimination by rats. Nature 224:918–919.

Piaget, J. 1970a. Genetic Epistemology. Columbia University Press, New York.

Piaget, J. 1970b. Piaget's theory. In P. H. Mussen (ed.), Carmichael's Manual of Child Psychology, Vol. 1, pp. 703–732. John Wiley & Sons, New York.

Piaget, J., and B. Inhelder. 1969. The Psychology of the Child. Routledge & Kegan Paul, London.

Poppen, R., J. Stark, J. Eisenson, T. Forrest, and G. Wertheim. 1969. Visual sequencing performance of aphasic children. J. Speech Hear. Res. 12:288–300.

Ricks, D. M. 1972. The beginnings of vocal communication in infants and autistic children. Unpublished doctorate of medicine thesis, University of London.

Ricks, D. M. 1975. Vocal communication in pre-verbal normal and autistic children. *In* N. O'Connor (ed.), Language, Cognitive Deficits, and Retardation, pp. 75–80. Butterworths, London.

Rosenthal, W. S. 1972. Auditory and linguistic interaction in developmental aphasia: Evidence from two studies of auditory processing. Papers and Reports on Child Language Development (Special Issue: Language Disorders in Children), No. 4, pp. 19–34. Stanford University Institute for Childhood Aphasia.

Ryan, J. 1974. Early language development: Towards a communicational analysis. *In* M. P. M. Richards (ed.), The Integration of a Child into a Social World, pp. 185–213. Cambridge University Press, Cambridge.

Sachs, J. 1971. The status of developmental studies of language. *In* J. Eliot (ed.), Human Development and Cognitive Processes, pp. 381–394. Holt, Rinehart and Winston, New York.

Schlesinger, I. M. 1971a. Learning grammar: from pivot to realization rule. *In* R. Huxley and E. Ingram (eds.), Language Acquisition: Models and Methods, pp. 79–89. Academic Press, London.

Schlesinger, I. M. 1971b. Production of utterances and language acquisition. *In* D. I. Slobin (ed.), The Ontogenesis of Grammar: A Theoretical Symposium, pp. 63–101. Academic Press, New York.

Schlesinger, I. M. 1974. Relational concepts underlying language. *In* R. L. Schiefelbusch and L. L. Lloyd (eds.), Language Perspectives— Acquisition, Retardation, and Intervention, pp. 129–151. University Park Press, Baltimore.

Schlesinger, I. M. Production and Comprehension of Utterances. In press.

Seuren, P. A. M. (ed.) 1974. Semantic Syntax. Oxford University Press, Oxford.

Sheehan, J. G., S. Aseltine, and A. E. Edwards. 1973. Aphasic comprehension of time spacing. J. Speech Hear. Res. 16:650–657.

Sinclair, H. 1969. Developmental psycholinguistics. *In* D. Elkind and J. H. Flavell (eds.), Studies in Cognitive Development, pp. 315–336. Oxford University Press, New York.

Sinclair, H. 1971. Sensorimotor action patterns as a condition for the acquisition of syntax. *In* R. Huxley and E. Ingram (eds.), Language Acquisition: Models and Methods, pp. 121–130. Academic Press, London.

Slobin, D. I. 1966. The acquisition of Russian as a native language. *In* F. Smith and G. A. Miller (eds.), The Genesis of Language, pp. 129–148. M.I.T. Press, Cambridge, Mass.

Slobin, D. I. (ed.) 1971a. The Ontogenesis of Grammar: A Theoretical Symposium. Academic Press, New York.

Slobin, D. I. 1971b. Psycholinguistics. Scott, Foresman & Company, Glenview, Ill.

Slobin, D. I. 1973. Cognitive prerequisites for the development of grammar. *In* C. A. Ferguson and D. I. Slobin (eds.), Studies of Child Language Development, pp. 175–208. Holt, Rinehart and Winston, New York.

Smith, S. M., H. O. Brown, J. E. P. Toman, and L. S. Goodman. 1947. The lack of cerebral effects of d-tubocurarine. Anethesiology 8:1–14.

Spiker, C. C. 1963. Verbal factors in the discrimination learning of children.

In J. C. Wright and J. Kagan (eds.), Basic Cognitive Processes in Children. Monographs of the Society for Research in Child Development 28:53–69.

Stark, J. 1966. Performance of aphasic children on the ITPA. Exceptional Children 33:153–158.

Tallal, P., and M. Piercy. 1973. Developmental aphasia: Impaired rate of non-verbal processing as a function of sensory modality. Neuropsychologia 11:389–398.

Tallal, P., and M. Piercy. 1974. Developmental aphasia: Rate of auditory processing and selective impairment of consonant perception. Neuropsychologia 12:83–93.

Vygotsky, L. S. 1962. Thought and Language. M.I.T. Press, Cambridge, Mass.

Withrow, F. B. 1964. Immediate recall by aphasic, deaf, and normally hearing children for visual forms presented simultaneously or sequentially in time. Asha 6:386.

Wolff, P. H. 1969. The natural history of crying and other vocalizations in early infancy. *In* B. M. Foss (ed.), Determinants of Infant Behavior, Vol. 4, pp. 81–109. Methuen & Co., Ltd., London.

Yehle, A. L., and J. P. Ward, 1969. Cross-modal transfer of a specific discrimination in the rabbit. Psychonomic Sci. 16:269–270.

Observations on the Operational and Figurative Aspects of Thought in Dysphasic Children

BÄRBEL INHELDER[1]

The Genevan Group, headed by Jean Piaget, Bärbel Inhelder, and Hermina Sinclair, are internationally known for their work on the development of thought and language in the child. What is less well known, particularly in this country, is the extensive work by Inhelder and her colleagues on atypical children. Her first major work in this area, published in French in 1943, provides a detailed description of the reasoning processes of retarded children (Inhelder, 1968), and a summary of her more recent research with other populations has appeared in a review article (Inhelder, 1966). The article reprinted here is of general theoretical interest because it describes children who develop more basic aspects of intelligence at a normal rate in the absence of a comparably developed linguistic system. Inhelder interprets her findings as strong evidence for the primacy of thought over language. She also reports that these dysphasic children usually show a representational deficit in several areas of symbolic behavior in addition to language—an observation that has been reported elsewhere in the literature (de Ajuriaguerra, 1966; Lovell, Hoyle, and Siddal, 1968). This second proposition provides the only hypothesis that specifies the exact nature of certain linguistic deficits and their relationship

Original article: Inhelder, B. 1963. Observations sur les aspects opératifs et figuratifs de la pensée chez des enfants dysphasiques. *In* Problèmes de Psycholinguistique, Vol. 6, pp. 143–153. Presses Universitaires de France, Paris. Reprinted with permission from Presses Universitaires de France. Translated by Ann E. Morehead and Donald M. Morehead with the assistance of Kate Cooper.

[1]Professor at the Institute of Educational Sciences, Geneva, in collaboration with E. Siotis.

to intellectual development—a position that reflects Piaget's (1962) view that language is but one aspect, albeit an important one, of a more general symbolic capacity for representation.

—DMM

The examination of a group of dysphasic children has revealed two facts, among others, which deserve closer analysis:

1. The majority of children with language problems—not just phonetic problems but syntactic and semantic ones as well—seem to develop certain concrete operations of thought, corresponding to age level.
2. Their language deficit is often accompanied by deficiencies in figurative symbolism. These facts place in a new perspective the problem of the relationship between the operative aspect of thought and its symbolic supports, such as linguistic signs and imagery.

DEVELOPMENT OF OPERATIVITY

In the case of a difference in the rate of development between operativity or thought and language, the question is: what direction will operative development take when it is being supported only by a rudimentary language, and, in particular, how will the child succeed in compensating for his linguistic deficiencies so that he can develop the elementary operations of thought?

Both the detailed analysis of early developmental processes and the adaptation of the clinical method for use in situations involving deficiencies in verbal communication will demonstrate ways in which the operativity of linguistically deficient children is both comparable to and distinct from that of children with normal language development.

Rather than analyzing the reasoning of older children who inadequately formulate concepts which are already established, wouldn't it be more worthwhile to trace the development of young children who are in the process of constructing elementary thought operations?

As an example, here is the case of a boy Y, age 5:7 (5 years, 7 months). In a language examination administered by a language clinician, we observe considerable difficulties in both the recital of a story—spontaneous or elicited—and in the imitation of words and sentences. In particular, one observes frequent suppression and inversion of terms. In response to the question, "What did you do at school?" Y replied something like this, "Fait te lète, se, te ménosélétation fait tes seu," which seems to mean, "Fais des lettres, c'était la récréation, fais des jeux" (You do writing, recess, do some games).

To examine the development of operativity, Y was first given a battery of tests in which the comprehension of instructions and the solution of problems required only an elementary level of verbal communication. The tests dealt with the arrangement of direct and inverse alignment of objects and with certain aspects of concrete classifications.

Despite his language deficiencies, Y was capable of solving each problem in the same way as the most advanced children of his age group. He succeeded in arranging a group of objects in direct and inverse order, according to the model presented. He restored the order of three beads placed on a straight rod passing through a tube and anticipated the order of their reappearance, both direct and inverse, when the tube had been rotated 180°. He even seemed to understand that two semi-rotations would restore the direct order. (During the experiment the child can see the model with the direct order and can arrange the beads according to his expectations.)

Y spontaneously classified geometric shapes according to the criterion of color. Then, the experimenter simply had to contrast a circle with a square for the child to make a classification based on the criterion of shape without hesitation. The following day he discovered in the same way a third criterion, that of size.

Likewise, Y solved some problems of class intersection presented in the form of matrices, by correctly choosing images which unite two criteria at once in order to rule out other possibilities. He even succeeded in drawing—not simply choosing—a picture which located the intersection of two classes.

Tasks that transform direct linear order into an inverse order, that classify forms according to successive or simultaneous criteria, involve processes which require that action schemes, or thought, are mobile and therefore capable of reversibility, a condition necessary for operational thinking.

The fact that some young dysphasic children do attain this level of operativity at the same age as children with normal language development seems to be an argument in favor of the hypothesis that the "logic of action," or thought, acts as a precursor to language.

But the question that immediately arises is: how are these same children going to go about solving operational problems, the solutions of which presuppose the understanding of verbal constructs such as the numerical quantifiers, "as much as," "more," and "less" or the logical quantifiers, "some" and "all"?

Our experience has shown us that it is possible to encourage attempts at operative solutions by adjusting our questions to these children's level of verbal comprehension.

In testing the notion of equivalence of numerical groupings, which is generally established in young children by one-to-one correspondence, we avoid the terms "as much as" or "the same thing," which are often misunderstood or ambiguous. The majority of children already know how to tell whether or not one person has more things to eat, to sell, etc. than another. After making a one-for-one exchange of merchandise for money, Y seemed to understand the equivalence between the two groups and resisted the suggestion that one person could have more than the other, describing with gestures the changes which had been carried out: "I took everything; you sold (i.e., received in exchange) all the money." When the exchange was reversed and then interrupted, Y discovered that the amount of money which remained was equal to the amount of merchandise at his disposal. He pointed to the objects to sell: "You can buy one, two, three (counting them on his fingers); you have one, two, three 'sous' (coins)."

The equivalence between two groups of eggs and egg cups, established again by a one-to-one correspondence, was also obtained. Despite the fact that the eggs were separated from each other by wide intervals, Y could see that there weren't more eggs than egg cups. He was quite indignant when we took away one element from one of the groups in order to establish an overall figurative correspondence instead of a numerical one. From then on, he himself used this process in various experiments on conservation of quantity in order to show that one group was equivalent to another.

In a test which was to examine an aspect of logical inclusions which presupposes the presence of the quantifiers "some" and "all," Y demonstrated through his operational actions that he was capable of solving the problem in spite of his inadequate vocabulary. The experiment is based on the following principle: if class A is included in class B (and class A′ is not null), all the members of class A are in class B, without the reverse being true. The problem is presented in a concrete form, avoiding the use of the ambiguous term "some": the child is presented a collection of small tokens, blue and red square ones and square and round blue ones. After a preliminary classification assuring us that the child understands the instructions, we ask questions in the following way:

1. "A little boy said, 'All the square ones are red' (all B's are A's); was he right?"

   Y answered, "No," pointing to the two square red tokens and separating out the other square tokens.

   And so on:

2. "All the round tokens are blue" (All A's are B's). Y said, "All blue and round," to separate the round blue tokens from the others (composed of blue and red squares).

3. "All the blues are round" (all B's are A's). Formulated in this way, Y did not seem to understand.

   A similar case, "Everything that is blue is round."

   He did, however, immediately grasp the formula, "All the blue things are round," replying. "No, [there are] still squares," gathering together all the round blue tokens and separating them from the others.

4. "All the red things are square" (all A's are B's). Y immediately answered, "Yes." He took the two red squares and separated them from the other square tokens.

It seems, then, that the child treats the classes of objects not as concepts but as "schemes of action" capable of grouping the objects and then separating them into their respective subgroups.

Because of this transfer of conceptual problems to the level of operational activity, some children succeed in compensating for their linguistic deficiencies, thereby reaching the threshold of concrete operations. In older children who have more developed, although still deficient, linguistic ability, we find in a residual form the same recourse to actual physical action. One boy, Z, age 11:6, struggling with the difficulties presented by class inclusion, tried to compare the extension of subclass A (brown beads) with that of class B (wooden beads) by striking each bead against the table to determine if it was wooden.

It appears, then, that the young children who accompany or replace their deficient linguistic schemes with schemes of actual physical action are more successful in attaining a normal operational level than are those who do not. If a systematic study done on a group of children with a comparable level of operative development and linguistic deficit were to confirm this finding, one could hypothesize that, even in the solution of conceptual problems that depend on language, it is still the operational schemes that assure the transition between the sensorimotor coordinations and those operations which can properly be called thought operations.

DEVELOPMENT OF FIGURATIVE SYMBOLISM

It could be assumed that dysphasic children compensate for their linguistic deficiency by a more highly developed figurative and imaginal symbolism. But, in the majority of cases studied, we find, on the contrary, a striking correspondence between deficits in language and those of figurative representation. All spatial relations are not affected, but the possibilities of evoking and anticipating transformations in spatial configurations are. It seems as though the formation of mental images—figurative symbols—is inhibited or even disturbed. It is commonly known that in some forms of aphasia the problems of the symbolic function are not limited to language but also affect spatial representation. It is interesting to note that some dysphasic children who don't seem to have any detectable neurological problems do have problems with the figurative aspect of thought, while the operational aspect is relatively unaffected.

To illustrate, here are a few observations on the behavior of a child Z, whose development we followed from the age of 9:6 to 11:6. Among the persistent problems noted during his language training, we found semantic confusions—confusions between members of the same class or association (e.g., apple and pear; figs and dates)—and phonetic confusions for both comprehension and production (e.g., "libraire" [bookseller] and "livreur" [delivery man]). Syntax seems to be particularly disrupted; there is an incoherent use of tense and an apparent inability to use the conditional. There is also a general difficulty in arranging narrative events according to their temporal succession.

However, development of the operative aspect of thought seems to be almost normal. Problems for which the solution requires only a minimum of symbolic representation—on the linguistic level as well as on the level of spatial imagery—are solved in the same manner as by normal children of the same age. Without any difficulty Z recognized the conservation of weight and substance of a ball of clay, regardless of the transformations and divisions it underwent. His linguistic productions are somewhat incomplete but adequate. "It [the ball] got long; nothing was taken away." Z also was able to make equivalent geometric constructions on the surfaces of different dimensions, using an operational system of measure. In contrast, Z seemed stumped by real obstacles each time the solution to the problems required the use of representational imagery. One such problem is that of conservation of volume which requires the anticipation of displacement of water as a function of immersed objects. Likewise, Z was able to understand the concept of weight conservation when sugar was dissolved in water but was unable to comprehend the process of dissolution itself.

As the development of the figurative aspect of thought is clearly impeded, it is interesting to note how operations, once established, succeed to some extent in directing the figurative representations so that they partially compensate for their deficiencies.

This progressive subordination of deficient figurative representations to thought operations is first illustrated in Z's behavior in an experiment involving the liquid levels in tilted glass jars. Asked to describe the direction of the level of the water, Z, at age 9:6, seemed to have difficulties comparable to those we have found in a majority of 7-year-old children; he was unable to disassociate the horizontal direction of the water from the inclined position of the container. At 11:6, he finally succeeded in solving the problem, but only when he was able to make explicit all of the physical conditions necessary to reveal the law of horizontality.

The anticipatory representation of the shadow of a rod or a circle as a function of its position and inclination in relation to a light source presented the same problems. Only after a delay of 2 years was Z able to imagine the successive modifications in a shadow, and even this success was due to operative seriation.

The coordination of perspectives by an observer drawing a group of mountains from different viewpoints presented a particularly difficult problem. Asked to choose the pictures that corresponded to different points of view, Z seemed incapable at first of putting himself in a perspective other than his own; little by little, he overcame his difficulties by operational reasoning which led to an understanding of left-right, up-down spatial relations.

Finally, the use of some techniques designed to study the mechanisms needed in the formation of mental images—images not easily reducible to geometric constructions—permits us to detect Z's particular problems in anticipating the transformation of spatial configurations. The anticipation of the rotation of a square in relation to a fixed frame of reference, as well as the anticipation of the trajectory of beads strung on a rod which is rotated 180°, hardly seemed possible at first. By gestures and by constant comparison of his attempts at a graphic representation (drawing) and of the actual physical displacement of the figures, the child tried to overcome the deficiencies of his mental imagery.

These fragmentary observations reveal the problem of the respective roles of operativity and of its support by images. The clinical evidence for the existence of a conflict between operativity and figurative symbolism and the more or less fruitful attempts of some children to by-pass their deficiencies in spatial representation by operational constructions seem to indicate that the figurative and operative do not represent two successive stages but rather that they are two complementary aspects of thought. Moreover, their roles seem to vary as a function of the level of operativity. It is clear that the problems of figurative representation can, in certain cases, slow down the process of formation of certain operations. But, once these operations are established, they seem not only to supplement the shortcomings in mental imagery but also to contribute to its development. At no time in its development does operativity seem to derive from figurative symbolism. It is, rather, through operativity itself that images lose their initial static character and gain mobility. This hypothesis, already suggested by our developmental data, seems to be confirmed by clinical facts.

The apparently frequent correspondence between language problems and difficulties with spatial representations suggests a possible link between the dysfunctions which affect the formation of figurative symbols and those which retard or disturb the formation of verbal symbols in language acquisition. If we only consider language in its finished form as a system of arbitrary signs combined in a way which is essentially conceptual, this possibility loses its meaning. But, we mustn't forget that initially language is part of a broader symbolic system that a child uses to express himself—means such as ludic gestures, posture, imagery—which all develop out of imitation. The very important role of symbolic play during the preoperational period shows in effect that, because of the lack of adequate conceptualization, the child needs to combine his use of collective or social language with a kind of personal or individual language which incorporates symbolic activity and mental imagery. Language and thought, before attaining a certain autonomy, have in common the characteristic of being partially figurative or representational.

The only aim of these questions and hypotheses is to direct future research. Our present knowledge of the origin and laws that govern language development is far too rudimentary to allow us to assign a place to language deficiencies in relation to the total symbolic function and linguistic structures. Research should, it seems to us, continue in two directions:

What are the relations between the first forms of language and the other modes of symbolic expression such as spontaneous and imitated gesture? We expect a great deal from the research undertaken by Lezine (1973)[2] on the development of sensorimotor actions and imitations and their correspondences to the onset of language within the total symbolic function.

What are the hierarchical aspects of syntactic development and, in particular, which levels of language development are compatible with which operational constructions? In order to approach such questions, shouldn't we look to some of the models furnished by contemporary linguistics? It is true that the gap between abstract models and the complexity of psychological data is still such that we might hesitate to use these models for analysis of child language, but some research done by Brown (1973) and his team at Harvard reveals interesting results. This research was based on Chomsky's (1965) linguistic models and shows, among other things, that the syntax of 3-year-olds obeys adult simplification rules, yet maintains a maximum of information. It is, then, not an idle hope that the addition of linguistics to genetic and clinical psychology will one day allow us to understand better the complex relation between language and thought.

REFERENCES

Brown, R. 1973. A First Language. Harvard University Press, Cambridge, Mass.

Chomsky, N. 1965. Aspects of a Theory of Syntax. M.I.T. Press, Cambridge, Mass.

Lezine, I. 1973. The transformation from sensorimotor to earliest symbolic function in early development. *In* Early Development, Vol. 51, pp. 221–232. Association for Research in Nervous and Mental Disease. Williams & Wilkins, Baltimore.

---

[2]The original citations have been updated to reflect the most current relevant research by Lezine, Brown, and Chomsky.

The Development and Prognosis of Dysphasia in Children

J. de AJURIAGUERRA, A. JAEGGI,
F. GUIGNARD, F. KOCHER,
M. MAQUARD, S. ROTH, and E. SCHMID

One of the shortcomings of recent research on language-deficient children is that most studies focus on purely linguistic aspects of the deficiency while neglecting other, equally significant areas of development. The longitudinal study of de Ajuriaguerra and his colleagues follows the long-established tradition (elaborately reviewed in Luchsinger and Arnold, 1965) of evaluating the global nature of the dysfunction as well as methods for its remediation. What differentiates their work within this tradition is that de Ajuriaguerra et al. also include recent developments in linguistics, cognition, and social and affective behavior. The study reprinted here is one of a series representing the most comprehensive body of research on the assessment and training of children with language deficiencies. According to de Ajuriaguerra et al., the failure to develop an adequate linguistic system appears to have its most serious repercussions during early adolescence in nonlinguistic areas of development, such as intelligence and social behavior. Specifically, they report that the failure to develop language at a normal rate precludes the development of adult thought or formal operations. Thought at this level of development becomes propositional since it coordinates itself with a highly developed linguistic system, though the latter still remains subordinate to it (also, see Furth and Youniss, 1971, reprinted this volume; Lenneberg, 1967; Fromkin et al., 1974; and Weiner, 1974, for extensive reviews of

Excerpted from de Ajuriaguerra et al. 1965. Évolution et pronostic de la dysphasie chez l'enfant. *In* La Psychiatrie de l'Enfant, Vol. 8, pp. 391–452. Presses Universitaires de France, Paris. Reprinted with permission from Presses Universitaires de France. Translated by Donald Morehead and Ann Morehead with the assistance of Kate Cooper.

language deficiencies and their relationship to critical periods for language acquisition).

—DMM

In a paper delivered to the April 1962 Congress of the Association for Scientific Psychology of the French Language we presented a study concerning dysphasic children, in which language was considered as a system in the process of development. Our approach differed, then, from those of phoneticians, linguists, and cyberneticians who study language as a pre-formed system.

Through a multi-dimensional study we attempted to characterize the subjects' language by considering it not as a function in itself, but rather in connection with mental and affective dynamics (de Ajuriaguerra et al., 1963). The conclusions that we reached presented new problems, the understanding of which required that these children be observed longitudinally. The findings of our subsequent observations comprise the present paper. We offer the summary of our first study below as an introduction.

LINGUISTIC ASPECTS

The term *dysphasic* was applied to subjects in this study to distinguish them, on the one hand, from aphasics and deaf (whose linguistic impairment is much more serious) and, on the other, from dysarthritics and anarthritics (for whom essentially articulation is affected).

1. We studied the organic and functional factors that affect the quality of linguistic development and the different aspects of verbal communication.
2. Following the established terminology, we used the term *speech* to refer to everything related to oral expression—in other words, the phonetic or articulatory aspect by which meanings are conveyed—and the term *language* was used to refer to varying semantic aspects of verbal communication—signifiers or words, the coordination of signifiers or words to express complex ideas (syntax), and the coordination of ideas (narrative, dialogue).

The articulatory system of each of our subjects was anatomically normal. Functionally, 40% of the cases presented some inadequacies but these were not sufficient to explain the extent of their deficit.

Tonal audiograms indicated that none of our subjects had any sensory deficit, but these tests were not sufficient to establish

whether or not the sounds of the language had been fully differentiated by the child. The synthesis of acoustical data and the
establishment of a system of classification and differentiation of
phonemes depend, among other things, on a central process which
develops only progressively during childhood, leading to what we call
auditory-verbal *perception*.

Even when we tested phonemes that had already been acquired
and nonsense words which presented no difficulty in articulation,
we still found a deficit in auditory-verbal perception for all of the
dysphasics. An 18-month-old child with normal language development which does not yet conform to the adult role may have better
auditory-verbal perception than some 5-year-old dysphasics who
nevertheless use language to communicate.

Five tests were particularly significant: the test for auditory-
verbal perception, the test for narration, the test for articulation, the
test for synonyms, and the test for vocabulary usage (this last test was
significant only when the subject failed it and his general language
development was seriously delayed). Success or failure on these tests
was the criterion for determining normal or deficient language.

There was a relative homogeneity among the deficits of comprehension, production, articulation, and semantics. Two previous
observations supported this: the verbal comprehension of dysphasics
is almost never normal and all of the subjects had articulation problems.

The different linguistic classifications made from the quantitative
data led in part to an impasse (subjects often recovered or their
linguistic organization was at times rapidly modified under the influence of, say, para-linguistic factors). On the other hand, a more
qualitative study permitted us to establish a correlation between
linguistic organization and expression (method of communication).
In this sense two prominent types of subjects were distinguished:

1. The "verbally restrained" or reserved: this restraint appeared to
coincide with the use of simple sentences and with narration in which
enumeration or description predominated. Further, these subjects
showed little discrepancy between the comprehension of language
and the construction of sentences and narrations (at least when the
comprehension was inadequate). Besides, within the tests themselves, we found little variation in performance.
2. The "verbally unrestrained": this condition appeared with the
intermittent use of complex sentences, variant word order, and a
more complex but generally incoherent narration. These subjects

showed a rather large discrepancy between comprehension and production. In addition, variations in performance—generally more important in this case than for the verbally restrained—were found.

Nevertheless, we varied this dichotomy slightly, recognizing that at times certain apparently fundamental behavior such as telegraphic style, use of function words, and laconism might represent unstable productions; however, some types of apparently opposing behavior can co-exist.

ASPECTS OF PSYCHOLOGICAL ORGANIZATION

We attempted to characterize the psychological profiles of our population of dysphasic children with a composite battery of tests, without excluding those in which language is used. In fact, to call certain tests "nonverbal" seemed to us to constitute a kind of misrepresentation, since presenting a child with a situation not requiring an explicit verbal expression still does not indicate that language plays no role in his comprehension of meaning and in his making a response. Careful evaluation of tests with verbal components provides valuable information about the adaptive use of deficient language.

For the majority of our subjects, establishing intellectual level did not pose any problems since their performance on standardized tests was normal. Yet, most of them presented uneven psychological profiles with poor performance in certain verbal tests and marked difficulties with spatial structuralization. Moreover, about half of the subjects presented rhythmic movement and minor psycho-motor difficulties.

Analysis of various tests showed that certain subtests designated as "verbal" were reliable in establishing intellectual level despite language problems.

In attempting to determine the role of language in the acquisition of the reference system, we were surprised to find a high percentage of failures in tasks where the form of the verbal message played a salient role in understanding its meaning. Apparently our subjects had little linguistic resource at their disposal; language for them was not a very economical means of communication because of the difficulties which it presented. Close attention to the relative importance of different elements in a verbal message was probably no longer adequate when the message was particularly rich in information. In this instance, the differentiation of the signals, or rather, the establishment of the relation of identity-contrast features which are at the base of coding and decoding, could no longer be executed rapidly enough by the subject as he was processing the entire set of factors.

The techniques of Inhelder and Piaget (1958) were used to analyze reasoning processes in order to specify operative functions.

Our examination included, then, operative aspects of thought (logical-mathematical, spatial-temporal, conceptual, classification and seriation), as well as figurative aspects (symbolic function of representation and anticipatory imagery). Each of the tests used involved language, either as an aspect of understanding a logical process assigned to internalized language or as an aspect of communication.

We found normal reasoning in 70% of our subjects at the level of concrete operations (none of our subjects had attained the age of formal operations). On the other hand, 85% of our subjects had clear and admittedly important problems in the realm of spatial representation.

It is interesting to note that in our dysphasics neither the problems of spatial structuralization established above nor those of anticipatory imagery—that is, an aspect of figurative thought—seemed seriously to disturb the efficiency of reasoning, at least at the stage of concrete operations. However, two qualifications must be made: these children always performed better in the tests with flexible content, especially in those situations which necessitated no complex verbal construction.

We wondered whether or not the strategies employed by these handicapped children differed in specific ways from those of children with normal language. We were at least able to establish that the most efficient subjects on the operative plane always used language to resolve the problems posed to them. This language—which, we must remember, was deficient—was selected either as a system of preferred reference or joined with operational thought.

AFFECTIVE AND SOCIAL ORGANIZATION

We questioned whether or not severe retardation of language, a deficiency having important repercussions on the development of social relations, was consistent with a normal affective organization. We were able to distinguish three groups among our subjects: 1) children who had a personality organization *within normal limits* except for verbal dialogue; 2) children who showed developmental disequilibrium with free-floating anxiety characteristic of *an affective retardation or of a so-called preneurotic state*; 3) children who had a *neurotic, prepsychotic, or psychotic* organization of personality— with solidly constructed defense mechanisms and a relatively rigid, almost closed personality structure.

Relying on this classification, we found:

1. *The appearance of language* was clearly less delayed in group 1 than in the other groups.
2. There was a significant relationship between the *need* for linguistic and para-linguistic *communication* and the affective structure.
3. The role of affective contribution was more clearly a determinant in the formation of personality structure of dysphasic children than were sociocultural or even linguistic contributions.
4. No children in the first group had experienced *separation* from the parents or *serious illnesses* at a young age, whereas in group 2, 47% of the subjects had been separated or were ill at the time of the onset of language. This percentage rose to 72% for the severely disturbed group. These figures conform to the findings of Spitz (1945) and Bowlby (1952) concerning the destructive role of prolonged early separations.
5. We found no relation between the severity of the dysphasia and the affective structure of our subjects. However, it seemed to us that there was a certain relationship between verbal communication and affective structure. Most of the affectively well-adapted children had a verbally restrained form of communication whereas most of the children having serious affective problems fit into the verbally unrestrained category.
6. The intellectual organization was more integrated in children who did not present notable affective difficulties.
7. No significant relationship could be established between the organization of personality and the seriousness of previously determined spatial-temporal problems.

After having reached these conclusions, we re-examined 17 of the 40 children. An average period of 2 years passed between the first and the second observation, in which some children had benefited from considerable training given them on linguistic and academic levels.

The age range of our 17 subjects was: at the first test, 4:3–10:10 years; at the retest, 7:2–12:9 years.

These children were classified according to the degree of progress in various areas of the written and spoken language.

Throughout our description, the observations are given according to this scale of progress. The major factors are presented in Table 1.

We will focus on aspects of verbal communication, intellectual development on the academic level, and socio-affective organization in the course of development of these dysphasics.

STUDY OF VERBAL COMMUNICATION

General Development

Regardless of level of intellect, age, affective structure, verbal behavior, or intensity of training, each subject developed in a majority of the areas studied.

The verbal behaviors had generally changed little; if anything, a reduction in the previously established characteristics was noted.

The defective semantic factor appeared even more in the retests than in the first tests, independent of intellectual and affective characteristics; thus, on the first test several of the subjects showed a thought structure that was just as deficient as the linguistic structure. On the retest, the thought structure was often improved due, in part, to linguistic development, and the discrepancies between thought and language appeared more on the explicit level of language. Yet it was often found that when the deficit related to thought structure, it was provoked by a specific linguistic deficiency. This seems to agree with the fact that many of our dysphasics had no operative difficulties on the nonverbal level (for example, in classifications) whereas these difficulties were marked when it was necessary to explain these same concepts verbally. An additional fact made clear at the retest was a specific aspect of the semantic problem—that the act of reading aloud seriously affected the comprehension of that which was read. In the end, spelling remained one of the most deficient activities.

Overall progress was often made because of a positive change in general attitude. This explains in part why such areas as "Comprehension" and "Narration" developed well, why the comprehension of the sentence often developed more than that of words, why difficulties of evoked imagery were still frequent, why syntactic structures developed better than morphological aspects, and why "Rhythm" developed better than "Auditory-Verbal Perception."

Table 1.

Observation No.	Age test (retest)	Language problems in other family members[a]	Illness or serious accidents in infancy	Prolonged separation early placement	Family atmosphere[a]	Sentences (appearance of)	Intellectual level test (retest) I to II[b]		Affective structure test (retest) I to III[c]		Linguistic structure restrained-unrestrained	Severity of deficit at the outset 1-3[d]	Logical operations test (retest)[b]
1 ♀	4:10 (7:3)	+	0	0	++	2-3 yrs	++	(+)	I	(I)	++	3 p	(+)
2 ♀	5:7 (7:2)	0	0	0	+	2-3 yrs	+	(++)	I	(I)	++	1 p	++ (++)
3 ♂	6:6 (9:1)	+	+	+	+	4 yrs	++	(+)	III	(III)	+	3	(+-)
4 ♂	4:3 (7:3)	+	0	0	+	2-3 yrs	+	(+)	I	(II)	++	2 p	(+)
5 ♀	5:5 (7:6)	+	0	0	+	2 yrs	-	(+)	I	(I)	+	1 p	(+-)
6 ♂ ♂	5:10 (8:)	0	+	0	-	2-3 yrs	+	(+)	II	(II)	++ In function of the situation	2	(+-)
7 ♂	6:9 (7:8)	?	0	++	{ - / + after 3 yrs }	4 yrs	+	(+)	III	(III)	++	2	+- (+)
8 ♂	10:10 (12:10)	+	0	0	++	4-5 yrs	+	(+)	I	(I)	++	3	++ (+)
9 ♀	6:3 (8:10)	+	0	0	-	4 yrs	-	(±)	II	(II)	+	3	- (++)
10 ♂	6:4 (8:1)	+	0	0	++	3-4 yrs	±	(++)	I	(I)	++	3	+ (+)
11 ♂	9:8 (11:7)	0	+	0	-	3-4 yrs	±	(±)	II	(II)	+	3	+ (+-)
12 ♀	7:5 (9:8)	+	0	0	-	4 yrs	±	(-)	III	(III)		3	+ (-)
13 ♀	7:7 (8:6)	(+)	0	0	+	3-4 yrs	±	(+)	II	(II)	++	2	+ (--)
14 ♂	8:0 (10:4)	?	0	+	-	3-4 yrs	+	(±)	II	(II)		2	- (+)
15 ♂	5:10 (7:2)	0	0	+	-	2-3 yrs	+	(-)	II	(III)	++	2	+ (-)
16 ♀	6:11 (9:3)	?	?	+	{ + after 4:6 }	4 yrs	±	(-)	III	(III)	++	3	- (--)
17 ♀	7:7 (8:6)	(+)	0	0	+	3-4 yrs	±	(±)	II	(II)		3	- (-)

[a] ++, good; +, average; -, inadequate.
[b] ++, superior level; +, normal; +-, borderline; -, inadequate; --, severely inadequate.
[c] I, well adapted; II, minor affective problems; III, serious affective problems.
[d] p, essentially phonetic problems.

Developmental Disabilities Related to Verbal System

We distinguished three groups: 1) those in which certain developments proved to be very important for the majority of these 17 subjects (these were in order: Verbal Comprehension, Narration, Syntax, Reading, Spatial Concepts, and Speech); 2) those in which progress was minimal for many, indeed most of our subjects: Vocabulary and Motor-Speech Coordination; 3) that in which there was practically no development for half of our subjects (and, as a result, retardation had increased); this was the auditory-verbal perception group where only three subjects made any significant progress.

Conclusions Relative to Study of These Disabilities

The progress of the dysphasics seemed to depend less upon their individual characteristics than upon the linguistic areas considered; in fact, when a given linguistic area had developed fully in a majority of the children (e.g., linguistic comprehension, narration, syntax), we did not find any subjects in which this particular area was not developed at all. Conversely, in an area in which there was practically no progress for most of the children (e.g., auditory-verbal perception), we found very few subjects who had made any significant progress in that area.

The development of each area seemed to depend more upon its degree of functional utility and upon the relative importance that it played in linguistic interaction than, for example, upon the intensity of the exercises completed in training. Thus, linguistic comprehension was the area that progressed the most. Therefore, we found that a young child's comprehension could be affected as a result of situational context. With the expansion and especially the improvement of social relations, this intuitive comprehension quickly proves to be restrictive. The restricted indices, then, necessarily diminish with the appearance of socially based word concepts; in fact, the phonetic quality of speech in our retested dysphasics remained defective, but it was intelligible enough for a third person to understand their language. The slow development of motor-speech coordination and of auditory-verbal perception seems to confirm this hypothesis; all of our dysphasics acquired a level of at least 4 or 5 years in these two areas, which was sufficient for rather broad linguistic exchange.

The deficits in the tests of Narration, Auditory-Verbal Perception, and Speech retained their diagnostic significance even for the trained dysphasics in that not one of them performed well on these tests, whereas in other areas (Spatial Concepts, Vocabulary, Linguistic Comprehension), certain previously established inadequacies were completely overcome.

Role of Training

Can training in itself be a determinant factor for the development of the linguistic system as a whole? It proved difficult to determine the *specific* role of training; in order to do so, it would have been necessary to have two nearly equivalent groups, one treated, the other not treated, and in each group we would have had to have subjects of about the same age, the same intellectual potential, and equal motivation, and to have a comparable number of training sessions, etc.

For each child we correlated the number of training sessions provided with the developmental level established during the retests in the various areas. The general conclusions are the following:

1. Only those children receiving many sessions of training showed important changes in development and these developmental changes appeared in almost every area tested.
2. The children receiving moderate, little, or no subsequent training made little progress and developed only in three to five of the nine areas observed.
3. It was in the development of the following four areas that training seemed to play a clear role for most of the subjects (70%): Vocabulary, Motor-Speech Coordination, Auditory-Verbal Perception, and Spelling.

It should be emphasized, however, that one-third of the children hardly progressed at all in Motor-Speech Coordination, Vocabulary, and Auditory-Verbal Perception, despite intense training. On the other hand, a marked improvement in the spelling of some of the children who had little or no training was noted. We shall try to further analyze this apparent discrepancy in relation to those factors other than training.
4. For four other areas (Syntax, Reading, Spatial Concepts, Speech), training did not seem to be an important factor unless the treatment had been particularly intensive.
5. And finally, for two areas (Comprehension and Narration), development seemed to be affected independent of training: almost all of the children—whether they had considerable, little, or no follow-up therapy—progressed significantly in these areas when we considered their initial deficit.

These last three conclusions indicated, then, that training was only one factor among many which determined the development of our dysphasics in certain aspects of verbal activity.

Thus, some of the children who had received little treatment progressed in almost all of the considered areas due, in part, to extra-training conditions.

Let us begin by analyzing those conditions which seem to us to have played an important role:

1. Verbal Behavior—among the four children who developed the most, three were verbally restrained.

2. Specific impairment of the linguistic system—when the semantic aspect was clearly defective, development had a tendency to be less favorable than when the dysphasic had a predominantly articulatory basis.

3. The language level of the dysphasic rather than his verbal potential at the beginning of training. In fact, the actual developments proved to be generally proportional to the original level of the child in the different areas; practically speaking, we observed no marked or spectacular development. Many of the changes which indicated significant progress remained in fact very inferior to the normal child and several changes suggesting minimal progress were obtained by children who originally had had only relatively minor problems. This finding demonstrates once again that our entire group of subjects retained after-effects characteristic of dysphasia. Consideration of verbal potential is important because several children showed relatively favorable development (intellectual level, training, affectivity, verbal behavior, age, etc.) but progressed only in those areas where all of the children had also developed. On the other hand, certain children presented less favorable prognoses but nevertheless developed; these subjects presented no serious dysphasia. Verbal potential is also important because the majority of the children showed results comparable to their test performance; the same test activities always proved difficult (e.g., auditory-verbal perception) or easy (e.g., comprehension).

INTELLECTUAL DEVELOPMENT

In this area two essential questions were asked: 1) Would the *overall mental efficiency* as originally tested be modified after training? 2) Would the *characteristics of the psychological profiles* of these children remain the same or would they be modified, and, if modified, could we reasonably discriminate between the effects of training and those of other factors?

Overall Mental Efficiency

To resolve the first question, our subjects were grouped into five classes according to their overall mental level established at the first test, and at the retest; because we wanted to use a level indicator which had few pejorative implications as far as the specific problems of language were concerned, we excluded the "Intellectual Verbal Quotient" of the Wechsler Intelligence Scale for Children, yet we retained the Total Intellectual Quotient of this test (= Verbal+Performance), deciding that it would be misleading to completely exclude from our evaluation the indicators of intelligence utilizing language, even when language was disturbed. This choice was equalized by including the results of a nonverbal test in our assessment (Raven's Progressive Matrices, 38 or 47 according to age) and a test indicating the state of the spontaneous intellectual development for each age level (Rey's Test, unpublished).

The following evaluations on the 17 subjects retested were obtained:

	Superior mental level	Normal mental level	Borderline mental level	Deficient mental level	Very deficient mental level
Test I	3	6	6	2	0
Test II	3	7	5	0	2

Thus, we can see that there was relatively little movement from one mental level to another.

In considering the development of each of these 17 children, we found that for eight of them (about half) the evaluation of the mental level was the same at the initial test as at the retest. But we must point out that it was the superior, normal, or "borderline" levels that did not change, never the deficient levels.

For the nine subjects whose mental level varied between the first test and the retest, it is necessary to point out that: 1) these variations most often affected the "borderline" and "inferior" levels; 2) these variations indicated improvement for four of the subjects and regression for five of them; and 3) the variations were particularly pronounced and significant for four cases, two of these indicating improvement and two, regression. It may be interesting to note that these four cases had been classified as both verbally restrained and rather unstable personalities with three of them showing unique histories (two hospitalizations, one situation involving twins).

Without being able to establish a clear relation between mental level and effected progress in language training, we can say that with one exception the 10 subjects who showed the most progress during training were all considered at the retest to have a normal or superior mental level, even though two of them were considered "borderline" and "deficient" on the first test. Since two low-level children were very young (5:5 and 6:9 years) as well as very infantile and unstable at the time of the first test, training may have coincided with a period of extensive personality organization that allowed the rather remarkable development of their potential intellectual efficiency.

Characteristics of Psychological Profile

First, on the retest we found the same dichotomy between different subtests of the WISC that had been established during the first examination; more specifically, our subjects continued to perform within the norm on "Comprehension" and "Similarity" items, whereas they were clearly inadequate in "Information," "Vocabulary," and "Arithmetic." The degree of variation between the first and second testings of the verbal WISC was minimal, with a slight tendency toward improvement rather than regression.

It would seem then that we were beginning to determine one of the essential characteristics of the psychological structure of dysphasics. The study of our subjects' linguistic system showed that, in spite of important modifications due, in part at least, to training, their linguistic systems remained rigid and unchanged. We observed the same persistence in the particular *form* in which language was used in given intellectual situations. We recall here the hypothesis that we formulated in our first study on these subjects concerning the bipolar distribution of their performance on verbal WISC:

> In the tests of comprehension, or in those implying a deduction of relations (e.g., similarity), the formal linguistic structure was not of prime importance—function words could be omitted and to some degree word order could be ignored. The child could easily grasp the key elements of the message, and because of this the message was easily retained and used, even by subjects of very limited linguistic competencies. On the other hand, in the second group of tests the perfor-

mance implied a search for and a definition of exact words and an understanding dependent upon the syntax of the message, which in turn was not separable from the semantic content of the message.

If we found the characterized deficits on this type of subtest to persist after these children had been trained in language, it would be necessary to deduce that training had had hardly any influence at all on the form of organizing intellectual activity per se, at least when this activity took place on a linguistic level. In other words, whatever the general mental efficiency of these children, and although very often language as a means of communication had been reinstated during training, it seemed clear that attention to the relative importance of the different elements of a verbal message remained inadequate for these subjects as soon as the message was extremely rich in information. The activity of coding and decoding retained a certain "haziness" which distorted the focus of identity-contrast and "banalized" the meaning of the message. This difficulty resulted in a kind of inefficiency in evaluating and in categorizing the elements of the verbal message in both speaking and listening. Therefore, one might well expect—and it was clearly established by the arithmetic subtest—a decrease in the number of possibilities of putting things in relation to one another, particularly on a verbal basis.

What does the study of reasoning using the methods of Inhelder and Piaget (1958) contribute to this crucial problem? Can we hope to establish with test-retest comparison that standardized mental testing is as useful as testing the processes of reasoning to provide a *prognosis of intellectual development*?

Let us first examine the difference between test and retest at the level of what is called mental operativity. It must be remembered that our comparison related to 11 of our 17 subjects, since certain subjects were not examined with the Inhelder and Piaget (1958) tests at the time of the first test.

Seven subjects out of 11 (around 65%) varied hardly at all between test and retest; three of them retained normal, even superior signs of reasoning, whereas the remaining four demonstrated the same difficulties at the retest that they had on the first test. In fact, five of these seven children persistently presented a general mental efficiency that was similar to their operative reasoning. The remaining two cases, which manifested marked inadequacies in their reasoning processes, continued to develop a general intellectual adaptation which was nearly normal. We expected a marked decrease in their mental efficiency and a stabilization at a level of operative deficiency.

Four subjects out of 11 showed important changes in their reasoning abilities between the test and the retest. Three subjects indicated notable regression except in the operative abilities considered normal at the first test. Since two of these children fell on the lower border of the norm on the first test, the prognosis for development towards an operative disability seemed certain for them. The third subject became psychotically disorganized between the first test and the retest due to hospitalization; as a result, the prognosis of intellectual development was more difficult to establish but still guarded considering the young age of the subject and the insignificant gains made in training.

However, one child progressed rapidly in an extremely positive way with the development of mobile operative processes (between 6:9 and 7:8 years), just at the beginning of logical concrete operations. For this child, who had a very sensitive and disturbed personality, it seemed that training in the intellectual processes was a good investment. It is interesting to note that, of all of the training formats, this format was the least systematic and the most psychotherapeutic in character, since the child never allowed the completion of a continuous and organized activity.

The establishment of a *prognosis for intellectual development* of our dysphasic subjects posed considerable problems. However, for several of them, at least, the observational data available allowed us, we thought, to make a prognosis with some certainty. In this evaluation we took into account factors other than the results from the psychological and operative tests: namely, the age of the subject, certain factors of personal history such as hospitalization or educational deficiencies, the development during language training, and finally, the organization of the personality. These elements were evaluated differently in each case.

Two groups could be distinguished among our 17 subjects: 1) a group in which the prognosis was relatively easy to establish; and 2) a group in which the prognosis was extremely difficult.

Besides, we think that because of the age attained by the majority of our subjects at the time of the retest (i.e., between 7:2 and 12:9 years) it had to be possible to distinguish in most cases a prognosis relating to the development of the *operative processes* as such, and a prognosis relating to the *efficient utilization* of these processes, notably translated in academic performance.

However—and we had already raised this problem at the time of our first study—it did not seem possible to us, given our older subjects, to eliminate the effects of inadequate academic training (owing to dysphasia) on the difficulties that they might have encountered during the transition to formal operations. We will return to this point later. Let us now see how our subjects were distributed:

Relatively Easy Prognosis to Establish from Point of View of Intellectual Development Ten subjects out of 17 presented reasonably clear characteristics of development: two subjects for whom we made an equally favorable prognosis as regards the development of the operative processes and the possibilities of efficient use of those processes; two subjects for whom we predicted with reasonable certainty that they would not succeed in developing formal or abstract logical processes; and finally, six subjects whom we classified as having relatively accentuated operative disabilities.

Prognosis of Intellectual Development Posing Difficult Problems For three subjects the heterogeneity of their performance—some performances being clearly superior—paired with the unstable structure of their personalities and disturbed personal histories did not allow us to predict the degree to which their intellectual processes could be used. If a deficit existed, it would have been more on the level of mental efficiency than that of potentiality, but such a distinction turned out to be artificial given the interaction of factors typical of human development. Moreover, these subjects greatly progressed during training. This indicated that they simultaneously developed language as a means of communication and improved the instrumental aspect of their language. The prognosis, although difficult to establish, seemed to be rather favorable.

One subject for whom psychological results were excellent at both the test and the retest progressed very little while in language training. Since this child had not yet attained the age of formal operations, certain hypotheses were posed: whether the progress in language would appear abruptly and develop rapidly at an unspecified time, or whether—and this was more plausible—the linguistic deficiencies would subsist until the period of formal thought, at which point the form and degree of efficiency in logical operations could be ascertained.

On the first test two subjects showed extreme deficits in the verbal sphere and deficits similar to the categorical dysfunctions described by Gelb (1937) and Goldstein (1948). However, these two children performed very well on the psychological examinations; their performance was at the level of concrete operations. One of these two cases (age 12:9 years) showed completely normal results at the retest except for real difficulties at the level of formal logical reasoning. These difficulties were demonstrated on both the standardized tests and those of Piaget. This did not indicate, however, that certain compensations would not permit this subject later access to formal operations. Yet, we were able to hypothesize that, since the language deficiency was largely retained and since heterogeneous intellectual performance dominated just at the moment when the integration of language into the mental processes was necessary for the appearance of formal operations, the subject would present an eccentric intellectual organization at best. The problem of knowing at what point logical operations would become part of this organization—an organization in which language had little direct role—remained open (see clinical observation number 8).

One subject posed an interesting problem. In fact, she was a little girl who progressed the best of our entire population and for whom mental efficiency and socio-affective adaptation were excellent. Yet, she reached only a mediocre level on the tests of operativity. We therefore only noted the excellent use that she made of her adaptive potential, still not being in a position to predict to what point this potential would develop. Nevertheless, we questioned whether or not this potential, fully utilized, would be sufficient for this subject to reach the stage of formal operations, since at 7:3 years she already presented some inadequacies in the concrete operative processes.

ACADEMIC DEVELOPMENT

After 4 years of observation, we completed our investigation concerning the academic progress of our subjects.

Table 2 contains the information that we obtained. In this table the children are classified according to their birthdates, and we have considered their academic development, characterized by the types of program (regular or specialized) that they completed and by whether or not they were delayed in those programs relative to their age group.

The five children born in 1955 still attended regular school; three of them are in a grade corresponding to their age, and the other two are delayed by 1 year each. Placement in a special class was considered for one of these subjects because he had made no academic progress and was developing psychotic symptoms. Of the 12 subjects born between 1950 and 1954, only two remained in regular school and they showed a delay of 1 year each.

Table 2. Scholastic development

Observation No.		Year of birth	Scholastic channel	Scholastic delay	Severity of problem[a]	Intensity of training[b]	Present affective status	Present overall intellectual level
4	♂	1955	Normal	0	2 p	++	II	+
1	♀	1955	Normal	0	3 p	++	I	+
5	♀	1955	Normal	0	1 p	(+)	I	+
2	♀	1955	Normal	1	1 p	++	I	++
15	♂	1955	Normal	1	2	(+)	III	±
10	♂	1954	Adapted	2	3	+	I	++
6	♂	1954	Normal	1	2	(+)	II	+
9	♀	1954	Special	2	3	++	II	±
7	♂	1953	Adapted	1	2	(+)	III	++
3	♂	1953	Adapted	2	3	++	III	+
12	♀	1953	Special	more than 3	3	(+)	III	±
16	♀	1953	Special	3	3	+	III	−
13	♀	1952	Special	3	2	0	II	−
17	♀	1952	Special	3	3	0	II	−
14	♂	1952	Normal	1	2	(+)	II	+
11	♂	1950	Adapted	3	3	++	II	±
8	♂	1950	Adapted	3	3	(+)	I	+

[a] 1, average; 2, important; 3, very important; p, essentially phonetic problems.
[b] ++, intense training; +, average training; (+), weak training; 0, no training.

We foresaw that these two subjects would laboriously pursue a primary school program in regular classes but would not be able to acquire a secondary education.

The other 10 cases were enrolled in special classes; their academic delay increased in significance as the children advanced in age. The prognosis for academic development was, therefore, most unfavorable, even for those subjects whose intellectual level stayed within the norms.

In conclusion, our study showed that academic stagnation did not depend entirely on factors of intellect, affectivity, or intensity of linguistic deficit; in our opinion, it was the result of the interaction of these different elements.

SOCIO-AFFECTIVE DEVELOPMENT

Social and affective development is an important element in evaluating long-term prognosis including entry into society as well as in determining immediate form of therapy.

We were concerned with the following questions:

1. Would only those children with serious handicaps regress or would they stabilize within the three categories outlined earlier?
2. Would the children with nearly normal personalities benefit most from language training?
3. Would we be able to determine their behavior based on their psycho-affective structure (in fact, two different kinds of behavior were empirically determined during training—the first was more pedagogical, while the second was more psychotherapeutic—each independent of the personalities of the therapists)?

For each of our subjects we reevaluated socio-affective development on the basis of a new clinical examination of each child and information from parents, teachers, and therapists. Out of 17 subjects, six belonged to the first group; seven subjects with very unstable affective structures were assigned to the intermediate group, and, finally, four of our retested subjects with seriously disturbed personalities made up the third group.

According to the criteria used to establish the three groups, 15 of the 17 reexamined subjects did not have a significantly modified affective structure. However, we were able to verify small changes, both negative and positive, within each of the three groups.

On the 17 subjects retested, we obtained the following evaluations:

	Group I	Group II	Group III
Test I	6	7	4
Test II	5	7	5

We can see, then, that there was little movement from one group to another.

One child in group I was examined at a point in his development (4:3 years) in which his instability and symbiotic behavior largely derived from his language deficiency although symbiotic tendencies were also noted in his mother and younger brother. On reexamination he demonstrated preneurotic behavior and was placed in group II.

Another child that we had placed in the intermediate group had clearly regressed toward psychotic behavior. In fact, this child, whose personality was characterized by disequilibrium and free-floating anxiety, became disorganized; this disorganization was partially related to his past experience and in part to his chaotic living conditions. In the child's home we observed the final collapse of an already crumbling family structure.

The six children assigned to group I at the first evaluation—the "well-adapted" group—were placed among the 10 subjects who had made good progress in verbal communication. Two children in each of the other two groups had also developed favorably despite their disturbed affective structures. The following conclusions were drawn from the group as a whole:

Eight children developed favorably through a reorganization of their personalities; for some of them this was done through better control of their obsessive tendencies, whereas, for others, improvement resulted from better integration of their fantasy lives, allowing them to relate better and even to create an identity which had been absent before. Language seemed to provide a perspective separate from their fantasy world and thereby gave them a better understanding of the real world.

Six children hardly modified their affective structures at all. The effective organization of three children clearly deteriorated.

It is interesting to note that seven of the 17 children experienced changes in family structure; the families of two of our subjects underwent restructuralization and the other five experienced family dissociation. With one exception, these changes did not have any significant effects on the psycho-linguistic development of our subjects.

Five children in group I received only standard training. We observed a discrepancy between the linguistic affective development in one child and included psychotherapy for both the mother and the child.

This discrepancy was also observed in three of the four disturbed children and their training included a good deal of psychotherapy.

To sum up, remembering that all of our subjects remained dysphasic: 1) they progressed in communication, whether or not they benefited from training; 2) no single factor accounted for their progress in language; 3) the following factors, in order of importance, determined the amount of progress in language: a) intellectual level and age at the onset of training; b) intensity of training and the subject's potential for socio-affective development; and c) the subject's posture toward language as a means of communication; 4) the degree of initial linguistic deficiency, then, at least if the problem was not essentially phonetic, was not an important determinant in the development for all of these children; 5) auditory-verbal perception deficiencies remained almost unchanged.

The linguistic behavior of our subjects remained essentially unchanged with a tendency toward leveling. The verbally restrained subjects, who represented children with the best affective development, acquired the most language and an improved verbal fluidity.

In these children we sometimes noticed the use of enriched language as a formal construction without significant communicative value; it was as though their language had lost that spontaneity which allowed the inclusion of the most subtle affective aspects.

In other children of the same group, this kind of language— poorly constructed and consequently unstable (susceptible at times to suffering a true "dislocation")—was capable of disorganizing thought.

However, the appearance of inhibition in the verbally unrestrained subjects, who for the most part had been placed at the other end of the affective distribution, coincided with progress in the opposite direction; they began to use a less nebulous language, and therefore communicated better. When they removed from their language excessive "noise," they were better able to control this reduced linguistic structure, a structure which was more manageable and allowed their separation from an isomorphic signifier-signified system. As a result, their symbolic references became more socialized, and, consequently, instruments for designating thought.

For most of our subjects *the affective structure* remained stable. However, within this same relative stability we also witnessed a tendency toward leveling in the extreme groups.

A certain number of the well adapted children presented neurotic traits consistent with previously unknown deficits and with repeated academic failures; however, for the majority of the seriously disturbed children, this condition, in whatever form it took, resulted in a decrease of their problems and consequently a better socio-affective adjustment.

The academic future of the dysphasic children seemed to us to be severely jeopardized. We witnessed an academic entrophy in the oldest members of the group. Only the youngest subjects who had early training continued to make some progress.

We feared that none of them would reach the level of the secondary school and, furthermore, that they would not be able to enter into an occupation requiring the use of complex language.

From the intellectual point of view, our two oldest subjects did not reach formal operations at the normal age (this despite good or even excellent pre-formal operativity). We expected that all our subjects would have these same problems.

DISCUSSION

It is erroneous to consider language an entity in itself. As soon as it is acquired, language takes on a social structure. It is relational and derives its form from the spoken language. The amount of information does not increase significantly with age in a given environment; however, as the child continues to develop language, he categorizes and abstracts a larger part of previously unavailable information. Aside from the quantity of current information, the school gives the child new sources of information which are both quantitative and qualitative. Both kinds of information change language structures by introducing new rules and concepts. As a result, the method of formulating language becomes less random and more general.

In human communication, we can distinguish between linguistic and para-linguistic functions that serve as a background in front of which the precise formulations that constitute dialogue unfold. In normal development, the characteristics of good communication seem to reflect a balance between the ground and the figure, the essential and the accessory being equally necessary.

If the language of the normal child develops in this way, the language of the dysphasic is formed in the frame of his personal universe; because of his deficit, the dysphasic child, even in the presence of others, is not open to verbal communication. The two codes (linguistic and para-linguistic) used in dialogue each have their own reality and interfere with each other but share a common experience in meeting external demands. Even though what one code expresses does not exactly correspond to what the other expresses, agreement is usually reached through shared reality. The dysphasic's language is unique in that it has become a constituent part of his personality. His language has meaning (though we are not saying that the language of the others has not), for he understands it without being aware of it, feels it without showing the need to internalize it. These two languages are not coherent with each other, but they do correspond in certain situations. One might say that there is an overlapping of the areas which surround each of them. If the organization of each one of these languages has its own distinct structure, then the aura is common to them and is formed from historical factors which are similar for both. Still, the dysphasic cautiously makes contact with society and maintains this contact by denying his inadequacies and by attempting a global approach which allows him to overcome some of his deficits. Subject meanings are not the same for both the dysphasic and the normal subjects. In fact, the dysphasic understands even more than our study would lead us to believe. Out of his inadequacy, he creates for himself an original totality that utilizes a personal code of reference. In a school setting, the dysphasic child can make a choice only from reference to this original totality. The immediacy of his thought does not allow him to follow the unfolding of the logic underlying verbally expressed operations. Since this internal logic of the message is not grasped, the learning of the operation is confused. It is in the gist of what is said, in the gray of what is transmitted, and in the fringes of the formulated or of the unformulated implied in communication that the dysphasic finds his mode of reference; it is in this way that, even if the dysphasic does not understand the exact form, he will nevertheless receive the message.

We must keep these characteristics in mind when we undertake training, for it is by attacking the communication strategies as well as the language deficiency that we can effect change. It is necessary to adapt our code to the code of the distinct dysphasic universe. Our formulations are not theirs. For these children it is not a question, as it is for children with a simple language delay, of slow maturation; the problem here is a specific (poor) structuralization. Therefore, training the dysphasic does not simply consist of developing an inadequate language, as is the case with pre-low-verbal children, because with the dysphasic we are dealing with a particular form of defective organization which was constructed very early.

Our study shows that dysphasics live in a linguistic frame that is peculiar to them and that, once formed, is difficult to change because of: 1) the actual organization of the dysphasic personality; 2) the difficulties in which this organization places the child in dialogue; 3) the difficulties that this linguistic posture creates in the organization of the cognitive sphere, which is certainly different from that of the normal child. With regard to this last point, the dysphasic child in fact presents some difficulties in the area of representational imagery and figurative anticipation. The lack of mobility of his thought prevents him from handling abstract concepts and from putting the appropriate distance between himself and the problem to be solved; 4) the problems of investment in a personal verbal sphere. Their form of contact is made either by retraction or by a more or less sterile activity. They would satisfy themselves with their personal code if they did not encounter the resistance of another code, notably academic requisites. It is reality which draws them out of a rather striking, self-absorbing world.

Our research in general shows that the dysphasic universe is presented as a closed form which requires treatment of the entire personality. Perhaps the method to discover is one which will tell us how to gain access to this world which has its own peculiar field of experience.

What the language clinician does in the course of training is probably over and above what he believes he is doing. In fact, if in training he considers the dysphasic as "retarded," he is making the mistake of addressing himself to a level of development rather than to a peculiar organization; if on the other hand he seeks to enter the universe of the dysphasic, he will be affecting what the child is more than what the child does. He will open unrestrained dialogue.

The ultimate goal of training is to bring these children nearer the norm in language as well as in intellectual mobility and affective exchanges. But is this possible? We believe that with the methods we employ, within certain limits, we arrive at substitutes rather than a reconstruction. In this frame we might ask if, instead of attempting an ideal that the child cannot attain, we might not better use tasks that are possible for him without binding him by normative values attached to standardized tests.

Moreover, we have seen that our subjects do not obtain a formal level of operativity described by Piaget (Inhelder and Piaget, 1958). Perhaps an effort should be made in this direction. The attempts made (see the technique in observation number 8) to overcome the difficulties that the dysphasic experiences in adopting an anticipatory attitude when presented formal problems at a hypothetico-deductive level have proven fruitless. Perhaps it would have been necessary to relate training to the construction of formal operations themselves. However, we can pose the hypothesis that, since these children failed to develop an adequate perceptual-verbal system at the end of the concrete operations period, they were forced to continue to use their already-constructed modes of handling reality.

These cognitive modes, because of their prolonged usage, developed horizontally and, as a result, prevented the integration of linguistic input. To comprehend reality by infraverbal means alone does not allow the subject to mediate and therefore to decenter.

Concerning treatment, this study poses primarily three problems: early detection, development of communication (a function of the psychological characteristics of the dysphasic), and verbal behavior.

Early Detection

Early detection seems to be imperative because: 1) the youngest children have the best prognosis; 2) when auditory-verbal perception is disturbed, it does not develop beyond a certain stage; 3) the form the deficit takes is predominantly phonetic in younger children; since syntax and semantics are only minimally structured at this level, any phonological acquisition will enhance the development of syntax and semantics. On the other hand, as in communication, phonetic problems are the most aggravating; consequently, therapeutic intervention is valued by the community and even by the child; 4) school performance is, in the majority of the cases, impeded by verbal problems if they persist when the child begins to read and spell; 5) the longer the delay in intervention, the more difficulties there are in restricting the comprehension of reality in the dysphasic child.

Development of Communication

Moreover, we have observed by comparing children who received training with those who have not that the development of verbal communication in all of our dysphasics was made in a syncretic manner. Their language developed better in utilizing context at the level of comprehension and relations, thereby allowing a better adaptation to the agreed upon code without, however, conforming to it; training had to encourage the child to structure an analysis by synthesis approach to auditory-perceptual reality. But, since we established that language developed as an isolated system, failure to modify the syncretic comprehension of reality meant working at a preverbal level. We knew that we would eventually have to confront the problem of how the child would make a rapid adaptation to the speech community and to an educational experience where the teaching would be essentially linguistic.

Verbal Behavior

Below we describe the therapeutic posture to be taken with verbally restrained and verbally unrestrained subjects. For the verbally restrained, we have seen that training proceeds in the direction of an expansion which, if begun early enough, facilitates total development. This point seems essential to us. In fact, training by its structured and systematic approach reassures these children, but it also risks being constrained and over-structured, thereby not allowing spontaneous development of an expression which might be incorrect but, nevertheless, communicative.

Thus, given the psychological organization of the verbally restrained subject, therapy will give language a significance of something to be improved, separate from the dynamic development of the personality.

The usefulness of joint psychotherapeutic intervention is still debatable even when the child is self-reflective, a point which is particularly delicate for the verbally restrained subject because of the frequent catastrophic reactions and the discouragement that he experiences when he realizes his deficit and his academic failures.

The verbally unrestrained subjects have a problem essentially of ordering; besides, the intensity of training is much less a determinant of their progress. Moreover, their unstable behavior makes a social contact difficult and the orderly activity of the clinician, who often sees no satisfactory or long-lasting results, can be thwarted by their apparent facility in verbal expression, leading the clinician to consider his contribution futile. Now, in these cases, the clinician can give the child the opportunity to express his past experiences through language. It is the meaningful presence of the clinician, serving as a point of reference during the reconstitution of experience into linguistic code, that allows the ideational and syntactic arrangement of language.

To conclude, we must take up the problem posed by the peculiar structure of the dysphasic personality. In our first study we emphasized the importance that must be given to affective factors, but we still should ask if these disorders are primary or secondary. Let us add that each subject seems to be individual, but that all of them arrived at a specific level of language usage. At what point is it that language, based on a defective auditory-perceptual problem, first takes on a noncommunicative form embedded in total development with a denial of direct and engaged discourse and later becomes an autonomous core with its own laws? We must note that for certain subjects production deficiencies apply not only to the linguistic realm but also to the realm of cognitive operations.

Can we expect something from a psychotherapeutic approach? Such an approach should give results at an early stage of development, whether the affective deficit is primary or secondary. Communicative relations in the normal child cannot be completely constructed apart from personality development, any more than language can be considered a purely instrumental function. For certain dysphasic children the psychotherapeutic approach opens general communications and for others it stimulates the need for language.

When language takes on the characteristics of a closed system, the effects of psychotherapy seem to us to be more problematic. In cases where a psychotherapeutic approach is considered, a broad-based intervention is necessary because after a certain stage the unused potential becomes rigid and loses its original flexibility. When this approach is effective, the child will need language training in order to acquire the shared code of verbal communication which has its own particular rules.

Psychotherapy must in any case be ready to stand by the family and the child when he discovers his defective state.

Dysphasia, then, is not reducible to an obstruction in the development of language, but it represents a particular form of language disorganization in development. It is necessary to attack the problems at an early stage when language is still flexible and simple, allowing it to take on social importance and to conform to the code of a well organized linguistic system.

As an example, here is one of our observations which seems to us fairly representative of the clinical setting and of the development of these dysphasic children:

Observation Number 8   Charles was brought to us at the age of 8 years, 10 months because of his inability to handle an academic program corresponding to his age.

Born in 1950, he was 4 years older than his only sibling. His father had had difficulties in elementary school similar to those of his son. French lessons had been "a real pain" for him too. His spelling remained poor and his wife edited all of his correspondence. Mr. R. served an apprenticeship as a sheet-metal worker. Not really satisfied with a position that he considered beneath his true capacities, he took a correspondence course at the age of 33 and succeeded in passing an examination for mechanics. He had a lot of trouble in memorizing his courses; in particular, he could never remember an algebraic formula. At the time of the first consultation, one of his inventions (a system of differential braking for the automobile) had just been patented by the factory where he worked. Afterwards, we learned that Mr. R. had been promoted to the higher position of technical designer. Mr. R. had always been very frank about the academic problems of his child.

Mrs. R. worked as a secretary until the birth of Charles. Afterwards, she occupied herself exclusively with the household and with the education of her children. An intelligent woman, she appeared to be very lucid and indulgent regarding Charles' academic difficulties, difficulties of such magnitude that Mrs. R. felt obliged to preside constantly over his school work and thus assumed an overprotective attitude in this area. Otherwise, the child was able to acquire good autonomy in all of his activities outside school.

Charles' sister had never presented any language problems. It was interesting to us to note that two uncles (one maternal and the other paternal) were left-handed.

The pregnancy progressed normally, with the exception of one small hemorrhage in the 2nd month of gestation. The birth was assisted by forceps because of inadequate contractions. The infant cried immediately and he weighed 7.2 pounds. His psycho-motor development was within the norms, and he was a lively baby who was curious about his environment and who early sought to communicate in an extra-verbal way. On the other hand, though Charles said his first words at around 8–9 months, he did not begin to use short sentences until the age of 4 or 5. Although during this period he strived hard to be understood, he only succeeded in expressing his needs and desires through gestures and isolated words such as *hungry, chocolate,* etc.

He never had any digestive problems nor did he have problems with sleeping. Well integrated in his family milieu, his socio-affective adaptation in the school community was initially totally satisfactory. A gay and boisterous child who liked outdoor games, he was well accepted by his peers.

Although we had no reason to suspect complacency on his parents' part regarding his "baby talk," he did make notable progress through contact with other children of his own age.

In the clinical examination we observed a child of an asthenic-athletic build. The neurological examinations revealed nothing pathological; gross motor coordination corresponded to his age, and he was right-handed.

The child seemed shy for his age; yet, we were surprised to see that, despite a marked deficiency in verbal expression, he was able to express his conflicts in subtle manner to his teachers, displaying a self-criticism rare in young children. His games, his interests, and his emotional life conformed to his age. He had a good identification with his father with whom he liked to tinker around the house.

In conclusion, at the time of the first examination, we found him to be a child who seemed to be developing in a harmonious manner with the exception of his linguistic inadequacy.

LANGUAGE EXAMINATIONS

First Examination

Language Use

Articulation   The phonemes were well articulated in isolation, but individualization and temporal segregation were defective for the retention of complex phonetic units ("presgiditateur" for "prestidigitateur").

Meaning   The vocabulary was nearly adequate but often could not be implemented at will; there were problems of recall when the context did not suggest the word. He held back his response for long periods of time in order to avoid being wrong.

The coordination of words relative to the idea to be expressed revealed a defective syntax at the level of sentences with several propositions (inversions in the word order, errors in the use of the tenses, etc.). One of the reasons for this kind of confusion was that the child expressed his thought as soon as it came to mind, without taking time to subordinate it to the verbal code; an analysis of this behavior revealed that he feared losing midway a part of the information that he wanted to transmit. Linguistic formulation was impeded at the level of the sentence by the recall problems mentioned above. He made up for this deficiency at times—in order to maintain a rapid delivery—by a slight paraphrase; furthermore, he did not lose control of this paraphrase, with the result that he frequently corrected himself and stammered. He often used a telegraphic style that enabled him to reduce the time lag between the speed of his thought which required complete sentences and the slowness of his verbal production. The key element of the message was often placed at the beginning of the sentence, even if this arrangement violated syntactic rules.

The coordination of ideas (narration) was peculiar in the sense that the child furnished only a few reference points, which were often logical, supposedly giving us an idea of the story that he wanted to narrate; it was up to the interlocutor to discover the child's precise but unstated meaning. At times the child became aware of his sequential omissions and he would then produce apparent anachronisms or disconnected discourse as corrections or additions. Just as at the syntactic level, this was another example of the child's need for immediate expression without adequate anticipation. As a result, the interlocutor arrived at an often partial, even erroneous, understanding of what the child was saying.

Language Comprehension

Vocabulary General understanding was slightly below the norm, but the deficit was more significant in the comprehension of words expressing temporal relations.

Comprehension of Verbal Units (Sentences and Narration) Here understanding was also derived from a limited number of reference points allowing holistic perception (we found here again the tendency toward a telegraphic style). This strategy was explained in part by the difficulties of perception, analysis, and retention of the whole and its composite parts. Since the child only retained certain elements—from which he attempted to form a synthesis—he was often led to a partial or even erroneous comprehension, all the more significant because the semantic value of certain syntactic forms and morphological variations escaped him.

Reading In all respects, reading reflected the development in spoken communication; reading was nearly fluent for simple texts; the child was unaware of the phonetic value of certain groups of letters and there were adjunctions, omissions, and confusions of voiced and unvoiced sounds in the reading of texts appropriate to the child's chronological age. The narration that he gave from such texts was badly structured and indicated a nonsynthetic understanding of the material which he was reading.

Spelling Successful performance on this test required a close analysis of the data and a precise understanding of the function of words; the means of substitution mentioned above and employed by this child on the level of spoken language evidently could not be utilized here, and so his performance proved to be even lower than that in reading. The problems of segregation and individualization that we have already mentioned were displayed in a more basic way (inversion of letters, lack of individualization of certain words). A study of grammatical knowledge showed that the recorded failures did not stem from an inadequate marking of concepts but from a more fundamental problem in the comprehension of grammatical categories and connected discourse (confusion between verb and adjective, for example).

Motor-Speech Coordination This was clearly deficient for his age (a little below 7 years), characterized by slowness and poor diction and intelligibility.

Auditory-Verbal Perception There were major problems both in immediate and deferred imitations of easily pronounced words; there was confusion between the nasal sounds (m-n), between the nasal sounds and their oral correspondents (un-e), and a modification of the rhythmical pattern (omission of syllables).

Second Examination

The second examination was 2 years later and included 40 sessions of training relating in particular to reading and writing. Marked progress was established on the tests of Verbal Comprehension, Narration, Syntax, and Reading: these were tests in which the content, by way of the substitutions that it allowed, facilitated the understanding and the structuring of data. The need to be explicit (in narration, for example) was more thoroughly understood, resulting in a more logical description of the facts; but the synthesis, at least in the formal area, was poor. We might compare the child's narration to a whole comprised of puzzle pieces, a whole finally forming a picture, but with the contour of each piece of the picture remaining visible. At times, the transitions between the sequences were still abrupt; they were sometimes related to difficulty in internal imagery or recall of the rest of the story, and sometimes related to the effort needed to connect one sequence to a following sequence (as with the verbal translation of ideas). From the syntactic point of view, the *sentences* were generally simple, concise, and correct. The frequent use of complex sentences seemed beyond his abilities, as indicated by simplifications made in the test of sentence repetition and in the poor performance on the test for finding syntactic errors. Inarticulate speech and stammering previously noted were no longer in evidence, but we still observed compensatory behavior: rather frequent pauses even in the middle of a sentence; relatively slow delivery; left-to-right arm movements during the production of sentences; infrequent use of pronouns so that complex sentences could be avoided and the verbal language could retain direct concrete contact with that which was designated. In *reading* there was proportionately more progress at the level of deciphering the code than at the level of understanding the content of the code (predominance of semantic difficulties).

Progress was less marked in the following tests noted in decreasing order: Vocabulary, Spatial Concepts, Speech, and Spelling. The *problems of evocation* or *recall* were still evident; there was a maximum use of his basic vocabulary. There was no clear understanding of the right and left dimensions of the body itself; the child could not easily handle two *spatial* coordinates at the same time (e.g., "lower right"). The same results were found at the *temporal* level ("before" and "after"). *Pronunciation* was correct for common words. *Spelling* showed the most residue of the former dysphasia (in view of the difficulty of making substitutions at this level in ways that were not specifically verbal); there were still some difficulties in morpheme division of words ("nais" for "n'est") and some errors of auditory-graphic correspondence ("siète" for "sieste").

There was no progress on the tests of Motor-Speech Coordination and Auditory-Verbal Perception, though these were two activities fundamental to the acquisition of language; however, a performance level of 6 years in these two areas allowed complex verbal exchange in simple situations.

In conclusion, the verbal behavior remained restrained, yet the method of explaining was much better though peculiar (e.g., descriptions made by piecing together information and by using juxtapositions that were otherwise logical).

There was more homogeneity in performance and progress in most of the areas tested; yet, the child was still dysphasic and still had spelling problems. Just as in other cases, some difficulties existed even at the level of verbal comprehension, despite an adequate intellectual level and training.

As he became less "concrete," there was a decrease in the following behaviors noted earlier: telegraphic style, the important element placed at the beginning of a sentence, self-styled disconnected discourse, "materialization" of verbal language ("much strong" for "very strong"), gestural language, and language use which could not separate itself from the concrete material that it signified; for example, "Make a sentence with milk and orangeade." Response: "You can't." The continued examination showed that the child thought that the two beverages did not go together.

The decrease of these kinds of behavior made the child's language much more socialized and comprehensible; yet, at the same time, new means of compensation appeared. Relative to the earlier ones, they indicated better self-regulation, but they nevertheless showed that the child had not overcome certain difficulties: rather long pauses (latency periods) between the verbal propositions, a somewhat slow delivery, and gestural support for the verbal production.

Semantic confusions predominated, but it is possible that to a significant degree they had been brought on in early childhood by *phonetic* problems related to afferent (difficulty of individualization, segregation and fixation of the phonemes—a difficulty that was still in evidence on the Auditory-Verbal Perception test) and efferent (problems of mobility and synchronization of movements necessary to speech) conduction. Motor-speech coordination remained poor.

PSYCHOLOGICAL EXAMINATIONS

Psychological examinations were given at ages 8:10, 10:10, and 12:9.

Behavior

Consistencies across Three Examinations   These included reserved attitude, difficulties of verbal expression, tendency to hurry over the work as soon as the tasks seemed easy to him; nevertheless, an apparent good nature.

Changes across Three Examinations   Changes included appearance beginning at the age of 10:10 of a defeatist attitude in difficult situations which led the child to cease all real effort. At 12:9 this passivity and dissatisfaction were even more marked and gave the interlocutor an impression of socio-affective infantilism contrasting with the child's favorable intellectual level.

Results

Overall Mental Level   At 8:10, all of the tests providing an index of mental level and efficiency yielded excellent results (superior quartile). The battery of tests given did not include a test requiring an explicit verbal expression from the child.

At 10:10, the mental level was within the normal range but reflected inconsistencies in performance on the various tests: Progressive Matrices 38: Centile 45; Verbal Quotient of the WISC: 97; Performance Quotient of the WISC: 102; total WISC IQ: 99.

At 12:9, the overall level remained normal; performance became more consistent, moving toward a weak average mental efficiency: Progressive Matrices 38: Centile 70; Verbal Quotient of the WISC: 85; Performance Quotient of the WISC: 98; total WISC IQ: 91.

Spatial-Temporal Organization   At 8:10, the results to Rey's Complex Figures (unpublished) were altogether normal.

At 10:10, the results to the Bender Test were inadequate (7–8-year level), and there was a complete incapacity to adapt himself in Stambak's Test of Rhythms (level lower than 5 years), a test in which the child said: "I am not able to understand how that taps."

At 12:9, the child's performance was disorganized on the Rey Complex Figure Test; in absolute value, the score was lower than it had been at 8:10. On the Bender Test, the child showed the same degree of retardation as at 10:10 (9–10-year level). There was again almost total incapacity on Stambak's Test of Rhythms (level lower than 5 years).

Memorization   At 8:10, the learning of visual material (Plateaux and the Rey Complex Figure Test) was satisfactory, whereas the memorization of auditory-verbal data (15 words, Rey) was very inadequate.

We no longer found this dichotomy in the two subsequent examinations in which the potential for learning had become disorganized even at the level of visual data. The child failed as soon as the use of symbols was required.

Coordination and Lateral Organization   The child was clearly right-handed. There were moderate movements with paratonia accompanying speech which persisted up to the age of 12:9. There was only average ability to coordinate facial movements. There were also a slight trembling and obvious difficulties in tests involving subtle eye-hand coordination. He demonstrated a general slowness, with an inability to suddenly change the rate of rhythmical movement. At 12:9, the Kwint test showed that certain movements were impossible in the right half of the face. At 10:10, left-right orientation had been learned; at 12:9, these concepts were completely disorganized.

Conclusions of Three Psychological Examinations

At 8:10 he was an intelligent child, who showed peculiar difficulties in organizing and assessing auditory-verbal data.

At 10:10 he was a child with normal intelligence who showed, aside from the language characteristics mentioned above, problems of spatial-temporal structuralization and problems at the level of forming symbols as a result of difficulties in evocation or imagery. It was noted that:

1. In every instance, the child seemed to proceed more by trial and error than by anticipatory action.
2. In general, he did not remember having completed certain tests which were taken again as a control.
3. The slightly longer questions were not understood unless the essentials could be understood in a few words.
4. The child was practically incapable of repeating verbatim even a brief order or statement; he often inverted the main elements: for example, he would say: "Seven boys have forty-two balls" for "Four boys have seventy-two balls." He could neither isolate an idea from its context nor keep in mind several ideas at the same time.
5. Reaction times to verbal tests were consistently long.
6. There were difficulties in seriation as much in rhythms as in visual tests (Borel-Maisonny signs).

At 12:9 his mental efficiency was satisfactory and even slightly above average on the tasks where there were numerous cues, primarily visual, and where these cues remained present throughout the course of operating on the task, thus allowing constant control; mental efficiency was also above average when *seriating* elements in time and space was not essential to understanding the whole and discovering the solution.

On the other hand, extreme difficulties were encountered every time the unfolding of logical reasoning involved a rigorous order of operations.

There was confusion in the ideas themselves and almost an inability to carry out subtle analysis of a whole in order to rearrange its parts, either at the level of linguistic or logical-mathematical operations.

When a test did not require a thorough analysis of the existing elements, the forming of synthetic recombinations improved.

However, it is interesting to note that at the logical-linguistic level the child understood the concept of a class as it relates to concrete nouns, but had difficulties when it was a question of actions (verbs), and was totally incapable of understanding class as it relates to qualities (adjectives).

Results on Inhelder-Piaget Tests

Behavior   At 10:6, Charles did not respond spontaneously and avoided manipulating test items although he used gestures as a substitute for his deficient language. At 12:6 years, he was even more passive and no longer responded at all; he seemed to have lost all interest in making appropriate and exact responses, and he remained impervious to all stimulation. He spoke more easily but in a disconnected way and did not attempt to make an effort in this area.

Development of Operative Reasoning   At the time of the first examination, we concluded that he had normal intelligence with superior performance on concrete tests. However, when we analyzed the form of his reasoning, we observed rigid expression and a very limited vocabulary. We also noted difficulties in the area of "symbolic representation," the specific nature of which remained to be determined.

At the time of the second examination, the age of the child (12:6) allowed systematic exploration of the formal aspects of reasoning. At this age level, reasoning must be able to rely upon specific hypotheses and conclusions must be derived from certain deductions. Following an experiment, a child usually gives proof for his particular line of reasoning. This is a sign of the degree of mobility in the thought of the subject. The essentially concrete mode of reasoning successfully used by Charles in the first examination could not be very useful to him at the level of formal operations if he had not developed these abilities in the interim. But:

1. No progress was recorded in the area of *operative explanation*. The explanation given on certain tests 2 years before was used again with no change and, more important, without any possibility of change. These interpretations were affirmative and not explanatory. We observed little potential for anticipation. There was even a regression relative to the first examination when the child gave some indication of anticipatory abilities normal for his age. The varied performance came from the fact that the child still passed certain tests when he was able to use alternate methods such as in trial and error and

successive corrections. On the other hand, whenever *planning* and *anticipation* had to be applied before the action or whenever *generalization* was necessary, Charles always started the task over without being able to use deduction and failed.

2. The discovery of mathematical and physical laws was possible only in situations which were well structured at the start and where it was simply a matter of applying reason. However, the generalization of this reasoning was not possible for Charles since he did not understand or use deduction. In this instance, we observed a reasoning process which was barely systematic and most obviously revealed in stereotyped responses.

3. Representational imagery and spatial transformations—Charles passed the tests when the anticipated movements were suggested by the examiner or when the expected transformations were part of already structured wholes with highly perceptible parts. On the other hand, he completely failed, as he had 2 years before, a test in which he had to analyze the movement of a projected shadow. Charles could not decenter himself from the real object in favor of its possible projection; he had not developed at all in this area during the previous 2 years and his thought had become rigid.

This child's condition posed a particularly interesting theoretical problem because of his excellent performance at the level of concrete operations at 10:6 and because of his total incapacity 2 years later to gain access, however slight, to formal operations or adult thinking. Could the problems which he presented with symbolic representation and anticipation—problems whose frequency we noted in our first study of the dysphasics—be reduced by a specific therapeutic procedure? If so, would we thus succeed in "raising" the operative process to the level of hypothetico-deductive reasoning?

In an attempt to specify this problem, we tried an unprecedented experiment which was carried out by a psychologist in our group, Mrs. E. Schmid. For 8 months, at the rate of one session per week, she attempted to train Charles in representational imagery and anticipatory exploration. She found the following: disconnected behavior; neither opposition nor enthusiasm; hardly ever present, no real interest in what was asked of him; briefly, a total lack of involvement. Neither his difficulties nor the errors that he made in training seemed to bother him, almost as if he recognized his mistakes all too well and understood that he could do nothing about them.

We attempted to teach the child to structure activity and in so doing strongly reinforced any signs of anticipatory behavior and showed him how to assume a healthy perspective given what he had to accomplish.

In the area of *experimental activity* (mechanical, physical, or mathematical problems presented on a concrete level) we attempted not to make him state the mathematical or physical laws, but to have him take into consideration and order all of the elements comprising a given system. The results were very unsatisfactory. When the child was able to acquire something in a clearly defined situation, he would still demonstrate an incapacity to generalize the reasoning process to plan and anticipate the solution in an analogous problem. The experimental exploration was generally done by trial and error. Charles experimented very little, and it was almost impossible to motivate him to take a more active attitude. Because of all of this, his potential to plan was very poor even when he applied the trial and error and the successive corrections methods. In a perseverative way, he almost always applied old procedures to new problems.

In the *graphic* area (imagining transformations of figures, sketching the different stages of change in a structure or of a given scene, structuring a whole from its parts, etc.) the results were similar. Imagery was not possible for Charles, regardless of the activity. When we gave him elements to be organized, we found once again the same behavior that he demonstrated in the area of experimental activity; he placed the elements one by one with neither a plan nor a design for the whole. The only transformations that he succeeded in making were topological displacements within a structured assembly.

In conclusion, this experiment was not very satisfactory from the therapeutic point of view. The anticipation and planning potential of the subject remained just as inadequate as it had been previously. We were to an extent simply confirming, first, the deterioration not only of the symbolic function but also of all anticipatory activity, and, second, Charles' inability to attain the level of formal operations or thought.

ACADEMIC DEVELOPMENT

Following the examinations that he took when he was 8:10 years old, the child changed classes during the school year. His behavior and his work were markedly better; however, his new teacher, although more tolerant than the preceding one, thought that the child should repeat third grade. It seemed to us during this same year that it was impossible to keep the child in the regular classroom. In fact, he had become conscious of his deficiencies and had become aware that, even though he was repeating the program, he was not capable of keeping up the work pattern of his classmates. He had real catastrophic reactions in situations where he had to complete a task alone in a specified period of time. Therefore, he was placed in a class with a small enrollment and individualized teaching.

Despite real progress, it proved impossible to reinstate Charles in the regular classroom. At the age of 12:6, he was 3 years behind the academic program.

AFFECTIVE DEVELOPMENT

Throughout the period of our observation (1958–1963), Charles' familial and social adaptation was satisfactory.

In frequent contacts with this child, we found a boy who was open, cheerful, and sociable, but who maintained a certain reserve. However, the child who surprised us at 8 and 9 years by an unusual maturity for his age seemed relatively infantile at 13 and 14 years. Despite a tolerant family and academic milieu, the child was distressèd each time that he became conscious of his difficulties; he reacted in an impulsive manner and we observed small pranks resulting from school situations that the child felt were inextricable. Charles was not capable of acquiring any autonomy in his work and the symbiotic relationship with his mother could not be overcome.

At 8 years of age, this child presented a striking imbalance between, on the one hand, a very extensive language deficit which affected all linguistic construction, and, on the other, an intellectual development and an affective maturity superior to his age.

Several years of academic, familial, and language training permitted him to compensate partially for his deficit. However, improvement of verbal behavior—which, we must remember, remained deficient and encumbered with numerous compensatory devices—was not accompanied by a parallel development in the intellectual and affective areas. On the contrary, we noted a progressive leveling of his whole personality.

We can hypothesize that Charles' intellectual development was dominated for a long time by processing reality through the mode of visual perception. This mode was already structured when language appeared; thus, language seems to have developed as a relatively isolated system of verbal stereotypes which were only initially coordinated with the existing psychological structures when their complexity paralleled those structures. Following this initial coordination, these stereotypes then tended to disorganize the general psychological structures by making their approach to reality rigid. Charles "spoke as he saw." He did not acquire a logical referent system allowing him to separate himself from the concrete; his strategies continued to be controlled by immediacy and impulsivity.

SUMMARY

In this report, which is an extension of an earlier study of 40 dysphasic children, we describe 17 of the original 40 children who were followed longitudinally for 2 years. We found that all of the children improved their communication skills, whether or not they benefited from language training. No single factor was responsible for this development.

The world of the dysphasic, then, seems to represent a closed system; dysphasia is not merely reducible to an obstruction in the development of the language, but rather seems to be a special kind of disorganization of language spanning its entire development.

We found that the linguistic behaviors of these children (verbally restrained or verbally unrestrained) remained essentially the same, with a tendency toward leveling in the two extreme groups. This same leveling phenomenon was found in their affective development.

The adaptive use of language for these children also assumed a special form in intellectual tasks. Certain aspects of their psychological profiles indicated to us that they would not be able to reach the level of formal operations. This general prognosis was further supported by their academic failures, which increased over the years.

Consequently, we recommend early detection and a therapeutic program which treats the entire personality of the dysphasic.

REFERENCES

de Ajuriaguerra, J., F. Guignard, A. Jaeggi, F. Kocher, M. Maquard, A. Paunier, D. Quinodoz, and E. Siotis. 1963. Organisation psychologique et troubles du développement du langage. *In* Problèmes de Psycholinguistique, pp. 109–140. Presses Universitaires de France, Paris.
Bowlby, J. 1952. Maternal Care and Mental Health. World Health Organization Monograph Series, Vol. 2. Geneva.

Gelb, A. 1937. Zur medizinischen Psychologie und philosophischen Anthropologie. Acta Psychol. 3:193.

Goldstein, K. 1948. Language Disturbances. Grune and Stratton, New York.

Inhelder, B., and J. Piaget. 1958. The Growth of Logical Thinking from Childhood to Adolescence. Basic Books, New York.

Spitz, R. 1945. Hospitalism. Psychoanalytic Study of the Child, Vol. 1. International Universities Press, New York.

Formal Operations and Language: A Comparison of Deaf and Hearing Adolescents

HANS G. FURTH and JAMES YOUNISS

It was not generally recognized until the 1920's that the assessment of intellectual potential in deaf children could best be determined by nonverbal methods (Herderschee, 1919, cited in Luchsinger and Arnold, 1965). The theory of Piaget makes a clear distinction between basic operational intelligence and the symbolic activities, including language, which support it. Deaf children present natural cases for testing the validity of this distinction and the early work of Vincent and Borelli (1951) and the research of Oléron (1957) represent the first attempts to do so. Furth and his colleagues (1966) have continued this research and the article by Furth and Youniss reprinted here raises an interesting theoretical issue which directly parallels the findings of Inhelder (1963, reprinted this volume) and de Ajuriaguerra et al. (1965, reprinted this volume) that language-deficient children with normal intellectual growth show a general representational deficit, including language, and fail to develop abstract thinking or adult thought. What is significant in the Furth and Youniss paper is that deaf populations do not show a general representational deficit in such areas as imagery but do show a specific linguistic deficit. An important theoretical question, then, is whether it is general symbolic functioning or language itself which precludes the onset of adult intelligence. Their research indicates that in purely formal tests, such as combinatorial functions, deaf subjects perform as well as

This investigation was supported in part by Grant No. 14-P-55084 from the United States Social and Rehabilitation Services and Grant No. 02026 from the United States National Institute of Child Health and Human Development.
    Originally published in the *International Journal of Psychology,* 1971, 6:49–64. Reprinted with permission from the International Union of Psychological Science.

normal adolescents, suggesting that general symbolic functions in the absence of highly developed language may be sufficient for aspects of adult thinking. However, on tasks related to symbolic logic, the deaf group's performance is inferior to that of their normal counterparts. What is striking is that deaf subjects—generally considered to be severely handicapped—do not appear to be as limited as children with general symbolic deficiencies but with normal pre-formal intelligence in developing abstract or formal thought.

—DMM

Traditionally psychologists have viewed the acquisition and eventual internalization of the natural language as the key to the emergence of intellectual operations. The critical role of the linguistic system in thinking has become axiomatic. Indeed most current theories, whether based on information processing models or social reinforcement, are incomplete without positing a linguistic system with which the user is thoroughly familiar. Our experimental findings of the past 10 years with respect to intellectual development of deaf persons (Furth, 1964, 1971) seriously call into question this traditional linguistic orientation. Many of our results have shown intellectual normality in children who could not adequately comprehend nor express the natural system of language in oral or written form. With these data in hand, it became clear that most psychological theories of thinking were inapplicable to the special case of deafness and hence lacked generality if not, in fact, an adequate basis.

In distinction from these, Piaget's theory seemed to provide a proper perspective in which to view deafness and its usual concomitant of linguistic deficiency. Piaget's position stands in clear contrast to others, especially with regard to the role attributed to language on the development of thinking. His theory can dispense with language to the extent that it or any other symbolic system is not conceived as integral to thinking structures. The conception of "thinking without language" (Furth, 1966) appears to many as a philosophical *tour de force*, and in fact Piaget's theory does imply a philosophical revolution. An appreciation of this novel insight comes from Piaget's distinction between operative and figurative aspects of thinking. Any perceptual or symbolic functioning can be viewed primarily under one or the other of these inseparable aspects, depending on one's choice and purpose. The figurative aspect focuses on the static, momentarily given "configuration" of an external event or an internal symbolic medium. The operative aspect of thinking, on the other hand, refers to the mental action or "operation" towards a given input. For instance, operative functioning assimilates a sensory cue or a symbolic medium into an adaptive response sequence or into a meaningful mental structure. Operativity and assimilation are Piaget's key terms for the essential aspect in every form of understanding, meaningful knowing and perceiving, and adaptive action. Operation and its adjective operatory are less inclusive terms than operativity and denote the developmentally later forms of operative functioning, in particular, the concrete operations of middle childhood and the formal operations of adolescence.

The present paper focuses on formal operatory thinking and represents our ongoing project to assess the functioning of deaf persons beyond the stages of concrete operations (Furth and Youniss, 1969). Concrete operations rely on perceptually present or representable situations, and can dispense with symbols altogether. In formal operatory functioning (Inhelder and Piaget, 1955), however, a symbolic medium is regularly present as the figurative aspect of that functioning. Without having to attribute to symbols a basic explanatory role, Piaget is bound to view the relation of symbolic to operative functioning as being much closer in formal than in concrete operations. Hence, the serious problem arises whether deaf adolescents are limited in formal operatory functioning even though in concrete operations they were not. We compared deaf persons to hearing language users of two types—one, a typical middle class suburban sample who employ language in academically and socially sophisticated ways and the other, a rural sample who, although thoroughly familiar with language, use it in more restricted ways. In earlier work this methodology has proved to be effective since it allows evaluation of language within its proper social context. The following pages after a short review of some prior work on concrete operations present a partial report of an investigation on thinking in deaf adolescents. Performance for three formal operatory tasks, Symbol Logic, Probability, and Combinations, is described. This is followed by a more detailed description of three typical deaf adolescents and a final theoretical section which attempts to clarify a position on language within Piaget's general development theory.

CONCRETE OPERATIONS AND DEAF CHILDREN

In line with the above rationale for studying deaf children, we designed a number of studies to measure the growth of concrete

operatory intelligence and the possible influence of linguistic deficiency. Generally we have observed that deaf perform like hearing
children during this phase of development. At times they required
additional instructions or repeated exposure to problems; essentially
they demonstrated the same growth patterns of operatory skills as
linguistically sophisticated subjects.

Two studies on visual imagery (Robertson and Youniss, 1969;
Youniss and Robertson, 1970) illustrate this point. Four tasks pat-
terened after Piaget and Inhelder (1966) were used: Horizontality of
Liquid, Shadow Projection, Visual Perspective, and Rotation of
Square. Results for hearing and deaf subjects of ages 8–9 and 11–12
are summarized in Table 1 in terms of successful anticipations of
images. The reader is referred to the two published papers for
procedural details and full results.

Table 1 illustrates the following major points. 1) Hearing and deaf
subjects at the same age levels performed alike in terms of percentages of success. 2) For both groups of subjects performance varied
systematically as a function of figurative input: those transformations
on which hearing children had difficulty were the same as those which
proved difficult for deaf subjects. 3) Deaf subjects began to achieve
operatory success, that is, they consistently subordinated figurative
variations to stable operative structures at the same age as their
hearing counterparts.

From data of this type we conclude that concrete operatory
intelligence cannot have its primary origin in a social language. Deaf
children come to apply self-consistent operations to physical objects
or events in the same way and at the same time as children immersed
in a societal language. Operativity, up to this late concrete operatory
stage, derives mainly from the child's own physical actions, and in
this respect deaf children are not deficient.

FORMAL OPERATIONS IN DEAF ADOLESCENTS

Subjects

Deaf Subjects   From a residential school 40 students were
selected. They were profoundly deaf from earliest childhood with no
other known neurological or physical disease, of at least average
measured intelligence and a chronological age of not less than 14
years. One-half of the sample consisted of students who were consid-

Table 1. Percentages of correct answers on the second presentation of four imagery problems for deaf (D) and hearing (H) children at two age levels

| | | Horizontality | | Shadow projection | |
| | | | | Vertical | Horizontal |
Subjects	N	Vert.-Horiz.	Diagonal	Vertical	Horizontal
D 8–9	16	88	61	85	67
H 8–9	16	98	55	97	66
D 11–12	16	100	86	89	78
H 11–12	16	100	85	95	85

Perspective

	135° L	90° L	45° L	0°	45° R	90° R	135° R	180° R
D 8–9	21	33	88	100	83	50	38	46
H 8–9	46	54	100	100	75	79	58	58
D 11–12	75	58	100	100	88	75	75	75
H 11–12	67	63	100	100	75	96	83	88

Rotation of square

	45°	90°	135°	180°	225°	270°	315°	360°
D 8–9	83	75	67	88	17	92	33	58
H 8–9	88	88	75	67	13	79	21	54
D 11–12	96	96	96	88	29	100	63	75
H 11–12	96	92	83	92	33	96	58	79

(N = 24 for Perspective and Rotation of square)

ered to be academically quite poor: their level of knowing language (as measured on reading tests) was below grade 3.5. The reading scores of the other half ranged from grade 4.0 to 7.2.

Can this sample of deaf adolescents, ranging in age from 14 to 20 years, be considered typical? No definite answer to this question can be given, perhaps for the one major reason that deaf people do not constitute one homogeneous group. On the other hand, all of these youngsters grew up without being able to assimilate during their early years the linguistic system of the environment. Moreover, they did not have the opportunity to acquire informally the adult deaf person's language of signs. They were exposed to formal language teaching, beginning around age five, and reached a certain level of competence which can be considered marginal for the better students and less than marginal for the other half of the sample. In sum, the better readers of the sample were better than average deaf students; but even their mastery of English language was poor compared to an ordinary hearing population. The poorer readers represented a more typical sample of deaf persons. In their case it would be unreasonable to claim even marginal linguistic competence: they knew a number of words, a small number of stock phrases, but they did not know the English language according to any reasonable criterion. Since this kind of linguistic deficiency is unknown in any other population, some examples of linguistic performance will be presented in a later section. It is understood that we are here referring not to the skill of articulated speech or lipreading but to the knowing of a language; consequently reading seems to be a fair measure of the extent to which a deaf person knows language.

Hearing Subjects   As one type of control subjects, 40 students in a rural high school were selected. They all attended 10th grade and had a chronological age around 16–17 years, corresponding to the mean age of the deaf sample. They were sampled on the basis of normal health and at least average measured intelligence. One-half was above, the other half was below average scholastic achievement. These youngsters came from homes that could be considered educationally less motivating than the typical middle class homes. The majority of fathers were engaged in semi-skilled or unskilled occupations. In addition to this rural sample another control group of 40 middle class hearing youngsters from a surburban region was used on some tasks. They were comparable in age and class placement to the rural control group.

Symbol Logic

One principal task to which the deaf and the rural hearing sample was exposed dealt with logical expressions. We devised a symbol-picture task which required practically no verbal knowledge but nevertheless provided a means through which to observe operatory functioning.

Briefly, the task made use of symbols, followed by the picture of an object and an arrow ($\rightarrow$) or a crossed arrow ($-/\rightarrow$) in between. The symbols were letters that referred to classes, e.g., H referred to the class House, T to the class Tree, B to Blue, Y to Yellow. Moreover, a bar above the alphabet symbol referred to Negation, so that $\bar{H}$ referred to a class of things other than House, and $\bar{B}$ to a color other than Blue. The classes of Things and Colors were symbolically connected by symbols for conjunction ($\cdot$) or disjunction (v). By means of the symbols the following six positive concept types were generated: H $\cdot$ B (Both House and Blue, i.e., Blue House); $\bar{H}$ $\cdot$ B (Both something not a House and Blue, e.g., Blue Tree); $\bar{H}$ $\cdot$ $\bar{B}$ (Both something not a House and not Blue, e.g., Yellow Tree). Corresponding to these three conjunctive concepts, there were three disjunctive concepts: H v B (Either a House or Blue or both, e.g., Yellow House); $\bar{H}$ v B (e.g., Yellow Tree, which satisfies $\bar{H}$); $\bar{H}$ v $\bar{B}$ (e.g., Yellow House, which satisfies $\bar{B}$). Finally, there were two negated connectives: H $\div$ B ("Not Blue-House") and H $\bar{v}$ B ("Neither House nor Blue nor Blue-House"). These eight concept types were systematically matched against four instance types that corresponded (T) or did not correspond (F) to the symbolized classes. For instance, in relation to the symbols $\bar{H}$ v B, the picture of a blue house is a FT instance, yellow house is an FF instance, a yellow tree is a TF instance and a blue tree a TT instance. With regard to the FT instance, a house is a false (F) instance of $\bar{H}$, while the blue color is a true (T) instance of B. A specific symbol pattern and an instance type were put on the blackboard; the problem consisted of making the logical judgment of correct ($\rightarrow$) or incorrect ($-/\rightarrow$) between symbol and picture. As an illustration, given the picture of a "blue house," the concept H $\cdot$ B requires $\rightarrow$, H $\cdot$ $\bar{B}$ $-/\rightarrow$, $\bar{T}$ $\cdot$ $\bar{B}$ $-/\rightarrow$, T v B $\rightarrow$, $\bar{H}$ v B $\rightarrow$, $\bar{T}$ v $\bar{B}$ $\rightarrow$ × T $\div$ B $\rightarrow$, T $\bar{v}$ B $-/\rightarrow$.

Training on this symbol-picture logic consisted of daily classroom sessions of about 35 minutes. The teacher put a problem on the blackboard that required some completion or modification. For instance, "$\bar{H}$ v B $\rightarrow$" was put on the board and students in turn were called to the board to draw a picture to the right of the arrow that would complete the symbol-picture sequence. Corrections were provided. Note that a variety of pictures could be drawn that satisfied the logical sequence, e.g., "a blue house," "a yellow tree," "a blue tree," but not "a yellow house."

In a previous study (Furth, Youniss, and Ross, 1970) we described four developmental stages in mastering this task. In stage I, children had difficulty with coordinating the negation of a symbol ($^-$) and the pictured presence or absence of a class; "$\bar{H} \rightarrow$ a tree" was hard, whereas the equivalent "H —/→ a tree" was easy, because in the difficult case a pictorial *absence* of the house went with a *correct* judgment, but in the easy case the same absence went with an *incorrect* judgment. A second stage showed mastery of this particular difficulty and an equivalent performance across the positive concept types for TT and FF instances, but difficulty with the discordant TF and FT instances. This stage was followed by stage III in which success was observed on all instances of the six positive concept types including TF and FT instances; however, the negated concepts, H · B and H v B, were poorly understood. Success on these negated concepts thus constituted stage IV and completed the developmental sequence. We found that after some training 52% of students at age 12 reached stage III but only a small fraction level IV; on the other hand, 79% of children between ages 6 and 9 did not perform beyond stage I. On the basis of these findings and supporting theoretical considerations we argued that stage III performance corresponded to the full establishment of concrete operatory mastery of classes whereas stage IV indicated formal operatory functioning.

In the present investigation we asked the question whether deaf adolescents after five weeks of training would reach level IV on our

Table 2. Number of subjects at various developmental stages on final test of symbol-picture logic

Subjects		Final stage			
		I	II	III	IV
Deaf	High achievers	3	4	5	8
	Low achievers	10	4	3	3
	Total	13	8	8	11
Hearing	High achievers	—	—	7	13
	Low achievers	3	6	3	8
	Total	3	6	10	21

Table 3. Initial stage of subjects who reached stages IV or III on final test in symbol-picture logic

	N At final test	I	II	III	IV
Deaf	10 at stage IV	2	6	1	1
	6 at stage III	3	3	—	—
Hearing	21 at stage IV	—	2	15	4
	10 at stage III	—	2	8	—

Symbol Logic task and thus give evidence of formal operations. Table 2 summarizes the results on the final logic test that had two items for each of four instance types so that there were eight problems for each of the eight concept types. On the 48 positive problems with conjunction or disjunction we used criterion scores as in Furth et al. (1970): a score of 42 or better was criterion of stage III, a score of 34 to 41 was criterion of stage II, and performance below that was referred to as stage I. In addition, for those subjects who fulfilled criterion of stage III, a score of 13 or more on the 16 items of *negated* conjunction or disjunction was considered criterion for stage IV. Table 3 summarizes the initial stage of those subjects who finally reached stages III or IV. The initial test, identical in form to the final test, was given after one week's training. Three deaf subjects from the final test were not present at the initial test.

Leaving other considerations for later, from a global viewpoint one can point to a clear overall deficit of the deaf versus the hearing sample. On the final test the number of deaf subjects reaching stage IV was significantly smaller than the number of hearing subjects, and in turn the number of deaf subjects performing at stage I was significantly larger than the number of hearing subjects. Significant differences were also found in the initial test: most hearing were at stage III and most deaf at stages II and I. This result corresponds to previous observations (Furth and Youniss, 1965; Youniss and Furth, 1967) and clarifies the relation of social-linguistic environment to performance on Symbol Logic. However, from an individual viewpoint, the data give positive evidence that three deaf adolescents whose language achievement was low (paragraph meaning score of grade 2.8 to 3.2) reached stage IV on the logic test. Two of these adolescents who performed at stage I on the initial logic test manifested after a few week's training a mature capacity to deal with formal logical structures—in striking contrast to having failed on linguistic structures after more than twelve years intensive training. Moreover, the eight deaf high achievers who reached stage IV had reading scores in the two highest cases of grades 6.5 and 7.2, respectively. Among hearing subjects at stage IV only three of the 21 students had a reading score as low as these two highest scores of deaf students. In other words, all deaf adolescents had less facility with language than any of the hearing students excepting two cases, but performed equally well on a formal logical symbol task.

Probability

To measure probability concepts we borrowed a task from our colleague Ross (1966) in which a subject was given balls of two colors which he then had to draw out of a box in series one-by-one. Starting with the given numbers of each color he had to predict which color he would pull out of the box and, while seeing the actual results, had to continue to predict and pull until the box was empty. Thus, there was the general requirement of continuously predicting the color that would most likely be drawn from the box under these conditions: odds changed with each draw and the actual results did not consistently reinforce correct predictions.

Each subject was given 15 starting situations consisting of the following initial odds: 2:2, 3:3, 4:4, once, and 2:1, 3:2, 4:2, 4:3, 5:3, and 5:4, twice. In all, a subject made 94 predictions and draws. Each time he drew out a ball, of course, the odds difference between the two colors changed; thus, over the 94 situations a subject faced varying odds. While with uneven odds the results of his draws were more frequently in accord with the rule of probability, they could in each single case turn out differently, except when there was only one color left.

The procedure can be illustrated by a starting situation of 3 green and 2 yellow balls. The subject put these 5 balls into the box; the experimenter then shook the box and the subject was told to reach in and, before drawing, to make his prediction. He should, of course, predict "green"—if he did so, a correct judgment was scored. If he in fact pulled a green ball, there would be 2 green and 2 yellow balls left in the box. Thus, his next prediction with even odds could be equally "green" or "yellow." Suppose he again pulled a green ball, there would now be 1 green and 2 yellow balls remaining. His next prediction should be "yellow"; however, suppose he pulled the green ball.

Now there would be two yellow balls remaining. Both remaining predictions then should be yellow.

It can be seen that this procedure has three specific requirements: 1) the subject must comprehend the probabilistic nature of the problem; 2) he must on the one hand keep a record of the actual draws, but on the other hand ignore results of drawing out the less likely colors; and 3) he must recalculate odds after each draw.

Table 4 presents results in terms of frequencies of pass-fail relations according to different odds for the 40 deaf, 40 rural hearing, and the 40 suburban adolescents. The top part of the table compares all situations in which odds favoring one color were >0.71 and all situations in which they were <0.67, but >0.50. To be given a pass, subjects had to make better than 80% correct predictions across all trials with similar odds; anything less was a failure. Three important results were evident. First, comparable proportions of deaf and hearing subjects passed both odds situations—18 deaf, 19 rural hearing, and 23 suburban subjects passed both kinds of odds situations. Second, for those subjects who were successful in only one of the two situations ($N = 48$) the overwhelming majority ($N = 44$) passed the situation when odds differences were large and failed when they were small. In other words, as odds differences approached 0.50, some subjects were unable to maintain a probabilistic outlook, even though they gave evidence that they had some grasp of probability in the >0.71 situations. Third, in all the subject groups high achieving subjects performed better than their low achieving counterparts.

The middle and bottom portions of the table expand these findings by showing pass-fail patterns for pairs of comparable odds situations. For instance, the pair 2:4 and 1:2 had identical odds, 0.33:0.67. In 2:4, however, there were *two* more balls of one color than the other, while in 1:2 there was only *one* more. Logically these were identical situations with regard to prediction, but they differed on the nonprobabilistic factor or absolute numbers. Generally, more suburban than rural hearing or deaf adolescents were equally successful with either situation of the pair. Further, of the 37 subjects who passed only one of these odds situations, 31 passed 2:4 but failed 1:2. Similarly, in the bottom part of Table 4, of 47 subjects who passed only one of the odds pairs, 39 passed 3:5 but failed 3:4.

In sum, about one-half of all the subjects manifested some formal comprehension of probabilistic concepts, i.e., they maintained a high level of successful prediction as odds differences continued to vary.

Table 4. Frequencies of pass-fail relations on probability as a function of odds or ball numbers for subject groups of high and low achievement

Odds		Deaf			Hearing rural			Hearing suburban		
		High	Low	Both	High	Low	Both	High	Low	Both
(0.71)	(0.67)									
+	+	10	8	18	10	9	19	16	7	23
+	−	8	10	18	6	7	13	4	9	13
−	+	0	0	0	1	2	3	0	1	1
−	−	2	2	4	3	2	5	0	3	3
(4:2)	(2:1)									
+	+	11	4	15	12	7	19	17	9	26
+	−	7	6	13	5	8	13	0	5	5
−	+	1	4	5	0	0	0	0	1	1
−	−	1	6	7	3	5	8	3	5	8
(5:3)	(4:3)									
+	+	6	9	15	8	7	15	14	6	20
+	−	7	5	12	6	5	11	3	5	8
−	+	4	2	6	1	3	4	1	5	6
−	−	3	4	7	5	5	10	2	4	6

The majority of the remaining subjects had some grasp of probability, which apparently was not on a formal level. Probability performance was contingent upon the sheer number of balls weighted in favor of one versus the other color, as is evident when one considered odds generally (>0.71 vs. <0.67) or when specific situations were analyzed (2:4 vs. 1:2 and 3:5 vs. 3:4).

It is tempting to argue that the less successful subjects not only relied on the figurative feature of numerical differences but, apparently, confounded probabilistic more and less with numerical more and less. With advanced age, however, these two factors become separated and operatory control subordinated the figurative factor. That is to say, no matter how much more numerous one color was than the other, the principle of probability was applied consistently. Importantly, according to our analyses, deaf and rural hearing adolescents reached this point in the same way at about the same time.

Combinations

Combinatorial thinking is one of the chief characteristics of the formal operatory stage. Following Piaget's example, two tasks were therefore designed to observe combinatorial behavior of our deaf adolescents in comparison with the same two hearing controls used with Probability. On the first combination task, Numbers, subjects had to lay out all possible permutations of pairs of ordered material starting with numbers 1 and 2, to which were added successively numbers 3 to 6. The second task, Colors, was presented following Numbers and required laying out all the possible permutations of triplets for unordered chips of three colors.

For Numbers, little cards with the written numbers 1 and 2 were prepared and spread out on a table. A subject was encouraged to make pairs; he was shown the pair 1-2 and asked for "another, different one." When the subject, often with the experimenter's help, had correctly made the other pairs—1-1, 2-1, 2-2—cards with the number 3 were added and he was instructed to do as before, namely, to make as many different pairs as possible. From this point on, as soon as he had made one pair, it was removed from his view. This removal was aimed at making the task depend more on operative memory and less on perceptual guessing. Subjects were encouraged to complete the task if fewer than the nine possible pairs were made; moreover, when they had finished, they were asked how many pairs they had made and required to answer from memory since the pairs were removed during the performance. Cards with the number 4 were now added; a subject had first to predict the number of possible pairs, then make permutations of pairs based on 1, 2, 3, 4 and again recall how many pairs he had actually made after indicating that he had finished. Next, cards with the number 5 were added and a subject's prediction of the number of possible pairs was noted; then he made as many pairs as he could, and, as before, each pair was noted by the experimenter and removed from the subject's view. As a final trial, the subject was handed a piece of paper and pencil and asked to write down pairs of numbers, based on the six numbers 1 to 6. Before proceeding with this request, he wrote down the number of pairs he thought he would be able to make.

This task was most instructive from the viewpoint of operative structure. With many deaf adolescents one could observe how the combinatorial structure took shape during the experiment. Since earlier trials included corrections of redundant or absent choices, a subject could proceed on the following trials with a better and more consistent strategy than before. At times he started with one strategy, only to change it midway and thereby fail to complete all permutations. Some individual examples of performance are presented in the next section.

For purposes of quantification, a subject's performance on the last trial—writing down of all permutations of pairs based on the first six numbers—was scored in terms of strategy, production, and prediction. In terms of strategy a score of 7 indicates use of the following perfect system of anchoring: 1-1, 1-2, 1-3 . . . 2-1, 2-2 . . . 5-1 . . . 5-6, 6-6; a score of 6 was given to that system when the doubletons 1-1, 2-2 . . . 6-6 were put ahead of the rest of the pairs; a score of 5 was given to forward and reverse anchoring: doubletons followed by 1-2, 1-3, 1-4, 1-5, 1-6; 2-1, 3-1 . . . 6-1; 2-3, 2-4 . . . 2-6; 3-2, 4-2 . . . ; a score of 4 consisted of a complete system of anchoring with pair reversals: 1-2, 2-1, 1-3, 3-1 . . . 2-3, 3-2, 2-4, etc.; a score of 3 was one-half of system 6: 1-2, 1-3 . . . 1-6, 2-3 . . . 2-6, 3-4 . . . , that is, no pairs were made in the reverse directions; a score of 2 included some efforts at pairing 1-2, 2-1, 2-3, 3-2, but not consistently following through as in strategy 4; finally, a score of 1 indicated a random performance.

In terms of production, a score of 4 was given for a complete writing of 36 pairs, a score of 3 for the same with four omissions or redundancies, a score of 2 for more than 18 pairs, and a score of 1 for fewer. In terms of prediction, a score of 3 indicates the correct

Table 5. Percentages of subjects obtaining different scores in terms of strategy, production, and prediction on two combinatorial tasks

	Numbers			Colors		
		Hearing			Hearing	
Score	Deaf	Rural	Suburban	Deaf[a]	Rural	Suburban
Strategy						
7	43	28	30	3	—	10
6	18	23	25	18	20	30
5	5	18	5	18	28	28
4	10	20	28	23	23	8
3	13	8	5	12	18	12
2	5	5	8	18	2	5
1	8	—	—	9	10	8
Production						
4	65	78	65	32	40	68
3	18	8	25	41	58	30
2	18	15	10	18	—	—
1	—	—	—	9	3	3
Prediction						
3	33	53	58	6	3	10
2	43	25	23	26	3	12
1	25	23	20	68	95	78

[a]$N = 34$ for the deaf subjects on this task; $N = 40$ for all other samples.

number 36, a score of 2 some other number between 30 and 40, and a score of 1 any other number.

Table 5 summarizes the data of the deaf and the two hearing samples with the following notable results. A larger percentage of hearing subjects (38% and 33%) used strategies 4 and 5 than did deaf subjects (15%); in turn, more deaf subjects used strategy 7 (43% vs. 28% and 30%). In terms of production there was no difference, whereas in prediction the hearing excelled the deaf sample (53% and 58% vs. 33% with a perfect score of 3).

Table 5 also lists the comparative results on the color chips task, consisting of three colors, white (W), red (R), and blue (B). In this task, subjects were instructed to make all possible triplets. Because it dealt with unordered material this task was considerably more difficult than Numbers, although all triplets were left in full view. A scoring system comparable to Numbers but with greater leniency was devised, so that strategy scores 7-4 indicated potentially successful systems with some overall order, even if not completed. A score of 7 was assigned for a combinatorial strategy in which subjects grouped triplets beginning with one color, e.g., WWW, WWB, WWR, WBW, WBR . . . and maintained a systematic ordering of triplets within each subgroup. A score of 6 was given to other types of subgrouping with systematic ordering. A score of 5 referred to subgroupings similar to 7 or 6 but with only partial ordering within subgroups. A score of 4 was assigned to an overall grouping that showed no ordering within subgroups. A score of 3 corresponded to an inadequate grouping. A score of 2 was given for pairing and a score of 1 for a random production of triplets (individual subjects in the next section illustrate strategy scores of 6 and 5).

A production score of 4 was given if at least 20 triplets were produced in substantially complete sequence, i.e., four or fewer triplets out of order; a score of 3 indicated the same number of triplets but with more than four triplets out of order. Scores of 2 or 1 were given to production of less than 20 triplets, 2 being a substantially complete, 1 an incomplete sequence. A prediction of 27 was rated as 3, another number between 20–30 was rated as 2, and anything else obtained a prediction score of 1. On this Color task the deaf sample was similar to the rural hearing and only the suburban hearing sample with a production score of 4 was better (68%) than the other two groups (32% and 40%).

In sum, on two combinatorial tasks linguistically deficient deaf adolescents used similar strategies, produced similar results, and predicted number of combinations like hearing adolescents. One difference was that a considerable number of hearing subjects were able to perform successfully with strategy 4 or 5 as if they were less in need than deaf adolescents of a systematic strategy in order to perform well. Other small differences were that more hearing subjects predicted the correct number of permutations on Numbers, and the suburban hearing sample produced more triplet permutations on Colors than did the deaf group. However, in general the comparability between the hearing and deaf groups was quite striking.

It should be added that deaf subjects on the initial Number task, as was pointed out, frequently started from a very low level of performance and with a few trials and corrections were observed to discover a logical system with which they were heretofore unfamiliar.

Such discovery was much less frequent with hearing samples who in any case have been exposed to much more mathematical training.

Three Individual Subjects

Subject **F.G.** was a 19-year-old male, deaf from birth with a present severe hearing loss of 95 db. in the better ear. *On Symbol Logic* he achieved stage IV success, or only one error in 64 problems. With *Numbers* he was successful in dealing with three and four numbers, but through a system of partial grouping. With four numbers he began by giving all doubletons (11, 22, etc.), then gave 12, 13, 14, 21, 31, 41 following a reversal strategy (scored 5) which many of the hearing but hardly any of the deaf subjects used successfully. This subgrouping was followed with five numbers and produced an inadequate result with many pairs missing. He was not able to predict how many pairs he would have with five or six numbers.

On the combinatorial task with three *Colors* he obtained a strategy score of 5. He began with tripletons, WWW, BBB, RRR, then switched to patterns of one of each color, WRB, RWB, BRW, BWR . . . , then doubletons, WWB, WWR, RRB . . . , finally doubletons separated by another color, WRW, WBW, RWR . . . He made 19 of the 27 possible triplets and predicted he would make 48. In sum, his performance was indicative of an attempt to be systematic but open to the influence of each preceding production; in this way he was only partially systematic within his groupings. As new combinations were made these partially determined which combinations would come next. On *Probability* he made only four errors out of 73 judgments with uneven odds. Two of these errors were due to memory and occurred with predicting the color of the last ball in the box. He was consistently correct on the critical comparisons 2:1 vs. 2:4 and 3:3 vs. 3:5.

This student who gave evidence of formal operatory thinking in Symbol Logic and Probability achieved a paragraph meaning score equivalent of grade 4.3. He was considered of average academic calibre among his fellow pupils and was enrolled in the field of woodworking. Neither he nor his teachers considered him going on to further schooling. This expectation was based on his rather low achievement in the English language. It was easy to confirm that he had failed to master English. On our own test with simple written sentences he showed minimal comprehension. For instance, to the sentence, "What part of a plant cannot be seen?" he wrote, "Grass" and to the sentence, "How does a newborn baby spend most of his time?" he wrote, "New Year's Day," or for "What causes the moon to shine?" he wrote, "Night." All of these answers seem to indicate that English was for him a paired association concoction-plant-grass, baby-time-New Year's Day, and moon-night.

This very weak grounding in English contrasts sharply with other data available on this student. For instance, we observed him playing basketball in an official game where he demonstrated excellent bodily coordination and above average teamwork. In the Symbol Logic train-ing sessions he proved to be a serious worker who paid little heed to his classmates but attended carefully to the teacher. However, he never asked questions publicly and, when corrected for mistakes, studiously reworked his lessons. Finally in terms of social background, he came from an intact family of middle income; his parents and four brothers were hearing. He entered school at CA 5 and in fourteen school years attended three different schools for the deaf. According to the WISC performance scale IQ he was in the normal range.

Subject B.M. was a male of CA 18 who according to the Stanford Achievement test was reading at grade 2.8. In *Symbol Logic* he made only eight errors out of 64 items, three of which occurred with the negated connectives—thus he achieved stage IV. With *Numbers* he was consistently systematic in producing all possible pairs in an obviously ordered plan. He could not, however, predict how many pairs he would make. On *Colors* he began with WWW and proceeded with permuta-tions containing two W's, e.g., WWR, RWW, WRW . . . then he pro-ceeded similarly with RRR and BBB. Moreover, within each color subgroup he maintained a systematic order of triplets and therefore received a strategy score of 6. He failed to produce all 27 combinations, however, and was unable to predict how many he would make. His poorest performance was on *Probability* with 19 erroneous predictions in 71 uneven odds cases. Fourteen of these errors occurred when odds were less than 0.67–0.33. He was clearly influenced by the frequency factor, making six errors in 13 attempts with odds 1:2 versus only one error in six attempts with odds 2:4.

As noted he was reading at a grade 2 level and expectedly his answers to our sentences manifested this weakness. To the *moon* question he answered with associate "Night." To the question, "How many sides does a cube have?" he answered, "Two sides" and to the question "What is the name of the month that follows Christmas?" he, as did most deaf adolescents, wrote, "December."

B.M. was deaf from birth and currently showed a db loss of 98. His middle income family is intact with one brother and two sisters one of whom is also deaf. His WISC performance IQ was 100 and his academic record for the past years showed little progress in the linguistic realm— grade equivalents for word meaning = 3.5, for word study skills = 2.7, for total language = 3.7. In mathematics, however, he was much better with computation = grade 8.6 and arithmetic concepts = grade 6.5. Socially, he is a well liked student and president of his class. His teachers call him a serious student and during the Symbol Logic sessions he was persistent and motivated. He, as opposed to F.G., attempted to speak in class even though his speech was not understandable. The school does not expect him to continue academically and his regular classes are preparing him for the printer's trade.

Subject J.M. was an 18-year-old male and is of special interest in a number of respects. He achieved only stage III in *Symbol Logic* with four errors on the negated connectives. Over all 64 test items he made just these four errors. When the training sessions began, he was in the infirmary with pneumonia and missed exactly two-thirds of the training sessions. On his own he asked the teacher and fellow students for past lessons and rapidly caught up with the class. Thus, his logic performance, while not as excellent as F.G.'s, is quite outstanding. With *Numbers* he achieved the highest possible scores for systematic planning. He correctly predicted he would make 36 combinations with six numbers and when performing consistently followed his plan. With *Colors* his performances dropped off slightly. He used systematic groupings—e.g., tripletons, doubletons, doubletons separated, etc.—but failed to complete each grouping systematically and received a strategy score of 5. On *Probability* he made but two errors in 65 situations of uneven odds. This almost perfect performance is interesting for the additional fact that 40 of his 65 predictions occurred with odds <0.67.

He is not considered academically oriented and takes his vocational course in shoe repair. He is called an "easy-going" classmate and is the heavyweight wrestler on the school team. His family background is difficult to reconstruct. He comes from an economically poor background, his father is unknown, and he has lived with various guardians. His reading grade level is 3.7, with word meaning of 2.9 and word study skills of 1.8. His responses to our sentence test were mixed. He answered the *baby* question with the word "one" and to the question *moon* with "night." He answered, "Are there more deaf people in Pennsylvania or in Philadelphia?" with "Yes." On the other hand, he answered the *plant* question correctly with "*root*" and a few other questions precisely and correctly. His other academic skills were also low; on the Stanford Achievement mathematics test he obtained computation = grade 5.9 and concepts = grade 4.3.

In summary, these three adolescent boys, profoundly deaf from birth, clearly manifest severely limited mastery of English—a school subject to which they were exposed for at least twelve years—but at the same time show better than average success on measures of formal operatory thinking. Each showed, in addition, a healthy, presently functioning, social life within the school; not knowing they were deaf, one would judge them to be typical older adolescents in appearance and demeanor. More importantly, all three demonstrated a definite capacity to learn in our training sessions with Symbol Logic. In contrast, schooling seems to have had minimal effects on their progress in the English language, either oral or written.

GENERAL DISCUSSION

The presence of concrete operations among healthy adults in all societies has never been called into question. Nor would anyone seriously assert that a deaf adult person in spite of severe linguistic deficiency would be lacking in concrete operations. The reasons for the ubiquitousness of these operations—with varying rates of emergence—are without doubt the essential communality found in the human organism with its developmental potential and in the physical and social environment. The case of formal operations, however, is different, and the question of their presence in all normal adults can be legitimately raised. On this point Piaget has made a few cautious statements in which he refers to the special interest and professional activity of an individual. He sees no contradiction in observing individuals of any age who function quite logically in the limited area of their speciality, but are quite retarded and on a very inferior level in those fields that are outside their speciality (Piaget, 1970). Thus, formal operations appear to require for their development more specialized occasions within the environment than is the case with concrete operations. This is understandable since the "objects" of formal operations are within the realm of symbolic functioning. Exposure to a logical symbolic environment is, of course, less general and more subject to individual circumstances than is exposure to the concrete physical and social world. Further, as the verbal language of society is apparently the most common and important symbol system it would not be unreasonable to assume that language is a prerequisite for formal operations and that deaf persons severely deficient in linguistic knowledge would not reach the formal operatory stage.

Before discussing the general implications of our reported findings on this question, it is imperative to establish that the procedures used actually involved formal operations. Symbol Logic and Combinations explicitly used formal operatory thinking. Thus, the difference between mastering a negated class (e.g., $\bar{H}$) and a negated logical connective (e.g., $\bar{\cdot}$) seems to be the characteristic difference between concrete and formal operations and a person who masters this distinction functions on a formal operatory level. In Probability, the evidence is not equally compelling, but the combination of memory and recalculation of odds argues strongly in favor of considering success on the task as formal operatory functioning.

Consideration must also be given to our use of training and correction on various tasks. Did our procedure merely teach adolescents a certain strategy or mode of responding? This possibility was ruled out by procedural controls. A second question arises, whether the formal operations observed at five weeks were entirely absent initially? The most convincing response to this question comes from a careful look at what happened during training: many subjects on Symbol Logic did not reach the criterion of mastery after five weeks while others did. It appears that a training procedure is at best a favorable occasion for the manifestation of an operatory mechanism. Both in Symbol Logic and in Combinations, we observed that for many subjects our investigation provided such a favorable environmental occasion. But our procedure made sure that there was no way in which a subject could mechanically learn the performance and succeed on all the changing trials. In other words, operations are not simply figurative items of information which one person transmits to another, but they are operative mechanisms of general understanding that come with gradual development in interaction with particular environmental factors.

Two general points concerning formal operatory functioning follow from our data. First, in every subject sample there were numerous cases of success on one task accompanied by failure on other formal operatory tasks. This finding suggests that for most people the stage of formal operations should not be likened to an overall, across-the-board accomplishment but rather to a potential that requires personal interest and environmental occasions. The second point is related to this phenomenon and deals with the particular effect of language. The results on the three tasks demonstrated rather large differences between subject groups on Symbol Logic, but only small differences on Probability or Combinations. Yet there were successes on Logic in the low achieving deaf group, just as there were failures on Combinations in the suburban hearing group. How could one explain the differences observed in Logic and the lack of differences on the other tasks?

It is reasonable to put more weight on Logic than on other tasks as manifesting the operatory potential of a subject for the simple reason that extended training preceded the final test. According to the suggested criterion 28% of deaf subjects showed formal operatory success compared to 53% of the rural hearing sample. From evidence not reported here, we know that the percentage from a suburban hearing sample would be considerably higher (around 75%) than for the rural sample. These observations support a view that sees in a special environment, including its verbal aspect, a powerful factor in motivating individuals toward selective formal operatory functioning without, however, making language the determining cause underlying these operations. This view stresses three points for further clarification concerning 1) a special environment as conducive to selective formal operations, 2) language as part of that environment, and 3) language as underlying the operations.

With regard to points 1 and 2, it is striking that the suburban in comparison to the rural environment did not substantially facilitate formal operatory functioning on Combinations or Probability. It is likely that the way language is used at the suburban home and at school affords more direct opportunity for developing skill in logical symbol use than in combinatorial or probabilistic thinking. However, it would be overly simplifying matters to single out language as the main difference between the two hearing samples. Of course, one can employ the word "language" in the sense of "linguistic use" and interpret verbal behavior as a reflection of more global environmental forces that include the social, vocational, and cultural aspirations and values of the environment. What we are trying to stress here is the non-trivial difference between knowing a language and using a language. Failure to observe this distinction weighs down any efforts at clarifying the role of language in behavior (Furth, 1970b). The rural sample, in contrast to the deaf sample, certainly knew language and its different language use—in contrast to the suburban sample—was due to a multitude of social factors that were reflected in, rather than being caused by, the use of language.

With regard to point 3, the evidence of the deaf sample, as documented especially in the individual examples, is compelling in that verbal language is not a prerequisite for formal operatory functioning, not even for Symbol Logic, and hence cannot be regarded as an underlying causal determinant. This statement does not deny that linguistic use can be a facilitating environmental occasion in logical symbol use. In that sense the greater accomplishment of the rural hearing over the deaf sample can be assumed to be due to the lack of symbolic use in the deaf sample. Linguistic use and particularly reading afforded training in the use of symbols for the hearing groups, the same medium in which our Symbol Logic task was expressed. In this connection the relative lack of linguistic influence on Probability and Combinations is interesting. Apart from formal training in school mathematics, the daily use of language or reading rarely focuses on these operations. It would be fully in accord with Piaget's operatory theory to assume that, in an environment that stresses these particular skills, more adolescents would be found applying formal operatory functioning to this area than was the case in our investigation. In fact, even though the two combinatorial tasks required basically the same operations, hardly one among all the 120 adolescents did anywhere near as well on Colors as on Numbers. This was a clear case of not applying an already demonstrated operation in another situation that gave less figurative support to the operative functioning.

Two final remarks are in order. Our study indicated the facilitating effect of linguistic *use* on certain formal operations that were expressed in a symbolic medium, but not on other formal operations. From experimental evidence as well as for theoretical reasons we would deny an analogous facilitating effect of linguistic use to concrete operatory functioning. Deaf youngsters in the concrete operatory period function at least as well as hearing youngsters from an educationally low-motivating environment; the occasional superiority of children from an educated environment is reasonably attributed to the greater motivation to foster general thinking rather than simply to language. Moreover—and here we turn to theoretical reasons—for the functioning of concrete operatory structures physical events, not verbal propositions, are primary objects of thinking (Furth, 1970a). Language is more closely related to formal than to concrete operations in that it provides a figurative medium for symbolic statements. Symbolic propositions are the proper object for thinking that has reached the formal operatory stage. In other words, whereas language is never a sufficient or necessary condition of operatory functioning, the evidence from our work with linguistically deficient persons indicates that it may have, at best, an indirect facilitating effect for concrete operations, but can have a direct facilitating effect on certain formal operations precisely because of the close relation between formal operations and symbolic functioning.

A final question can be asked about the many subjects in both the deaf and the hearing rural sample who did not reach a formal operatory criterion in any of the three areas investigated. Do those deaf subjects with poor linguistic skills and those hearing subjects in a rural setting who have not shown formal operatory structures ever develop them? This question obviously relates back to the generality of formal operatory functioning as discussed earlier where the emergence of formal structures was seen to be partly dependent on interest and environmental occasions. Our speculation is that they would be able to manifest formal operatory thinking once they are seriously engaged in some speciality. It seems consonant with Piaget's theory to hold that the mere absence of a conventional language or of an educationally stimulating environment is not sufficient to terminate prematurely the normal operative development that is species-specific to humans.

REFERENCES

Furth, H. G. 1964. Research with the deaf. Implications for language and cognition. Psychol. Bull. 62:145–164.

Furth, H. G. 1966. Thinking without language. Psychological implications of deafness. Free Press, New York.

Furth, H. G. 1970a. Piaget for teachers. Prentice-Hall, Englewood Cliffs, N.J.

Furth, H. G. 1970b. On language and knowing in Piaget's developmental theory. Hum. Dev. 13:241–257.

Furth, H. G. 1971. Linguistic deficiency and thinking. Research with deaf subjects 1964–1969. Psychol. Bull. 76:58–72.

Furth, H. G., and J. Youniss. 1965. The influence of language and experience on discovery and use of logical symbols. Br. J. Psychol. 56:381–390.

Furth, H. G., and J. Youniss. 1969. Thinking in deaf adolescents. Language and formal operations. J. Commun. Disord. 2:195–202.

Furth, H. G., J. Youniss, and B. M. Ross. 1970. Children's utilization of logical symbols. An interpretation of conceptual behavior based on Piagetian theory. Dev. Psychol. 3:36–57.

Inhelder, B., and J. Piaget. 1955. De la logique de l'enfant à la logique de l'adolescent. Presses Universitaires de France, Paris.

Piaget, J. 1970. Seminar notes. Catholic University, Washington, D.C., June (mimeograph).

Piaget, J., and B. Inhelder. 1966. L'image mentale chez l'enfant. Presses Universitaires de France, Paris.

Robertson, A., and J. Youniss. 1969. Anticipatory visual imagery in deaf and hearing children. Child Dev. 40:123–135.

Ross, B. M. 1966. Probability concepts in deaf and hearing children. Child Dev. 37:917–928.

Youniss, J., and H. G. Furth. 1967. The role of language and experience on the use of logical symbols. Br. J. Psychol. 58:435–443.

Youniss, J., and A. Robertson. 1970. Projective visual imagery as a function of age and deafness. Child Dev. 41:215–234.

Pragmatics and Sociolinguistics in Child Language

ELIZABETH BATES

Interest in communication as a socializing force in children's language and thought was a central concern in the early work of Piaget (1926) and Vygotsky (1934, translated 1962). For Vygotsky in particular, the mediating force between the linguistic community and language and thought was word meaning. Similarly, the recent emphasis on meaning in generative semantics has again led to the study of communication, divided in this paper between pragmatics (individual language use in social context) and sociolinguistics (language use in context by social groups). In child language research, Gruber (1967) was the first to use extensive contextual data to analyze the syntactic form of children's two-word utterances as discernible speech acts. However, it was not until Parisi and Antinucci (1970) adapted more recent work in generative semantics to child language that the focus of pragmatic analysis changed to meaning. Bates gives an extensive review of the developments leading to current research in pragmatics and locates the foundations of this area in the philosophy of meaning. She argues that contextual information is not only a source for determining semantic interpretations of an utterance but that it is also an aspect of competence that needs to be accounted for in the child's grammar. Although the study of pragmatics in children's language is a new area of research, studies on sociolinguistic aspects of child language have been going on for some time. Initially, sociolinguistic research focused on class, race, and sex differences; more recent work has studied the nature of linguistic input to the child (see Andersen, 1975, for a bibliography of these studies) and ways in which children talk to adults and to one another. Bates also introduces a number of issues on language use which are relevant to the study of language-deficient children, one of which—conversational postulates—is already being used in language training (Lee, Koenigsknecht, and Mulhern, 1975).

—DMM

> "To say something is to do something."   —J. L. Austin

No one would deny that language is acquired and used in a social context. But there is a great deal of disagreement about the relationship between language and context. For decades, British empiricists and American learning theorists claimed that language was entirely determined by the environment: the child selects speech models from the environment, imitates them, and is reinforced for those imitations that most closely approximate the model (e.g., Skinner, 1957; Mowrer, 1960). In the late 1950's and early 1960's, linguists (Chomsky, 1957) and psychologists (Lenneberg, 1967; McNeill, 1966) moved away from the empiricist approach to a nativist model of language: the child is biologically equipped with certain clues about the nature of language and sets out actively searching his speech environment for structures that correspond to those clues. In this latter model, the effect of context on language is minimal. Although a rich or impoverished environment can affect the *rate* of development, the crucial structural aspects of language are not derived from the speech input but are imposed on it.

Of course, both of these models must account for the fact that French infants end up speaking French and Chinese infants end up speaking Chinese. To that extent, at least, both empiricist and nativist models have attributed some causal role to the speech environment. Recently, however, a rather different model has been proposed for the relation between language and context. In this model, context does not just *cause* language, but is an integral part of the *structure* of language. Meanings are conveyed through a creative combination of utterances and social settings. This chapter is about the way that children master such a communicative system, learning how to do things in context through the use of words and other signals.

The terms "pragmatics" and "sociolinguistics" have both been used to describe this contextualist approach to language. "Sociolinguistics" is self-explanatory, combining sociology and language into a unified area of study. "Pragmatics" is a term taken from the American pragmatist philosopher, Charles Peirce (1932). In an analysis based on Peirce's work, Charles Morris (1946) divides the study of language into three areas: 1) *syntactics,* the relations holding among signs; 2) *semantics,* the relations between signs and their referents; and 3) *pragmatics,* the relations between signs and their human users. A brief history of recent linguistic and psycholinguistic research indicates that these three areas of language have been emphasized in precisely the above order historically. Furthermore, within child language research, the shift in emphasis from syntax, to semantics, to pragmatics has also involved some important changes in our view of the nature and source of linguistic knowledge.

BACKGROUND

First, from 1959 to the late 1960's, psycholinguistics was strongly influenced by Chomsky's theory of transformational grammar (Chomsky, 1957, 1965). From a psychological perspective, Chomsky's major contribution involved a rejection of the environmentalist approach that had characterized American verbal learning theory for decades. Chomsky had proposed that sentences are generated from abstract syntactic deep structures. These deep structures contain formal constituents, or "phrase markers," like "subject noun phrase" and "verb phrase," arranged in hierarchical relations. Through a series of operations called "transformations," deep structure phrase markers are permuted, deleted, and recombined into strings of lexical items called "surface structures." These surface structures are in turn transformed by a phonological component into strings of speech sounds. The general outlines of this system are now quite familiar—if only for historical reasons—to most students of child language. (For more details, see Brown, 1973; Slobin, 1971). The crucial point for psychologists rested in the fact that since deep structures and transformations are internal events, they can never be "observed" by a preverbal child. To explain the process by which children might derive something like a transformational grammar from their speech environment, it seemed necessary to suggest that children already know, in some sense, what they are looking for.

It is important to stress the fact that deep structures, according to Chomsky, are purely formal mathematical objects. Like the x and y variables in an algebraic formula, syntactic roles like subject and object can be manipulated and moved around by the operations of the transformational component of the grammar. And like algebraic variables, these syntactic roles are economical precisely because they are unconstrained by specific sentence meanings. Thus, a small number of rules can be used to create an infinite set of sentences. The semantic fact that subject and verb roles are often occupied by agents and actions is, according to Chomsky, merely a convenient coincidence from the point of view of syntax. Chomsky provides a separate semantic component which, through a series of lexical rules, *interprets* abstract syntactic structures into semantic notions like agent and action. But the syntactic structures themselves are primary. Subject and verb are neither isomorphic with nor derived from ideas like agent-action. In stressing this theoretical point, McNeill (1970) suggested that deep structure constituents may be "strong linguistic universals," innate concepts that are *supported by* cognitive-semantic knowledge of the world but are not derived from cognitive-semantic knowledge.

Because of the primacy of syntax in Chomskian theory and because child psychologists were using Chomsky's model to guide their research, semantics was neglected within child language research for several years. Studies focused on the emergence of syntactic constituents (e.g., subject, verb phrase) and transformations (e.g., interrogatives, negation, passives), particularly as these relations are expressed through word order (Braine, 1973; Brown, Cazden, and Bellugi, 1973; McNeill, 1966). Child research generally began around 20–24 months of age, the point at which children begin to combine two or more words systematically, within something like a syntax (Miller and Ervin-Tripp, 1973; Brown, Cazden, and Bellugi, 1973). With a few exceptions (e.g., Bever, 1970), little effort was made to relate these developments to emerging cognitive, perceptual, and social functions, probably because of the assumption within transformational theory that syntactic "competence" is unrelated to these psychological domains.

In many studies during this period, it was amply demonstrated that children learn language in creative ways, imposing strategies and hypotheses that they could not possibly have derived from passive observation and imitation of adult speech. Hence, again, researchers concluded that children must already know something about what they are looking for. It was, of course, still possible in principle that children derive their hypotheses about what to look for from their social, cognitive, and perceptual knowledge of the world, rather than from some innate language acquisition device. But the particular nature of Chomsky's syntactic theory made it very difficult to determine just what those connections between language and the rest of cognition might be.

By the late 1960's, many psychologists had become frustrated with the limitations of a purely syntactic theory. The innateness hypothesis left developmental psychologists with little else to offer. And the restricted role of semantics in Chomsky's theory offered no bridge between language development and the rest of cognitive psychology. Clearly, a linguistic theory that placed more emphasis on semantics might have provided more heuristics for research on the relationship between syntactic development and cognitive meanings. Although it was not easy to work within a linguistic paradigm without linguists, several psychologists in the late 1960's began to discuss the form that a semantically based transformational grammar might take and to suggest relationships between such a grammar and general cognitive development.

The most explicit effort in this direction came from Schlesinger (1971), who noted that early child utterances show consistent and simple semantic regularities. Schlesinger proposed a transformational grammar based on meaning, or "semantic intention markers," instead of Chomsky's syntactic phrase markers. For example, the relationship "agent-action-receiver of action" might be mapped directly into a string of lexical items, without passing through a separate syntactic level with relations like subject-verb-object. Later on in development the child would observe instances in which the mapping rules for agent-action were applied to other semantic concepts as well; from these instances, he could then infer the existence of such purely syntactic roles as subject-verb. But by that time the main outlines of a transformational grammar, with deep structure markers and transformations and surface structures, would already have been worked out on cognitive-perceptual grounds. In Schlesinger's approach there was no need to invoke an innate language acquisition device to account for early syntactic behavior. Instead, early syntactics was essentially early semantics, which, in turn, was early cognition.

Supporting evidence for a semantic approach to child language came from several other sources as well. Brown (1973) noted that the strict subject-verb order observed in very young speakers of English *could* also be explained by an (agent-vehicle)/action rule instead of a subject-verb rule. Brown (1973), Bowerman (1969), and Slobin (1970) all noted that child speech samples from diverse language communities (e.g., the Luo of Kenya, Samoan, Finnish, Hebrew) all seem to express the same limited set of meaning structures. Finally, Sinclair (1971) suggested that these kinds of simple sentence meanings are precisely the ones that would be predicted from patterns of sensorimotor intelligence in Piaget's theory of cognitive development. All of these writers retain Chomsky's idea that language involves deep structures and transformations. But they do not regard this deep structure as the esoteric creature of linguistics. Instead, they have proposed that the source of language deep structure is the logical structure of early thought. Transformations are, then, ways of ordering, lexicalizing, and expressing those thoughts.

Again, it must be stressed that these semantic-cognitive analyses of early speech were all worked out within the methods and assumptions of the linguistic paradigm. These psychologists were necessarily hampered by the lack of help from transformational grammarians in detailing how a linguistic transformation on a cognitive-semantic structure might work. One could sketch such a mapping rule at the relatively simple stage of two-word speech. But as Brown says in *A First Language* (1973), theories like Schlesinger's are too limited to describe the more complex speech of an older child. In general, psychologists in this transitional period (particularly Schlesinger, 1971; and Sinclair, 1971) suggested that early thought deep structures might later develop into the pure syntactic deep structures of Chomsky, e.g., the agent-action base for a mapping rule is replaced by subject-verb. In a sense, stage I grammar was reclaimed by cognitive psychology, but the rest of language development was left to be worked out by Chomskian linguists.

However, at the same time that psychologists began to express dissatisfaction over Chomsky's treatment of semantics, a parallel development took place within linguistics proper. Several of Chomsky's own students proposed a model of generative grammar in which the autonomous syntactic component was replaced by a set of semantic deep structures. The reasons for this shift had little to do with the psychologist's dilemma concerning language-thought relations. Instead, orthodox transformational grammar had failed to meet many of its own theoretical criteria. For example, many transformationalists had accepted Katz and Postal's (1964) proposal that transformations do not change meaning. Since the syntactic component was supposedly blind to particular kinds of semantic content, all sentences should react the same way to the same transformation. The two sentences:

(1) John kissed the girl
(2) The girl was kissed by John

mean approximately the same thing, although one is the product of an active transformation and the other is produced by a passive transformation. However, the sentence:

(3) All girls kiss some men

means something entirely different from the passivized version:

(4) Some men are kissed by all girls

Hence the passive transformation *does* change meaning for certain kinds of sentences. It does not operate "blindly" on meaning-free phrase markers. Such "exceptions" were not limited only to quantifiers like "some" and "all." Similar questions arose for pronominalization, reflexives, adverbs, and a wide set of other grammatical structures. As more and more of these problems arose, there seemed to be only two ways to account for them within the transformationalist model: 1) build the exceptions into the transformational component so that transformations create different kinds of meanings out of the same deep structure; or 2) account for the exceptions within the deep structure itself, replacing the meaning-free phrase markers with deep structures that are already semantic to begin with. In this second approach, transformations would then operate "blindly" on certain kinds of abstract semantic relations instead of syntactic phrase markers. The latter course essentially involves doing away altogether with Chomsky's pure, mathematical syntactic objects and with his separate semantic component, replacing both with a single set of abstract, logical structures containing all of the *semantic* relations holding among the lexical items in a sentence. This approach, espoused by several generative grammarians, including Fillmore (1968), Lakoff and Ross (1967), McCawley (1968), and Postal (1972), has been termed "generative semantics."

Within generative semantics, there have been several proposals regarding the nature of semantic deep structure (see Bowerman, this volume). The details of the particular models need not concern us here. What should be clear, however, is that transformational linguists had now proposed a model of generative grammar that was compatible with the efforts of psychologists like Schlesinger (1971) and Slobin (1970). Schlesinger's proposal for a system of semantic intention markers was of course far less detailed than the abstract semantic deep structures of linguists like Ross, Lakoff, etc. Nor were the generative semanticians themselves particularly concerned with the psychologists' desire to relate such deep structures to models of cognitive and perceptual functioning. But regardless of whether linguists were interested in helping psychologists, it is true that the kinds of deep structures described in these new semantic models look far more like "thought structures" than do the structures proposed by Chomsky. The various semantically based grammars have, in fact, provided psychologists with a whole new set of heuristics for exploring the relationship between language acquisition and general psychological development.

The first of the generative semantics models to be adopted by psycholinguists was Fillmore's case grammar (Fillmore, 1968), which provides a brief list of semantic "case" relations that hold between a verb and one or more noun phrases. For example, in the sentence

(5) John cut the salami with a knife

"John" takes the agentive case, "salami" takes the accusative case, and "knife" takes the instrumental case. This particular semantic model was sufficiently simple and brief to provide an excellent starting point for studies that involved writing semantic grammars for very early speech. The fact that a single noun phrase can be assigned a case interpretation meant that case grammar could also be applied to the earliest one-word utterances of small children, inferring the case relation that the child intended to express by observing the way that the utterance is used in a nonverbal or verbal context. Studies taking the case grammar approach to early semantics include Bowerman (1969), Ingram (1971), and Greenfield and Smith (1976).

In the period in which syntactics had been the focus of research, studies had generally begun with children 20–24 months of age. In semantically oriented research, studies have begun with the very first meaningful utterances of children, as early as 10–12 months of age. Also, the emphasis was no longer on the relationships among signs but on the meanings expressed by one or more lexical items and the possible relationship such meanings may have to the child's level of cognitive development. Some researchers have gone beyond Fillmore's more conservative list of case relations, using instead the detailed and complex "natural logic" analyses of generative semanticians like G. Lakoff (1970) and McCawley (1968). Antinucci and Parisi (1972; 1973) have applied a particularly detailed semantic model of their own to very early child speech. They describe utterances as brief as one word with elaborate deep structure "trees," capturing the child's intention in using the utterance, the aspects of the nonverbal context to which the child refers, the information presupposed by his utterance, and so forth. A similar approach is now being applied by Slobin and his colleagues (1975), to free speech samples from English-, Italian-, Turkish-, and Serbo-Croatian-speaking children.

At this point in recent history, the emphasis within both linguistics and psycholinguistics was on capturing in the semantic deep structure *all* of the meaning signaled in the surface form of utterances. Many linguists were confident that this could, in fact, be done. It was proposed that there may be a limited set of semantic components which can be continually recombined to yield a potentially infinite set of meanings. But as generative semanticians strove to incorporate more and more information about meaning into a formal semantic system, it became clear that more and more information was required concerning the context in which a sentence was used (e.g., R. Lakoff, 1972). The same sentence, with the same lexical items, can mean very different things depending on who uses the sentence, in what kind of social and conversational context. For example, the sentence

(6) Gee, it's cold in here

may be used as a simple declarative sentence. But in other instances it may clearly convey a request to close the window. Similarly, in the sentence

(7) The committee refused the group a permit because they are radicals

the antecedent of "they" can be either "committee" or "group" depending on what we know extralinguistically to be the politics of the two groups in question.

In the earlier stages of generative semantics, it was felt that this sort of contextual information could also be accounted for in a formal semantic model. In addition to the set of semantic components underlying lexical items like "John," "hit," and "ball," proposals were made for other kinds of semantic-pragmatic deep structures, containing information about the speaker, the listener, the information assumed to be true in a particular speech context, etc. Information about the identity of speaker and listener and the speaker's goal in using the sentence (e.g., as a command, as a question) was described in a type of formal structure called the "performative." Another set of structures called "presuppositions" were used to describe information that is not contained in the sentence itself but must be known and understood if that sentence is to make sense. A separate set of presupposition-like structures, called "conversational postulates," was suggested to describe assumptions about the nature of human conversation in general, especially as these assumptions are used to convey subtle messages to the listener. In this chapter, we examine these three kinds of pragmatic structures in more detail, with illustrations from research on the use of such structures by young children.

First, however, one further theoretical point should be made clear. As we have said, within both linguistics and psycholinguistics, the effort to formalize semantics led inevitably to an effort to formalize contextual information, or pragmatics. At first, it seemed that pragmatic information was ancillary to the rest of semantics, something that could be added on or studied separately. It is now far less clear that this is the case. *Pragmatics is perhaps best defined as rules governing the use of language in context.* As such, it does not define a separate kind of linguistic structure or "object." Rather, all of language is pragmatic to begin with. We choose our meanings to fit contexts and build our meanings onto those contexts in such a way that the two are inseparable, in the same way that "figure" is definable only in terms of "ground." According to this view, every act involved in the construction of meaning is in itself a pragmatic act. The act of reference, the selection of lexical items to stand for one or more referents, and the combination of acts of reference into the core unit of semantics, the proposition, are all contextually based uses of language.

In keeping with this approach, we discuss not three, but four kinds of pragmatic structure in this paper: performative, presuppositions, conversational postulates, and propositions. After we consider these four kinds of pragmatic structures, we then turn to some separate but related issues in sociolinguistics, as they are being investigated in child language. At the end of this exposition, it will hopefully be clear that context is an integral part of language.

As is shown, studies on the acquisition of pragmatics begin prior to speech itself, in the first year of life. These studies indicate that semantics emerges, developmentally and logically, from pragmatics, in much the same way that syntax has been shown to emerge from semantic knowledge.

PRAGMATIC STRUCTURES AND THEIR ACQUISITION

Propositions and Reference

A proposition can be defined for present purposes as a predicate-argument structure in which an attribute is predicated of one argument (e.g., "Mary is beautiful"), or a relationship is predicated between two or more arguments (e.g., "Mary hit the ball" in which "hit" is the predicate that relates "Mary" and "ball"). However, this sort of definition implies that propositions are entities, objects or things made up of smaller objects or things called predicates and arguments. In fact, this sort of an entity approach to meaning does characterize most generative semantic analyses, efforts to break sentences down into underlying components, or "atomic" predicates and arguments. There is another kind of approach to meaning in which "predication," the act of constructing a proposition, is considered an act rather than an object, a sort of mental operation that the speaker "does" rather than some possession that he "has." Although the field of language philosophy is certainly too intricate and complex to summarize with one issue, it is true that this one problem—the question of meaning as act vs. meaning as object—has been a central issue in most major theories. Since this issue has important implications for the pragmatics of child language, it may be worth our time to explore it briefly here.

At one extreme in the philosophy of meaning we find the positions of Austin (1962), Wittgenstein (1958, 1970) and Quine (1960). In *Philosophical Investigations* and *The Blue and the Brown Books,* Wittgenstein presents the concept of the language game. The meaning of the word "brick," according to this analysis, is not simply a referential correspondence between the sound "brick" and a reddish rectangular object. Rather, the meaning of the word is built up through the circumstances or "games" in which the word is used, e.g., handing certain kinds of objects back and forth while building houses, etc. Insofar as we all use the same sound in similar circumstances, there is a conventional "meaning" attached to that sequence of sounds. But the meaning is not restricted to a given "referent" or entity to which that name belongs. It consists of rules for using that name, in linguistic and nonlinguistic contexts. In *Word and Object,* Quine employs a similar analysis. He compares the network of meanings which different individuals may have for the same word to the arrangement of branches within garden hedges clipped to look like elephants. Viewed externally, they follow the same pattern. But we have no way of knowing what internal arrangement of action patterns have been joined to produce the conventional use of a word. This position on the nature of meaning essentially reduces all of semantics to rules of use so that pragmatics and semantics are indistinguishable levels of meaning.

This position was a reaction against another extreme view that meaning is an object—either an entity existing in the mind (what

Quine calls "the museum theory"), or a sound corresponding to an entity in the outside world. The view that names must correspond to something real was often quoted within ontological arguments such as St. Anselm's suggestion that the ability to think of an All-Perfect Being implies His existence. A more modern version of the meaning-as-entity theory, with completely different goals, can be found in Russell's theory of denoting (1905). In an effort to refine philosophy as a scientific tool, Russell claims that all sentences can be analyzed into minimal propositions with "atomic" predicates. An analysis is complete if the arguments, or values, in the proposition can each be tested for a corresponding referent in the real world. If there is a referent for each "name," then the proposition can be judged as true or false according to the operations of predicate calculus. If there is no referent for one of the values in the proposition, then the statement is meaningless. Since it cannot be computed, a meaningless statement is of no interest within a scientific language. The Russellian analysis has been used to criticize ontological arguments like that of St. Anselm, in which the very existence of a name is used to argue for the presence of a corresponding entity. But it is interesting that the concept of meaning-as-object is assumed in both approaches. The difference is simply that Russell limits possible object-referents to measurable or potentially observable phenomena in some "real" world of physical sensation, whatever that may be.

Within such entity theories of meaning, there are two ways of handling pragmatics. One is to construe rules-of-use as meaningless operations that need not be verified since they convey no information. For example, the operation equating "it" to "the ball" in "John hit it" adds no meaning and hence need not be verified. The other approach is to reduce rules-of-use to statements or descriptions that contain the pragmatic meanings, such as a statement describing the relationship of a pronoun to its antecedent in the situation where the pronoun is used. For example, the sentence "John hit it" would be analyzed into a set of minimal propositions, one of which is the statement "It = the ball in situation X." These pragmatic propositions must then be verified according to the same principles as other propositions.

There are several mixed proposals midway between the two extremes of referent-as-thing and referring-as-activity. Frege (1952), who had influenced Russell's earlier writings, distinguishes two types of meaning. One is "sense," the concept of meaning employed in most ordinary language. "Sense" is Frege's term for mental entities, indivisible experiences in the senses with which ordinary men grasp the meaning of words. "Reference," on the other hand, is the type of meaning of greatest interest to science, in which external, real-world entities are found to correspond to particular terms. It was the "sense" or mental aspect of meaning which Russell rejected in later work. Strawson (1950) agrees with Frege that not all meaning can be reduced to reference, and that there are mental experiences that cannot be ascribed truth values. However, Strawson's writings have a different flavor, in that he stresses the active role of speakers in the creation of meaning within different contexts, as opposed to more passive reception by sense "entities." Within the writings of Frege and Strawson, we find a concept of "referring" as an activity or use of language by speakers rather than an object or property of sentences.

The "object" approach to meaning has also characterized most research on early child speech, particularly those studies that discuss early utterances in terms of semantic features that are either present or absent for a given word (for a review of these approaches, see Clark, 1973). However, several more recent studies have taken the "meaning-as-act" approach to language acquisition, suggesting that early meanings are not static entities but based instead on actions carried out in context. Greenfield and Smith (1976), Antinucci and Parisi (1973), Ingram (1971), and others interested in the semantics of early speech have inferred the "rich" meanings underlying one-word speech by observing the context in which those words are used. Greenfield and Smith, and Parisi (1974) have explicitly discussed the contextual basis of early meaning structures as "combinatorial meanings." The child constructs his meanings on two levels. At the expressive level, he selects one aspect of the context (generally that aspect undergoing greatest change or emphasis) and encodes it explicitly into a one-word expression, e.g., "Daddy!" At a second, implicit level he constructs the rest of his meaning, those parts of the context to which the expression "Daddy" is related. The connection between the explicitly symbolized and encoded meaning and the implicit, perceptual-motor meaning is often indicated with such overt acts as pointing, orientation of the body, eye contact, etc. For example, when "Daddy!" is used within the combinatorial meaning "This is Daddy's shoe," the child will often point to the shoe or hold it up proudly for his listener to see. Where "Daddy" is used instead to mean "Daddy is coming," the child may perhaps run toward the door after hearing a car pull up outside. But regardless of whether the child explicitly indicates the contextual part of his meaning through pointing, etc., adults rarely have difficulty interpreting the richer meanings associated with one-word utterances. The question is, are these combinatorial meanings something the child *has*—a complete and articulated symbolic deep structure—or are they, at least in part, something the child *does,* in the same way that he relates toys together through his play activities or explores a new room through the actions of his hands and body? According to the "act" interpretation, at least part of the child's meaning may be sensorimotor, described "inside" the child as a set of action schemata rather than a set of deep structures in the traditional sense. Hence, most of the semantics of early child speech is in fact pragmatic; to understand it we must have knowledge of the context within which a sentence is used. Combinatorial meanings, or propositions, are not entities that the child has but performances, involving procedures for using words in contexts.

There is a further sense in which very early child speech is essentially pragmatic. In the above examples, at least part of the child's meaning—the expressed portion—can be described as a symbolic object that the child in some sense *has* as a semantic deep structure. But an examination of the first uses of reference by children leads to the conclusion that reference itself grows out of procedures for getting things done. There is a game, or activity of "referring," which emerges gradually as a distinct kind of operation among a set of pragmatic procedures for doing things to the world.

To illustrate this point, let us examine several longitudinal studies reporting the "first words" of very young children. Greenfield and Smith (1975) note that the first words used by their subjects are not truly referential in the sense of naming an object or event. Instead, they are words that are in themselves events or performances, like "hi" and "bye-bye." Piaget (1962) notes that the first word used by his daughter Jacqueline was "panama." Literally, this word means "grandfather." But as Jacqueline used it, the word was a procedure for requesting just about anything, whether grandfather was there or not. Piaget suggests that Jacqueline adopted this word to fill the request function because grandfather was "her most faithful servant," usually associated with doing things for her. Nevertheless, for Jacqueline the word does not "mean" or "stand for" grandfather. Bates, Camaioni, and Volterra (1973) report similar first words in their two subjects. Carlotta (12 months) used the sound "na-na" on all occasions in which she wanted something or someone. Marta (15 months) used the clear-cut sound "Ayi!" to accompany acts of pointing to objects or interesting events. In both cases, the word accompanies an act but does not actually represent or stand for a particular referent, any more than the act of pointing itself "represents" the thing to which it refers.

There are other examples that are even more "word-like," but are still not fully referential. Svachkin (1973) gives the example of an infant who used the word for "kitty" in a game in which she threw her kitty out of the crib, said the word, and waited for the adult to bring the kitty back. However, she did not use the word to name or ask for the kitty in any other context. Hence, the word remained embedded within the game context, as one of the routines or acts of which the game consisted. Similarly, Bates, Camaioni, and Volterra's subject Marta used the word "da" (Italian for "give") in all acts of giving and taking objects. But she never used the word to demand that an object be given to her, nor did she use it to describe an act of giving which she might have observed. Since adults regularly intone the word "da" while reaching out a hand during exchanges, it seems likely that Marta interpreted the sound as a routine that accompanies such activities. In the same study, the infant Carlotta was observed using the word "bam" as a regular part of any act of knocking down block towers or messing up arrangements of toys. In all these cases the word, while tied to the presence of particular objects or events, remained essentially an *act,* a routine or procedure, rather than a symbolic vehicle standing for or representing its referent.

Piaget (1962) gives still more complex examples of the way in which early words are embedded in action sequences. In one example, his daughter Jacqueline stood on a balcony, looking down at a dog passing underneath, and said the word for "dog." However, instead of extending the term later to other dogs or doglike creatures, she began to use the word to name anything that she saw passing below from her place on the balcony. Hence, in the game of naming, Jacqueline placed more emphasis on the context of the game rather than on the particular nature of the referents that she named.

All of these instances bring to mind Wittgenstein's concept of the language game, i.e., the meaning of a word like "brick" is not the reddish, rectangular object itself, but a set of circumstances in which the sound "brick" is used. Gradually those circumstances may be narrowed down to those in which the reddish rectangular object is physically or psychologically present. But the starting point is a context-based act rather than the object or referent itself. This process is not restricted to first words alone. Throughout our lives, vocabulary is mastered through observing the use of a given sound in a variety of circumstances. For example, in a study by Bates (1976), a 2-year-old Italian child first used quantifier terms (e.g., some, a few, many, etc.) as procedures for requesting cookies. He would shout out a long string of these quantifiers in seemingly random order, with no apparent regard for the notion of particular quantities, until a cookie was obtained at last. It seems likely that he had observed the use of quantifiers by adults in requests and exchanges of objects and had assumed that these were the defining circumstances for the use of those terms, rather than particular quantities or amounts. In the same study, Bates reports on a 5-year-old Italian boy who was asked about the meaning of formal vs. informal pronouns of address. The child replied without hesitation that "tu" (the informal pronoun) is used in the morning and "Lei" (the formal pronoun) is used in the afternoon. Obviously these circumstances must have coincidentally accompanied the distribution of the two pronouns in this child's particular social settings, so that he gradually defined the two pronouns in terms of time of day rather than social formality.

The point of these illustrations is that *all* of semantics is *essentially* pragmatic in nature. Children do not learn a set of isomorphic sign-referent relations. Rather, they learn how to do things with sounds, continually redefining the appropriate contexts for various language "games." With older child speakers, as with adult speakers, we can usually assume that we all employ more or less the same rules of use for a given lexical item. If we did not, communication simply would not take place. But as Quine (1960) says, meanings are mental acts rather than specifiable object-referents. Hence, we can never be entirely certain that we have all arrived at the same conventional, observable *use* through the same mental pathways. We only know that we manage to *do* more or less the same things with words.

Performatives

We have just proposed that, logically and ontogenetically, all of semantics and syntactics are derived ultimately from pragmatics, from "language games" that consist in the use of signals in contexts to carry out some function. Reference itself is, according to this approach, a context-based, pragmatic act of "referring." Accordingly, propositions—the "stuff" of which semantic deep structures are made—also have a pragmatic base. However, the other three formalisms introduced earlier—performatives, presuppositions, and conversational postulates—are the ones that are traditionally defined as "pragmatic structures." Hence, most research on pragmatic aspects of speech in children and adults has been organized around these three concepts.

The first major category of pragmatic structures, or rules of use, is the speaker's goal in using a proposition. This structure has been discussed as the "speech act," "performative," or "illocutionary force" associated with a sentence. It describes the speaker's intention to issue a command, ask a question, make a promise, etc.

The concept of "speech act" was first introduced into modern language philosophy by J. Austin, in his 1962 book *How to Do Things with Words*. The speech act analysis was in part a response to the "entity" approach to meaning discussed earlier, as espoused by philosophers like Russell, who claimed that all language could be analyzed into atomic propositions with corresponding truth values. Austin proposed instead that some utterances—such as "I order you ... ," "I christen you ... ," or "I now pronounce you man and wife"—are events in themselves. While one could determine whether a speech act had or had not occurred (e.g., a drunk smashing a bottle against the Queen Mary has not actually christened the Queen Mary no matter what words he uses), it would be senseless to call such a sentence true or false. In fact, not only these special sentences but all utterances can be analyzed into three kinds of speech acts: *locutions, illocutions,* and *perlocutions.*

Locutionary acts include all the acts that are required for the making of speech, e.g., constructing propositions and uttering sounds. In an example offered by Austin (1962, p. 100), a person who just witnessed a locutionary speech act might describe the act as follows:

> He said to me, "Shoot her!" meaning by "shoot" shoot and referring by "her" to her.

Essentially, locutionary acts are the procedures or acts that underlie the pragmatics of reference that we have just discussed—the use of a sound to carry out the function of referring in a given context.

An illocutionary speech act is a conventional social act, recognized as such by both speaker and hearer, that takes place when a sentence is uttered, e.g., a command is issued, a child is baptized. The same man who witnessed the above *locutionary* act, according to Austin, might describe the concomitant *illocutionary* act as follows:

> He urged (or advised, ordered, etc.) me to shoot her.

In other words, an illocution is a conventional social act such as ordering, advising, urging, baptizing, promising, etc.

Finally, a perlocutionary act creates the effects, planned or unplanned, of having used a sentence; e.g., the listener is annoyed, the married couple lives happily ever after, etc. Austin continues his example by suggesting that the same person who witnessed the above *locution* and *illocution* might describe the resulting *perlocution* as follows:

He persuaded me to shoot her.

"Persuades" differs from "ordering," "advising," etc. in that the persuasion might have been a by-product, perhaps even an unintentional by-product, of any number of locutions and illocutions. For example, the speaker might have unintentionally persuaded the listener to shoot the woman by reporting that she was about to blow up a local munitions plant.

In "What is a Speech Act?", Searle (1965) carries these distinctions even further, dividing all sentences into two parts, a speech act and a proposition. The same proposition expressed in

(5) John is leaving the room

can be carried with a variety of illocutionary forces, yielding sentences like

(8) Is John leaving the room?
(9) John, leave the room!
(10) If only John would leave the room!

and so forth. The illocutionary act is signaled by a series of elements: intonation, the mood of the verb, the presence of an explicit performative verb (e.g., "I order you . . ."), plus, of course, punctuation in written language or extralinguistic context in spoken language. Searle underlines, furthermore, that not all illocutionary acts have a propositional content and offers as examples such expressions as "Hurray!" or "Hello." While Austin had originally specified that all three aspects of a sentence—illocutionary, locutionary, perlocutionary—are speech acts, the word "speech act" has generally been reserved for the illocutionary force of an utterance. Searle's distinction between propositional content and illocutionary force contributes to this usage of the term.

Readers familiar with transformational grammar will note the strong parallels between Searle's analysis and linguistic issues pertaining to deep structure and transformations. It was perhaps inevitable that attempts would be made to incorporate the performative analysis into a generative grammar. The first such effort is Ross's "On Declarative Sentences" (1970), in which he claims that even the relatively "neutral" simple declarative sentence is dominated in deep structure by a higher sentence "I say to you . . . ," that takes as its complement the neutral proposition, e.g., Leave (John). The so-called performative analysis has been used extensively by generative semanticists since Ross's article. Evidence for the syntactic reality of a performative hypersentence has been drawn from issues like pronominalization, reflexivization, and the behavior of certain adverbials. The procedure generally involves: 1) selecting a syntactic phenomenon that occurs in subordinate clauses; 2) demonstrating that main clauses also show this behavior under certain circumstances; and 3) explaining the behavior of those main clauses as the product of the usual subordinate clause rules operating from a higher performative main clause. For example, reflexive pronouns are generally permissible only when the antecedent has previously been specified—

(11) John said that the book was for Bill and himself.
(12) *The book was for Bill and himself.

Yet the rules seem to differ for first and second person pronouns—

(13) John said that the book was for Bill and myself.
(14) The book was for Bill and myself.

These exceptions can be made to follow one general, economical rule for pronominalization if we admit the existence of a performative hypersentence ("I say to you . . .") in deep structure. If this structure is implicit in all sentences, then the speaker and listener are already specified in the dominant, performative clause. Hence no special exceptions are required to the rule for pronominalizing subordinate clauses. Fraser (1971) and others have offered extensive criticisms of the syntactic arguments for performative hypersentences. The matter is by no means settled within generative grammar. However, the performative analysis continues to be a popular solution to syntactic problems that involve information about the speaker, the listener, and the speech act itself.

There is very little research on pragmatics in child speech. But by far the greater proportion of what work there is has centered on the acquisition of performatives. In a sense, of course, much of the work carried out in the 1960's on the acquisition of transformations (e.g., interrogatives, negation) is related to the acquisition of speech acts, or at least the explicit means for carrying out speech acts. However, there is a difference between acquisition of a performative *function* and acquisition of the means for expressing that function in a particular language. For example, Bates (1976) notes that Italian infants acquire interrogatives at the one-word stage—not surprising, since the Italian language expresses questions by the use of intonation contours only, with no particular changes in word order, etc. Bellugi (1968) has shown that although English children have interrogative intonation fairly early, they master the various other aspects of the interrogative transformation—e.g., reordering sentence constituents, adding auxiliaries like "did," etc.—a little at a time. Bowerman (1969) reports that in Finnish, where interrogatives are expressed through the addition of a question particle "ko," without particular intonation, children seem to express interrogatives fairly late. The differences among English, Italian, and Finnish children suggest that the relative complexity of surface mechanisms for expressing speech acts will determine to some extent the age at which those speech acts can be performed through conventional means.

However, when early child utterances are viewed within their nonverbal contexts, it becomes clear that at least a few performative *functions* are established at the very beginning of speech, although the child may adopt idiosyncratic means for expressing those functions. Halliday (1973) classifies a series of social functions of speech that emerge in the first 2 years of life. Ingram (1971) analyzed the one-word stage in the speech records of Leopold's subject Hildegard, from the point of view of a case grammar, describing semantic case notions like "agent" as well as pragmatic "modalities" like interrogative, emphasis, etc. Ingram reports that separate imperative, interrogative, and declarative functions are already expressed through gesture, tone of voice, etc. even within one-word utterances. Gruber (1973) has suggested that one-word utterances may express one of several performative functions, so that the one-word sentence "Shoe!" can mean "I order you to give me the shoe," "I indicate to you a shoe," and so forth. Antinucci and Parisi (1973) have applied the generative semantic performative analysis to one-word speech, describing imperative and declarative functions in terms of an "I say to you (proposition X)" format in the deep structures written for various utterances. Greenfield and Smith (1976) find the same sorts of performative functions in the one-word utterances of their subjects. In addition, they also report that the very first words used by these children were so-called "pure performatives," the utterances "hi!" and "by-bye!" similar to Searle's examples of pure, proposition-free illocutions like "Hurray!"

On the basis of such findings, Bates, Camaioni, and Volterra (1973) were led to the conclusion that certain simple performatives—since they are clearly established in the child's first utterances—must have developed in the period prior to speech, through the use of gesture and nonverbal vocal signals. To examine this hypothesis, they undertook a longitudinal study of the development of performatives prior to speech. Using the quasi-longitudinal format suggested by Slobin (1967), the authors selected three infants, at 2 months, 6 months, and 12 months of age, respectively, at the beginning of the study. The children were visited in their homes and videotaped in bi-weekly sessions, for approximately 8 months, until they had overlapped each other in development. The home visits included the administration of informal "games" and other interventions based on Piaget's theory of sensorimotor development, to determine the kinds of cognitive developments that may be prerequisite to preverbal communication. Bates, Camaioni, and Volterra conclude that there are three stages in the development of communication, corresponding to Austin's perlocutionary, illocutionary, and locutionary functions.

In the perlocutionary stage, from birth to about 10 months of age, the child is not aware a priori of the communicative value of his signals. For example, he does not point or reach toward objects while looking up at the adult in apparent anticipation of help. Nor does he use objects intentionally to obtain adult attention—showing them, giving them, etc. Instead, his signals are perlocutions in the sense that they are signals that are not recognized *by both sender and receiver* as conventional communications.

In the illocutionary stage, from 10 months to between 12 and 15 months, the authors report the emergence of what are termed "proto-imperatives" and "proto-declaratives." The proto-imperative is defined as the intentional use of an adult as the means of obtaining a desired object. The proto-declarative is defined instead as the intentional use of an object as the means of obtaining adult attention—in showing, giving, pointing, etc. Bates, Camaioni, and Volterra report that these two functions seem to emerge around the same time that the child also uses one object as the means to obtaining another, e.g., pulling a cloth support toward him in order to take an object resting on that support. All three functions—use of an object to obtain an object, use of an adult to obtain an object, use of an object to obtain adult attention—may be viewed as aspects of a single concept of tool use, corresponding to Piaget's sensorimotor stage V.

The locutionary stage began around 12 months for one subject and at around 15–16 months for the oldest of the three subjects. At this point, the two infants began to use words with a referential value (e.g., naming the object that they wanted, labeling an object while pointing to it) within the same performative schemes that had developed during the illocutionary phase. However, this locutionary stage seemed to require a further cognitive development, corresponding to Piaget's sensorimotor stage VI, the capacity for symbolic representation. For example, at around the same time that the two infants used locutions within their performative acts, they also showed the beginnings of symbolic play (e.g., pretending that a spoon is a telephone), memory for absent objects and locations, etc.

Bates, Camaioni, and Volterra are currently engaged in a study of 25 infants, followed from 9 to 14 months, to determine whether the above findings will generalize to a larger sample. In the meantime, however, several other studies of preverbal performatives have appeared. All of these studies reach similar conclusions concerning the importance of the period from 10 to 12 months in the acquisition of performative functions.

Sugarman (1973) investigated the cognitive basis for preverbal imperatives, using the Hunt and Uzgiris scales for sensorimotor development and observing communicative behavior in a set of somewhat standardized situations (e.g., presenting an object out of a child's reach when the child is sitting in a highchair). She also reports that Piaget's stage V, particularly the causal developments typified by the use of a support to obtain an object, seems to be prerequisite to the intentional use of imperative signals.

Carter (1974) and Lock (1972) have observed the use of eye contact, reaching, and other signals indicating that the child understands the communicative value of his gestures, cries, and other commands. Dore (1973) undertook a particularly extensive study of preverbal performatives and early one-word speech acts. Like Carter, Lock, and Sugarman, Dore also reports that a particularly clear, controlled use of nonverbal signals begins around 10 months of age. Bruner (1975) is now engaged in research on these and other prerequisites to speech as they develop in the first year of life. He traces the development of performatives back still further, to around 3 months of age. At this point, according to Bruner and Scaife (in press), an infant will follow the line of his mother's gaze, resulting in shared visual attention to objects. Bruner suggests that his shared attention is the beginning of joint reference, a prerequisite for all later communication.

Recall that in the section on the pragmatics of reference we discussed the distinction between meaning as object and meaning as act. The same issue can be raised with regard to performative structure. The studies just described suggest that something like a performative intention or function is established prior to speech, during the sensorimotor period. However, this does not automatically mean that 10-month-olds "have" performatives in the sense of symbolic objects or deep structure "trees" of the type proposed by generative semanticians. Instead, these early performatives might best be described as action schemes, procedural blueprints containing the communicative goal, the identity of the intended listener, and the kinds of signals that can be used to reach both.

In addition to the action-object issue, a second distinction can be made between performative intentions and performative conventions. The above studies indicate that performative intentions are established quite early, in some cases even prior to speech. But as we noted earlier, the acquisition of conventional means for expressing those intentions may take years, depending on the complexity and difficulty of those conventions in a given language community.

There are also a number of studies on later performatives, particularly the use of polite request forms by older children. However, since these studies also involve questions of presuppositions and conversational postulates, we will discuss them later on.

Presuppositions

Another construct that has been used extensively in pragmatic analyses is the concept of presupposition. There is considerable controversy regarding the nature of presuppositions (Kiefer, 1973). Because the term is used in so many different ways by different authors, a careful understanding of these different uses is essential for anyone interested in research in this area.

There are three possible definitions of presupposition: 1) semantic or logical presupposition (P_1); 2) pragmatic presupposition (P_2); and 3) psychological presupposition (P_3). As in the case of "reference" vs. "referring," these definitions differ primarily on the issue of presuppositions as objects, or properties of sentences, versus presupposing as an activity of speakers.

Semantic Presupposition Presuppositions were originally described in language philosophy with respect to the problem of verifiability. The information available in a given sentence can be divided into three types: asserted meaning, entailed meaning, and presupposed meaning. These three types of information differ insofar as they have different truth conditions.

First, the meaning *asserted* by a sentence is true if the sentence is true, and false if the sentence is false. Take the example,

(15) John has a sister.

Our knowledge of the meaning of the word "sister" enables us to construct the paraphrase

(16) John has a female sibling.

We know that these sentences take the same assertions because the negation of (15)—

(17) John does not have a sister

requires the negation of (16)—

(18) John does not have a female sibling.

The truth conditions for two equivalent assertions can be formalized as follows:

$$T(15) \Rightarrow T(16)$$
$$F(15) \Rightarrow F(16)$$

However, in addition to the information that is actually asserted by sentence (15), we can deduce further information such as

(19) John's parents had more than one child.

Sentences (15) and (19) do not make the same assertions, since even if sentence (15) is false, sentence (19) can still be true. For example, John may have 12 brothers even though he has no sisters. In this case we say that the truth of sentence (19) is *entailed by* the truth of (15), but not asserted by (15). If a given sentence (Y) is entailed by a sentence (X), then Y is true if X is true, but Y is not necessarily affected if X is false. The entailment relation for the above sentences can be formalized as follows:

$$T(15) \Rightarrow T(19)$$
$$F(15 \Rightarrow \text{no conclusion.}$$

Finally, there is one further kind of information which can be deduced from both sentence (15) and its negation, (17). Both the positive and negative forms of the statements require that, within whatever world (15) and (17) are relevant, sentence (20) must be true:

(20) John exists.

If there were no entity called John, then neither (15) nor (17) could be verified. And according to Russell (1905), a sentence which cannot be computed is by definition nonsense. Thus, the truth of sentence (20) is *presupposed by* both (15) and (17). This set of relations yields one of the definitions of presupposition listed above. A logical or semantic presupposition (P_1) is a condition deducible from the meaning of a sentence, which must be true for that sentence to be either a true or a false proposition. For the above sentences, this relation can be formalized as

$T(15) \Rightarrow T(20)$
$F(15 \Rightarrow T(20)$.

By this definition, any information implied by a sentence which is affected by the negation of that sentence is not a presupposition. This relation can be used as a test to determine whether entailed information is logically presupposed by a sentence.

Pragmatic Presupposition   The above definition of presupposition was originated for a restricted purpose, to facilitate the computation of true and false information from a given set of sentences. Theoretically, this concept completes a closed system of logical relations that can hold between sentences. But there are other types of information deducible from a given sentence, which have to do with the relationship between that sentence and the context in which it is used. This information is neither asserted, entailed, nor presupposed in the sense outlined above, because it is not a property of the sentence itself. For example, the utterance

(21) Mr. Smith, can I get your coat?

usually indicates that the listener is an adult male, and may also suggest that the listener is either a social superior or a distant acquaintance of the speaker. If (21) were used with a small child or with a close friend, it would probably be for purposes of humor, an intentional violation of expectations. Similarly, the sentence

(22) Do you want your din-din?

suggests that the listener is a child or possibly a pet. In our culture, sentence (23)

(23) I simply love your tie

indicates that the speaker is either female, or as R. Lakoff (1973) suggests, a male who shares the peripheral power and status of females. However, none of these conditions in any way affects the truth or falsity of the propositions contained in these sentences. Instead, they are pragmatic presuppositions, conditions necessary for a sentence to be appropriate in the context in which it is used (P_2).

These conditions were originally described by Austin (1962), with regard to speech acts, or performatives. Austin had claimed that there is a class of sentences which cannot be either true or false, since they are events in themselves, e.g., "I now pronounce you man and wife." However, while such sentences cannot be verified, we can determine whether they have functioned properly or not. For example, the sentence "I now pronounce you man and wife" fails to function if the speaker has no legal right to perform marriage ceremonies. Austin calls these constraints on speech acts "felicity conditions." By the definition furnished above, felicity conditions are also pragmatic presuppositions.

At first glance, pragmatic and semantic presupposition seem to be separate categories. However, there are ambiguous cases in which what seems to be a semantic presupposition will vary according to the context in which the sentence is used. This is frequently the case with lexical presuppositions. The meaning of lexical items can often be divided into presupposed meaning and asserted/referential meaning. Fillmore (1971) offers as an example the sentence

(24) I blamed John for burning the dinner.

In this sentence, the speaker presupposes that John burnt the dinner, while he asserts that it was wrong to do so. By contrast the sentence

(25) I accused John of burning the dinner

presupposes that burning the dinner is wrong, while asserting that John did it. According to such an analysis, the two verbs "blame" and "accuse" contain the same information, but distributed differently between presupposed and asserted meaning. These presuppositions generally obey the logical test for presuppositions, in that they hold true for both the assertion and the negation of the same sentence. Hence

(26) I did not accuse John of burning the dinner

still presupposes that burning the dinner is wrong.

However, in some cases lexical presuppositions shift according to the context in which the lexical item is used. Take the example

(27) John is a bachelor.

The meaning of bachelor includes the information that John is an unmarried adult male. Under normal circumstances the information "unmarried" is the asserted portion of the meaning, while the information "adult male" is presupposed by the use of the word "bachelor." For example, "John is a bachelor" would be a very peculiar answer to the question "How old is John?" or "Is John your son or your dog?" By the same token, the sentence

(28) John is not a bachelor

asserts that John is not unmarried, while the speaker usually takes for granted (i.e., pragmatically presupposes) that John is an adult male. However, this kind of presupposition fails the test for logical presuppositions outlined above. If John is a 2-year-old boy, and I tell my neighbor "John is not a bachelor," my neighbor will probably assume that John is an adult, unless he knows otherwise. Should he find out later that he was wrong, he is justified in accusing me of being uncooperative, or of misleading him. But he cannot accuse me of lying. Sentence (28) is not false even though John is only 2 years old. The condition "adult male" is necessary for the assertion of (27) to be true, but not for (28) to be true. Hence, by the logical definitions outlined above, the condition "adult male" is semantically entailed by sentence (27), but it is not a semantic presupposition (P_1) of (27). Instead, it is a pragmatic presupposition, a condition necessary for both (27) and (28) to be *appropriate*.

The shifting nature of pragmatic presuppositions may be clearer in the following example. Suppose that I have a single girlfriend who is anxious to marry. She has been invited to visit the home of some older friends, who mention that a neighbor's son John will be present. When she explains this fact to me, we both assume that the neighbor's son John will be a little boy. When my friend comes over the next day, I ask her "How was the party?" She smiles and responds

(27a) John is a bachelor.

In this instance, sentence (27) asserts not only that John is unmarried, but that he is an adult male. The usual division of the lexical meaning of "bachelor" is

assert: unmarried
presuppose (P₂): adult male.

In this particular context, the meaning of the predicate "bachelor" is redivided into

assert: unmarried, adult
presuppose (P₂): male.

The problem of pragmatic presupposition reintroduces the speaker into a theory of sentences. Insofar as pragmatic presuppositions vary according to the context and the beliefs of the interlocutors, they cannot be defined by reference to the sentence alone. Semantic presuppositions are conditions which are necessary for a sentence to be true or false. Pragmatic presuppositions are conditions which are necessary for a sentence to be appropriate in a given context. Hence, by definition, pragmatic presuppositions are the property of speakers. This is true for lexical presuppositions such as the "bachelor" example, as well as for the conditions of use for polite forms, baby-talk forms, or "female" forms in examples (21) through (23). However, insofar as pragmatic presuppositions include Austin's felicity conditions, then they also include the felicity conditions of the speech act "declare." One of the felicity conditions of declaring is that the speaker believes what he is saying to be true, or at least wants to indicate that he believes it to be true. Untrue assertions are uncooperative (albeit common) and hence inappropriate speech acts. This means that the pragmatic definition of presupposition (P₂) *subsumes* the semantic definition (P₁). The conditions necessary for a sentence to be true or false are included among conditions necessary for a sentence to be appropriate in most contexts.

George Lakoff (1973) has suggested that pragmatic presuppositions can be reduced to normal semantics if we describe them as part of the structure of the performative. As such, they make up part of the semantic tree structure underlying every sentence, and can therefore trigger the application of different sentence forms. However, the same criticism that has been made of the performative analysis in general can also be lodged against this proposal. Insofar as pragmatic presuppositions are relations between a sentence and the speaker's beliefs about the context, they involve not only mental "objects," but rules for sentence use. If we use propositional notation to describe presuppositions, we must be careful to define the special psychological nature of such a propositional structure.

Psychological Presuposition "Presupposing" is the act of using a sentence to make a comment about some information assumed to be shared or verifiable by speaker and listener. This presupposition can be distinctly signaled by some constituent of surface structure. Or it can be left locally unmarked. When the presupposed material affects the surface form of the sentence, it can be handled within a grammar of sentences. But a *speaker* can presuppose information in using a sentence, even if his *sentence* does not. The presupposition will carry as long as the speaker and the listener construct the same "topic-comment" relationship between the asserted information and the assumed information.

This definition differs from Lakoff's proposal in one important respect. In Lakoff's model, once the presupposition is described in the deep structure, the grammar is automatically sensitive to it. If the grammar includes a transformation (e.g., a particular word order, or a kind of intonation pattern) that is sensitive to a given presupposition, and that transformation has not been applied with a given sentence, then according to the generative semantic model we must conclude that the presupposition was never constructed as part of the meaning of the sentence. Hence, even though presupposition is defined in terms of appropriateness as well as truth, it is still defined in terms of sentence form instead of speaker intentions. In the model used in this chapter, a presupposition can be psychologically present regardless of its phonetic expression, as long as both the speaker and the listener share the *act* of presupposing, or as long as the speaker *thinks* that the act is shared. This definition of presupposition makes the concept potentially unverifiable within a linguistic theory, since "presupposing" can be carried out without affecting the external form of sentences. For this reason, I have grouped psychological presuppositions as a separate class (P_3), to distinguish it from the definitions of presupposition used in most linguistic models. However, just as pragmatic presupposition (P_2) subsumes semantic presupposition (P_1), the class of psychological acts of presupposing (P_3) subsumes all cases in which the presupposing act is signaled in sentence form (P_1 and P_2).

Let us take an example of a psychological presupposition which is not necessarily signaled in surface form. My friend George and I walk into a party where we are expecting to meet Fred's new girlfriend. Fred is just back from the Orient, and has brought his girlfriend with him from there. He told us over the telephone that her name is Mai Ling. George and I assumed that she was Oriental. We walk into the room and are introduced to Mai Ling, who is a tall Swedish blond. George turns to me several moments later and says "She's blonde." Given our shared beliefs earlier in the day, the sentence serves as a comment on the expectation that Mai Ling would be Oriental. It is possible, even likely, that Goerge would use an intonation pattern of surprise with his comment. In that case, the psychological presupposition (P_3) would also be a linguistic-pragmatic one (P_2), in that there would be an explicit phonetic signal of surprise. But even if he does *not* use a special intonation pattern, the presupposition can still carry. There may be nothing in the surface form of the sentence itself that in any way presupposes, semantically or pragmatically, that I expected Mai Ling to be Oriental, and that Orientals are expected to have dark hair. But the sentence nonetheless bears a topic-comment relationship to the presupposition that Mai Ling would be Oriental, because George and I have created that presupposition as a psychological event.

There is one particularly important reason to define presuppositions as psychological operations, regardless of their grammatical expression. As in the case of the child's limited propositions discussed earlier, it is also true that young children may presuppose information that they are unable to signal in the surface form of their utterances. In order to understand the child's eventual mastery of conventions for signaling presupposed material, we must be willing to infer, if possible, the psychological presence of presuppositions prior to their syntactic expression. We can recover the child's presuppositions in the same way that we recover underlying proposition meaning, by examining the use of sentences in a given context. But once again, the emphasis is on the pragmatic intention as opposed to the pragmatic convention.

Another important point in using this psychological definition of presupposing is to emphasize the difference between presupposing as a procedure, and presupposition as a mental object. We will suggest further on that the first acts of presupposing arise automatically out of some lower level psychological processes. We cannot be certain that the child has constructed the information in a presupposition *as a symbolic object* (in Piaget's sense, as internally represented information) until he can use recognizable surface signals (conventional or idiosyncratic) that demonstrate his cognitive control of the presupposition. Very young children seem to move from unmarked but appropriate use of presuppositions (as in the "She is blonde" example), to the explicit marking of presuppositions in speech. This ontogenetic move from P_3 presuppositions is based on an overall increase in the amount of material a child can control in a given moment of processing vs. the amount of material that must be left at a perceptual-motor level. The child begins to control his own procedures of "taking for granted" as symbolic structures in themselves.

After this lengthy introduction to the concept of presupposition, it would be appropriate to present a series of studies on acquisition of the various types of presuppositions by children. Given the enormous number of heuristic descriptions available for presuppositional structure, there is certainly sufficient material for a great deal of developmental research. However, there is at this writing very little work directly related to the acquisition of presuppositions.

One of the few developmental studies explicitly discussing the question of presupposition is by Antinucci and Volterra (1973) on the presuppositions of negation in one-word speech. The authors point out that a negation is *not* a description of a nonevent. Rather, speakers use negations to cancel out some kind of information that the listener supposedly believes or might believe. As such, negations are always comments on a presupposition. For example, the statement "It is not raining" makes sense only if someone believed, feared, or otherwise presupposed that it might rain in the first place. Antinucci and Volterra discuss four kinds of presuppositions that underlie early negations, concluding that such use of listener presuppositions is already well established between $1^{1}/_{2}$ and 2 years of age.

Maratsos (1973, 1974) has investigated the acquisition of several structures that semanticians generally describe in terms of presupposition. For example, Maratsos (1973) discusses the difficulty that young children have with stress patterns indicating pronominal coreference. Take the two sentences

(29) John hit Harry and then he hit Sarah
(30) John hit Harry and then *he* hit Sarah

in which the italicized pronoun receives contrastive stress. In sentence (29) "he" refers to John, while in sentence (30) "he" refers to someone other than John. Sentences like (30) require more presupposed information by the listener than (29), and Maratsos demonstrates, in fact, that the latter are more difficult for young children to process than the former. In another article, Maratsos (1974) investigates comprehension of specific vs. nonspecific articles (i.e., "the" vs. "a") by young children, and concludes that both of these forms are clearly understood as early as 3 years of age. Definite and indefinite articles have traditionally been described in terms of presuppositions about the listener's familiarity with a given referent, e.g., "the boy" vs. "a boy" (see Parisi and Antinucci, in press). Hence, this would be another case in which certain kinds of presuppositions are readily understood by young children. Maratsos himself does not explicitly relate either of these studies to the theoretical question of presupposed vs. asserted information as it has been discussed here. However, just as we can examine the old literature on acquisition of transformations from the point of view of performatives, there are also a great many studies of grammatical development, similar to these two by Maratsos, which are relevant to the acquisition of presuppositions.

Since presuppositions are an open, potentially infinite class of structures, it would be impossible to investigate the acquisition of presuppositions exhaustively in the same way that we investigate the acquisition of verb tense or quantifiers. Any kind of information can, at least in the P_3 sense outlined above, serve as a presupposition for another kind of information. It would still be useful to examine studies like those of Maratsos from the point of view of presuppositional processing; it would be still more useful to design future studies around particular questions regarding asserted, entailed, and presupposed information. However, since we are at the very beginning of research into the pragmatics of child speech, it may be most useful at this point to examine the *function* served by the proposition-presupposition relationship in general and the way in which that general function develops in young children.

Viewed in the most general sense, the relationship between presupposition and proposition is analogous to the relation between topic and comment. Viewed still more abstractly, both presupposition-proposition and topic-comment can be seen as linguistic variants of the more pervasive relationship of ground and figure. The analogy may in fact be more than a metaphor. There is some evidence indicating that the "new" information in one-word speech usually presupposes "old" information in the context in which it occurs. Greenfield and Smith (1976) and Veneziano (in preparation, 1975) have examined the information value of one-word utterances and find that the element of the situation which the child chooses to encode is almost invariably the element undergoing greatest change or emphasis. For example, if the child is putting a series of objects in a bucket, he chooses to encode the names of the changing objects rather than "bucket" or "put." If a series of agents are taking turns carrying out the same activity, the agent is the element most likely to be encoded. If one agent is executing a series of different acts, the verb is the element that will usually appear in one-word utterances. And so forth. Similar observations can be found in the works of De Laguna (1927), Sechehaye (1926), and Vygotsky (1962), who note that "monorhemes" or one-word sentences tend to express comments rather than topics (cited in MacWhinney, 1975).

Bates (1976) has suggested that this tendency is the automatic product of two basic processes in the child's nervous system. One is the operation of the orienting system (Sokolov, 1958). From the first few days of life, the child's orienting system selects novel stimuli for his attention from a background of old information. It is, then, not surprising that early speech follows the same pattern, with novel or important elements chosen for encoding against a background of unchanging objects and events. The other process, perhaps derived from the same physiological sources as the first, is the operation of figure/ground principles in all perceptual channels. A comment can be viewed as a figure selected for encoding against a ground, or "topic." Viewed from these two perspectives, it would indeed be surprising if children did *not* regularly focus on important, changing, high-information events and encode those with their limited verbal capacity rather than some bit of older, background information. In fact, the opposite tendency—to express old information first, perhaps because a listener does not share that information—should be far more difficult for young children.

The division of new and old information at the one-word stage may, then, be viewed as the beginning of the proposition-presupposition relationship. Gradually, as the child's encoding capacity increases, he will be able to encode more and more explicit information in his comments, leaving less of the original message implicit in the context. But the new/old, comment/topic division is still functional with longer, more complex messages.

There has been a limited amount of research on topicalization in child speech. Hornby, Hass, and Feldman (1970) asked kindergarten and second grade children to select the "most important word" in each of several sentences. The younger children varied considerably in their selection, and their choices were particularly related to semantic features of the words rather than sentence function. The older children, however, consistently selected the grammatical predicate (generally a verb) as the "most important" or focal part of the sentence. Hornby and Hass (1970) showed preschool children pairs of pictures in which all but one element was held constant, e.g., a picture of a girl petting a dog followed by a picture of the same girl petting a cat. They found that children have a strong tendency to use contrastive stress to describe the changing element in the second picture (e.g., "The girl is petting the *cat*"). Also, the sentence subject (also the semantic agent) was more likely to receive contrastive stress than other sentence elements. This latter finding is particularly interesting given the fact that in English, under neutral, noncontrastive conditions, the subject generally contains the "topic" or "old information." Hence, when the subject is the new or focal element, it has to receive contrastive marking of some sort to cancel the standard expectation that subject is old or topicalized information.

Gruber (1967) has examined the topic-comment distinction in the speech of a 28-month-old English-speaking child. He finds a strong tendency for topic to be ordered first, with comment second, and suggests that this distinction may be the ontogenic predecessor of a later distinction into subject and predicate. Note, however, that in English the respective orders topic-comment, subject-verb, and agent-action are all high-frequency constructions, and all three relationships tend to overlap in the simple sentences addressed to children. Hence, in English, it is difficult to determine exactly what kind of strategy a child is using when he selects a preferred word order.

There are other languages, however, in which children do not receive such clear-cut ordering models from their environment. For example, in Italian the ordering for subject and predicate, agent and action, tends to vary according to the pragmatic demands of the situation. Hence a subject that is also the sentence topic (as is often the case in English as well) will generally precede the verb. But when the subject is new or important information with respect to the predicate, it tends to be placed at the end of the sentence. Baroni, Fava, and Tirandola (1973) and Bates (1976) claim that for Italian children the very first ordering rules adopted by children are in fact pragmatic rules. In particular, very young Italian children tend to follow the rule "new information first/old information second," regardless of the syntactic or semantic role of the new vs. old information from an adult perspective. MacWhinney (1974) reports similar findings for the first stages in the acquisition of Hungarian. Adult word order varies in both Italian and Hungarian. Hence, children in these two language communities do not receive the same consistent ordering models that English children receive from English adults. Bates (1976) has suggested that, in the absence of clear-cut models for semantic ordering (e.g., agent first/action second), child speakers will tend to adopt pragmatic ordering principles. Furthermore, the order "new first/old second" may be a more "natural" strategy, in that the novel, high-information element is essentially "blurted out" first, with other information added on with the child's remaining processing capacity. Hence the new/old order at the two-word level can be seen as a continuation of the new-only rule described by Greenfield and Smith (1976) and others for the one-word stage. (See MacWhinney, 1975 for a more detailed discussion of the concept of focus in child speech.)

Until more data are available on topic-focus relations, and on the acquisition of presuppositions in general, these proposals are primarily speculative. However, it should at least be clear that presuppositions are not ancillary structures that are "added onto" propositions. Children do not acquire presuppositional "trees" one at a time in the same way that they acquire vocabulary items. Every time the child selects a piece of information for encoding, he automatically presupposes the contextual information from which his comment was selected. Hence, presupposing is an integral part of every act of speech. In fact, insofar as presupposing is "taking information for granted," it is probably easier for young children than the reciprocal action of proposing. In the course of pragmatic development, the major task for children will be to learn when *not* to presuppose, i.e., when it is necessary to provide the listener with explicit clues about the information that is being assumed as background for a comment.

This also means that the development of presuppositions is tied to the decline of egocentrism in early childhood. As the child learns to distinguish between his own viewpoint and that of his listeners (i.e., as he learns to "role-take"), he will gradually realize that his own presuppositions may not be readily available to his listeners. Hence, he will learn to expand and rearrange his utterances, so that *both* the asserted and the presupposed information are clear to others.

To illustrate, recall the example offered earlier for P_3 presuppositions. Suppose I had said, "She's blonde!" to my friend George, assuming that he remembers our expectation that the woman in question would be Oriental. If George failed to understand my comment, I would be required to backtrack and provide one or more of the presuppositions upon which my statement was based. Instead of repeating "She's blonde," I might say something like

(7) We thought she would be Oriental, but she's not. In fact, she's even blonde.

Communication failures with young children can often be traced to the failure of this particular function. First, preschool children are not skilled in predicting differences between their own viewpoint and those of others (for illustrations, see Flavell et al., 1968; Krauss and Glucksberg, 1969). Hence, they are likely to use P_3 presuppositions inappropriately, in situations in which the listener does not have the prerequisite information. Second, when misunderstandings do occur, young children also have difficulty in back-tracking, locating the source of the misunderstanding; instead of tracing the point at which presuppositions misfired, they may simply repeat or paraphrase their original statement, adding no more of the necessary background information than they did the first time. A particularly fruitful area for future research in pragmatics will involve the relationship between role-taking, egocentrism, and both the production and comprehension of messages with presupposed information.

Conversational Postulates

There is a particular class of pragmatic presuppositions that have been used extensively in recent attempts to formalize the pragmatic system. These are a set of assumptions about the nature of human discourse, referred to as conversational postulates. The concept of conversational implicature was originally introduced by Grice (1968) to describe some systematic aspects of language that cannot be reduced to true or false statements. It is assumed that normal human beings who enter into a conversation have agreed to be cooperative. This general principle of cooperation means that speakers will tell each other the truth, that they will only offer information assumed to be new and relevant to the listener, that they will only request information that they sincerely want to have, and so forth. Of course, this boy scout code of conversation rarely holds constant across a given sample of real dialogue, nor has Grice suggested that it will. Rather, he claims that we will use the set of standard rules in such a way that our deviations from the code will be recognized as violations and hence contribute additional information. Take the example of the truth principle. If I have just come home from walking through a torrential rain, and my spouse says to me, "You look terrific," we both know that the utterance is not true. Because the sentence is false, and we both know it to be false, and because we assume that there is a conversational rule against blatant falsehoods, the sentence serves in this context as an ironic statement that I am soaking wet and look horrible.

The same principle of contrast operates in much of polite speech as well. For example, a woman at a bus stop says to me, "Do you know what time it is?" There is a conversational rule which says that speakers do not request irrelevant information from their listeners, and I know that my own knowledge of the time is in itself irrelevant to a stranger waiting for a bus. I therefore conclude from this clear violation that the woman wants more than she has actually requested. I cannot simply answer, "Yes, I do know." I must also add "It is 4:30."

Gordon and Lakoff (1971) have incorporated Grice's system into a general semantic-pragmatic theory of sentences. The conversational postulates, which Grice himself left unformalized, have been formalized within the grammar as a set of semantic components such as (*sincere*) and (*relevant*). These components are contained within the performative structure of a sentence in a form something like "I say to you (*relevant*) (proposition X)." These components can be grouped together and replaced by other components, permitting pragmatically equivalent clusters to be interchanged. Hence, the listener can compute the overall intention of the speaker by canceling out contradictory components. This translation of Grice's rules into semantic primitives is an interesting conflation of semantic and pragmatic analysis, but in itself adds little to a psychological theory of pragmatics. Regardless of the particular formal notation used to describe them, in a psychological system we must define the conversational postulates as intentions, or rules for using utterances. As with other psychological presuppositions, the speaker uses a sentence to comment upon or intentionally violate an assumed rule of conversation. This usage may or may not be marked in the surface form of the utterance. Indeed, there is a kind of humor which depends crucially upon the unmarked nature of a pragmatic violation. If a comedian laughs out loud at his own jokes, for many native speakers the joke fails. When I walk into the house bedraggled from a rainstorm, my spouse's comment, "You look terrific," is much funnier if delivered with a completely sincere expression. On the other hand, the same deadpan joke is a disaster if uttered insincerely at a time when I do not share the knowledge that not even my mother could love me now. The ability to predict whether or not the listener shares a given assumption and to plan one's utterances accordingly is one of the highest achievements in pragmatic development. Much of verbal art will depend upon the multi-level use of sentences to say one thing and mean another, without losing the primary goal of communicating with the listener. While it will be useful to learn linguistic conventions associated with such operations, the same playful violations of conversational rules can be carried out psychologically without invoking the usual set of syntactic contrasts. Hence, conversational postulates also divide into P_3 presuppositions and P_2 presuppositions, marked and unmarked in the surface form of sentences.

Ervin-Tripp (1976; in press) has suggested that the understanding and production of request forms by children will proceed from direct imperatives (e.g., "Gimme the blanket") to indirect requests that are presumably based on conversational postulates (e.g., "Gee I'm cold" or "Can you reach that blanket?"). With regard to the issue of *comprehension* of requests, Bates (1971) analyzed videotaped mother-child conversations with 36 2-, 3-, and 4-year-olds, in both a task-oriented and a free play situation. In one analysis, she compared request forms by mothers in terms of likelihood of both behavioral compliance and verbal response by children. Mothers employed a variety of directives, including many of the subtle request forms discussed by Grice and by Gordon and Lakoff. Children were just as likely to comply with indirect requests as they were with direct commands, although they were significantly more likely to respond verbally (e.g., "Okay") to commands that were framed as questions. Shatz (1974, 1975) analyzed behavioral and verbal responses to direct vs. indirect commands in naturalistic home observations with mothers and 2-year-olds. Shatz also reports no differences in likelihood of compliance to direct vs. indirect requests, although she notes that question directives (e.g., "Can you shut the door?") were occasionally misunderstood as literal questions rather than commands. Both Shatz and Bates conclude that children as young as 2 years of age can recognize the command that is implicit in a variety of subtle requests and statements of need by mothers. However, both authors also suggest that very young children may be relying in large measure on nonverbal cues from the mother, and on a shared understanding of the context (e.g., knowledge of what action is expected next in a given game, at lunchtime, etc.). (However, compare Garvey, in press.)

With regard to *production* of indirect forms, Aksu (1973) reviews requests by Turkish children, and reports that Gricean requests (e.g., "We haven't had any cookies in a long time") are among the last to develop in children. Bates (1971) also reports that virtually all of the requests by the children in her study were either straight commands, "Can I have . . ." requests, or simply statements of desire (e.g., "I want that!"). Similarly, in a longitudinal study of two Italian children,

Bates (1976) reports that requests based on conversational postulates do not appear until at least 3^{1}/$_{2}$–4 years of age. She does, however, note that certain kinds of indirect requests—particularly the simple question imperative, e.g., "You open door?"—appear as early as 1/^{1}$_{2}$ years. According to Gordon and Lakoff (1971), this sort of question-request is also based on use of conversational postulates. Why, then, would other uses of indirect commands be delayed until 4 years of age? One possible explanation can be found in an analysis of speech acts by Sadock (1974), who suggests that certain indirect requests may be idiomatic expressions, similar to such phrases as "kicked the bucket." Idioms are learned arbitrarily through their use in context in much the same way that the connection between lexical items and their referents is learned. The question-directive would be one such idiomatic request form, requiring no recourse to rules of conversation to be understood. Other indirect request forms, on the other hand, are not idioms and do require use of conversational rules in order to be understood. Bates (1976) notes that the direct speech acts that appear between 1/^{1}$_{2}$ and 2 years of age are Italian versions of Sadock's idiomatic requests, while the structures that appear between 3/^{1}$_{2}$ and 4 are more likely to require use of conversational postulates.

These studies lead to the conclusion that comprehension precedes production for various kinds of directives. To examine this hypothesis further, Bates (1976) administered a pragmatic comprehension-production task to 60 Italian preschool children, between 3 and 7 years of age. First, the children were introduced to an old woman hand puppet, "Signora Rossi," who was described as the proprietress of a visible mound of wrapped candies. The child was told that if he asked the woman for a piece of candy, she would give him one. After the first request was elicited, the experimenter pretended to whisper with the puppet, and said "Signora Rossi wants to give you a piece of candy, but she likes children to ask very, very nicely. Could you ask her once again even nicer?" This task elicited both the child's spontaneous request forms, and his ability to increase the degree of politeness in his requests. If the child was not frustrated or distracted, this procedure was administered twice. In all cases, the children were given the candy, regardless of the nature of their response. In the second part of the task, the child was told that now he would play the role of Mrs. Rossi and decide who asked most nicely for candy. He was presented two identical puppets who took turns making requests. The child heard a series of paired requests—e.g., "I want a piece of candy'' vs. ''I would like a piece of candy''—and was asked each time to decide ''Who asked nicest?'' Also, after each decision the child was asked ''Why was he nicer? What did he say that was better?''

The results confirmed the suggestion in Bates (1971) that comprehension of polite forms precedes production. In the first part of the experiment, eliciting children's own request forms, 3-year-olds were rarely capable of changing their original request at all. And yet on the comprehension part of the experiment they did make significantly correct judgments on two types of items: presence/absence of please, and soft vs. harsh intonation. Older children discriminated some of the more difficult Italian structures (e.g., conditionals) as more polite but did not use them in their own speech. Instead, among older children, the instruction to ask ''nicer'' resulted primarily in addition of ''please'' and shifts toward softer intonation. In fact, some children actually repeated their first request in a whisper, without changing the grammatical form at all. Also, the older children would occasionally ask for less candy in their second request (e.g., ''Give me a piece of candy'' became ''Give me just a little candy''). Finally, there was a tendency for children to shift from imperative to interrogative in their second request. However, it should be noted that question-directives in Italian involve nothing more than an interrogative intonation, e.g., ''Give me!'' is changed to ''Give me?'' There are no changes in word order for interrogatives as there are in English, nor do Italian question-directives require modal verbs like ''could,'' ''would,'' ''will,'' etc. Also, these question-directives are among the forms that correspond to Sadock's notion of idiomatic requests, and hence do not necessarily imply mastery of Gricean principles.

Judgment of complex polite forms, such as conditional verbs (e.g., ''I would like'' vs. ''I want'') and formal levels of address, did not reach significance until $5^1/2$–6 years of age. Also, it is interesting that the item contrasting imperative with interrogative was not discriminated significantly by children in any of the age groups, even though Italian children use such forms as early as $1^1/2$. It is possible that the children have learned idiomatically that the question-directive is more *effective* in drawing adult attention to their needs but have not analyzed it as a ''softer'' or more polite form.

Finally, the questions, ''Why was he nicer? What did he say that was better?'' yielded a particularly interesting pattern of results, supporting the notion of a comprehension-production lag. Younger children were significantly able to make a *passive* judgment that one form was "better," but generally could not explain their decision in any way. Among 4–5-year-olds, a child would often correctly choose something like, "I would like some candy" as nicer, and then, when asked to explain the choice, answer with something like, "Because he said 'gimme some candy.' " Hence, the child understands the structure *imperative + polite,* but regenerates that structure as *imperative* only. This tendency was particularly pronounced between 4 and 4¹/₂. Between 4¹/₂ and 5 a slightly more complex pattern emerged. Again, given the item "I would like" versus "I want," a child might correctly discriminate "I would like." But when asked to explain "What did he say that was better?" the child would respond with something like "Because he said 'please.' " It seems that a child may understand the entire structure *imperative + polite* but then regenerate the *polite* portion by substituting the polite forms that are more readily available in his own repertoire.

The area of politeness judgments is just one application of conversational postulates. Other areas of interest are ironic jokes and insults, and "softeners," statements that assert information while limiting the speaker's responsibility for the truth of that information. A great deal of research remains to be done on children's understanding and production of many of these subtle, indirect uses of conversational rules and contextual information.

PRAGMATICS VS. SOCIOLINGUISTICS

At the beginning of this chapter it was stated that the terms "pragmatics" and "sociolinguistics" have both been used to describe the contextualist approach to language. The acquisition of various pragmatic structures was then described, as though pragmatics and sociolinguistics were interchangeable names for precisely the same thing. Indeed, many writers do use the terms interchangeably, and it is difficult to locate a clear boundary between the two.

However, a number of rather different questions, only remotely related to the pragmatic issues just discussed, do fall within the area of sociolinguistics. For example, the study of dialectology, different versions of the same language that are spoken in different communities, is an area that properly belongs to the sociology of language. Since research in both pragmatics and sociolinguistics is expanding at such a rapid rate, some sort of working definition distinguishing the two fields may be quite useful. For present purposes, let us say that pragmatics is the study of rules for using language in context—rules that can, at least in principle, be part of the linguistic competence of a single speaker. Sociolinguistics, on the other hand, is the study of differences between social groups in the use of a given language or set of languages. Hence sociolinguistic studies, comparing two or more ethnic groups, social classes, etc., can focus on differences between those groups in *any* area of language: phonology, syntax, semantics, or pragmatics. To illustrate, a study of differences in pronunciation of the letter "r" by upper class vs. lower class New Yorkers would be a sociolinguistic study of phonological differences. A study of the use of polite address forms in New York, without regard to group differences, would be a pragmatic study. Finally, a study of differences between upper class and lower class New Yorkers in the use of those same address forms would be considered a sociolinguistic study of pragmatics.

According to these definitions, sociolinguistics is closely related to sociology, since it involves the study of social groups rather than individuals. Pragmatics is more closely allied with language philosophy and psychology, focusing on context-based linguistic processes within real or hypothetical individuals.

There is, however, one border area between the two fields in which the distinctions are once again blurred. Individual speakers do have access to group differences in their own language community. As a result, an individual can use his knowledge of group differences to identify himself more closely with a given social group or to increase the distance between himself and members of that group. For example, a little girl who wants to play with the boys in her neighborhood may affect the "tough" speech style that the boys require as a badge of group membership. A lower class speaker seeking a job in a white-collar establishment may tune his speech toward the middle-class style that he feels is expected of him. A teenager may increase his use of adolescent jargon when in adult company to emphasize his sense of estrangement from the adults. And so forth. A particularly elaborate version of this process has been studied by Gumperz and Hymes (1964) and others, with regard to the bilingual's knowledge of the proper settings for switching from one language to another. In this sense, sociolinguistic differences can also become part of the pragmatic competence of single individuals.

There are many straightforward sociolinguistic studies of child language although they are not always classified as such by their authors. Decades of research on sex, social class, and racial differences in verbal ability represent one approach to the sociolinguistics of child speech. (For a discussion of racial and social class differences, see Williams (1970). For a review of sex differences in language, see Cherry (1975)). These studies tend to report quantitative differences on various standardized measures; hence, the results are often either difficult to interpret or simply uninteresting from a structural point of view.

An exception is the work of Bernstein (1966) on social class differences in the use of restricted vs. elaborated codes. A restricted code, according to Bernstein, is a highly context-based use of language, involving a high frequency of idioms and clichés to express global concepts, plus extensive use of elliptical references to shared knowledge, frequent substitution of pronouns and other deictic expressions in place of explicit noun phrases, etc. In other words, the restricted code is highly pragmatic, maximally exploiting implicit, presupposed, contextual information. The elaborated code, on the other hand, is a highly explicit version of the same language, involving expressions that are interpretable in a variety of contexts without a great deal of prior knowledge about speakers, listeners, and speech settings.

Actually, these are not two separate codes but rather opposite poles on a continuum from implicit to explicit uses of the same language. The advantage of the restricted code is its economy; if and when the speaker can assume a great deal of shared information, the restricted code is more efficient. The elaborated code is preferable when the speaker knows very little about his listener and the particular setting in which messages are exchanged. The elaborated code is particularly useful in writing and is more likely to be mastered by speakers engaged in a great deal of written communication. Bernstein (1966) notes that middle- and upper-class school children generally speak both the elaborated and the restricted codes and can switch from one to the other according to the demands of the setting. Lower-class children, on the other hand, are generally familiar only with the restricted code. While this code works perfectly well in their home settings, it places them at a disadvantage in the school situation, particularly when written communication is required.

Parisi and Gianelli (1974) have examined the acquisition of Italian in a longitudinal study comparing two lower-class, rural children acquiring Italian dialect, with two middle-class children acquiring the standard code. Their findings are related to Bernstein's concept of restricted vs. elaborated social class differences. Parisi and Gianelli observe that the acquisition of logical-semantic structures (e.g., embedded expressions, adverbial modifiers) follows the same sequence at approximately the same rate in all four children. Also, between 1¹/₂ and 2¹/₂ years of age, there are no social class differences in the absolute number and type of verbs, adverbials, and adjectives. There is, however, one interesting social class difference in their study. Middle-class children use considerably more nouns than lower-class children. Also, the lower-class children were more likely to use pronouns and other deictic expressions (e.g., "Give me that") in situations in which the middle-class children used explicit noun descriptions (e.g., "Give me the airplane"). Parisi and Gianelli suggest that between 1¹/₂ and 2¹/₂ years of age the middle-class children have already begun to depend less on the context to carry their meanings. Since verbs, adverbs, and adjectives cannot be easily replaced by deictic expressions (e.g., "that"), children from both classes are forced to find and use the explicit term for such concepts. But, since noun phrases are easily substitutable by pronouns in context, lower-class children rely more on the context to express noun phrases, and hence develop less extensive noun vocabularies.

Bernstein's work was carried out in England in urban settings where the only difference in social groups was a socioeconomic difference. The problem in the U.S. is more complex in that socioeconomic groups also tend to have very different racial and ethnic backgrounds. This problem has been particularly acute in research on the speech of black children (Labov, 1970). For years Black English was viewed as an inferior, substandard, or somehow "disadvantaged" version of Standard American English. Black children were often described as "nonverbal" on the basis of their reticence in interview settings; differences in grammatical usage by black children were described as grammatical errors. Labov has contested both these interpretations. With regard to the first, he has demonstrated that "nonverbal" black children are in fact quite verbally fluent when the testing situation is made to seem less formal and foreboding. Labov manipulated the formality of the setting by introducing a few simple changes, e.g., having the interviewer sit on the floor with the child and one of his friends with a bag of potato chips to share among them. The wealth of linguistic data derived from such situations was also used to refute the second interpretation, that black grammatical structures are "errors." Labov argues instead that grammatical differences between Black English and Standard American English are in fact dialect differences. In short, Black English is a different language, with several consistent differences in grammatical rules. It may also be the case that many black children are disadvantaged and may even speak something like Bernstein's restricted code. But, such issues are not to be confused with the separate question of differences in dialect. Black English in itself is not a substandard code, any more than the Spanish spoken by Chicano children is a substandard version of English.

The question of social class differences brings us to a related issue that lies in the border area between sociolinguistics and pragmatics. Social class groups are not entirely isolated from one another. Lower-class speakers may not have total productive mastery of middle-class speech, but they are aware of its existence. Mitchell-Kernan (1969) reports that black adults in Oakland, California, can make consistent judgments of "good" vs. "country" speech in audiotaped recordings from various black speakers. Lambert (1967) reports that both English and French-Canadian adults in Canada judge an English speaker (presented on audiotape only) as more intelligent and trustworthy than a speaker with French-Canadian pronunciation. Such findings suggest that many adults have learned to value their own dialect negatively in comparison with the "standard" dialect of the larger community. At what age do children become aware of dialect and class differences? And when do they acquire such negative judgments of their own code?

At this writing, the only study I am aware of that examines this question directly is by Cremona and Bates (in preparation). Cremona and Bates studied Italian children, from the first to the fifth grade, in a small rural community outside of Rome. On a series of production measures, they established that the children were all speakers of the local rural dialect, although their speech was increasingly "Italianized" as a function of school attendance. Subjects were asked to listen to a series of audiotaped sentence pairs, in which the same sentence was given in both standard Italian and in the local dialect. The instructions were simply to decide "Which one spoke better." At the beginning of first grade, children showed up to 80% preference on some items for standard Italian over their own dialect. In the fifth grade, preference for the standard forms reached 100% on almost all items. Hence, by 6 years of age rural Italian children have already developed a sense of linguistic inferiority, a negative evaluation of their own dialect in comparison with the national standard.

Within this border of sociolinguistic judgments by individual speakers, there are also a number of recent studies on children's understanding of sex and age group differences in language. Garcia-Zamor (1973) presented 4-year-old children of both sexes with a series of sentences containing lexical items that are generally identified with speech by either males or females (e.g., use of expletives). The 4-year-olds could already discriminate male speech from female speech at a significant level.

Shatz and Gelman (1973) and Sachs and Devlin (1973) report that 4-year-olds adjust their speech appropriately to the age level of their listeners; they use simpler, shorter phrases, with exaggerated intonation contours, when speaking to a 2-year-old listener as compared with a 4-year-old listener. These are the same effects that have been noted in the speech of mothers to children of different ages (e.g., Phillips, 1970; Drach, 1969). Some critics have suggested that this effect, at least in 4-year-old children, does not really indicate control of age-appropriate codes, but rather some kind of spontaneous reaction at the moment of conversation to feedback from the 2-year-old listener (e.g., the 2-year-old's failure to understand the game). To test this hypothesis, Sachs and Devlin also instructed their 4-year-olds to role-play a conversation with two types of dolls, one described as a 4-year-old peer, the other described as an infant who was just learning to talk. In play conversations with the infant doll, the 4-year-olds again showed the patterns of simplified, age-appropriate speech that they had shown with real 2-year-olds. Sachs and Devlin concluded that these children do have some kind of a priori knowledge of age group differences in language and are not simply reacting to failed communications with 2-year-olds.

Given the tremendous growth in the area of sociolinguistics in the last few years, the amount of developmental research on sociolinguistic issues is still surprisingly small. Clearly, each and every pattern of language use identified by sociologists must have been adopted by children in that community at some stage in development. A better understanding of the acquisition of sociolinguistic patterns may be useful for the development of intervention programs, if and when such programs are politically and morally appropriate. Above all, however, an understanding of the way that children acquire pragmatic and sociolinguistic rules should lead to an improved understanding of the relationship between social, cognitive, and linguistic development in general.

CONCLUSION: PRAGMATICS AND SOCIOLINGUISTICS IN LANGUAGE-DEFICIENT CHILDREN

There is to date only a limited amount of psychological research on pragmatics and sociolinguistics. It is therefore not surprising that even less work has been carried out on pragmatics and language deficiency. Given the variety of linguistic models that are now available for language-context relations, there are a great many questions for future research on pragmatics in both normal and language-deficient children.

To summarize briefly the points covered in this chapter, some fruitful areas for future research include the following.

Pragmatics of Reference   It was suggested earlier that there is no "one moment" in which a child forms a bond between a word and its referent. Instead, children acquire word meanings gradually, using sounds in a variety of contexts until the "language game" appropriate for a given word has been mastered. Clearly, this functional approach to the acquisition of meaning has implications for language pathology. How well does a language-impaired child control the contextual aspects of word use (both connotative and denotative)? Does he use a given lexical item in a wider or a more restricted range than normal children? Or are the pragmatics of reference the same for both normal and impaired children?

Performatives   What is the illocutionary range in language-deficient children? Are they more restricted in the variety of performatives they are willing to use? Do their limitations extend only to the conventions used to express performatives, or are they also limited in the range of performative intentions? These questions also apply to the ability of language-deficient children to modify their performatives, to violate or conform to conversational postulates. For example, do these children have devices for softening requests and assertions? If they have no strictly linguistic devices to accomplish this goal, do they have nonverbal means (e.g., loudness vs. softness, change in facial expression, etc.) for the same purpose? Are they aware of violations of conversational postulates by others?

Presuppositions   How do language-deficient children handle presupposed and entailed information? Do they provide clues to the background of their utterances when the listener may not have that background? Or do they assume too much from their listeners? What is the relationship between the mastery of presuppositions and relative egocentrism (i.e., ability to take the listener's perspective) in this population of children? How do they handle the old/new, topic/focus relationship in their communications? If they are unable to use standard linguistic means for this purpose, do they invent their own means to express the new/old relationship?

Sociolinguistics   Are language-deficient children aware of subgroup differences in language use? Do they account for these differences in their own speech? For example, how does a child with a language problem handle a situation in which he is required to communicate with a very young child vs. an older listener?

Comprehension and Production   On all of these issues, what is the relationship between comprehension and production of pragmatic and sociolinguistic information? It is possible, for example, that children with specific language defects may, when compared with normals, have relatively higher comprehension of implicit, context-based vs. explicit or "elaborated" speech. If their problem lies not in communication in general, including the use of context, but in particular structural aspects of speech, then language-deficient children may have become particularly competent at pulling information out of contextual uses of speech. Alternatively, a language defect may extend beyond syntactic-semantic processing into general, pragmatic aspects of communication.

I am aware of only one study at this writing which specifically investigates pragmatic issues in language-deficient children. Snyder (1975) has compared language-delayed vs. normal children on the development of prelinguistic and early verbal performatives and presuppositions. Using a set of standardized tasks for eliciting communication, Snyder is examining 1) the means used by the two populations in expressing declarative and imperative functions, and 2) the differences between the two samples in handling new vs. old information. The children are matched on mean-length-of-utterance; hence, the normals are a good deal younger than the delayed children. Measures of cognitive development are taken for all subjects to compare cognitive maturity with pragmatic competence in both groups. Snyder has hypothesized that language-delayed children will have difficulty not only with the content of language, but with the pragmatic rules for early communication.

If, as more recent linguistic models suggest, context is an essential aspect of the very structure of language, then an investigation of pragmatics should be a crucial aspect of future developmental studies. Furthermore, a comparison of normal and language-deficient children should yield particularly rich data concerning the role of context in the acquisition of language.

REFERENCES

Ainsworth, M. D. S. 1964. Patterns of attachment behavior shown by the infant in interaction with its mother. Merrill-Palmer Quart. 10:51–58.

Aksu, A. 1973. Request forms used by Turkish children. Mimeographed. University of California, Berkeley.

Antinucci, F., and D. Parisi. 1972. Early Language Development: A second stage. *In* Proceedings of the Conference on Present Problems of Psycholinguistics, Paris.

Antinucci, F., and D. Parisi. 1973. Early language acquisition: A model and some data. *In* C. Ferguson and D. Slobin (eds.), Child Language Development, pp. 607–619. Holt, Rinehart and Winston, New York.

Antinucci, F., and V. Volterra. 1973. Lo sviluppo della negazione nel linguaggio infantile: uno studio pragmatico. *In* Studi per un modello del linguaggio, Quaderni della Ricerca Scientifica, CNR, Rome.

Austin, J. L. 1962. How to Do Things with Words. Oxford University Press, Cambridge.

Baroni, A., E. Fava, and G. Tirondola. 1973. L'Ordine delle parole nel linguaggio infantile. University of Padova.

Bates, E. 1971. The Development of Conversational Skill in 2, 3 and 4 year olds. Unpublished master's thesis, University of Chicago.

Bates, E. 1976. Language and Context: the Acquisition of Pragmatics. Academic Press, New York.

Bates, E., L. Camaioni, and V. Volterra. 1973. The acquisition of performatives prior to speech. CNR Laboratory Technical Report No. 129. Rome. (Revised version in Merrill-Palmer Quart., 1975, 21:3.)

Bellugi, U. 1968. Linguistic mechanisms underlying child speech. *In* G. M. Zale (ed.), Proceedings of the Conference on Language and Language Behavior. Appleton-Century-Crofts, New York.

Bernstein, B. 1966. Elaborated and restricted codes: Their social origins and some consequences. *In* A. G. Smith (ed.), Communication and Culture. Holt, Rinehart and Winston, New York.

Bever, T. 1970. The cognitive basis for linguistic structure. *In* J. Hayes (ed.), Cognition and the Development of Language, pp. 279–362. John Wiley and Sons, New York.

Bowerman, M. F. 1973. Early Syntactic Development: A Cross-linguistic Study with Special Reference to Finnish. Cambridge University Press, Cambridge.

Braine, M. D. S. 1973. The ontogeny of English phrase structure. *In* C. Ferguson and D. Slobin (eds.), Studies in Child Language Development, pp. 407–421. Holt, Rinehart and Winston, New York.

Brown, R. 1973. A First Language. Harvard University Press, Cambridge, Mass.

Brown, R., C. Cazden, and U. Bellugi. 1973. The child's grammar from I to III. *In* C. Ferguson and D. Slobin (eds.), Studies in Child Language Development, pp. 295–333. Holt, Rinehart and Winston, New York.

Bruner, J. 1975. The ontogenesis of speech acts. J. Child Lang. 2:1.

Bruner, J., and M. Scaife. The capacity for joint visual attention in the infant. Mimeographed. Oxford University. In press.

Carter, A. L. 1974. The development of communication in the sensorimotor period: a case study. Unpublished Ph.D. dissertation, University of California, Berkeley.

Cherry, L. 1975. Sex differences in child speech: McCarthy Revisited. Educational Testing Service. Princeton, N.J.

Chomsky, N. 1957. Syntactic Structures. M.I.T. Press, Cambridge, Mass.

Chomsky, N. 1965. Aspects of a Theory of Syntax. M.I.T. Press, Cambridge, Mass.

Chomsky, N. 1968. Language and Mind. Harcourt, Brace and World, New York.

Clark, E. 1973. What's in a word? On the child's acquisition of semantics in his first language. In T. Moore (ed.), Cognitive Development and the Acquisition of Language, pp. 65–110. Academic Press, New York.

De Laguna, G. A. 1927. Speech: Its Function and Development. University Press, Bloomington, Ind.

Dore, J. 1973. The Development of Speech Acts. Unpublished Ph.D. dissertation, City University of New York.

Dore, J. 1974. A pragmatic description of early development. J. Psychol. Res. 3(4):343–350.

Drach, K. 1969. The language of the parent: a pilot study. In Working Paper #14: The structure of linguistic input to children. Language Behavior Research Laboratory, University of California, Berkeley.

Ervin-Tripp, S. 1976. Wait for me, roller-skate. In C. Mitchell-Kernan and S. Ervin-Tripp (eds.), Child Discourse. Academic Press, New York.

Ervin-Tripp, S. Is Sybil there? Language in Society. In press.

Fillmore, C. 1968. The Case for Case. In E. Bach and R. T. Harms (eds.), Universals in Linguistic Theory, pp. 1–87. Holt, Rinehart and Winston, New York.

Fillmore, C. 1971. Types of lexical information. In D. Steinberg and J. Jakobovitz (eds.), Semantics. Cambridge University Press, Cambridge.

Flavell, J. N., P. Botkin, C. Fry, Jr., J. Wright, and P. Jarvis. 1968. The Development of Role-Taking and Communicative Skills in Children. John Wiley and Sons, New York.

Fraser, B. 1971. An Examination of the Performative Analysis. Mimeographed. Harvard University. (Available from the Indiana University Linguistics Club.)

Frege, G. 1952. Philosophical writings. P. Geech and M. Black (eds.). Basil Blackwell, Oxford.

Garcia-Zamor, M. 1973. Child's awareness of sex-role distinctions in language use. Presented to the Meeting of the Linguistic Society of America.

Garvey, C. Requests and responses in the speech of preschool children. J. Child Lang. In press.

Gordon, D., and G. Lakoff. 1971. Conversational postulates. In Proceedings from the 7th Regional Meeting of the Chicago Linguistic Society, University of Chicago.

Greenfield, P. M., and J. Smith. 1976. The Structure of Communication in Early Language Development. Academic Press, New York.

Grice, H. P. 1968. The Logic of Conversation. Mimeographed. University of California, Berkeley.

Gruber, J. 1967. Topicalization in child language. Found. Lang. 3:37–65.

Gruber, J. 1967. Correlations between the syntactic construction of the child and adult. Presented to the Society for Research in Child Development. (Reprinted in C. Ferguson and D. Slobin (eds.), Studies in Child Language Development, pp. 440–445. Holt, Rinehart and Winston, New York, 1973).

Gumperz, J., and D. Hymes (eds.). 1964. The Ethnography of Communication. Am. Anthrop. 66(6):Pt. 2.

Halliday, M. A. K. 1975. Learning How to Mean: Explorations in the Development of Language. Edward Arnold, London.

Hornby, P., W. Hass, and C. Feldman. 1970. A developmental analysis of the psychological subject and predicate of the sentence. Lang. Speech 13:182–193.

Hornby, P., and W. Hass. 1970. Use of contrastive stress by preschool children. J. Speech Hear. Res. 13:395–399.

Ingram, D. 1971. Transitivity in child language. Language 47:888–910.

Katz, J., and P. Postal. 1964. An Integrated Theory of Linguistic Descriptions. M.I.T. Press, Cambridge, Mass.

Keenan, E. 1974. Conversational competence in children. J. Child Lang. 1(2):163–183.

Kiefer, F. 1973. On Presuppositions. In F. Kiefer and N. Ruwet (eds.), Generative Grammar in Europe. Reidel, Dordrecht.

Krauss, R., and S. Glucksberg. 1969. The development of communication: competence as a function of age. Child Dev. 40:255–266.

Labov, W. 1970. The logic of non-standard English. In F. Williams (ed.), Language and Poverty. Markham, Chicago.

Lakoff, G. 1970. Linguistics and natural logic. In Studies in Generative Semantics #1. Phonetics Laboratory, University of Michigan.

Lakoff, R. 1972. Language in context. Language 48(4):907–927.

Lakoff, R. 1973. Language and a woman's place. Lang. Soc. 2:45–80.

Lambert, W. E. 1967. A social psychology of bilingualism. J. Soc. Issue 23:91–109.

Lenneberg, E. H. 1967. The Biological Foundations of Language. John Wiley and Sons, New York.

Lock, A. J. 1972. From out of nowhere. Presented to the Second International Symposium on Child Language, Florence. (Revised version in M. von Raffler-Engel and Y. Lebrun (eds.), Baby Talk and Infant Speech. Swets and Zeitlinger, Holland.

MacWhinney, B. 1974. How Hungarian children learn to speak. Unpublished Ph.D. dissertation, University of California, Berkeley.

MacWhinney, B. 1975. Topicalization and focusing in Hungarian child language. Presented at the Stanford Child Language Forum, Stanford.

Maratsos, M. 1973. The effects of stress in the understanding of pronominal coreference in children. J. Psycholin. Res. 2:1–8.

Maratsos, M. 1974. Preschool children's use of definite and indefinite articles. Child Dev. 45:446–455.

McCawley, J. 1968. The role of semantics in a grammar. In E. Bach and R. T. Harms (eds.), Universals in Linguistic Theory. pp. 124–169. Holt, Rinehart and Winston, New York.

McNeill, D. 1966. The creation of language by children. In J. Lyons and R. J. Wales (eds.), Psycholinguistic Papers: Proceedings from the 1966 Edinburgh Conference. pp. 99–132. Edinburgh University Press, Edinburgh.

McNeill, David. 1970. Explaining linguistic universals. University of Chicago.

Miller, W., and S. Ervin-Tripp. 1973. The development of grammar in child language. *In* C. Ferguson and D. Slobin (eds.), Studies in Child Language Development, pp. 355–380. Holt, Rinehart and Winston, New York.

Mitchell-Kernan, C. 1969. Language Behavior in a Black Urban Community. Doctoral dissertation, University of California, Berkeley.

Morris, Charles. 1946. Signs, Language and Behavior. Prentice-Hall, Englewood Cliffs, N.J.

Mowrer, O. H. 1960. Learning Theory and the Symbolic Process. John Wiley and Sons, Inc., New York.

Parisi, D., and F. Antinucci. Elements of Grammar. Academic Press, New York. In press.

Parisi, D., and W. Gianelli. 1974. Language and social environment at 2 years. Unpublished manuscript, Institute of Psychology, National Council of Research, Rome, Italy.

Peirce, Charles Sanders. 1932. Collected Papers. C. Hartshorne and P. Weiss (eds.). Harvard University Press, Cambridge, Mass.

Phillips, J. 1970. Formal characteristics of speech which mothers address to their young children. Unpublished doctoral dissertation, Johns Hopkins University.

Piaget, J. 1954. The Construction of Reality in the Child. Translated by Margaret Cook. Ballantine, New York.

Piaget, J. 1962. Play, Dreams and Imitation in Childhood. W. W. Norton and Company, New York.

Postal, P. 1972. The Best Theory. *In* S. Peters (ed.), Goals in Linguistics. Prentice-Hall, Englewood Cliffs, N.J.

Quine, W. V. 1960. Word and Object. John Wiley and Sons, New York.

Ross, J. R. 1970. On declarative sentences. *In* R. A. Jakobs and P. S. Rosenbaum (eds.), Readings in English Transformational Grammar. Ginn, Waltham, Mass.

Russell, B. 1905. On denoting. Mind 14:479–93.

Sachs, J., and Devlin, J. 1973. Young children's use of age-appropriate speech styles in social interaction and role-playing. Presented to the Linguistic Society of America.

Sadock, J. 1972. Speech act idioms. *In* Proceedings of the 8th Regional Meeting of the Chicago Linguistic Society, Chicago.

Sadock, J. 1974. Towards a Linguistic Theory of Speech Acts. Seminar Press, New York.

Schlesinger, I. M. 1971. Production of utterances and language acquisition. *In* D. Slobin (ed.), The Ontogenesis of Grammar, pp. 63–101. Academic Press, New York.

Searle, J. 1965. What is a speech act? *In* M. Black (ed.), Philosophy in America. Allen & Unwin, Cornell.

Sechehaye, M. A. 1926. Essai sur la structure logique de la phrase. Champion, Paris.

Shatz, M. 1974. The comprehension of indirect directives: can 2 year olds shut the door? Presented to the Linguistic Society of America.

Shatz, M. 1975. How young children respond to language: procedures for answering. Presented to the Stanford Child Language Forum, Stanford.

Shatz, M., and R. Gelman. 1973. The development of communication skills: modifications in the speech of young children as a function of the listener. Monographs of the Society for Research in Child Development 38(5).

Sinclair de Zwart, H. 1971. Acquisition of language, linguistic theory and epistemology. Presented to Colloque Internationale du C.M.R.S., Problems Actuele en Psycholinguistique, Paris.

Skinner, B. F. 1957. Verbal Behavior. Appleton-Century-Crofts, New York.

Slobin, D. 1967. Field Manual for the Cross-Cultural Study of the Acquisition of Communicative Competence. University of California at Berkeley Bookstore, Berkeley.

Slobin, D. I. 1970. Universals of grammatical development in children. In G. B. Flores d'Arcais and W. J. M. Levett (eds.), Advances in Psycholinguistics, pp. 174–186. North Holland, Amsterdam.

Slobin, D. I. 1971. Psycholinguistics. Scott, Foresman and Co., Glenview, Ill.

Slobin, D. 1975. On learning about language by watching it change through time. Invited address, Stanford Child Language Forum, Stanford.

Snyder, L. 1975. Pragmatics in language-deficient children: prelinguistic and early verbal performatives and presuppositions. Unpublished Ph.D. thesis, University of Colorado.

Sokolov, E. N. 1958. Perception and the Conditioned Reflex. University of Moscow Press, Moscow.

Strawson, P. F. 1950. On referring. Mind 59.

Sugarman, S. 1973. A description of communicative development in the prelanguage child. Honors thesis, Hampshire College.

Svachkin, N. 1973. The development of phonemic speech perception in early childhood. In C. Ferguson and D. Slobin (eds.), Studies in Child Language Development, pp. 91–128. Holt, Rinehart and Winston, New York.

Vygotsky, L. S. 1962. Thought and Language. M.I.T. Press, Cambridge, Mass. (Russian first edition 1934.)

Williams, F. (ed.) 1970. Language and Poverty. Markham, Chicago.

Wittgenstein, L. 1958. The Blue and the Brown Books. Harper and Row, New York.

Literature Cited in Preface and Editorial Comments

de Ajuriaguerra, J. 1966. Speech disorders in childhood. *In* C. Carterette (ed.), Brain Function: Speech, Language and Communication, pp. 117–140. University of California Press, Los Angeles.

de Ajuriaguerra, J., A. Jaeggi, F. Guignard, F. Kocher, M. Maquard, S. Roth, and E. Schmid. 1965. The development and prognosis of dysphasia in children. La Psychiatrie de l'Enfant 8:391–452 (excerpted this volume).

Andersen, E. 1975. A selected bibliography on language input to young children. Stanford University Committee on Linguistics Papers and Reports on Child Language Development 9:75–86.

Anderson, S. 1974. The Organization of Phonology. Academic Press, New York.

Berko, J. 1958. The child's learning of English morphology. Word 14:150–177.

Bloom, L. 1970. Language Development: Form and Function in Emerging Grammars, M.I.T. Press, Cambridge, Mass.

Bowerman, M. 1973. Structural relationships in children's utterances: Syntactic or semantic? *In* T. Moore (ed.), Cognitive Development and the Acquisition of Language, pp. 197–213. Academic Press, New York.

Bowerman, M. 1974. Learning the structures of causative verbs: A study in the relationship of cognitive, semantic, and syntactic development. Stanford University Committee on Linguistics Papers and Reports on Child Language Development 8:142–178.

Brown, R. 1973. A First Language. Harvard University Press, Cambridge, Mass.

Brown, R., and C. Fraser. 1963. The acquisition of syntax. *In* C. Cofer and B. Musgrave (eds.), Verbal Behavior and Learning, pp. 158–201. McGraw-Hill, New York.

Chomsky, N. 1957. Syntactic Structures. Mouton, The Hague.

Chomsky, N., and M. Halle. 1968. The Sound Pattern of English. Harper and Row, New York.

Compton, A. 1975. Generative studies of children's phonological disorders: A strategy of therapy. *In* S. Singh (ed.), Measurement Procedures in Speech, Hearing, and Language, pp. 55–90. University Park Press, Baltimore.

Crystal, D., P. Fletcher, and M. Garman. 1975. The Grammatical Analysis of Language Disability: A Procedure for Assessment and Remediation. Arnold, London.

de Villiers, P., and J. de Villiers. 1973. A cross-sectional study of the acquisition of grammatical morphemes in child speech. J. Psycholin. Res. 2:267–278.

Ferguson, D., and C. Farwell. 1975. Words and sounds in early language acquisition: English initial consonants in the first 50 words. Language 51:419–439.

Furth, H. 1966. Thinking without Language. The Free Press, New York.

Furth, H., and J. Youniss. 1971. Formal operations and language: A comparison of deaf and hearing adolescents. Int. J. Psychol. 6:49–64 (reprinted this volume).

Fromkin, V., S. Krashen, S. Curtiss, D. Rigler, and M. Rigler. 1974. The development of language in Genie: A case of language acquisition beyond the 'critical period.' Brain Lang. I: 81–107.

Garvey, C. 1975. Requests and responses in children's speech. J. Child Lang. 2:41–63.

Gruber, J. 1967. Topicalization in child language. Found. Lang. 3:37–65.

Ingram, D. 1974. Phonological rules in young children. J. Child Lang. 1:49–64.

Ingram, D. 1976. Phonological Disability in Children. Arnold, London.

Inhelder, B. 1963. Observations on the operational and figurative aspects of thought in dysphasic children. Problèmes ,de Psycholinguistique 6:143–153 (reprinted this volume).

Inhelder, B. 1966. Cognitive development and its contribution to the diagnosis of some phenomena of mental deficiency. Merrill-Palmer Quart. 12:299–319.

Inhelder, B. 1968. The Diagnosis of Reasoning Processes in the Retarded. John Day, New York.

Inhelder, B., and J. Piaget. 1964. The Early Growth of Logic in the Child. Norton, New York.

Jakobson, R. 1968. Child Language, Aphasia, and Phonological Universals. Mouton, The Hague.

Lackner, J. 1968. A developmental study of language behavior in retarded children. Neuropsychologia 6:301–320 (reprinted this volume).

Ladefoged, P. 1971. Preliminaries to Linguistic Phonetics. University of Chicago Press, Chicago.

Lee, L. 1966. Developmental sentence types: A method for comparing normal and deviant syntactic development. J. Speech Hear. Disord. 31:311–330.

Lee L., R. Koenigsknecht, and S. Mulhern. 1975. Interactive Language Development Teaching. Northwestern University Press, Evanston, Ill.

Lenneberg, E. 1962. Understanding language without ability to speak: A case report. J. Abnorm. Soc. Psychol. 65:419–425.

Lenneberg, E. 1964. Speech as a motor skill with special reference to nonaphasic disorders. In The Acquisition of Language. Monograph of the Society for Research in Child Development 29:115–127.

Lenneberg, E. 1964. Language disorders in childhood. Harv. Educ. Rev. 34:152–177.

Lenneberg, E. 1967. Biological Foundations of Language. John Wiley, New York.

Lenneberg, E., I. Nichols, and E. Rosenberger. 1964. Primitive stages of language development in mongolism. *In* Disorders of Communication, Vol. 42, pp. 119–137. Research Publications, A.R.N.M.D.

Lenneberg, E., G. Rebelsky, and I. Nichols. 1965. The vocalization of infants born to deaf and to hearing parents. Vita Humana 8:23–37.

Lovell, K., and B. Bradbury. 1967. The learning of English morphology in educationally subnormal special school children. Am. J. Ment. Defic. 71:609–615.

Lovell, K., H. Hoyle, and M. Siddall. 1968. A study of some aspects of the play and language of young children with delayed speech. J. Child Psychol. Psychiatry 9:41–50.

Luchsinger, R., and G. Arnold (eds.). 1965. Voice-Speech-Language. Wadsworth Publishing Co., Belmont, Calif.

McNeill, D. 1970. The Acquisition of Language: The Study of Developmental Psycholinguistics. Harper and Row, New York.

McReynolds, L., and D. Engmann. 1975. Distinctive Feature Analysis of Misarticulations. University Park Press, Baltimore.

Menn, L. 1971. Phonotactic rules in beginning speech. Lingua 26:225–251.

Menyuk, P. 1964. Comparison of grammar of children with functionally deviant and normal speech. J. Speech Hear. Res. 7:109–121.

Menyuk, P. 1969. Sentences Children Use. M.I.T. Press, Cambridge, Mass.

Morehead, D., and D. Ingram. 1973. The development of base syntax in normal and linguistically deviant children. J. Speech Hear. Res. 16:330–352 (reprinted this volume).

Moskowitz, A. 1970. The two-year-old stage in the acquisition of English morphology. Language 46:426–441.

Newfield, M., and B. Schlanger. 1968. The acquisition of English morphology by normal and educable mentally retarded children. J. Speech Hear. Res. 11:693–706.

Oléron, P. 1957. Studies of the Mental Development of Deaf-Mutes. Monograph of the Centre National de la Recherche Scientifique, Paris.

Oller, D. 1973. Regularities in abnormal child phonology. J. Speech Hear. Disord. 16:36–47.

Parisi, D., and F. Antinucci. 1970. Lexical competence. *In* G. Flores d'Arcais and W. Levelt (eds.), Advances in Psycholinguistics, pp. 197–210. North Holland, Amsterdam.

Parker, F. 1976. Distinctive features in speech pathology: Phonology or phonemics? J. Speech Hear. Disord. 41:23–39.

Piaget, J. 1926. The Language and Thought of the Child. Harcourt Brace, New York.

Piaget, J. 1952. The Origins of Intelligence in Children. Humanities, New York.

Piaget, J. 1962. Play, Dreams, and Imitation in Childhood. Norton, New York.

Schane, S. 1973. Generative Phonology. Prentice Hall, Englewood Cliffs, N.J.

Schlesinger, I. 1971. Production of utterances and language acquisition. *In* D. Slobin (ed.), The Ontogenesis of Grammar, pp. 63–101. Academic Press, New York.

Scholes, R. 1970. On functors and contentives in children's imitations of word strings. J. Verb. Lear. Verb. Beh. 9:167–170.

Shatz, M., and R. Gelman. 1973. The development of communication skills: Modifications in the speech of young children as a function of listener. Monograph of Society for Research in Child Development 38.

Sinclair, H. 1971. Sensorimotor action patterns as a condition for the acquisition of syntax. *In* R. Huxley and E. Ingram (eds.), Language Acquisition: Model and Methods, pp. 121–130. Academic Press, New York.

Singh, S. 1976. Distinctive Features: Theory and Validation. University Park Press, Baltimore.

Slobin, D. 1973. Cognitive prerequisites for the development of grammar. *In* C. Ferguson and D. Slobin (eds.), Studies in Child Language Development, pp. 175–208. Holt, Rinehart and Winston, New York.

Slobin, D., and C. Welsh. 1973. Elicited imitation as a research tool in developmental psycholinguistics. *In* C. Ferguson and D. Slobin (eds.), Studies in Child Language Development, pp. 485–497. Holt, Rinehart and Winston, New York.

Smith, N. 1973. The Acquisition of Phonology: A Case Study. Cambridge University Press, Cambridge, Mass.

Stampe, D. 1969. The acquisition of phonetic representation. Papers from the Fifth Regional Meeting of the Chicago Linguistic Society, pp. 443–454. Chicago.

Vincent, M., and M. Borelli. 1951. La naissance des opérations logiques chez des sourd-muets. Enfance 4:222–238.

Vygotsky, L. 1962. Thought and Language. M.I.T. Press, Cambridge, Mass.

Walsh, H. 1974. On certain practical inadequacies of distinctive feature systems. J. Speech Hear. Disord. 39:32–43.

Weiner, P. 1974. A language-delayed child at adolescence. J. Speech Hear. Disord. 39:202–212.

Index